The Essential Writings of Merleau-Ponty

The
Essential
Writings of
Merleau-Ponty

edited by Alden L. Fisher

St. Louis University

 Harcourt, Brace & World, Inc.

New York   Chicago   San Francisco   Atlanta

ISBN: 0-15-524240-7

Library of Congress Catalog Card Number: 69-17417

PREFACE

This book includes selections from all of Maurice Merleau-Ponty's major writings and strands of thought. While the book is primarily intended for the use of college undergraduates, it will provide useful background reading for graduate students and the general reader.

Most of the selections included are whole chapters or articles; the few necessary exceptions were taken from works that lent themselves to subdivision. The book thus confronts the reader with Merleau-Ponty's thought itself and introduces little editorial filtering.

While the shortcomings of this collection are wholly my own responsibility, I should like to thank Professors James Collins, Herbert Spiegelberg, and John Wild for their very generous suggestions, criticisms, and encouragement. I should also like to thank Mr. Dennis O'Connor and my wife for their help in preparing the manuscript.

Alden L. Fisher

CONTENTS

INTRODUCTION

The following biographical note appears at the beginning of a recent book devoted to the thought of Maurice Merleau-Ponty:

Merleau-Ponty was born in 1908. His father died prior to World War I, and he and a brother and sister were raised in Paris by their mother. His education followed a familiar pattern: secondary education at the Lycée Louis-le-Grand, and then L'Ecole Normale, from which he graduated in 1930. During the next five years he taught in a lycée at Beauvais, held a grant for research from the Caisse de la Recherche Scientifique for a year, and then taught again—this time at the lycée in Chartres. In 1935 he returned to Paris as a junior member—*agrégé répétiteur*—of the faculty at L'Ecole Normale. In the winter of 1939 he entered the army and served as a lieutenant in the infantry. After demobilization and during the German occupation he taught again and labored over what was to be his major work: *Phenomenology of Perception*. With the end of the occupation he joined the faculty of L'Université de Lyon and at the same time became co-editor with Sartre of the periodical *Les Temps modernes*. By 1950 his reputation was established, and he came to the Sorbonne as Professor of Psychology and Pedagogy. He was to remain in this post—not at all well suited to him—for only two years. In 1952 he was appointed to the Collège de France, to the chair that had been left vacant by the death of Louis Lavelle and that had previously been occupied by Henri Bergson and Edouard Le Roy. He was the youngest philosopher ever to hold this position—one of the more exalted in French academic life—and he retained it until his death in May, 1961.[1]

[1] John Bannon, *The Philosophy of Merleau-Ponty* (New York: Harcourt, Brace & World, 1967), pp. 2–3.

3

This note includes the minimal essential data concerning Merleau-Ponty's life and career. Further information would be very helpful; much in his works will not be fully clarified, for example, until we know who his teachers were, what books he used, and what figures in classical and contemporary philosophy were most influential in his formation. However, only a little was written about Merleau-Ponty the man while he was alive, for he led a quiet and discreet life, in marked contrast to his sometime friend and collaborator Jean-Paul Sartre.[2] Since he left few papers and no known autobiographical materials, the best remaining source of information would be interviews with his contemporaries. Until a major biographical work is undertaken, we shall have to be content with the above brief facts and the following incidental information.

Merleau-Ponty was reared as a Catholic; his mother was a devout woman, and one has the impression that Merleau-Ponty was equally so in his youth and early adult years. Sometime during the 1930's Merleau-Ponty became disaffected with the established Church and ceased to practice his faith. On one occasion—at the *Rencontres internationales* in Geneva, September, 1951—he even admitted that the label "atheist" could be applied to him. One had the impression, however, that he did so with reluctance and under considerable pressure of the moment.[3] During his last years he refused to accept the designation and seemed rather an open and "waiting" agnostic. His final position with regard to religion is not known; what is clear is that some degree of reconciliation with the Church of his early years must have been realized prior to his sudden death from a coronary thrombosis in May of 1961, for a Catholic Mass was said at his funeral. Considering the attitude of the French hierarchy in matters of this kind, there can be little room for doubt.

According to the testimony of his own writings, Merleau-Ponty's childhood was happy, so happy that his adult years never quite provided as complete a sense of rich fulfillment. The death of his father while he was still very young must have affected him greatly, however, for he became extremely close to his mother and remained com-

[2] One of the richest documents available, which gives a feeling for Merleau-Ponty the man, is Sartre's account of their friendship and professional collaboration, written at the time of Merleau-Ponty's death: Jean-Paul Sartre, "Merleau-Ponty," in *Situations* (New York: George Braziller, 1965), pp. 227–326.
[3] See the discussion of his paper "Man and Adversity" in *La Connaissance de l'homme au xxᵉ siècle* (Neuchatel: Éditions de la Baconnière, 1951), pp. 249–52.

pletely devoted to her until her death only a few years prior to his own. He was happily married to a physician and psychiatrist, a woman of considerable prominence in her own right; they had one child, a daughter.

Merleau-Ponty was a man of medium stature with a striking Gallic face filled with character. A well and neatly groomed man, he had neither the flamboyant nor the disheveled appearance affected by so many European intellectuals. Indeed, he had the external appearance of a successful French business executive, however quickly his eyes and speech dissipated such an impression. He was essentially timid and seemed happiest to live quietly with a few intimate friends rather than in the larger circle his eminence would easily have made possible. Nevertheless, he was a most impressive lecturer and a very effective teacher with an obvious interest in his students and in younger people generally. Extremely gentle and polite, he took the time and effort to put people at their ease; a good listener, he left the impression of being genuinely interested in his interlocutor.

These brief impressions will fill in the bare bones of Merleau-Ponty's "official" biography for students of his thought until more complete accounts become available.

Merleau-Ponty's first major work, *The Structure of Behavior*, was completed in 1938 when he was only thirty years old (although it was not published until 1942). Seven years later, in 1945, his second and most important work, *Phenomenology of Perception*, was completed. When one realizes that these seven years included his military service, the German occupation, and his activities in the Resistance, the accomplishment of so long and sustained a work seems even more remarkable. Two collections of essays followed, one devoted to writings in the philosophy of politics and given the pregnant title of *Humanism and Terror*, the other a brilliant collection of essays on various general topics entitled *Sense and Non-Sense*, published in 1948. His next work was his powerful inaugural address on the occasion of his assuming the chair of philosophy at the Collège de France in 1952 and called *In Praise of Philosophy*, large parts of which are included in these selections.

Evidence now indicates that Merleau-Ponty was working on more than one major philosophical work during these years. One work was provisionally entitled *Vérité et Existence*, the other *La Prose du monde*. The former may have been part of the work that later was entitled

La Visible et l'invisible, only partially complete at the time of Merleau-Ponty's death and published posthumously. Of *La Prose du monde* we have only one unfinished introductory section that was discovered recently and published as an article.[4] Merleau-Ponty's complete disaffection for the French Communist party and his intellectual break with Jean-Paul Sartre were the occasion for a very polemical political work, *Les Aventures de la dialectique,* published in 1955.

Only one other personal work was published during Merleau-Ponty's life—again a collection of essays, called *Signs,* that contains several important articles and many incidental pieces. This work was published in 1960, a year before his death. In 1955 and 1956 he edited an anthology called *Les Philosophes célèbres.* Many of his own contributions to this work are republished in *Signs.* Thus, most of Merleau-Ponty's philosophical articles were later published in one collection or another. A few of the major ones that remained uncollected in any French volume were gathered together by James Edie and published in English under the title of *The Primacy of Perception.* Some minor writings have still not been reprinted,[5] but it is clear that all of Merleau-Ponty's principal writings are quite accessible to the student and scholar.

The great shock caused by Merleau-Ponty's death was not simply because one of the most important philosophers of our time had died. One also felt a deep and terrible loss because Merleau-Ponty was so young; as philosophers go, he had barely reached his prime. It is almost certain that, had he lived, his philosophical contribution would have grown well beyond its present size, impressive as that is.

This is not the place to evaluate in detail the background intellectual influences on Merleau-Ponty's thought and writings. As we have already indicated, a great deal of detective work has still to be done before these influences can become entirely clear. Nevertheless, it is evident from Merleau-Ponty's writings that these influences fall primarily into three categories: Husserl, Marx, and existentialism. With regard to the last, existentialism is both an influence and a result of Merleau-Ponty's work, for, while he was clearly influenced by such writers as Gabriel Marcel and especially Martin Heidegger and Sartre, it is equally clear that Merleau-Ponty was himself one of the leading

[4] *Revue de métaphysique et de morale,* Vol. 72 (1967), pp. 139–53.
[5] Merleau-Ponty did a great deal of writing for newspapers in France, but so far these short essays have not been republished in more permanent form.

formative exponents of existentialism. The close friendship for many years between Merleau-Ponty and Jean-Paul Sartre and their collaborative work on *Les Temps modernes* could not have failed to affect the thinking of both men. Always less dramatic and extreme, both personally and philosophically, than Sartre, Merleau-Ponty is just as authentically existentialist in his philosophy.

Sartre introduced Merleau-Ponty to the writings of Edmund Husserl, but it is probably true that Husserl exercised an even more profound influence on Merleau-Ponty than on Sartre. While just as committed as Sartre to the concrete, Merleau-Ponty made Husserl's phenomenology, especially that of the last years, much more integrally a part of his own philosophical method. In many ways Merleau-Ponty's philosophy is a genuine synthesis of the best in existentialism and phenomenology; the term existential phenomenology probably applies better to Merleau-Ponty's thought than to the thought of any other philosopher.

Marx undoubtedly exercised a deep influence on Merleau-Ponty's political thinking. Never a committed Communist, Merleau-Ponty nevertheless felt very close to French Marxist and Communist thinking during and immediately following the Second World War. However, he became increasingly critical of contemporary communism until his radical break with it and with Sartre, marked by the publication of his *Les Aventures de la dialectique*. But Marx remained a permanent influence on Merleau-Ponty's political and social thought.

Important as Husserl, Marx, and existentialism are as influences on Merleau-Ponty's thinking, their role should not be exaggerated. Merleau-Ponty, much more than Sartre or Heidegger, impresses the reader as a man who has meditated on the whole of the history of philosophy, especially on the great classical moderns. An ardent and sustained critic of all idealisms and rationalisms, Merleau-Ponty was nevertheless profoundly influenced by Descartes, Kant, and Hegel. His criticisms always take the form of trying to distill out of these writers what is of lasting importance and of incorporating this into his own philosophical position. This is perhaps most dramatically illustrated in the final chapter of *The Structure of Behavior,* which is included in these selections.

Of all the classical moderns, Hegel perhaps influenced Merleau-Ponty most deeply—not, certainly, the Hegel of absolute mind, but the Hegel of the dialectic and of the phenomenology. In his lectures at the Collège de France, Merleau-Ponty devoted a sustained and systematic analysis to Hegel alone among the moderns. As a matter of fact, since Hegel occupied Merleau-Ponty's time in the historical part of his lectures from about 1955 until the time of his death, it is perhaps true to say that Hegel's influence on him was growing. However, it was present from the very beginning, as evidenced by *The Structure of Behavior*.

At a time when the focus of much of contemporary philosophy was becoming more and more restricted—with first the positivists directing the interest of philosophers primarily to logic and science, and later the linguistic analysts focusing philosophy's attention primarily on ordinary linguistic usage as it appears either in everyday language or in various technical language uses—Merleau-Ponty represents a return to a more comprehensive philosophy in the classical tradition. For him philosophy must be a completely unrestricted reflection on the whole of human experience including, certainly, science and language but also man himself and all his activities, among them art, politics, society, and religion. At the same time that he resisted modern efforts to restrict the subject matter of philosophy, Merleau-Ponty carried out a sustained critique of the great rationalists, not because of any irrationalism or arbitrary restriction of reason on his part, but because of the rationalists' tendency to build closed systems. Merleau-Ponty is impatient with conceptual system building; for him, philosophy is the application of reason's full powers to the task of disengaging the structures of experience and making manifest all their hidden intelligibilities. Merleau-Ponty is skeptical of the possibility of reason's completing its work—reality is too rich to be fully captured by one mind and one set of categories—but philosophy's task is to exercise reason to its fullest possible capacity. No limits are set on the potentialities of reason except its own inner limitations and the limits of reality itself.

Having said this, it is also fair to say that, for Merleau-Ponty, reality never presents itself without some degree of ambiguity, and he is highly sensitive to this irrational side of things. His philosophy has in fact been called a philosophy of ambiguity. But, for him, recognizing the irrational is not the same as capitulating to it, and a main thrust of his philosophy is precisely to enlarge reason, to make reason adequate to and inclusive of the non-rational and the irrational. Philosophy's attention to the contingent, the vague, the dark underside of things is for Merleau-Ponty only a way to be more faithful to the task of reason itself, the task of unrestricted reflection.

One of the places where Merleau-Ponty first brings into play the full powers of critical reflection is in his critique of science. It is often asserted, and with some reason, that existentialism is antiscientific. But this is most certainly not true of the thought of Merleau-Ponty. As a matter of fact his work contains implicitly a whole philosophy of science in which the contributions of science are given full weight. What Merleau-Ponty is exhaustively critical of, especially in the social sciences, is the frequent pretension of science to being the only valid mode of knowing. Also, and again especially in the social sciences, Merleau-Ponty is acutely critical of the assumption implicit in most sciences that their theories, frequently reductionistic, constitute a truer account of reality than one theory based on direct experience.

He shows definitively that every effort on the part of science to substitute its own account for the structure of the real is essentially circular. For science, as all other modes of human knowledge, must begin with direct perceptual experience and return to it. In other words, science must in its own way be an account and an elucidation of direct perceptual experience, a "moment of lived experience," or it is not an explanation of anything at all. This is Merleau-Ponty's doctrine of the *primacy of perception* and his own version of Husserl's famous phenomenological maxim that philosophy, for its part, must be a return "to the things themselves."

The process of human perception that Merleau-Ponty regards as so fundamental is not simply the passive registering of the data provided by the external world. Rather, the act of perceiving is shown to be co-constitutive of the human world—the only primary world—in all its rich contours. For this reason, the act of perceiving itself and the objects of perception come to be the central object of study. In addition to a sustained criticism of all scientistic and reductionistic views, for Merleau-Ponty it becomes necessary to carry out a direct examination of perception and perceived reality—hence *The Phenomenology of Perception*.

Two other features of Husserl's thought that Merleau-Ponty made use of are the idea that the natural attitude about "reality" must be overcome by a series of reductions, and the notion of the radical intentionality of human consciousness. The natural tendency to view the world as "out there" in itself, independent of and uninvolved with human life and knowledge, and the further assumption that this world is *really* like an account which can be given of it by science, are both shown to be prejudices of the uncritical mind. These prejudices must be overcome by sustained critiques designed to lay bare the unfounded assumptions of common sense and of science. These analyses are the equivalent in Merleau-Ponty's philosophy of the phenomenological reductions of Husserl; both are intended to bring us back to the primarily real, the world of direct perception.

Secondly, the notion of the radical intentionality of human consciousness is fundamental to Merleau-Ponty's thought. When one reflects carefully on perception and its objects, and especially when one discovers through such reflection that perception is not a passive affair but an active taking hold and a molding of one's own world, one sees the need for a careful noematic-noetic analysis—an analysis of the "noema" and the "noesis"—in Husserl's terms.[6] That is, I must first look at the full complexity and variety of the objects of perception. And this will necessarily lead to an analysis of the acts of perceiving themselves. Furthermore, it will show me not only that the perceptual world is primary, the only truly given world, but also that this given is always *given for* a perceiving consciousness. Thus is rediscovered and confirmed Husserl's doctrine of intentionality: that every object is an object for an intending mind, that this is the primary reality, and hence that the mind is radically intentional in structure. The world is both revealed and shaped by the acts of perception in which it is grasped.

But Merleau-Ponty carries the analysis of perception further by showing that there are at least two distinct levels of perception. There are the objects of perception and the acts of perceiving which are directly available to reflection. I can sit back and look at my desk. If I attend carefully to the way in which the desk is given to me I find that the desk presents itself to me as there in front of me with its qualities of color, size, shape, etc. It presents itself to me in the act of perceiving it. I can carry this reflection on the object and act of perception much further. I can show that the desk can never be perceived all at once but only in a series of profiles. Because this is so, no act of perception can ever exhaust the given of an object and, hence, an act of perceiving, while always veridical as an act of perceiving, can never give me apodictic but only presumptive knowledge of the object. The desk presents

[6] Most simply, and as a first approach, "noema" refers to what is presented to consciousness or the mind, while "noesis" refers to the acts of the mind directed toward or "intending" such objects or presentations.

itself to me as a cube-shaped object with a kneehole in it and uniformly colored. In fact one of the now unperceived sides could be missing or be of a different color.

Hence, I can, and in a sense I must, carry out an *intensive* analysis of the perceived desk, finding out more and more about it as it gives itself in successive and more detailed acts of perception. But it still remains the case that I can never exhaust the direct perception of an object since it will always and forever remain true that I can never perceive it all at once, spread out before me in all its intelligibility. Since perception is the primary act, that in and through which the real is given to me, and since no mode of knowing can definitively surpass its origins in direct perception, this will have important implications for Merleau-Ponty's theory of truth.

If it remains true that Merleau-Ponty is never a skeptic in the Humean sense—on the contrary, he holds that, in perception, one does genuinely achieve the object, that in each act of perception the dualism of the *pour soi* and the *en soi* is overcome—it remains equally true that the world is never exhaustively given to the perceiving or knowing mind. His is the complete antithesis of a kind of spectator realism and theory of truth. It is in this sense that the givens of perception cannot yield, for Merleau-Ponty, the kind of necessities required for the rationalist systems. Reality will yield some necessary structures, but its contingency can never be fully overcome.

I can also carry out an *extensive* analysis of the perceived desk by noting that it is in front of me and in this room. In looking at the desk I can perceive the walls of the room. In some sense I can even perceive the wall behind me; were I doubtful, I could try to imagine perceiving a desk in a room with the wall behind me missing. From this I would see that the wall behind me is present to me in a sense. Furthermore, the room is in a house, the house on a street in a town, in a state and a country, etc. I can carry on this analysis until I reach a kind of limit which I call the world. The world is thus not a thing but the horizon of all possible objects and things.

But this analysis is now at the level of explicit, thematic perception. Following Husserl, Merleau-Ponty distinguishes this level of perception from the level of unreflective, unthematic perception which also has its intentional objects. This distinction leads to the doctrine of the lived world—an idea developed by Husserl and exploited with enormous fruitfulness by Merleau-Ponty. As I go about my business, as I act and live in my world, I am always actively perceiving and shaping that world. But much of the time I am not attending to either the acts of perception nor the ways in which these acts are shaping the world in which I live. Hence, the world which seems to me to be (and in a real sense, according to Merleau-Ponty, is) always already there is also in a sense the product of a long series of constitutive acts of perception. To demonstrate this point Merleau-Ponty makes rich use of the findings of psychology; for example, he points to the way in which a child perceives his world prelinguistically. He also shows how affectivity is both tied to and influences the quality of my perception at this lived level. Thus, in reflection, I am always obliged to try to recover what has been built up at the level of unreflective perception. One of philosophy's primary and ongoing tasks then becomes a reflection upon the structures of this lived world, reflection trying to recover the unreflected.

It is in this context that Merleau-Ponty develops his philosophy of the body. Of all the objects of perception, the human body is perhaps the most ambiguous. Following ideas similar to those of Marcel, but not using exactly the same language, Merleau-Ponty distinguishes between my body for me and my body for others. It is possible to view the body "objectively" like any other object or thing. In this perspective the body is a functional organism with objective processes taking place within it. This is the body which can be examined by the physician and treated by chemical means. But this is not precisely the same body as my body for me as lived from within.

Rather my body for me is seen to be the means by which I am situated in a world. It is also that by which I am able to perceive a world. Thus the body for me or the lived body is that by means of which I am part of the world and at the same time that by means of which I have a perspective on the world. The perspectival character of perceptual objects has as a counterpart the situated character of acts of perceiving because of their participating in the situated character of the body.

Thus the lived body is that ambiguous reality which is not identical with the subject—it is not the subject but rather the means by which the subject is a real subject in a real world—but neither is it the same as external objects, for no other object in our experience is lived from within. Each person's own body then is a kind of third term, participating in the character of subject and object but being identical with neither. And, since each self is related to a body, must be embodied in order to be a real and not a fictive self, Merleau-Ponty can speak of an incarnate self or a besouled body. Each expression emphasizes one aspect of the same reality. And it is this lived body which is primary, the body for others being an abstraction from it.

It is also this body which, by means of behavior, is seen to be the expression of the subject. The body is the means then by which man perceives; it is also radically the means by which the subject can find expression in a real world. Spoken language, speech, is only the most important such mode of expression. All human gestures and all behavior toward objects are ways of expressing the subject as well as ways of being in and at the same time expressing a world.

Merleau-Ponty provides us with rich analyses of these dimensions of the expressivity of the human body, notably in human sexuality, one of man's ways of being affectively present to another; in his use of tools, one of man's ways of working to transform his world; and, of course, in human speech, the means by which one incarnate subject communicates with another.

From this point Merleau-Ponty will, then, go on to develop his philosophy of language, his philosophy of art, and even his views of society and history. For the lived body is also man's way of being with others and situated in a social condition and in a history. This is not to say that these modes of human existence are reducible to a theory of the body, or that they cannot be analyzed in their own right. Rather it is to say that each of these modes of existence shares in the fundamental human condition by being precisely dimensions of the existence of incarnate subjects, besouled bodies.

In all of this it is Merleau-Ponty's constant effort to make philosophy as concrete as possible, just as, at another level, it was Merleau-Ponty's constant concern that philosophy deal with the living problems of the time.

Each of these aspects of Merleau-Ponty's thought is represented in later selections in this volume. If these introductory remarks and these selections lead the reader to investigate the scope of Merleau-Ponty's thought in the full range of his writing, they will have accomplished their purpose.

ALDEN L. FISHER

Philosophy and Phenomenology

Merleau-Ponty was elected to the chair of philosophy at the Collège de France in 1952. The first selection, excerpted from In Praise of Philosophy, *constituted part of his inaugural lecture. It represents his reflections on the nature of philosophy and the situation of the philosopher. Socrates is taken as the model for the philosopher's relation to the established community.*

The second selection in Part One is the preface of Merleau-Ponty's major work, Phenomenology of Perception. *In it he attempts to give his response to that very difficult question: what is phenomenology? In so doing he locates his own thought with regard to that of the founder of contemporary phenomenology, Edmund Husserl.*

I. IN PRAISE OF PHILOSOPHY

The man who witnesses his own research, that is to say his own inner disorder, cannot feel himself to be the heir of the distinguished men whose names he sees on these walls. If, in addition, he is a philosopher, that is to say if he knows that he knows nothing, how could he believe himself justified in occupying this chair, and how could he even desire to do so? The answer to these questions is very simple. Since its foundation the Collège de France has been charged with the duty, not of giving to its hearers already-acquired truths, but the idea of free investigation. If, last winter, the Collège de France desired to maintain a chair of philosophy, it is because philosophical ignorance puts the crowning touch on the spirit of search to which it is devoted. If a philosopher solicits your votes, my dear colleagues, it is, you well know, in order to live the philosophical life more completely. And if you have elected him, it is to support this endeavor in his person. Although I feel unequal to the honor, I am nevertheless happy to undertake the task, since it is a great good fortune, as Stendhal said, for one "to have his passion as a profession." I have been touched at finding you so resolved, all other considerations aside, in desiring to maintain philosophy in your midst, and it is a pleasure to thank you for this today. . . .

The philosopher is marked by the distinguishing trait that he possesses *inseparably* the taste for evidence and the feeling for ambiguity. When he limits himself to accepting ambiguity, it is called equivocation. But among the great it becomes a theme; it contributes to estab-

Maurice Merleau-Ponty, *In Praise of Philosophy*, trans. by John Wild and James M. Edie (Evanston, Illinois: Northwestern University Press, 1963), pp. 3–5, 32–42, 58–64. Reprinted by permission.

lishing certitudes rather than menacing them. Therefore it is necessary to distinguish good and bad ambiguity. Even those who have desired to work out a completely positive philosophy have been philosophers only to the extent that, at the same time, they have refused the right to install themselves in absolute knowledge. They taught not this knowledge, but its becoming in us, not the absolute but, at most, our *absolute relation* to it, as Kierkegaard said. What makes a philosopher is the movement which leads back without ceasing from knowledge to ignorance, from ignorance to knowledge, and a kind of rest in this movement. . . . Thus it is the philosopher and he alone who is judge. Here we have come back to the self and to the tête-à-tête of the self with the true. Now we have said that there is no solitary truth. Are we therefore on a revolving wheel? We are, but it is not the wheel of the skeptics. It is true that in the last resort there is no judge, that I do not think according to the true alone, nor according to myself alone, nor according to the others alone, because each of the three has need of the other two and it would be a non-sense to sacrifice any one. A philosophical life always bases itself on these three cardinal points. The enigma of philosophy (and of expression) is that sometimes life is the same to oneself, to others, and to the true. These are the moments which justify it. The philosopher counts only on them. He will never accept to will himself against men, nor to will men against himself, nor against the true, nor the true against them. He wishes to be everywhere at once, at the risk of never being completely anywhere. His opposition is not aggressive; he knows that this often announces capitulation. But he understands the rights of others and of the outside too well to permit them any infringement. If, when he is engaged in external enterprises, the attempt is made to draw him beyond the point where his activity loses the meaning which inspired it, his rejection is all the more tranquil in that it is founded on the same motives as his acceptance. Hence the rebellious gentleness, the pensive engagement, the intangible presence which disquiet those who are with him. As Bergson said of Ravaisson in a tone so personal that one imagines him to be speaking of himself: "He gave no hold. . . . He was the kind of man who does not even offer sufficient resistance for one to flatter himself that he has ever seen him give way."

If we have recalled these words of Bergson, not all of which are in his books, it is because they make us feel that there is a tension in the relation of the philosopher with other persons or with life, and that this uneasiness is essential to philosophy. We have forgotten this a little. The modern philosopher is frequently a functionary, always a writer, and the freedom allowed him in his books admits an opposite view. What he says enters first of all into an academic world where the choices of life are deadened and the occasions for thought are cut off. Without books a certain speed of communication would be impossible, and there is nothing to say against them. But in the end they are only words expressed a bit more coherently. The philosophy placed in books has ceased to challenge men. What is unusual and almost insupportable in it is hidden in the respectable life of the great philosophical systems. In order to understand the total function of the philosopher, we must remember that even the philosophical writers whom we read [and of whom we are one] have never ceased to recognize as their patron a man who never wrote, who never taught, at least in any official chair, who talked with anyone he met on the street, and who had certain difficulties with public opinion and with the public powers. We must remember Socrates.

The life and death of Socrates are the history of the difficult relations that the philosopher faces—when he is not protected by literary immunity—with the gods of the City, that is to say with other men, and with the fixed absolute whose image they extend to him. If the philosopher were a rebel, it would be less shocking. For in the last analysis each one of us knows for his own part that the world as it is, is unacceptable. We like to have this written down for the honor of humanity, though we may forget it when we return to our affairs. Hence rebellion is not displeasing. But with Socrates it is something different. He teaches that religion is true, and he offered sacrifices to the gods. He teaches that one ought to obey the City, and he obeys it from the very beginning to the end. He is reproached not so much for what he does as for his way of doing it, his motive. In the *Apology* there is a saying which explains it all, when Socrates says to his judges: *Athenians, I believe as none of those who accuse me.* Revealing words! He believes *more* than they, but also he believes in another way, and in a different sense. True religion for Socrates is a religion in which the gods are not in conflict, where the omens remain ambiguous—since, in the last analysis, says the Socrates of Xenophon, it is the gods, not the birds, who foresee the future—where the divine reveals itself, like the *daimon* of Socrates, only by a silent warning and a reminder to man of his ignorance. Religion is, therefore, true, but true in a sense that it does not know—true as Socrates thinks it, not as it thinks.

And in the same way when he justifies the City, it is for his own reasons, not for *raisons d'Etat*. He does not run away. He appears before the tribunal. But there is little respect in the reasons he gives for this. First of all, he says, at my age the lust for life is not in place; furthermore, one would not put up with me much better elsewhere; finally, I have always lived here. There remains the celebrated argument for the authority of the laws. But we need to examine it more closely. Xenophon makes Socrates say that one may obey the laws in wishing for them to change, as one fights a war in wishing for peace. Thus it is not that the laws are good but that they pertain to order, and one needs order in order to change it. When Socrates refuses to flee, it is not that he recognizes the tribunal. It is that he may be in a better position to challenge it. By fleeing, that is, he would become an enemy of Athens and would make the sentence against him true. By remaining, he has won, whether he be acquitted or condemned, for he will prove his philosophy either in leading his judges to accept it, or in his own acceptance of the sentence.

Aristotle, seventy-five years later, will say, in leaving the city of his own accord, that there is no sense in allowing the Athenians to commit a new crime against philosophy. Socrates, on the other hand, works out for himself another idea of philosophy. It does not exist as a sort of idol of which he would be the guardian and which he must defend. It exists rather in its living relevance to the Athenians, in its absent presence, in its obedience without respect. Socrates has a way of obeying which is a way of resisting, while Aristotle disobeys in seemliness and dignity. Everything that Socrates does is ordered around the secret principle that one is annoyed if he does not comprehend. Always to blame by excess or default, always more simple and yet less abstract than the others, more flexible and less accommodating, he makes them ill at ease, and inflicts upon them the unpardonable offense of making them doubt themselves. He is there in life, at the assembly of the people, and before the tribunal, but in such a way that one can make nothing of him. He gives them no eloquence, no prepared rhetoric. By entering into the game of respect, he would only justify the calumny against him. But even less any show of defiance! This would be to forget that in a certain sense the others can hardly judge otherwise than they do. The same philosophy obliges him to appear before the judges and also makes him different from them. The same freedom which brings him among them frees him from their prejudices. The very same principle makes him both universal and singular. There is a part of him by which he is the kinsman of them all. It is called *reason* and is invisible to them. For them, as Aristophanes says, it is cloudy, empty chattering. The commentators sometimes say it is all a misunderstanding. Socrates believes in religion and the City, in spirit and in truth. They believe in them to the letter. He and his judges are not *on the same ground*. If only he had been better understood, one would have seen clearly that he was neither seeking for new gods, nor neglecting the gods of Athens. He was only trying to give them a sense; he was interpreting them.

The trouble is that this operation is not so innocent. It is in the world of the philosopher that one saves the gods and the laws by understanding them, and to make room on earth for the life of philosophy, it is precisely philosophers like Socrates who are required. Religion interpreted—this is for the others religion suppressed. And the charge of impiety—this is the point of view of the others towards him. He gives reasons for obeying the laws. But it is already too much to have reasons for obeying, since over against all reasons other reasons can be opposed, and then respect disappears. What one expects of him—this is exactly what he is not able to give—is assent to the thing itself, without restriction. He, on the contrary, comes before the judges, yes, but it is to explain to them what the City is. As if they did not know! As if they *were not* the City! He does not plead for himself. He pleads the cause of a city which would accept philosophy. He reverses the roles and says to them: it is not myself I am defending; it is you. In the last analysis the City is in him and they are the enemies of the laws. It is they who are being judged, and he who is judging them—an inevitable reversal in the philosopher, since he justifies what is outside by values which come from within.

What can one do if he neither pleads his cause nor challenges to combat? One can speak in such a way as to make freedom show itself in and through the various respects and considerations, and to unlock hate by a smile—a lesson for our philosophy which has lost both its smile and its sense of tragedy. This is what is called irony. The irony of Socrates is a distant but true relation with others. It expresses the fundamental fact that each of us is only himself inescapably, and nevertheless recognizes himself in the other. It is an attempt to open up both of us for freedom. As is true of tragedy, both the adversaries are justified, and true irony uses a double-meaning which is founded on these facts. There is therefore no self-conceit. It is irony on the self no less than on the others. As Hegel well says, it is *naïve*. The story of Socrates is not to say less in order to win an advantage in showing great mental power, or in suggesting some esoteric knowledge. "Whenever I convince anyone of his ignorance," the *Apology* says with melancholy, "my listeners imagine that I know everything that he does not know." Socrates does not know any *more* than they know. He knows only that there is no absolute knowledge, and that it is by this absence that we are open to the truth.

To this good irony Hegel opposes a romantic irony which is equivocal, tricky, and self-conceited. It relies on the power which we can use, if we wish, to give any kind of meaning to anything whatsoever. It levels things down; it plays with them and permits anything. The irony of Socrates is not this kind of madness. Or at least if there are traces of bad irony in it, it is Socrates himself who teaches us to correct Socrates. When he says: I make them dislike me and this is the proof that what I say is true, he is wrong on the basis of his own principles. All sound reasoning is offensive, but all that offends us is not true. At another time, when he says to his judges: I will not stop philosophizing *even if I must die many times,* he taunts them and tempts their cruelty. Sometimes it is clear that he yields to the giddiness of insolence and spitefulness, to self-magnification and the aristocratic spirit. He was left with no other resource than himself. As Hegel says again, he appeared "at the time of the decadence of the Athenian democracy; he drew away from the externally existent and retired into himself to seek there for the just and the good." But in the last analysis it was precisely this that he was self-prohibited from doing, since he thought that one cannot be just all alone and, indeed, that in being just all alone one ceases to be just. If it is truly the City that he is defending, it is not merely the City in him but that actual City existing around him. The five hundred men who gathered together to judge him were neither all important people nor all fools. Two hundred and twenty-one among them thought he was innocent, and a change of thirty votes would have saved Athens from the dishonor. It was also a question of those after Socrates who would run the same danger. He was perhaps free to bring down the anger of the fools

upon himself, to pardon them with a certain contempt, and then to
pass beyond his life. But this would not absolve him in advance from
the evil he might bring on others and would not enable him to pass
beyond *their* lives. It was therefore necessary to give to the tribunal its
chance of understanding. In so far as we live with others, no judgment
we make on them is possible which leaves us out, and which places
them at a distance. *All is vain,* or *all is evil,* as likewise *all is well,*
which are hard to distinguish, do not come from philosophy.

It is possible to fear that our time also is rejecting the philosopher
that dwells within it, and that once again philosophy will evaporate
into nothing but *clouds.* For to philosophize is to seek, and this is to
imply that there are things to see and to say. Well, today we no longer
seek. We "return" to one or the other of our traditions and "defend"
it. Our convictions are founded less on perceived values and truths
than on the vices and errors of those we do not like. We love very few
things, though we dislike many. Our thinking is a thought in retreat or
in reply. Each of us is expiating for his youth. This decadence is in
accord with the course of our history. Having passed a certain point
of tension, ideas cease to develop and live. They fall to the level of
justifications and pretexts, relics of the past, points of honor; and
what one pompously calls the movement of ideas is reduced to the
sum of our nostalgias, our grudges, our timidities, and our phobias. In
this world, where negation and gloomy passion take the place of
certitude, one does not seek above all to see, and, because it seeks to
see, philosophy passes for impiety. It would be easy to show this in
connection with two absolutes which are at the center of our discussions: God and history. . . .

Let us show, in conclusion, that views like these justify philosophy
even in its weakness.

For it is useless to deny that philosophy limps. It dwells in history
and in life, but it wishes to dwell at their center, at the point where
they come into being with the birth of meaning. It is not content with
what is already there. Since it is expression in act, it comes to itself only
by ceasing to coincide with what is expressed, and by taking its distance
in order to see its meaning. It is, in fact, the Utopia of possession at a
distance. Hence it can be tragic, since it has its own contrary within
itself. It is never a *serious* occupation. The serious man, if he exists, is
the man of one thing only, to which he assents. But the most resolute
philosophers always wish the contrary—to realize, but in destroying;

to suppress, but also to conserve. Always, they have an afterthought. The philosopher pays attention to the serious man—of action, of religion, or of passion—perhaps more acutely than anyone. But precisely in doing this, one feels that he is different. His own actions are acts of witness, like the "signifying acts" by which the companions of Julien Sorel at the seminary sought to prove their piety. Spinoza writes *"ultimi barbarorum"* on the tyrants' gate. Lagneau took legal action before the University authorities to rehabilitate an unfortunate candidate. Having done these things, each returns home, and remains there for years. The philosopher of action is perhaps the farthest removed from action, for to speak of action with depth and rigor is to say that one does not desire to act.

Machiavelli is the complete contrary of a machiavellian, since he describes the tricks of power and, as we say, "gives the whole show away." The seducer and the politician, who live in the dialectic and have a feeling or instinct for it, try their best to keep it hidden. It is the philosopher who explains that dialectically, under given conditions, an opponent becomes the equivalent of a traitor. This language is the precise opposite of what the powers say. The powers omit the premises and speak more succinctly. They simply say: here there are nothing but criminals. The manichees, who throw themselves into action, understand one another better than they understand the philosopher, for there is a certain complicity among them. Each one is the reason for the being of the other. But the philosopher is a stranger to this fraternal melée. Even if he had never betrayed any cause, one feels, in his very manner of being faithful, that he would be able to betray. He does not take sides like the others, and in his assent something massive and carnal is lacking. He is not altogether a real being.

This difference exists. But is it really between the philosopher and the man? It is rather the difference in man himself between that which understands and that which chooses, and every man, like the philosopher, is divided in this way. There is much that is artificial in the portrait of the man of action whom we oppose to the philosopher. This man of action is himself not all of one piece. Hate is a virtue from behind. To obey with one's eyes closed is the beginning of panic; and to choose against what one understands, the beginning of skepticism. One must be able to withdraw and gain distance in order to become truly engaged, which is, also, always an engagement in the truth. The same author who wrote one day that all action is manichean, having become involved in action soon after, familiarly answered a journalist who reminded him of what he had said: "all action is manichean, *but don't overdo it!*"

No one is manichean before himself. It is an air that men of action have when seen from the outside, and which they rarely treasure in their memories. If the philosopher helps us to understand, henceforth, something of what a great man says in his own heart, he saves the truth of all, even for the man of action, who needs it, for no real statesman has ever seriously said that he was not interested in the truth. Later on, perhaps tomorrow, the man of action will rehabilitate the philosopher. As for those who are simply men, and not professionals in action, they are very far from classifying all others into the good and the evil, at least as long as they speak of what they have seen, and judge from close up. One finds them, when one looks, to be surprisingly sensitive to philosophical irony, as if it brought their silence and their reserve into the light, because here, for once, the word serves to open and release us.

The limping of philosophy is its virtue. True irony is not an alibi; it is a task; and the very detachment of the philosopher assigns to him a certain kind of action among men. Because we live in one of those situations that Hegel called diplomatic, in which every initiative risks being changed in meaning, we sometimes believe that we are serving the cause of philosophy by isolating it from the problems of the day, and Descartes has recently been honored for not having taken sides between Galileo and the Holy Office. The philosopher, it is said, should not prefer one rival dogmatism to another. He should occupy himself with absolute being beyond both the object of the physicist and the imagination of the theologian. But this is to forget that, by refusing to speak, Descartes also refuses to vindicate and to bring into action the philosophical order in its proper place. By remaining silent, he does not transcend these twin errors. He leaves them at grips with one another; he encourages them, particularly the victor of the moment. To be silent is not the same as to say why one does not wish to choose. If Descartes had acted, he could not have failed to establish the relative right of Galileo against the Holy Office, even if this were finally to subordinate ontology to physics. Philosophy and absolute being are never above the rival errors that oppose each other at any given time. These are never errors in quite the same way, and philosophy, which is integral truth, is charged with saying what in them it is able to integrate. In order that one day there might be a state of the world in which free thought would be possible, of scientism as well as of imagination, it did not suffice to bypass these two errors in silence. It was essential to speak against, and in this case to speak against the imagination. In the case of Galileo, the thought of physics carried the interests of truth. The philosophical absolute does not have any permanent seat. It is never elsewhere; it must be defended in each event. Alain said to his students: "Truth is momentary for us men who have a short view. It belongs to a situation, to an instant; it is necessary to see it, to say it, to do it at this very moment, not before nor after in ridiculous maxims; not for many times, for there are no many times." The difference here is not between the man and the philosopher. Both of them think the truth in the event. They are both opposed to the important one who thinks by principles, and against the roué who lives without truth.

At the conclusion of a reflection which at first isolates him, the philosopher, in order to experience more fully the ties of truth which bind him to the world and history, finds neither the depth of himself nor absolute knowledge, but a renewed image of the world and of himself placed within it among others. His dialectic, or his ambiguity, is only a way of putting into words what every man knows well—the value of those moments when his life renews itself and continues on, when he gets hold of himself again, and understands himself by passing beyond, when his private world becomes the common world. These mysteries are in each one of us as in him. What does he say of the relation between the soul and the body, except what is known by all men who make their souls and bodies, their good and their evil, go together in one piece? What does he teach of death, except that it is hidden in life, as the body in the soul, and that it is this understanding, as Montaigne said, which brings "a peasant and whole peoples to die, just as surely as philosophers?" The philosopher is the man who wakes up and speaks. And man contains silently within himself the paradoxes of philosophy, because to be completely a man, it is necessary to be a little more and a little less than man.

2. WHAT IS PHENOMENOLOGY?

What is phenomenology? It may seem strange that this question has still to be asked half a century after the first works of Husserl. The fact remains that it has by no means been answered. Phenomenology is the study of essences; and according to it, all problems amount to finding definitions of essences: the essence of perception, or the essence of consciousness, for example. But phenomenology is also a philosophy which puts essences back into existence, and does not expect to arrive at an understanding of man and the world from any starting point other than that of their 'facticity'. It is transcendental philosophy which places in abeyance the assertions arising out of the natural attitude, the better to understand them; but it is also a philosophy for which the world is always 'already there' before reflection begins —as an inalienable presence; and all its efforts are concentrated upon re-achieving a direct and primitive contact with the world, and endowing that contact with a philosophical status. It is the search for a philosophy which shall be a 'rigorous science', but it also offers an account of space, time and the world as we 'live' them. It tries to give a direct description of our experience as it is, without taking account of its psychological origin and the causal explanations which the scientist, the historian or the sociologist may be able to provide. Yet Husserl in his last works mentions a 'genetic phenomenology',[1] and

Maurice Merleau-Ponty, "Preface," *Phenomenology of Perception,* trans. by Colin Smith (New York: The Humanities Press, 1962), pp. vii-xvi. Reprinted by permission.

[1] *Méditations cartésiennes,* pp. 120 ff.

even a 'constructive phenomenology'.[2] One may try to do away with
these contradictions by making a distinction between Husserl's and
Heidegger's phenomenologies; yet the whole of *Sein und Zeit* springs
from an indication given by Husserl and amounts to no more than an
explicit account of the 'natürlicher Weltbegriff' or the 'Lebenswelt'
which Husserl, towards the end of his life, identified as the central
theme of phenomenology, with the result that the contradiction reappears in Husserl's own philosophy. The reader pressed for time will
be inclined to give up the idea of covering a doctrine which says
everything, and will wonder whether a philosophy which cannot
define its scope deserves all the discussion which has gone on around
it, and whether he is not faced rather by a myth or a fashion.

Even if this were the case, there would still be a need to understand
the prestige of the myth and the origin of the fashion, and the opinion
of the responsible philosopher must be that *phenomenology can be
practised and identified as a manner or style of thinking, that it existed
as a movement before arriving at complete awareness of itself as a
philosophy.* It has been long on the way, and its adherents have discovered it in every quarter, certainly in Hegel and Kierkegaard, but
equally in Marx, Nietzsche and Freud. A purely linguistic examination of the texts in question would yield no proof; we find in texts
only what we put into them, and if ever any kind of history has suggested the interpretations which should be put on it, it is the history of
philosophy. We shall find in ourselves, and nowhere else, the unity
and true meaning of phenomenology. It is less a question of counting
up quotations than of determining and expressing in concrete form
this *phenomenology for ourselves* which has given a number of present-
day readers the impression, on reading Husserl or Heidegger, not so
much of encountering a new philosophy as of recognizing what they
had been waiting for. Phenomenology is accessible only through a
phenomenological method. Let us, therefore, try systematically to
bring together the celebrated phenomenological themes as they have
grown spontaneously together in life. Perhaps we shall then understand why phenomenology has for so long remained at an initial stage,
as a problem to be solved and a hope to be realized.

It is a matter of describing, not of explaining or analysing. Husserl's
first directive to phenomenology, in its early stages, to be a 'descriptive

[2] See the unpublished *6th Méditation cartésienne,* edited by Eugen Fink, to
which G. Berger has kindly referred us.

psychology', or to return to the 'things themselves', is from the start a rejection of science. I am not the outcome or the meeting-point of numerous causal agencies which determine my bodily or psychological make-up. I cannot conceive myself as nothing but a bit of the world, a mere object of biological, psychological or sociological investigation. I cannot shut myself up within the realm of science. All my knowledge of the world, even my scientific knowledge, is gained from my own particular point of view, or from some experience of the world without which the symbols of science would be meaningless. The whole universe of science is built upon the world as directly experienced, and if we want to subject science itself to rigorous scrutiny and arrive at a precise assessment of its meaning and scope, we must begin by reawakening the basic experience of the world of which science is the second-order expression. Science has not and never will have, by its nature, the same significance *qua* form of being as the world which we perceive, for the simple reason that it is a rationale or explanation of that world. I am, not a 'living creature' nor even a 'man', nor again even 'a consciousness' endowed with all the characteristics which zoology, social anatomy or inductive psychology recognize in these various products of the natural or historical process—I am the absolute source, my existence does not stem from my antecedents, from my physical and social environment; instead it moves out towards them and sustains them, for I alone bring into being for myself (and therefore into being in the only sense that the word can have for me) the tradition which I elect to carry on, or the horizon whose distance from me would be abolished—since that distance is not one of its properties—if I were not there to scan it with my gaze. Scientific points of view, according to which my existence is a moment of the world's, are always both naïve and at the same time dishonest, because they take for granted, without explicitly mentioning it, the other point of view, namely that of consciousness, through which from the outset a world forms itself round me and begins to exist for me. To return to things themselves is to return to that world which precedes knowledge, of which knowledge always *speaks*, and in relation to which every scientific schematization is an abstract and derivative sign-language, as is geography in relation to the countryside in which we have learnt beforehand what a forest, a prairie or a river is.

This move is absolutely distinct from the idealist return to con-

[margin note: good working definition of science]

sciousness, and the demand for a pure description excludes equally
the procedure of analytical reflection on the one hand, and that of
scientific explanation on the other. Descartes and particularly Kant
detached the subject, or consciousness, by showing that I could not
possibly apprehend anything as existing unless I first of all experienced
myself as existing in the act of apprehending it. They presented consciousness, the absolute certainty of my existence for myself, as the
condition of there being anything at all; and the act of relating as the
basis of relatedness. It is true that the act of relating is nothing if
divorced from the spectacle of the world in which relations are found;
the unity of consciousness in Kant is achieved simultaneously with
that of the world. And in Descartes methodical doubt does not
deprive us of anything, since the whole world, at least in so far as we
experience it, is reinstated in the *Cogito,* enjoying equal certainty, and
simply labelled 'thought about . . .' . But the relations between subject and world are not strictly bilateral: if they were, the certainty of
the world would, in Descartes, be immediately given with that of the
Cogito, and Kant would not have talked about his 'Copernican
revolution'. Analytical reflection starts from our experience of the
world and goes back to the subject as to a condition of possibility
distinct from that experience, revealing the all-embracing synthesis as
that without which there would be no world. To this extent it ceases
to remain part of our experience and offers, in place of an account, a
reconstruction. It is understandable, in view of this, that Husserl,
having accused Kant of adopting a 'faculty psychologism',[3] should
have urged, in place of a noetic analysis which bases the world on the
synthesizing activity of the subject, his own *'noematic reflection'*
which remains within the object and, instead of begetting it, brings
to light its fundamental unity.

   The world is there before any possible analysis of mine, and it
would be artificial to make it the outcome of a series of syntheses
which link, in the first place sensations, then aspects of the object
corresponding to different perspectives, when both are nothing but
products of analysis, with no sort of prior reality. Analytical reflection
believes that it can trace back the course followed by a prior constituting act and arrive, in the 'inner man'—to use Saint Augustine's
expression—at a constituting power which has always been identical
with that inner self. Thus reflection itself is carried away and trans-

---

[3] *Logische Untersuchungen, Prolegomena zur reinen Logik,* p. 93.

(margin note:) What about the Stegosauras, only dimly aware it's alive—doesn't it perceive other things as well? or better?

planted in an impregnable subjectivity, as yet untouched by being and time. But this is very ingenuous, or at least it is an incomplete form of reflection which loses sight of its own beginning. When I begin to reflect my reflection bears upon an unreflective experience; moreover my reflection cannot be unaware of itself as an event, and so it appears to itself in the light of a truly creative act, of a changed structure of consciousness, and yet it has to recognize, as having priority over its own operations, the world which is given to the subject, because the subject is given to himself. The real has to be described, not constructed or formed. Which means that I cannot put perception into the same category as the syntheses represented by judgements, acts or predications. My field of perception is constantly filled with a play of colours, noises and fleeting tactile sensations which I cannot relate precisely to the context of my clearly perceived world, yet which I nevertheless immediately 'place' in the world, without ever confusing them with my daydreams. Equally constantly I weave dreams round things. I imagine people and things whose presence is not incompatible with the context, yet who are not in fact involved in it: they are ahead of reality, in the realm of the imaginary. If the reality of my perception were based solely on the intrinsic coherence of 'representations', it ought to be for ever hesitant and, being wrapped up in my conjectures on probabilities, I ought to be ceaselessly taking apart misleading syntheses, and reinstating in reality stray phenomena which I had excluded in the first place. But this does not happen. The real is a closely woven fabric. It does not await our judgement before incorporating the most surprising phenomena, or before rejecting the most plausible figments of our imagination. Perception is not a science of the world, it is not even an act, a deliberate taking up of a position; it is the background from which all acts stand out, and is presupposed by them. The world is not an object such that I have in my possession the law of its making; it is the natural setting of, and field for, all my thoughts and all my explicit perceptions. Truth does not 'inhabit' only 'the inner man',[4] or more accurately, there is no inner man, man is in the world, and only in the world does he know himself. When I return to myself from an excursion into the realm of dogmatic common sense or of science, I find, not a source of intrinsic truth, but a subject destined to be in the world.

[4] In te redi; in interiore homine habitat veritas (Saint Augustine).

All of which reveals the true meaning of the famous phenomenological reduction. There is probably no question over which Husserl has spent more time—or to which he has more often returned, since the 'problematic of reduction' occupies an important place in his unpublished work. For a long time, and even in recent texts, the reduction is presented as the return to a transcendental consciousness before which the world is spread out and completely transparent, quickened through and through by a series of apperceptions which it is the philosopher's task to reconstitute on the basis of their outcome. Thus my sensation of redness is _perceived as_ the manifestation of a certain redness experienced, this in turn as the manifestation of a red surface, which is the manifestation of a piece of red cardboard, and this finally is the manifestation or outline of a red thing, namely this book. We are to understand, then, that it is the apprehension of a certain _hylè,_ as indicating a phenomenon of a higher degree, the _Sinngebung,_ or active meaning-giving operation which may be said to define consciousness, so that the world is nothing but 'world-as-meaning', and the phenomenological reduction is idealistic, in the sense that there is here a transcendental idealism which treats the world as an indivisible unity of value shared by Peter and Paul, in which their perspectives blend. 'Peter's consciousness' and 'Paul's consciousness' are in communication, the perception of the world 'by Peter' is not Peter's doing any more than its perception 'by Paul' is Paul's doing; in each case it is the doing of pre-personal forms of consciousness, whose communication raises no problem, since it is demanded by the very definition of consciousness, meaning or truth. In so far as I am a consciousness, that is, in so far as something has meaning for me, I am neither here nor there, neither Peter nor Paul; I am in no way distinguishable from an 'other' consciousness, since we are immediately in touch with the world and since the world is, by definition, unique, being the system in which all truths cohere. A logically consistent transcendental idealism rids the world of its opacity and its transcendence. The world is precisely that thing of which we form a representation, not as men or as empirical subjects, but in so far as we are all one light and participate in the One without destroying its unity. Analytical reflection knows nothing of the problem of other minds, or of that of the world, because it insists that with the first glimmer of consciousness there appears in me theoretically the power of reaching some universal truth, and that the other

person, being equally without thisness, location or body, the Alter
and the Ego are one and the same in the true world which is the
unifier of minds. There is no difficulty in understanding how *I* can
conceive the Other, because the I and consequently the Other are not
conceived as part of the woven stuff of phenomena; they have validity
rather than existence. There is nothing hidden behind these faces
and gestures, no domain to which I have no access, merely a little
shadow which owes its very existence to the light. For Husserl,
on the contrary, it is well known that there is a problem of other
people, and the *alter ego* is a paradox. If the other is truly for himself
alone, beyond his being for me, and if we are for each other and not
both for God, we must necessarily have some appearance for each
other. He must and I must have an outer appearance, and there must
be, besides the perspective of the For Oneself—my view of myself and
the other's of himself—a perspective of For Others—my view of
others and theirs of me. Of course, these two perspectives, in each
one of us, cannot be simply juxtaposed, *for in that case it is not I
that the other would see, nor he that I should see.* I must be the
exterior that I present to others, and the body of the other must be the
other himself. This paradox and the dialectic of the Ego and the
Alter are possible only provided that the Ego and the Alter Ego are
defined by their situation and are not freed from all inherence; that is,
provided that philosophy does not culminate in a return to the self,
and that I discover by reflection not only my presence to myself, but
also the possibility of an 'outside spectator'; that is, again, provided
that at the very moment when I experience my existence—at the ultimate extremity of reflection—I fall short of the ultimate density
which would place me outside time, and that I discover within myself
a kind of internal weakness standing in the way of my being totally
individualized: a weakness which exposes me to the gaze of others as
a man among men or at least as a consciousness among consciousnesses. Hitherto the *Cogito* depreciated the perception of others,
teaching me as it did that the I is accessible only to itself, since it
defined *me* as the thought which I have of myself, and which clearly
I am alone in having, at least in this ultimate sense. For the 'other'
to be more than an empty word, it is necessary that my existence
should never be reduced to my bare awareness of existing, but that it
should take in also the awareness that *one* may have of it, and thus
include my incarnation in some nature and the possibility, at least, of

a historical situation. The *Cogito* must reveal me in a situation, and it is on this condition alone that transcendental subjectivity can, as Husserl puts it,[5] *be* an intersubjectivity. As a meditating Ego, I can clearly distinguish from myself the world and things, since I certainly do not exist in the way in which things exist. I must even set aside from myself my body understood as a thing among things, as a collection of physico-chemical processes. But even if the *cogitatio,* which I thus discover, is without location in objective time and space, it is not without place in the phenomenological world. The world, which I distinguished from myself as the totality of things or of processes linked by causal relationships, I rediscover 'in me' as the permanent horizon of all my *cogitationes* and as a dimension in relation to which I am constantly situating myself. The true *Cogito* does not define the subject's existence in terms of the thought he has of existing, and furthermore does not convert the indubitability of the world into the indubitability of thought about the world, nor finally does it replace the world itself by the world as meaning. On the contrary it recognizes my thought itself as an inalienable fact, and does away with any kind of idealism in revealing me as 'being-in-the-world'.

It is because we are through and through compounded of relationships with the world that for us the only way to become aware of the fact is to suspend the resultant activity, to refuse it our complicity (to look at it *ohne mitzumachen,* as Husserl often says), or yet again, to put it 'out of play'. Not because we reject the certainties of common sense and a natural attitude to things—they are, on the contrary, the constant theme of philosophy—but because, being the presupposed basis of any thought, they are taken for granted, and go unnoticed, and because in order to arouse them and bring them to view, we have to suspend for a moment our recognition of them. The best formulation of the reduction is probably that given by Eugen Fink, Husserl's assistant, when he spoke of 'wonder' in the face of the world.[6] Reflection does not withdraw from the world towards the unity of consciousness as the world's basis; it steps back to watch the forms of transcendence fly up like sparks from a fire; it slackens the intentional threads which attach us to the world and thus brings them to our

[margin handwritten notes:] One can't escape the fact that for all his subjectivity, his feeling of I' as separate from 'other', he is still a 'Being-in-the-world!'

reflection is a suspension of belief, stepping back and beholding essences.

[5]*Die Krisis der europäischen Wissenschaften und die transzendentale Phäno-menologie,* III (unpublished).

[6] *Die phänomenologische Philosophie Edmund Husserls in der gegenwärtigen Kritik,* pp. 331 and ff.

notice; it alone is consciousness of the world because it reveals that world as strange and paradoxical. Husserl's transcendental is not Kant's and Husserl accuses Kant's philosophy of being 'worldly', because it *makes use* of our relation to the world, which is the motive force of the transcendental deduction, and makes the world immanent in the subject, instead of *being filled with wonder* at it and conceiving the subject as a process of transcendence towards the world. All the misunderstandings with his interpreters, with the existentialist 'dissidents' and finally with himself, have arisen from the fact that in order to see the world and grasp it as paradoxical, we must break with our familiar acceptance of it and, also, from the fact that from this break we can learn nothing but the unmotivated upsurge of the world. The most important lesson which the reduction teaches us is the impossibility of a complete reduction. This is why Husserl is constantly re-examining the possibility of the reduction. If we were absolute mind, the reduction would present no problem. But since, on the contrary, we are in the world, since indeed our reflections are carried out in the temporal flux on to which we are trying to seize (since they *sich einströmen,* as Husserl says), there is no thought which embraces all our thought. The philosopher, as the unpublished works declare, is a perpetual beginner, which means that he takes for granted nothing that men, learned or otherwise, believe they know. It means also that philosophy itself must not take itself for granted, in so far as it may have managed to say something true; that it is an ever-renewed experiment in making its own beginning; that it consists wholly in the description of this beginning, and finally, that radical reflection amounts to a consciousness of its own dependence on an unreflective life which is its initial situation, unchanging, given once and for all. Far from being, as has been thought, a procedure of idealistic philosophy, phenomenological reduction belongs to existential philosophy: Heidegger's 'being-in-the-world' appears only against the background of the phenomenological reduction.

A misunderstanding of a similar kind confuses the notion of the 'essences' in Husserl. Every reduction, says Husserl, as well as being transcendental is necessarily eidetic. That means that we cannot subject our perception of the world to philosophical scrutiny without ceasing to be identified with that act of positing the world, with that interest in it which delimits us, without drawing back from our commitment which is itself thus made to appear as a spectacle, without

[margin, handwritten:] Husserl's transcendental remains suspended, it is never totally immersed in the world, but remains somewhat apart, retaining an identity

[margin, handwritten:] Like Russell trying to make a set of all those things that are part of the world.

passing from the *fact* of our existence to its *nature,* from the Dasein to the Wesen. But it is clear that the essence is here not the end, but a means, that our effective involvement in the world is precisely what has to be understood and made amenable to conceptualization, for it is what polarizes all our conceptual particularizations. The need to proceed by way of essences does not mean that philosophy takes them as its object, but, on the contrary, that our existence is too tightly held in the world to be able to know itself as such at the moment of its involvement, and that it requires the field of ideality in order to become acquainted with and to prevail over its facticity. The Vienna Circle, as is well known, lays it down categorically that we can enter into relations only with meanings. For example, 'consciousness' is not for the Vienna Circle identifiable with what we are. It is a complex meaning which has developed late in time, which should be handled with care, and only after the many meanings which have contributed, throughout the word's semantic development, to the formation of its present one have been made explicit. Logical positivism of this kind is the antithesis of Husserl's thought. Whatever the subtle changes of meaning which have ultimately brought us, as a linguistic acquisition, the word and concept of consciousness, we enjoy direct access to what it designates. For we have the experience of ourselves, of that consciousness which we are, and it is on the basis of this experience that all linguistic connotations are assessed, and precisely through it that language comes to have any meaning at all for us. 'It is that as yet dumb experience . . . which we are concerned to lead to the pure expression of its own meaning'.[7] Husserl's essences are destined to bring back all the living relationships of experience, as the fisherman's net draws up from the depths of the ocean quivering fish and seaweed. Jean Wahl is therefore wrong in saying that 'Husserl separates essences from existence'.[8] The separated essences are those of language. It is the office of language to cause essences to exist in a state of separation which is in fact merely apparent, since through language they still rest upon the ante-predicative life of consciousness. In the silence of primary consciousness can be seen appearing not only what words mean, but also what things mean: the core of primary meaning round which the acts of naming and expression take shape.

Seeking the essence of consciousness will therefore not consist in de-

---

[7] *Méditations cartésiennes,* p. 33.
[8] *Réalisme, dialectique et mystère,* l'Arbalète, Autumn, 1942, unpaginated.

veloping the *Wortbedeutung* of consciousness and escaping from existence into the universe of things said; it will consist in rediscovering
my actual presence to myself, the fact of my consciousness which is in
the last resort what the word and the concept of consciousness mean.
Looking for the world's essence is not looking for what it is as an
idea once it has been reduced to a theme of discourse; it is looking for
what it is as a fact for us, before any thematization. Sensationalism
'reduces' the world by noticing that after all we never experience any
thing but states of ourselves. Transcendental idealism too 'reduces'
the world since, in so far as it guarantees the world, it does so by
regarding it as thought or consciousness of the world, and as the mere
correlative of our knowledge, with the result that it becomes immanent in consciousness and the 'aseity' of things is thereby done away
with. The eidetic reduction is, on the other hand, the determination
to bring the world to light as it is before any falling back on ourselves
has occurred, it is the ambition to make reflection emulate the unreflective life of consciousness. I aim at and perceive a world. If I said,
as do the sensationalists, that we have here only 'states of consciousness', and if I tried to distinguish my perceptions from my dreams
with the aid of 'criteria', I should overlook the phenomenon of the
world. For if I am able to talk about 'dreams' and 'reality', to bother
my head about the distinction between imaginary and real, and cast
doubt upon the 'real', it is because this distinction is already made by
me before any analysis; it is because I have an experience of the real
as of the imaginary, and the problem then becomes one not of asking
how critical thought can provide for itself secondary equivalents of
this distinction, but of making explicit our primordial knowledge of
the 'real', of describing our perception of the world as that upon
which our idea of truth is forever based. We must not, therefore,
wonder whether we really perceive a world, we must instead say: the
world is what we perceive. In more general terms we must not wonder
whether our self-evident truths are real truths, or whether, through
some perversity inherent in our minds, that which is self-evident for
us might not be illusory in relation to some truth in itself. For in so
far as we talk about illusion, it is because we have identified illusions,
and done so solely in the light of some perception which at the same
time gave assurance of its own truth. It follows that doubt, or the
fear of being mistaken, testifies as soon as it arises to our power of
unmasking error, and that it could never finally tear us away from

truth. We are in the realm of truth and it is 'the experience of truth' which is self-evident.[9] To seek the essence of perception is to declare that perception is, not presumed true, but defined as access to truth. So, if I now wanted, according to idealistic principles, to base this *de facto* self-evident truth, this irresistible belief, on some absolute self-evident truth, that is, on the absolute clarity which my thoughts have for me; if I tried to find in myself a creative thought which bodied forth the framework of the world or illumined it through and through, I should once more prove unfaithful to my experience of the world, and should be looking for what makes that experience possible instead of looking for what it is. The self-evidence of perception is not adequate thought or apodeictic self-evidence.[10] The world is not what I think, but what I live through. I am open to the world, I have no doubt that I am in communication with it, but I do not possess it; it is inexhaustible. 'There is a world', or rather: 'There is the world'; I can never completely account for this ever-reiterated assertion in my life. This facticity of the world is what constitutes the *Weltlichkeit der Welt,* what causes the world to be the world; just as the facticity of the *cogito* is not an imperfection in itself, but rather what assures me of my existence. The eidetic method is the method of a phenomenological positivism which bases the possible on the real.

We can now consider the notion of intentionality, too often cited as the main discovery of phenomenology, whereas it is understandable only through the reduction. 'All consciousness is consciousness of something'; there is nothing new in that. Kant showed, in the *Refutation of Idealism,* that inner perception is impossible without outer perception, that the world, as a collection of connected phenomena, is anticipated in the consciousness of my unity, and is the means whereby I come into being as a consciousness. What distinguishes intentionality from the Kantian relation to a possible object is that the unity of the world, before being posited by knowledge in a specific act of identification, is 'lived' as ready-made or already there. Kant himself shows in the *Critique of Judgement* that there exists a unity of the imagination and the understanding and a unity of subjects *before the object,* and that, in experiencing the beautiful, for example, I am

9 *Das Erlebnis der Wahrheit* (*Logische Untersuchungen, Prolegomena zur reinen Logik*) p. 190.
10 There is no apodeictic self-evidence, the *Formale und transzendentale Logik* (p. 142) says in effect.

aware of a harmony between sensation and concept, between myself and others, which is itself without any concept. Here the subject is no longer the universal thinker of a system of objects rigorously inter-related, the positing power who subjects the manifold to the law of the understanding, in so far as he is to be able to put together a world —he discovers and enjoys his own nature as spontaneously in harmony with the law of the understanding. But if the subject has a nature, then the hidden art of the imagination must condition the categorial activity. It is no longer merely the aesthetic judgement, but knowledge too which rests upon this art, an art which forms the basis of the unity of consciousness and of consciousnesses.

Husserl takes up again the *Critique of Judgement* when he talks about a teleology of consciousness. It is not a matter of duplicating human consciousness with some absolute thought which, from outside, is imagined as assigning to it its aims. It is a question of recognizing consciousness itself as a project of the world, meant for a world which it neither embraces nor possesses, but towards which it is perpetually directed—and the world as this pre-objective individual whose imperious unity decrees what knowledge shall take as its goal. This is why Husserl distinguishes between intentionality of act, which is that of our judgements and of those occasions when we voluntarily take up a position—the only intentionality discussed in the *Critique of Pure Reason*—and operative intentionality (*fungierende Intentionalität*), or that which produces the natural and antepredicative unity of the world and of our life, being apparent in our desires, our evaluations and in the landscape we see, more clearly than in objective knowledge, and furnishing the text which our knowledge tries to translate into precise language. Our relationship to the world, as it is untiringly enunciated within us, is not a thing which can be any further clarified by analysis; philosophy can only place it once more before our eyes and present it for our ratification. *But by thinking about our relationship to the world (some people introspect more than others) doesn't this change our relationship to the world?*

Through this broadened notion of intentionality, phenomenological 'comprehension' is distinguished from traditional 'intellection', which is confined to 'true and immutable natures', and so phenomenology can become a phenomenology of origins. Whether we are concerned with a thing perceived, a historical event or a doctrine, to 'understand' is to take in the total intention—not only what these things are for representation (the 'properties' of the thing perceived, the mass of 'historical facts', the 'ideas' introduced by the doctrine)—but the unique mode of existing expressed in the properties of the pebble, the glass or the piece of wax, in all the events of a revolution, in all the thoughts of a philosopher. It is a matter, in the case of each civilization, of finding the Idea in the Hegelian sense, that is, not a law of the physico-mathematical type, discoverable by objective thought, but that formula which sums up some unique manner of behaviour towards others, towards Nature, time and death: a certain way of patterning the world which the historian should be capable of seizing upon and making his own. These are the *dimensions* of history. In this context there is not a human word, not a gesture, even one which is the outcome of habit or absent-mindedness, which has not some meaning. For example, I may have been under the impression that I lapsed into silence through weariness, or some minister may have thought he had uttered merely an appropriate platitude, yet my silence or his words immediately take on a significance, because my fatigue or his falling back upon a ready-made formula are not accidental, for they express a certain lack of interest, and hence some degree of adoption of a definite position in relation to the situation.

When an event is considered at close quarters, at the moment when it is lived through, everything seems subject to chance: one man's ambition, some lucky encounter, some local circumstance or other appears to have been decisive. But chance happenings offset each other, and facts in their multiplicity coalesce and show up a certain way of taking a stand in relation to the human situation, reveal in fact an *event* which has its definite outline and about which we can talk. Should the starting-point for the understanding of history be ideology, or politics, or religion, or economics? Should we try to understand a doctrine from its overt content, or from the psychological make-up and the biography of its author? We must seek an understanding from all these angles simultaneously, everything has meaning, and we shall find this same structure of being underlying all relationships. All these views are true provided that they are not isolated, that we delve deeply into history and reach the unique core of existential meaning which emerges in each perspective. It is true, as Marx says, that history does not walk on its head, but it is also true that it does not think with its feet. Or one should say rather that it is neither its 'head' nor its 'feet' that we have to worry about, but its body. All economic and psychological explanations of a doctrine are true, since the thinker never thinks from any starting-point but the one constituted by what he is. Reflection even on a doctrine will be complete only if it succeeds in linking up with the doctrine's history and the extraneous explanations of it, and in putting back the causes and meaning of the doctrine in an existential structure. There is, as Husserl says, a 'genesis of meaning' (*Sinngenesis*),[11] which alone, in the last resort, teaches us what the doctrine 'means'. Like understanding, criticism must be pursued at all levels, and naturally, it will be insufficient, for the refutation of a doctrine, to relate it to some accidental event in the author's life: its significance goes beyond, and there is no pure accident in existence or in coexistence, since both absorb random events and transmute them into the rational.

Finally, as it is indivisible in the present, history is equally so in its sequences. Considered in the light of its fundamental dimensions, all periods of history appear as manifestations of a single existence, or as episodes in a single drama—without our knowing whether it has an ending. Because we are in the world, we are *condemned to meaning,* and we cannot do or say anything without its acquiring a name in history.

Probably the chief gain from phenomenology is to have united extreme subjectivism and extreme objectivism in its notion of the world or of rationality. Rationality is precisely measured by the experiences in which it is disclosed. To say that there exists rationality is to say that perspectives blend, perceptions confirm each other, a meaning emerges. But it should not be set in a realm apart, transposed into absolute Spirit, or into a world in the realist sense. The phenomenological world is not pure being, but the sense which is revealed where the paths of my various experiences intersect, and also where my own and other people's intersect and engage each other like gears. It is thus inseparable from subjectivity and intersubjectivity, which find their unity when I either take up my past experiences in those of the present, or other people's in my own. For the first time the philosopher's thinking is sufficiently conscious not to anticipate itself and endow its own results with reified form in the world. The philosopher tries to conceive the world, others and himself and their interrelations. But the meditating Ego, the 'impartial spectator' (*uninteressierter Zuschauer*)[12] do not rediscover an already given rationality, they 'establish' them-

---

[11] The usual term in the unpublished writings. The idea is already to be found in the *Formale und transzendentale Logik,* pp. 184 and ff.
[12] *6th Méditation cartésienne* (unpublished).

selves',[13] and establish it, by an act of initiative which has no guarantee in being, its justification resting entirely on the effective power which it confers on us for taking our own history upon ourselves.

The phenomenological world is not the bringing to explicit expression of a pre-existing being, but the laying down of being. Philosophy is not the reflection of a pre-existing truth, but, like art, the act of bringing truth into being. One may well ask how this creation is *possible,* and if it does not recapture in things a pre-existing Reason. The answer is that the only pre-existent Logos is the world itself, and that the philosophy which brings it into visible existence does not begin by being *possible;* it is actual or real like the world of which it is a part, and no explanatory hypothesis is clearer than the act whereby we take up this unfinished world in an effort to complete and conceive it. Rationality is not a *problem.* There is behind it no unknown quantity which has to be determined by deduction, or, beginning with it, demonstrated inductively. We witness every minute the miracle of related experiences, and yet nobody knows better than we do how this miracle is worked, for we are ourselves this network of relationships. The world and reason are not problematical. We may say, if we wish, that they are mysterious, but their mystery defines them: there can be no question of dispelling it by some 'solution', it is on the hither side of all solutions. True philosophy consists in re-learning to look at the world, and in this sense a historical account can give meaning to the world quite as 'deeply' as a philosophical treatise. We take our fate in our hands, we become responsible for our history through reflection, but equally by a decision on which we stake our life, and in both cases what is involved is a violent act which is validated by being performed.

Phenomenology, as a disclosure of the world, rests on itself, or rather provides its own foundation.[14] All knowledge is sustained by a 'ground' of postulates and finally by our communication with the world as primary embodiment of rationality. Philosophy, as radical reflection, dispenses in principle with this resource. As, however, it too is in history, it too exploits the world and constituted reason. It must therefore put to itself the question which it puts to all branches of knowledge, and so duplicate itself infinitely, being, as Husserl says,

---

[13] Ibid.
[14] '*Rückbeziehung der Phänomenologie auf sich selbst,*' say the unpublished writings.

a dialogue or infinite meditation, and, in so far as it remains faithful to its intention, never knowing where it is going. The unfinished nature of phenomenology and the inchoative atmosphere which has surrounded it are not to be taken as a sign of failure, they were inevitable because phenomenology's task was to reveal the mystery of the world and of reason.[15] If phenomenology was a movement before becoming a doctrine or a philosophical system, this was attributable neither to accident, nor to fraudulent intent. It is as painstaking as the works of Balzac, Proust, Valéry or Cézanne—by reason of the same kind of attentiveness and wonder, the same demand for awareness, the same will to seize the meaning of the world or of history as that meaning comes into being. In this way it merges into the general effort of modern thought.

---

[15] We are indebted for this last expression to G. Gusdorf, who may well have used it in another sense.

PART TWO

Philosophy and the Sciences of Man

Merleau-Ponty's major philosophical contributions in The Structure of Behavior *and* Phenomenology of Perception *were preceded by a discussion and critique of the contribution of science. This critique constitutes a reduction, in the phenomenological sense, of the world of science to the primary world of the perceptually given. Merleau-Ponty defends the thesis that the perceptual world and hence perception is primary in the first selection. It was written after the completion of* Phenomenology of Perception *and constitutes Merleau-Ponty's presentation of the findings of this work to the Société française de philosophie in November of 1946.*

Concrete applications of the relation of phenomenology to the social sciences are presented by Merleau-Ponty in the two following selections, first to sociology and then to psychoanalysis. These findings can be generalized to other social sciences as well.

3 · THE PRIMACY OF PERCEPTION
AND ITS PHILOSOPHICAL CONSEQUENCES

The unprejudiced study of perception by psychologists has finally revealed that the perceived world is not a sum of objects (in the sense in which the sciences use this word), that our relation to the world is not that of a thinker to an object of thought, and finally that the unity of the perceived thing, as perceived by several consciousnesses, is not comparable to the unity of a proposition [*théorème*], as understood by several thinkers, any more than perceived existence is comparable to ideal existence.[1]

As a result we cannot apply the classical distinction of form and matter to perception, nor can we conceive the perceiving subject as a consciousness which "interprets," "deciphers," or "orders" a sensible matter according to an ideal law which it possesses. Matter is "pregnant" with its form, which is to say that in the final analysis every perception takes place within a certain horizon and ultimately in the "world." We experience a perception and its horizon "in action" [*pratiquement*] rather than by "posing" them or explicitly "knowing" them.

Maurice Merleau-Ponty, "The Primacy of Perception and Its Philosophical Consequences," *The Primacy of Perception and Other Essays,* Part I, Ch. 2, ed. by James M. Edie, trans. by James M. Edie (Evanston, Illinois: Northwestern University Press, 1964), pp. 12–27. Reprinted by permission.

[1] This address to the Société française de philosophie was given shortly after the publication of Merleau-Ponty's major work, the *Phenomenology of Perception;* and it represents his attempt to summarize and defend the central thesis of that work. . . . The discussion took place on November 23, 1946, and was published in the *Bulletin de la société française de philosophie,* vol. 49 (December, 1947), pp. 119–53.—*Trans.*

Finally the quasi-organic relation of the perceiving subject and the world involves, in principle, the contradiction of immanence and transcendence.

Do these results have any value beyond that of psychological description? They would not if we could superimpose on the perceived world a world of ideas. But in reality the ideas to which we recur are valid only for a period of our lives or for a period in the history of our culture. Evidence is never apodictic, nor is thought timeless, though there is some progress in objectification and thought is always valid for more than an instant. The certainty of ideas is not the foundation of the certainty of perception but is, rather, based on it—in that it is perceptual experience which gives us the passage from one moment to the next and thus realizes the unity of time. In this sense all consciousness is perceptual, even the consciousness of ourselves.

The perceived world is the always presupposed foundation of all rationality, all value and all existence. This thesis does not destroy either rationality or the absolute. It only tries to bring them down to earth.

. . . The point of departure for these remarks is that the perceived world comprises relations and, in a general way, a type of organization which has not been recognized by classical psychology and philosophy.

If we consider an object which we perceive but one of whose sides we do not see, or if we consider objects which are not within our visual field at this moment—i.e., what is happening behind our back or what is happening in America or at the South Pole—how should we describe the existence of these absent objects or the nonvisible parts of present objects?

Should we say, as psychologists have often done, that I *represent* to myself the sides of this lamp which are not seen? If I say these sides are representations, I imply that they are not grasped as actually existing; because what is represented is not here before us, I do not actually perceive it. It is only a possible. But since the unseen sides of this lamp are not imaginary, but only hidden from view (to see them it suffices to move the lamp a little bit), I cannot say that they are representations.

Should I say that the unseen sides are somehow anticipated by me, as perceptions which would be produced necessarily if I moved, given the structure of the object? If, for example, I look at a cube, knowing the structure of the cube as it is defined in geometry, I can anticipate the perceptions which this cube will give me while I move around it.

Under this hypothesis I would know the unseen side as the necessary consequence of a certain law of the development of my perception. But if I turn to perception itself, I cannot interpret it in this way because this analysis can be formulated as follows: It is *true* that the lamp has a back, that the cube has another side. But this formula, "It is true," does not correspond to what is given to me in perception. Perception does not give me truths like geometry but presences.

I grasp the unseen side as present, and I do not affirm that the back of the lamp exists in the same sense that I say the solution of a problem exists. The hidden side is present in its own way. It is in my vicinity.

Thus I should not say that the unseen sides of objects are simply possible perceptions, nor that they are the necessary conclusions of a kind of analysis or geometrical reasoning. It is not through an intellectual synthesis which would freely posit the total object that I am led from what is given to what is not actually given; that I am given, together with the visible sides of the object, the nonvisible sides as well. It is, rather, a kind of practical synthesis: I can touch the lamp, and not only the side turned toward me but also the other side; I have only to extend my hand to hold it.

The classical analysis of perception reduces all our experience to the single level of what, for good reasons, is judged to be true. But when, on the contrary, I consider the whole setting [*l'entourage*] of my perception, it reveals another modality which is neither the ideal and necessary being of geometry nor the simple sensory event, the *"percipi,"* and this is precisely what remains to be studied now.

But these remarks on the setting [*entourage*] of what is perceived enable us better to see the perceived itself. I perceive before me a road or a house, and I perceive them as having a certain dimension: the road may be a country road or a national highway; the house may be a shanty or a manor. These identifications presuppose that I recognize the truc size of the object, quite different from that which appears to me from the point at which I am standing. It is frequently said that I restore the true size on the basis of the apparent size by analysis and conjecture. This is inexact for the very convincing reason that the apparent size of which we are speaking is not perceived by me. It is a remarkable fact that the uninstructed have no awareness of perspective and that it took a long time and much reflection for men to become aware of a perspectival deformation of objects. Thus there is no deciphering, no mediate inference from the sign to what is signified, because the alleged signs are not given to me separately from what they signify.

In the same way it is not true that I deduce the true color of an object on the basis of the color of the setting or of the lighting, which most of the time is not perceived. At this hour, since daylight is still coming through the windows, we perceive the yellowness of the artificial light, and it alters the color of objects. But when daylight disappears this yellowish color will no longer be perceived, and we will see the objects more or less in their true colors. The true color thus is not deduced, taking account of the lighting, because it appears precisely when daylight disappears.

If these remarks are true, what is the result? And how should we understand this "I perceive" which we are attempting to grasp?

We observe at once that it is impossible, as has often been said, to decompose a perception, to make it into a collection of sensations, because in it the whole is prior to the parts—and this whole is not an ideal whole. The meaning which I ultimately discover is not of the conceptual order. If it were a concept, the question would be how I can recognize it in the sense data, and it would be necessary for me to interpose between the concept and the sense data certain intermediaries, and then other intermediaries between these intermediaries, and so on. It is necessary that meaning and signs, the form and matter of perception, be related from the beginning and that, as we say, the matter of perception be "pregnant with its form."

In other words, the synthesis which constitutes the unity of the perceived objects and which gives meaning to the perceptual data is not an intellectual synthesis. Let us say with Husserl that it is a "synthesis of transition" [synthèse de transition][2]—I anticipate the unseen side of the lamp because I can touch it—or a "horizonal synthesis" [synthèse d'horizon]—the unseen side is given to me as "visible from another standpoint," at once given but only immanently. What prohibits me from treating my perception as an intellectual act is that an intellectual act would grasp the object either as possible or as necessary. But in perception it is "real"; it is given as the infinite sum of an indefinite series of perspectival views in each of which the object is given but in none of which is it given exhaustively. It is not accidental

---

[2] The more usual term in Husserl is "passive synthesis," which designates the "syntheses" of perceptual consciousness as opposed to the "active syntheses" of imagination and categorial thought.—Trans.

for the object to be given to me in a "deformed" way, from the point of view [place] which I occupy. That is the price of its being "real." The perceptual synthesis thus must be accomplished by the subject, which can both delimit certain perspectival aspects in the object, the only ones actually given, and at the same time go beyond them. This subject, which takes a point of view, is my body as the field of perception and action [pratique]—in so far as my gestures have a certain reach and circumscribe as my domain the whole group of objects familiar to me. Perception is here understood as a reference to a whole which can be grasped, in principle, only through certain of its parts or aspects. The perceived thing is not an ideal unity in the possession of the intellect, like a geometrical notion, for example; it is rather a totality open to a horizon of an indefinite number of perspectival views which blend with one another according to a given style, which defines the object in question.

Perception is thus paradoxical. The perceived thing itself is paradoxical; it exists only in so far as someone can perceive it. I cannot even for an instant imagine an object in itself. As Berkeley said, if I attempt to imagine some place in the world which has never been seen, the very fact that I imagine it makes me present at that place. I thus cannot conceive a perceptible place in which I am not myself present. But even the places in which I find myself are never completely given to me; the things which I see are things for me only under the condition that they always recede beyond their immediately given aspects. Thus there is a paradox of immanence and transcendence in perception. Immanence, because the perceived object cannot be foreign to him who perceives; transcendence, because it always contains something more than what is actually given. And these two elements of perception are not, properly speaking, contradictory. For if we reflect on this notion of perspective, if we reproduce the perceptual experience in our thought, we see that the kind of evidence proper to the perceived, the appearance of "something," requires both this presence and this absence.

Finally, the world itself, which (to give a first, rough definition) is the totality of perceptible things and the thing of all things, must be understood not as an object in the sense the mathematician or the physicist give to this word—that is, a kind of unified law which would cover all the partial phenomena or as a fundamental relation verifiable in all—but as the universal style of all possible perceptions. We must make this notion of the world, which guides the whole transcendental deduction of Kant, though Kant does not tell us its provenance, more explicit. "If a world is to be possible," he says sometimes, as if he were thinking before the origin of the world, as if he were assisting at its genesis and could pose its *a priori* conditions. In fact, as Kant himself said profoundly, we can only think the world because we have already experienced it; it is through this experience that we have the idea of being, and it is through this experience that the words "rational" and "real" receive a meaning simultaneously.

If I now consider not the problem of knowing how it is that there are things for me or how it is that I have a unified, unique, and developing perceptual experience of them, but rather the problem of knowing how my experience is related to the experience which others have of the same objects, perception will again appear as the paradoxical phenomenon which renders being accessible to us.

If I consider my perceptions as simple sensations, they are private; they are mine alone. If I treat them as acts of the intellect, if perception is an inspection of the mind, and the perceived object an idea, then you and I are talking about the same world, and we have *the right* to communicate among ourselves because the world has become an ideal existence and is the same for all of us—just like the Pythagorean theorem. But neither of these two formulas accounts for our experience. If a friend and I are standing before a landscape, and if I attempt to show my friend something which I see and which he does not yet see, we cannot account for the situation by saying that I see something in my own world and that I attempt, by sending verbal messages, to give rise to an analogous perception in the world of my friend. There are not two numerically distinct worlds plus a mediating language which alone would bring us together. There is—and I know it very well if I become impatient with him—a kind of demand that what I see be seen by him also. And at the same time this communication is required by the very thing which I am looking at, by the reflections of sunlight upon it, by its color, by its sensible evidence. The thing imposes itself not as true for every intellect, but as real for every subject who is standing where I am.

I will never know how you see red, and you will never know how I see it; but this separation of consciousness is recognized only after a failure of communication, and our first movement is to believe in an undivided being between us. There is no reason to treat this primordial communication as an illusion, as the sensationalists do, because even then it would become inexplicable. And there is no reason to base it on our common participation in the same intellectual consciousness because this would suppress the undeniable plurality of consciousnesses. It is thus necessary that, in the perception of another, I find myself in relation with another "myself," who is, in principle, open to the same truths as I am, in relation to the same being that I am. And this perception is realized. From the depths of my subjectivity I see another subjectivity invested with equal rights appear, because the behavior of the other takes place within my perceptual field. I understand this behavior, the words of another; I espouse his thought because this other, born in the midst of my phenomena, appropriates them and treats them in accord with typical behaviors which I myself have experienced. Just as my body, as the system of all my holds on the world, founds the unity of the objects which I perceive, in the same way the body of the other—as the bearer of symbolic behaviors and of the behavior of true reality—tears itself away from being one of my phenomena, offers me the task of a true communication, and confers on my objects the new dimension of intersubjective being or, in other words, of objectivity. Such are, in a quick résumé, the elements of a description of the perceived world.

Some of our colleagues who were so kind as to send me their observations in writing grant me that all this is valid as a psychological inventory. But, they add, there remains the world of which we say "It is true"—that is to say, the world of knowledge, the verified world, the world of science. Psychological description concerns only a small section of our experience, and there is no reason, according to them, to give such descriptions any universal value. They do not touch being itself but only the psychological peculiarities of perception. These descriptions, they add, are all the less admissible as being in any way definitive because they are contradicted by the perceived world. How can we admit ultimate contradictions? Perceptual experience is contradictory because it is confused. It is necessary to think it. When we think it, its contradictions disappear under the light of the intellect. Finally, one correspondent tells me that we are invited to return to the perceived world as we experience it. That is to say that there is no need to reflect or to think and that perception knows better than we what it is doing. How can this disavowal of reflection be philosophy?

It is true that we arrive at contradictions when we describe the perceived world. And it is also true that if there were such a thing as a non-contradictory thought, it would exclude the world of perception as a simple appearance. But the question is precisely to know whether there is such a thing as logically coherent thought or thought in the pure state. This is the question Kant asked himself and the objection which I have just sketched is a pre-Kantian objection. One of Kant's discoveries, whose consequences we have not yet fully grasped, is that all our experience of the world is throughout a tissue of concepts which lead to irreducible contradictions if we attempt to take them in an absolute sense or transfer them into pure being, and that they nevertheless found the structure of all our phenomena, of everything which *is* for us. It would take too long to show (and besides it is well known) that Kantian philosophy itself failed to utilize this principle fully and that both its investigation of experience and its critique of dogmatism remained incomplete. I wish only to point out that the accusation of contradiction is not decisive, *if the acknowledged contradiction appears as the very condition of consciousness.* It is in this sense that Plato and Kant, to mention only them, accepted the contradiction of which Zeno and Hume wanted no part. There is a vain form of contradiction which consists in affirming two theses which exclude one another at the same time and under the same aspect. And there are philosophies which show contradictions present at the very heart of time and of all relationships. There is the sterile non-contradiction of formal logic and the justified contradictions of transcendental logic. The objection with which we are concerned would be admissible only if we could put a system of eternal truths in the place of the perceived world, freed from its contradictions.

We willingly admit that we cannot rest satisfied with the description of the perceived world as we have sketched it up to now and that it appears as a psychological curiosity if we leave aside the idea of the true world, the world as thought by the understanding. This leads us, therefore, to the second point which I propose to examine: what is the relation between intellectual consciousness and perceptual consciousness?

Before taking this up, let us say a word about the other objection which was addressed to us: you go back to the unreflected [*irréfléchi*]; therefore you renounce reflection. It is true that we discover the unreflected. But the unreflected we go back to is not that which is prior to philosophy or prior to reflection. It is the unreflected which is understood and conquered by reflection. Left to itself, perception forgets itself and is ignorant of its own accomplishments. Far from thinking that philosophy is a useless repetition of life I think, on the contrary, that without reflection life would probably dissipate itself in ignorance of itself or in chaos. But this does not mean that reflection should be carried away with itself or pretend to be ignorant of its origins. By fleeing difficulties it would only fail in its task.

Should we now generalize and say that what is true of perception is also true in the order of the intellect and that in a general way all our experience, all our knowledge, has the same fundamental structures, the same synthesis of transition, the same kind of horizons which we have found in perceptual experience?

No doubt the absolute truth or evidence of scientific knowledge would be opposed to this idea. But it seems to me that the acquisitions of the philosophy of the sciences confirm the primacy of perception. Does not the work of the French school at the beginning of this century, and the work of Brunschvieg, show that scientific knowledge cannot be closed in on itself, that it is always an approximate knowledge, and that it consists in clarifying a pre-scientific world the analysis of which will never be finished? Physico-mathematical relations take on a physical sense only to the extent that we at the same time represent to ourselves the sensible things to which these relations ultimately apply. Brunschvieg reproached positivism for its dogmatic illusion that the law is truer than the fact. The law, he adds, is conceived exclusively to make the fact intelligible. The perceived happening can never be reabsorbed in the complex of transparent relations which the intellect constructs because of the happening. But if this is the case, philosophy is not only consciousness of these relations; it is also consciousness of the obscure element and of the "non-relational foundation" on which these relations are based. Otherwise it would shirk its task of universal clarification. When I think the Pythagorean theorem and recognize it as true, it is clear that this truth is not for this moment only. Nevertheless later progress in knowledge will show that it is not yet a final, unconditioned evidence and that, if the Pythagorean theorem and the Euclidean system once appeared as final, unconditioned evidences, that is itself the mark of a certain cultural epoch. Later developments would not annul the Pythagorean theorem but would put it back in its place as a partial, and also an abstract, truth. Thus here also we do not have a timeless truth but rather the recovery of one time by another time, just as, on the level of perception, our certainty about perceiving a given thing does not guarantee that our experience will not be contradicted, or dispense us from a fuller experience of that thing. Naturally it is necessary to establish here a difference between ideal truth and perceived truth. I do not propose to undertake this immense task just now. I am only trying to show the organic tie, so to speak, between perception and intellection. Now it is incontestable that I dominate the stream of my conscious states and even that I am unaware of their temporal succession. At the moment when I am thinking or considering an idea, I am not divided into the instants of my life. But it is also incontestable that this domination of time, which is the work of thought, is always somewhat deceiving. Can I seriously say that I will always hold the ideas I do at present—and mean it? Do I not know that in six months, in a year, even if I used more or less the same formulas to express my thoughts, they will have changed their meaning slightly? Do I not know that there is a life of ideas, as there is a meaning of everything I experience, and that every one of my most convincing thoughts will need additions and then will be, not destroyed, but at least integrated into a new unity? This is the only conception of knowledge that is scientific and not mythological.

Thus perception and thought have this much in common—that both of them have a future horizon and a past horizon and that they appear to themselves as temporal, even though they do not move at the same speed nor in the same time. We must say that at each moment our ideas express not only the truth but also our capacity to attain it at that given moment. Skepticism begins if we conclude from this that our ideas are always false. But this can only happen with reference to some idol of absolute knowledge. We must say, on the contrary, that our ideas, however limited they may be at a given moment—since they always express our contact with being and with culture—are capable of being true provided we keep them open to the field of nature and culture which they must express. And this possibility is always open to us, just because we are temporal. The idea of going straight to the essence of things is an inconsistent idea if one thinks about it. What is given is a route, an experience which gradually clarifies itself, which gradually rectifies itself and proceeds by dialogue with itself and with others. Thus what we tear away from the dispersion of instants is not an already-made reason; it is, as has always been said, a natural light, our openness to *something*. What saves us is the possibility of a new development, and our power of making even what is false, true—by thinking through our errors and replacing them within the domain of truth.

But finally, it will be objected that I grasp myself in pure reflection, completely outside perception, and that I grasp myself not now as a perceiving subject, tied by its body to a system of things, but as a thinking subject, radically free with respect to things and with respect to the body. How is such an experience of self, of the *cogito,* possible in our perspective, and what meaning does it have?

There is a first way of understanding the *cogito:* it consists in saying that when I grasp myself I am limited to noting, so to speak, a psychic fact, "I think." This is an instantaneous constatation, and under the condition that the experience has no duration I adhere immediately to what I think and consequently cannot doubt it. This is the *cogito* of the psychologists. It is of this instantaneous *cogito* that Descartes was thinking when he said that I am certain that I exist during the whole time that I am thinking of it. Such certitude is limited to my existence and to my pure and completely naked thought. As soon as I make it specific with any particular thought, I fail, because, as Descartes explains, every particular thought uses premises not actually given. Thus the first truth, understood in this way, is the only truth. Or rather it cannot even be formulated as truth; it is experienced in the instant and in silence. The *cogito* understood in this way—in the skeptical way—does not account for our idea of truth.

There is a second way of understanding the *cogito:* as the grasping not only of the fact that I think but also of the objects which this thought intends, and as evidence not only of a private existence but also of the things which it thinks, at least as it thinks them. In this perspective the *cogito* is neither more certain than the *cogitatum,* nor does it have a different kind of certainty. Both are possessed of ideal evidence. Descartes sometimes presented the *cogito* in this way—as, for example, in the *Regulae* when he placed one's own existence (*se esse*) among the most simple evidences. This supposes that the subject is perfectly transparent for itself, like an essence, and is incompatible with the idea of the hyperbolic doubt which even reaches to essences.

But there is a third meaning of the *cogito,* the only solid one: the act of doubting in which I put in question all possible objects of my experience. This act grasps itself in its own operation [*à l'oeuvre*] and thus cannot doubt itself. The very fact of doubting obturates doubt.

The certitude I have of myself is here a veritable perception: I grasp myself, not as a constituting subject which is transparent to itself, and which constitutes the totality of every possible object of thought and experience, but as a particular thought, as a thought engaged with certain objects, as a thought in act; and it is in this sense that I am certain of myself. Thought is given to itself; I somehow find myself thinking and I become aware of it. In this sense I am certain that I am thinking this or that as well as being certain that I am simply thinking. Thus I can get outside the psychological *cogito*—without, however, taking myself to be a universal thinker. I am not simply a constituted happening; I am not a universal thinker [*naturant*].[3] I am a thought which recaptures itself as already possessing an ideal of truth (which it cannot at each moment wholly account for) and which is the horizon of its operations. This thought, which *feels* itself rather than *sees* itself, which searches after clarity rather than possesses it, and which creates truth rather than finds it, is described in a formerly celebrated text of Lagneau. Should we submit to life or create it, he asked. And he answered: "Once again this question does not pertai nto the domain of the intellect; we are free and, in this sense, skepticism is true. But to answer negatively is to make the world and the self unintelligible; it is to decree chaos and above all to establish it in the self. But chaos is nothing. To be or not to be, the self and everything else, we must choose" (*Cours sur l'existence de dieu*). I find here, in an author who spent his whole life reflecting on Descartes, Spinoza, and Kant, the idea—sometimes considered barbarous—of a thought which remembers it began in time and then sovereignly recaptures itself and in which fact, reason, and freedom coincide.

Finally, let us ask what happens, from such a point of view, to rationality and experience, whether there can be any absolute affirmation already implied in experience.

The fact that my experiences hold together and that I experience the concordance of my own experiences with those of others is in no way compromised by what we have just said. On the contrary, this fact is put in relief, against skepticism. Something appears to me, as to anyone else, and these phenomena, which set the boundaries of everything thinkable or conceivable for us, are certain as phenomena. There is meaning. But rationality is neither a total nor an immediate guarantee. It is somehow open, which is to say that it is menaced.

[3] The reference is to Spinoza's *natura naturans.—Trans.*

Doubtless this thesis is open to two types of criticism, one from the psychological side and the other from the philosophical side.

The very psychologists who have described the perceived world as I did above, the Gestalt psychologists, have never drawn the philosophical conclusions of their description. In that respect they remain within the classical framework. Ultimately they consider the structures of the perceived world as the simple result of certain physical and physiological processes which take place in the nervous system and completely determine the *gestalten* and the experience of the *gestalten*. The organism and consciousness itself are only functions of external physical variables. Ultimately the real world is the physical world as science conceives it, and it engenders our consciousness itself.

But the question is whether Gestalt theory, after the work it has done in calling attention to the phenomena of the perceived world, can fall back on the classical notion of reality and objectivity and incorporate the world of the *gestalten* within this classical conception of reality. Without doubt one of the most important acquisitions of this theory has been its overcoming of the classical alternatives between objective psychology and introspective psychology. Gestalt psychology went beyond this alternative by showing that the object of psychology is the structure of behavior, accessible both from within and from without. In his book on the chimpanzees, Köhler applied this idea and showed that in order to describe the behavior of a chimpanzee it is necessary, in characterizing this behavior, to bring in notions such as the "melodic line" of behavior. These are anthropomorphic notions, but they can be utilized objectively because it is possible to agree on interpreting "melodic" and "non-melodic" behaviors in terms of "good solutions" and "bad solutions." The science of psychology thus is not something constructed outside the human world; it is, in fact, a property of the human world to make the distinction between the true and the false, the objective and the fictional. When, later on, Gestalt psychology tried to explain itself—in spite of its own discoveries—in terms of a scientistic or positivistic ontology, it was at the price of an internal contradiction which we have to reject.

Coming back to the perceived world as we have described it above, and basing our conception of reality on the phenomena, we do not in any way sacrifice objectivity to the interior life, as Bergson has been accused of doing. As Gestalt psychology has shown, structure, *Gestalt,* meaning are no less visible in objectively observable behavior than in the experience of ourselves—provided, of course, that objectivity is not confused with what is measurable. Is one truly objective with respect to man when he thinks he can take him as an object which can be explained as an intersection of processes and causalities? Is it not more objective to attempt to constitute a true science of human life based on the description of typical behaviors? Is it objective to apply tests to man which deal only with abstract aptitudes, or to attempt to grasp the situation of man as he is present to the world and to others by means of still more tests?

Psychology as a science has nothing to fear from a return to the perceived world, nor from a philosophy which draws out the consequences of this return. Far from hurting psychology, this attitude, on the contrary, clarifies the philosophical meaning of its discoveries. For there are not two truths; there is not an inductive psychology and an intuitive philosophy. Psychological induction is never more than the methodological means of bringing to light a certain typical behavior, and if induction includes intuition, conversely intuition does not occur in empty space. It exercises itself on the facts, on the material, on the phenomena brought to light by scientific research. There are not two kinds of knowledge, but two different degrees of clarification of the same knowledge. Psychology and philosophy are nourished by the same phenomena; it is only that the problems become more formalized at the philosophical level.

But the philosophers might say here that we are giving psychology too big a place, that we are compromising rationality by founding it on the texture of experience, as it is manifested in perceptual experience. But either the demand for an absolute rationality is only a wish, a personal preference which should not be confused with philosophy, or this point of view, to the extent that it is well-founded, satisfies it as well as, or even better than, any other. When philosophers wish to place reason above the vicissitudes of history they cannot purely and simply forget what psychology, sociology, ethnography, history, and psychiatry have taught us about the conditioning of human behavior. It would be a very romantic way of showing one's love for reason to base its reign on the disavowal of acquired knowledge. What can be validly demanded is that man never be submitted to the fate of an external nature or history and stripped of his consciousness. Now my philosophy satisfies this demand. In speaking of the primacy of perception, I have never, of course, meant to say (this would be a return to the theses of empiricism) that science, reflection, and philosophy are only transformed sensations or that values are deferred and calculated pleasures. By these words, the "primacy of perception," we mean that the experience of perception is our presence at the moment when things, truths, values are constituted for us; that perception is a nascent *logos;* that it teaches us, outside all dogmatism, the true conditions of objectivity itself; that it summons us to the tasks of knowledge and action. It is not a question of reducing human knowledge to sensation, but of assisting at the birth of this knowledge, to make it as sensible as the sensible, to recover the consciousness of rationality. This experience of rationality is lost when we take it for granted as self-evident, but is, on the contrary, rediscovered when it is made to appear against the background of non-human nature.

The work[4] which was the occasion for this paper is still, in this respect, only a preliminary study, since it hardly speaks of culture or of history. On the basis of perception—taken as a privileged realm of experience, since the perceived object is by definition present and living—this book attempts to define a method for getting closer to present and living reality, and which must then be applied to the relation of man to man in language, in knowledge, in society and religion, as it was applied in this work to man's relation to perceptible reality and with respect to man's relation to others on the level of perceptual experience. We call this level of experience "primordial"—not to assert that everything else derives from it by transformations and evolution (we have expressly said that man perceives in a way different from any animal) but rather that it reveals to us the permanent data of the problem which culture attempts to resolve. If we have not tied the subject to the determinism of an external nature and have only replaced it in the bed of the perceptible, which it transforms without ever quitting it, much less will we submit the subject to some impersonal history. History is other people; it is the interrelationships we establish with them, outside of which the realm of the ideal appears as an alibi.

This leads us . . . to draw certain conclusions from what has preceded as concerns the realm of the practical. If we admit that our life is inherent to the perceived world and the human world, even while it re-creates it and contributes to its making, then morality cannot consist in the private adherence to a system of values. Principles are mystifications unless they are put into practice; it is necessary that they animate

[4] The *Phenomenology of Perception.—Trans.*

our relations with others. Thus we cannot remain indifferent to the aspect in which our acts appear to others, and the question is posed whether intention suffices as moral justification. It is clear that the approval of such or such a group proves nothing, since, in looking for it, we choose our own judges—which comes down to saying that we are not yet thinking for ourselves. It is the very demand of rationality which imposes on us the need to act in such a way that our action cannot be considered by others as an act of aggression but, on the contrary, as generously meeting the other in the very particularity of a given situation. Now from the very moment when we start bringing the consequences of our actions for others into morality (and how can we avoid doing so if the universality of the act is to be anything more than a word?), it appears possible that our relations with others are involved in immorality, if perchance our perspectives are irreconcilable —if, for instance, the legitimate interests of one nation are incompatible with those of another. Nothing guarantees us that morality is possible, as Kant said in a passage which has not yet been fully understood. But even less is there any fatal assurance that morality is impossible. We observe it in an experience which is the perception of others, and, by sketching here the dangerous consequences which this position entails, we are very much aware of its difficulties—some of which we might wish to avoid. Just as the perception of a thing opens me up to being, by realizing the paradoxical synthesis of an infinity of perceptual aspects, in the same way the perception of the other founds morality by realizing the paradox of an *alter ego,* of a common situation, by placing my perspectives and my incommunicable solitude in the visual field of another and of all the others. Here as everywhere else the primacy of perception—the realization, at the very heart of our most personal experience, of a fecund contradiction which submits this experience to the regard of others—is the remedy to skepticism and pessimism. If we admit that sensibility is enclosed within itself, and if we do not seek communication with the truth and with others except on the level of a disembodied reason, then there is not much to hope for. Nothing is more pessimistic or skeptical than the famous text in which Pascal, asking himself what it is to love, remarks that one does not love a woman for her beauty, which is perishable, or for her mind, which she can lose, and then suddenly concludes: "One never loves anybody; one loves only qualities." Pascal is proceeding like a skeptic who asks *if* the world exists, remarks that the table is only a sum of sensations, the chair another sum of sensations, and finally concludes: one never sees anything; one sees only sensations.

If, on the contrary, as the primacy of perception requires, we call what we perceive "the world," and what we love "the person," there is a type of doubt concerning man, and a type of spite, which become impossible. Certainly, the world which we thus find is not absolutely reassuring. We weigh the hardihood of the love which promises beyond what it knows, which claims to be eternal when a sickness, perhaps an accident, will destroy it . . . . But it is *true,* at the moment of this promise, that our love extends beyond *qualities,* beyond the body, beyond time, even though we could not love without qualities, bodies, and time. In order to safeguard the ideal unity of love, Pascal breaks human life into fragments at will and reduces the person to a discontinuous series of states. The absolute which he looks for beyond our experience is implied in it. Just as I grasp time through my present and by being present, I perceive others through my individual life, in the tension of an experience which transcends itself.

There is thus no destruction of the absolute or of rationality here, only of the absolute and the rationality separated from experience. To tell the truth, Christianity consists in replacing the separated absolute by the absolute in men. Nietzsche's idea that God is dead is already contained in the Christian idea of the death of God. God ceases to be an external object in order to mingle in human life, and this life is not simply a return to a non-temporal conclusion. God needs human history. As Malebranche said, the world is unfinished. My viewpoint differs from the Christian viewpoint to the extent that the Christian believes in another side of things where the *"renversement du pour au contre"* takes place. In my view this "reversal" takes place before our eyes. And perhaps some Christians would agree that the other side of things must already be visible in the environment in which we live. By advancing this thesis of the primacy of perception, I have less the feeling that I am proposing something completely new than the feeling of drawing out the conclusions of the work of my predecessors. . . .

4. THE PHILOSOPHER
AND SOCIOLOGY

Philosophy and sociology have long lived under a segregated system which has succeeded in concealing their rivalry only by refusing them any meeting-ground, impeding their growth, making them incomprehensible to one another, and thus placing culture in a situation of permanent crisis. As always, the spirit of inquiry has gotten around these interdicts; and it seems to us that both philosophy and sociology have now progressed far enough to warrant a reexamination of their relationships.

We would also like to call attention to the thought Husserl gave to these problems. Husserl seems to us to be exemplary in that he may have realized better than anyone else that all forms of thought are in a certain sense interdependent. We need neither tear down the behavioral sciences to lay the foundations of philosophy, nor tear down philosophy to lay the foundations of the behavioral sciences. Every science secretes an ontology; every ontology anticipates a body of knowledge. It is up to us to come to terms with this situation and see to it that both philosophy and science are possible.

The segregation of philosophy and sociology has perhaps nowhere been described in the terms in which we are going to state it. Fortunately, the practices of philosophers and sociologists are often less exclusive than their principles. Yet this segregation nevertheless constitutes a part of a certain common sense of philosophers and soci-

Maurice Merleau-Ponty, "The Philosopher and Sociology," *Signs,* Part II, Ch. 3, trans. by Richard C. McCleary (Evanston, Illinois: Northwestern University Press, 1964), pp. 98–113. Reprinted by permission.

ologists which, by reducing philosophy and the behavioral sciences to what it believes is their ideal type, ultimately endangers scientific knowledge just as much as philosophical reflection.

Even though all the great philosophies are recognizable by their attempt to think about the mind *and its dependency*—ideas and their movement, understanding and sensibility—there is a myth about philosophy which presents it as an authoritarian affirmation of the mind's absolute autonomy. Philosophy so conceived is no longer an inquiry. It is a certain body of doctrines, made to assure an absolutely *unfettered* spirit full possession of itself and its ideas. In another connection, there is a myth about scientific knowledge which expects to attain from the mere recording of facts not only the science of the things of the world but also the science of that science—a sociology of knowledge (conceived of itself in an empiricist fashion) which should make the universe of facts self-contained by including even the ideas we invent to interpret the facts, and thus rid us, so to speak, of ourselves. These two myths sustain one another in their very antagonism. For even though the philosopher and the sociologist are opposed to one another, they at least agree upon a delimitation of boundaries which assures them of never meeting. But if the *cordon sanitaire* were removed, philosophy and sociology would destroy one another. Even now, they battle for our minds. Segregation is cold war.

In this atmosphere, any investigation which seeks to take both ideas and facts into account is immediately bifurcated. Facts, instead of being taken as the spur and warrant for a constructive effort to reach their inner dynamics, are worshipped as a sort of peremptory grace which reveals all truth. And ideas are exempted as a matter of principle from all confrontation with our experience of the world, others, and ourselves. The movement back and forth from facts to ideas and from ideas to facts is discredited as a bastard process— neither science nor philosophy—which denies scientists the final interpretation of the very facts that they have taken the pains to assemble, and which compromises philosophy with the always provisional results of scientific research.

We must be fully aware of the *obscurantist* consequences of this rigid segregation. If "mixed" investigations really have the inconveniences we have just mentioned, then we shall have to admit that a simultaneously philosophical and scientific view of experience is impossible, and that philosophy and sociology can attain certain knowledge only if they ignore one another. We shall have to hide from the scientist that "idealization" of brute fact which is nevertheless the essence of his work. He will have to ignore the deciphering of meanings which is his reason for being, the construction of intellectual models of reality without which there would no more be any sociology today than there would formerly have been Galilean physics. We shall have to put the blinders of Baconian or "Millian" induction back on the scientist, even though his own investigations obviously do not follow these canonical recipes. Consequently, he will pretend to approach social fact as if it were alien to him, as if his study owed nothing to the experience which, as social subject, he has of intersubjectivity.

Under the pretext that as a matter of fact sociology is not yet constructed with this lived experience but is instead an analysis, an explicit formulation and objectification of it which reverses our initial consciousness of social relationships (and ultimately shows that these experienced social relationships are very special variants of a dynamics we are originally unaware of and can learn about only in contact with other cultural formations), objectivism forgets another evident fact. We can expand our experience of social relationships and get a proper view of them only by analogy or contrast with those we have lived. We can do so, in short, only by subjecting the social relationships we have experienced to an *imaginary variation*. These lived relationships will no doubt take on a new meaning in comparison with this imaginary variation (as the fall of a body on an inclined plane is put in a new light by the ideal concept of free fall), but they will provide it with all the sociological meaning it can have.

Anthropology teaches us that in such and such cultures children treat certain cousins as their "kin," and facts of this sort allow us ultimately to draw up a diagram of the kinship structure in the civilization under consideration. But the correlations thus noted give only the silhouette or contour of kinship in that civilization, a cross-section of behavior patterns which are nominally defined as those of "kinship" at certain significant but still anonymous points X . . . , Y . . . , Z . . . . In short, these correlations do not yet have a sociological meaning. As long as we have not succeeded in installing ourselves in the institution which they delimit, in understanding the style of kinship which all these facts allude to and *the sense in which* certain subjects in that culture perceive other subjects of their generation as their "kin," and finally, in grasping the basic personal and interpersonal structure and the institutional relationships with nature and others which make the established correlations possible, the formulas which sum up these correlations could just as well represent a given physical or chemical process of the same form. Let us make it perfectly clear that the underlying dynamics of the social whole is certainly not *given* with our narrow experience of living among others, yet it is only by throwing this experience in and out of focus that we succeed in representing it to ourselves, just as the generalized number remains number for us only through the link which binds it to the whole number of elementary arithmetic.

On the basis of Freudian conceptions of pre-genital sexuality, we can make up a list of all the possible modes of accentuation of the orifices of the child's body, and the ones which are realized by our cultural system and have been described by the Freudians appear on the list as singular variants among a great number of possible ones which are perhaps current in civilizations as yet unknown to us. But this list tells us *nothing* about the relationships with others and with nature which define these cultural types, as long as we do not refer to the psychological meaning of the mouth, the anus, or the genital equipment in our own experience, so as to see in the different uses which are made of them by different cultures, different crystallizations of an initial polymorphism of the body as vehicle of being-in-the-world. The list we are shown is only an invitation to imagine, on the basis of our experience of the body, other techniques of the body. The technique which happens to be actualized in us can never be reduced to simply one among all possible techniques; for it is against the background of this privileged experience, where we learn to know the body as a "structuring" principle, that we glimpse the other "possibles," no matter how different from it they may be.

It is essential never to cut sociological inquiry off from our experience of social subjects (which of course includes not only what we have experienced ourselves but also the behavior we perceive through the gestures, tales, or writings of our fellow men). For the sociologist's equations begin to represent something social only at the moment when the correlations they express are connected to one another and enveloped in a certain unique *view* of the social and of nature which is characteristic of the society under consideration and has come to be institutionalized in it as the hidden principle of all its overt functioning—even though this view may be rather different than the official conceptions which are current in that society. If objectivism or scientism were ever to succeed in depriving sociology of all recourse to significations, it would save it from "philosophy" only by shutting it off from knowledge of its object. Then we might do mathematics in the social, but we would not have the mathematics *of* the society being considered. The sociologist philosophizes every time he is required to not only record but comprehend the facts. At the moment of interpretation, he is himself already a philosopher. This means that the professional philosopher is not disqualified to reinterpret facts he has not observed himself, if these facts say something more and different than what the scientist has seen in them. As Husserl says, eidetic analysis of the physical thing did not begin with phenomenology but with Galileo. And reciprocally, the philosopher has the right to read and interpret Galileo.

The segregation we are fighting against is no less harmful to philosophy than to the development of scientific knowledge. How could any philosopher aware of the philosophical tradition seriously propose to forbid philosophy to have anything to do with science? For after all the philosopher always thinks *about something:* about the square traced in the sand, about the ass, the horse, and the mule, about the cubic foot of size, about cinnabar, the Roman State, and the hand burying itself in the iron filings. The philosopher thinks about his experience and his world. Except by decree, how could he be given the right to forget what science says about this same experience and world? Under the collective noun "science" there is nothing other than a systematic handling and a methodical use—narrower and broader, more and less discerning—of this same experience which begins with our first perception. Science is a set of means of perceiving, imagining, and, in short, living which are oriented toward the same truth that our first experiences establish an urgent inner need for. Science may indeed purchase its exactness at the price of schematization. But the remedy in this case is to confront it with an integral experience, not to oppose it to philosophical knowledge come from who knows where.

Husserl's great merit is that from the time he reached philosophical maturity, and increasingly so as he pursued his efforts, he made use of his "intuition of essences," "morphological essences," and "phenomenological experience" to mark out a realm and an attitude of inquiry where philosophy and effective knowledge could meet. We know that he began by affirming, and continued to maintain, a rigorous distinction between the two. Nevertheless, it seems to us that his idea of a psycho-phenomenological parallelism (or as we may say in generalizing, his thesis of a parallelism between positive knowledge and philosophy such that there is for each affirmation of one a corresponding affirmation of the other) leads him in truth to the idea of *reciprocal envelopment*. As far as the social is concerned then, the problem is to know how it can be both a "thing" to be acquainted with without prejudices, and a "signification" which the societies we acquaint ourselves with only provide an occasion for—how, that is, the social can exist both in itself and in us. Having entered this labyrinth, let us follow the stages by which Husserl makes his way toward his last conceptions, in which, moreover, these stages will be as much retained as gone beyond.

At the outset, he asserts philosophy's rights in terms which seem to abolish those of actual knowledge. Speaking of that eminently social relation, language, he states as a principle[1] that we could not possibly understand the functioning of our own language, or break away from the pseudo-certainties which result from the fact that it is ours and gain a true acquaintance with other languages, unless we had first constituted a schema of the "ideal form" *of* language and of the modes of expression which must in strict necessity pertain to it if it is to be language. Only then will we be able to understand how German, Latin, and Chinese participate (each in its own way) in this universal structure of essential meanings, and to define each of these languages as a mixture in original proportions of universal "forms of signification"—a "confused" and incomplete realization of the "general and rational grammar." The actually existing language was thus to be reconstructed by a synthetic operation which began with the essential structures of any possible language and enveloped it in their ideal clarity. Philosophical thought took on an air of absolute autonomy, it and only it being capable of attaining true understanding through recourse to essences which provided the key to things.

Generally speaking, this stage of Husserl's thought calls our whole historical experience of social relationships into question in the interest of determining essences. Historical experience does present us with many "social processes" and "cultural formations" such as forms of law, art, and religion. But as long as we stick to such empirical realizations, we do not even know the meaning of these headings we class

[1] *Logische Untersuchungen*, II, 4te Unters., p. 339.

them under. And, consequently, we know even less whether the historical changes in a given religion or a given form of law or art are really essential and provide a true standard of their value; or whether on the contrary this law, this art, this religion contain yet other possibilities. History, Husserl used to say at this point, cannot judge an idea; and when it does, this "evaluating" (*wertende*) history borrows surreptitiously from the "ideal sphere" the necessary connections which it pretends to bring forth from the facts.[2]

As for the "world-views" which submit to being no more than the balance of what the knowledge available at any given moment allows us to think, Husserl grants that the problem they raise is a real one, but he objects that it is raised in such a way as to block any serious solution. The real problem stems from the fact that philosophy would lose its meaning if it refused to judge the present. Just as a morality which was "as a matter of principle transfinite and endless" would no longer be a morality, a philosophy which as a matter of principle gave up taking any position in the present would no longer be a philosophy.[3] But the fact is that in wanting to face up to present problems, "to have their system, and in time enough to be able to live afterwards,"[4] the *Weltanschauung* philosophers miss everything. They can bring no more rigor to the solution of these problems than other men, because like them they are within the *Weltanschauung* and have no *Weltwissenschaft*. And in devoting themselves entirely to thinking about the present, they rob true philosophy of the unconditional devotion she demands. Now once constituted, true philosophy would allow us to think about the present as well as the past and the eternal. To go straight to the present is thus to relinquish the solid for the illusory.

When in the second part of his career Husserl returns to the problems of history, and especially to the problem of language, we no longer find the idea of a philosopher-subject, master of all that is possible, who must first put *his own* language at a distance in order to find the ideal forms of a universal language this side of all actuality. Philosophy's first task in respect to language now appears to be to reveal to us anew our inherence in a certain system of speech of which we make fully efficacious use precisely because it is present to us just as immediately as our body. Philosophy of language is no longer con-

---

[2] *Philosophie als strenge Wissenschaft,* p. 325.
[3] *Ibid.,* p. 332.
[4] *Ibid.,* p. 338.

trasted to empirical linguistics as an attempt at total objectification of language to a science which is always threatened by the preconceptions of the native language. On the contrary, it has become the rediscovery of the subject in the act of speaking, as contrasted to a science of language which inevitably treats this subject as a thing. Pos[5] has shown quite clearly how the phenomenological attitude is contrasted to the scientific or observational attitude. The latter, since it is directed toward an already established language, takes that language in the past and breaks it down into a sum of linguistic facts in which its unity disappears. The former has become the attitude that permits direct access to the living language present in a linguistic community which uses it not only to preserve but to establish, and to envisage and define a future. So here a language is no longer broken down into elements which can be added up piece by piece; it is like an organ whose tissues all contribute to its unified functioning, irrespective of the diversity of their origins and the fortuitousness of their original insertion into the whole.

Now if it is really the peculiar office of phenomenology to approach language in this way, phenomenology is no longer the synthetic determination of all possible languages. Reflection is no longer the return to a pre-empirical subject which holds the keys to the world; it no longer circumambulates its present object and possesses its constitutive parts. Reflection must become aware of its object in a contact or frequenting which at the outset exceeds its power of comprehension. The philosopher is first and foremost the one who realizes that he is situated in language, that he *is speaking;* and phenomenological reflection can no longer be limited to a completely lucid enumeration of the "conditions without which" there would be no language. It must show why there is speech—that paradox of a subject turned toward the future who speaks and understands—in spite of all we know about the accidents and shifts of meaning which have created the language. Present speech casts a light which is not found in any merely "possible" expression. It is an operation in our linguistic "field of presence" which, far from being a particular case of other possible systems of expression, serves as our model for conceiving of them. Reflection is no longer the passage to a different order which reabsorbs the order of present things; it is first and foremost a more acute awareness of the way in which we are

[5] H. Pos, "Phénoménologie et Linguistique," *Revue Internationale de Philosophie* (January, 1939).

rooted in them. From now on, the absolute condition of a valid philosophy is that it pass by way of the present.

To tell the truth, we do not have to wait until Husserl recognizes
that the *Lebenswelt* is phenomenology's principal theme to note the
repudiation of formal reflection in his thought. The reader of the *Ideen
I* will have already noticed that eidetic intuition has always been a
"confirmation," and phenomenology an "experience" (a phenomenology of seeing, Husserl said, should be constructed on the basis of a
Sichtigkeit which we have actually experienced to begin with; and he
generally rejected the possibility of a "mathematics of phenomena" or
a "geometry of what is lived"). It is just that the ascending movement
was not stressed. Thought barely supported itself on its actually existing structures in order to sift out its possible ones: a wholly imaginary
variation extracted a treasure of eidetic assertions from the lowest-
grade experience. When the recognition of the life-world, and thus too
of language as we live it, becomes characteristic of phenomenology (as
it does in the last wirtings), this is only a more resolute way of saying
that philosophy does not possess the truth about language and the
world from the start, but is rather the recuperation and first formulation of a Logos scattered out in our world and our life and bound to
their concrete structures—that "Logos of the aesthetic world" already
spoken of in the *Formal and Transcendental Logic.* Husserl will only
be bringing the movement of all his previous thought to completion
when he writes in a posthumous fragment that transitory inner phenomena are brought to ideal existences by becoming incarnate in
language.[6] Ideal existence, which at the beginning of Husserl's thought
was to have been the foundation for the possibility of language, is now
the most characteristic possibility *of* language.

But if philosophy no longer consists in passing to the infinity of
possibles or leaping into absolute objectivity, then it is understandable
that certain linguistic investigations should anticipate Husserl's own,
and that certain linguists should without knowing it tread upon the
ground of phenomenology. Husserl does not say it, nor does Pos, but it
is hard not to think of Saussure when Husserl insists that we return
from language as object to the spoken word.

In reality, philosophy's whole relationship to history changes in the
very movement of reflection which was trying to free philosophy from

[6] Ursprung der Geometrie," *Revue Internationale de Philosophie* (January,
1939), p. 210.

history. In proportion as he reflects further upon the relation between eternal and factual truths, Husserl finds it necessary to replace his initial delimitations with a far less simple relation. His meditations on transcendental reflection and its possibility, which he pursued for at least twenty years, show clearly enough that in his view this term did not designate some sort of distinct faculty which could be circumscribed, pointed out, and actually isolated side by side with other modalities of experience. In spite of all his trenchant formulations constantly reaffirming the radical distinction between the natural and the transcendental attitude, Husserl is well aware from the start that they do in fact encroach upon one another, and that every *fact of consciousness* bears the transcendental within it. As far as the relation of fact and essence is concerned, in any case, a text as old as *Philosophy as a Rigorous Science* (after having distinguished, as we have been recalling, the "ideal sphere" and historical facts) expressly foresaw the overlapping of the two orders. For it pointed out that the reason why historical criticism really shows that a given order of institutions has no substantial reality, and is actually only a common noun to designate a mass of facts with no internal relation, is that empirical history includes confused intuitions of essences, and criticism is always the reverse side or emergence of a positive assertion which is already there.

In the same article, Husserl was already admitting that history is precious to the philosopher *because it reveals the Gemeingeist to him.* It is not so hard to go from these first formulations to the later ones. To say that history teaches the philosopher what the *Gemeingeist* is, is to say that it gives him the problem of intersubjective communication to think about. It makes it necessary for him to understand how there are not only individual minds (each incumbent in a perspective on the world) which the philosopher can inspect by turns without being allowed (and even less required) to think of them *together,* but also a community of minds coexisting for one another and as a consequence invested individually with an exterior through which they become visible. As a result, the philosopher may no longer speak of mind in general, deal with each and every mind under a single name, or flatter himself that he constitutes them. Instead he must see himself within the dialogue of minds, situated as they all are, and grant them the dignity of self-constituting beings at the very moment that he claims that dignity for himself. We are on the verge of the enigmatic formulation Husserl will arrive at in the texts of the *Krisis der europäischen Wissenschaften,* when he writes that "transcendental subjectivity is intersubjectivity."

Now if the transcendental is intersubjectivity, how can the borders of the transcendental and the empirical help becoming indistinct? For along with the other person, all the other person sees of me—all my facticity—is reintegrated into subjectivity, or at least posited as an indispensable element of its definition. Thus the transcendental descends into history. Or as we might put it, the historical is no longer an external relation between two or more absolutely autonomous subjects but has an interior and is an inherent aspect of their very definition. They no longer know themselves to be subjects simply in relation to their individual selves, but in relation to one another as well.

In the unpublished manuscripts of the final period, the contrast between fact and essence will be explicitly mediated by the idea that the purest reflection discloses a "genesis of meaning" (*Sinngenesis*) immanent in its objects—the need for each manifestation of its objects to have a "before" and "after" and develop through a series of steps or stages in which each step anticipates and is taken up in a subsequent one that could not possibly exist "at the same time" as the preceding one yet presupposes it as its past horizon. Of course this intentional history is not simply the sum of all manifestations taken one by one. It takes them up again and puts them in order; in the actuality of a present, it reanimates and rectifies a genesis which could miscarry without it. But it can do so only in contact with what is given, by seeking its motives within it. It is no longer just through an unfortunate accident that the study of significations and the study of facts encroach upon one another. If it did not condense a certain development of *truth,* a signification would be empty.

It is to be hoped that we shall soon be able to read, in the complete works of Husserl,[7] the letter that he wrote to Lévy-Bruhl on March 11, 1935, after having read *La mythologie primitive.* Here he seems to admit that the philosopher could not possibly have immediate access to the universal by reflection alone—that he is in no position to do without anthropological experience or to construct what constitutes the mean-

---

[7] In the process of being published at The Hague by Martinus Nijhoff, under the direction of H. L. Van Breda. The editors have not granted us any rights to quote the few unpublished excerpts to be found here. Consequently we ask the reader not to expect any more than a foretaste of texts whose only authorized edition is being prepared by the Husserl Archives of Louvain.

ing of other experiences and civilizations by a purely imaginary variation of his own experiences. "It is a possible and highly important
task," he writes, "it is a great task to project ourselves into (*einzufüh-
len*) a human community enclosed in its living and traditional
sociality, and to understand it insofar as, in and on the basis of its
total social life, that human community possesses the world, which
is not for it a 'representation of the world' but the real world." Now
our access to archaic worlds is barred by our own world. Lévy-
Bruhl's primitives "have no history" (*geschichtlos*); for them "life is
only a passing present" (*ein Leben, das nur stromende Gegenwart ist*).
We on the contrary live in an historical world; a world, that is, which
"has a partly realized future (the national 'past') and a partly to be
realized future." No intentional analysis seeking to recover and reconstitute the structures of the archaic world could possibly limit itself to
making those of our own explicit; for what gives meaning to these
structures is the milieu or *Umwelt* of which they are the typical style,
and thus we cannot understand them without understanding how time
passes and being is constituted in these cultures. Husserl goes so far as
to write that "on the path of that already largely developed intentional
analysis, historical relativism is incontestably justified as an anthropological fact."

To bring things to a close, how does Husserl now conceive of philosophy? The last lines of the letter give us an idea: philosophy must
accept all the acquisitions of science (which have the first word concerning knowledge), and thus historical relativism along with them.
But as philosophy, it cannot be content to simply make note of the
variety of anthropological facts. "Although anthropology, like every
positive science and all these sciences as a whole, may have the first
word concerning knowledge, it does not have the last." Judging by
Husserl's later views, philosophy would gain autonomy after, not before, positive knowledge. This autonomy would not exempt the philosopher from gathering in everything anthropology has to offer us,
which means, basically, testing our effective communication with other
cultures. Nor could it withhold anything from the scientist's jurisdiction which was accessible to his methods of research. It would simply
set itself up in a dimension where no scientific knowledge can dispute
it. Let us try to show which one.

Suppose the philosopher no longer lays claim to the unconditional
power to think his own thought through and through. He agrees that

his "ideas" and his "certainties" are always to some extent naive, and that caught up as they are in the fabric of the culture he belongs to, they cannot be truly known by just being scrutinized and varied in thought, but must be confronted with other cultural formations and viewed against the background of other preconceptions. Then has he not from this moment on abdicated his office and handed his rights over to empirical investigation and the positive disciplines? No, he has not; that is just the point. The same dependence upon history which prohibits the philosopher from arrogating to himself an immediate access to the universal or the eternal prohibits the sociologist from taking the philosopher's place in this function and giving ontological value to the scientific objectification of the social. The concept of history in its most profound sense does not shut the thinking subject up in a point of space and time; he can seem to be thus contained only to a way of thinking which is itself capable of going outside all time and place in order to see him in his time and place.

Now it is precisely this presumption to absolute thought which is discredited by the historical sense. There can be no question of simply transferring to science the grand-mastery denied to systematic philosophy, as historicism does. "You believe you think for all times and all men," the sociologist says to the philosopher, "and by that very belief you only express the preconceptions or pretensions of your culture." That is true, but it is no less true of the dogmatic sociologist than it is of the philosopher. *Where does he speak from,* the sociologist who speaks in this way? The sociologist can only form this idea of an historical time which allegedly contains philosophers as a box contains an object by placing himself outside history in turn and claiming the privileged position of absolute spectator.

In reality, it is the very concept of the relationships of mind to its object that historical consciousness invites us to reshape. The point is that my thought's inherence in a certain historical situation of its own and, through that situation, in other historical situations which interest it—since it is the fundamental origin and original foundation of the objective relations which science speaks to us about—makes knowledge of the social self-knowledge, and calls forth and authorizes a *view of intersubjectivity as my own* which science forgets even as it utilizes it, and which is proper to philosophy. Since we are all hemmed in by history, it is up to us to understand that whatever truth we may have is to be gotten not in spite of but through our historical inherence. Super-

ficially considered, our inherence destroys all truth; considered radically, it founds a new idea of truth. As long as I cling to the ideal of an
absolute spectator, of knowledge with no point of view, I can see my
situation as nothing but a source of error. But if I have once recognized
that through it I am grafted onto every action and all knowledge which
can have a meaning for me, and that step by step it contains everything
which can *exist* for me, then my contact with the social in the finitude
of my situation is revealed to me as the point of origin of all truth,
including scientific truth. And since we have an idea of truth, since we
are in truth and cannot escape it, the only thing left for me to do is to
define a truth in the situation.

Knowledge will then be based upon the unimpeachable fact that we
are not in a situation like an object in objective space. Our situation is
for us the source of our curiosity, our investigations, and our interest in
first other situations as variants of our own and then in our own life,
illuminated by (and this time considered as a variant of) the lives of
others. Ultimately, our situation is what links us to the whole of human experience, no less than what separates us from it. "Science" and
"sociology" will designate the effort to construct ideal variables which
objectify and schematize the functioning of this effective communication. We shall call "philosophy" the consciousness we must maintain
as our consciousness of the ultimate reality whose functioning our
theoretical constructions retrace but could not possibly replace—of the
open and successive community of *alter egos* living, speaking, and
thinking in one another's presence and in relation to nature as we
sense its presence behind, around, and before us at the limits of our
historical field.

Thus philosophy is not defined by a peculiar domain of its own.
Like sociology, it only speaks about the world, men, and mind. It is
distinguished by a certain *mode* of consciousness we have of others, of
nature, or of ourselves. It is nature and man in the present, not "flattened out" (Hegel) in a derivative objectivity but such as they are
presented in our present cognitive and active commerce with them.
Philosophy is nature in us, the others in us, and we in them. Accord-
ingly, we must not simply say that philosophy is compatible with
sociology, but that it is necessary to it as a constant reminder of its
tasks; and that each time the sociologist returns to the living sources of
his knowledge, to what operates within him as a means of understanding the forms of culture most remote from him, he practices philosophy

spontaneously. Philosophy is not a particular body of knowledge; it is the vigilance which does not let us forget the source of all knowledge.

We are not claiming that Husserl would ever have agreed to some definition of this sort, since up until the end he always thought of the return to living history and the spoken word—the return to the *Lebenswelt*—as a preparatory step which should be followed by the properly philosophical task of universal constitution. Yet it is a fact that in his last published work, rationality is no longer more than one of two possible alternatives we face, the other being chaos. And it is precisely with an awareness of a sort of nameless adversity threatening rationality that Husserl searches for that which can stimulate knowledge and action. Reason as a summons and a task, the "latent reason" which must be changed into itself and brought to explicit consciousness, becomes the criterion of philosophy. "It is only in this way that it will be decided whether the end (*Telos*) innate in the European conception of man since the birth of Greek philosophy—his will to be human on the basis of philosophical reason (and his inability to be so in any other way), in an unending movement from latent to manifest reason, and in an unending attempt to govern himself through his own human truth and authenticity—whether all this is only the mere historical fact of an illusion, the accidental acquisition of one accidental human community among other wholly different human communities and histories. Or whether, on the contrary, there did not come to light for the first time in the Greek conception of man what is essentially inherent as entelechy in the quality of man as man. Taken in itself, the quality of man consists essentially in being human within human communities bound together generatively and socially. And if man is a rational being, he can be so only to the extent that the whole human community he belongs to is a rational community, either latently disposed to reason or openly disposed to an entelechy which has arrived at self-awareness or become evident to itself, and is thus consciously guiding human development according to its essential necessity. Philosophy and science would then be the historical movement of revelation of universal reason, 'innate' in the human community as such."[8] Thus the essence of man is not given, nor is his essential necessity unconditional. His essence will energize his actions only if the rationality first conceived for us by the Greeks does not remain accidental but

[8] "Die Krisis der Europäischen Wissenschaften und die transzendentale Phänomenologie," *Philosophia*, I (1936), p. 92.

proves to be essential by the knowledge and the action it makes possible, and gets itself recognized by irrational human communities. The
Husserlian essence is now borne by an "entelechy."

Philosophy's role as consciousness of rationality in contingency is
no insignificant residue. In the last analysis, only the philosophical
consciousness of intersubjectivity enables us to understand scientific
knowledge. Without this philosophical consciousness, scientific knowledge remains indefinitely in suspense, always deferred until the termination of discussions of causality which, having to do with man, are by
their nature interminable. We wonder for example whether social
relationships are (as psychoanalytic sociology would have it) only the
amplification and generalization of the sexual-aggressive drama, or
whether on the contrary this drama itself (in the form described by
psychoanalysis) is only a particular case of the institutional relationships of Western societies. These discussions have the value of induc-
ing the sociologists to make observations, of revealing facts, and of
giving rise to analyses and insights. But they admit of no conclusion as
long as we remain on the level of causal and "objective" thought, since
we can neither reduce one of the causal chains to nothing nor think of
them together as causal chains. We can hold that both these views are
true (as they are) only on the condition that we move to an a-causal
mode of thought, which is philosophy. For there are two truths which
much be grasped simultaneously. The individual drama takes place
among *roles* which are already inscribed in the total institutional structure, so that from the beginning of his life the child proceeds—simply
by perceiving the attentions paid to him and the utensils surrounding
him—to a deciphering of meanings which from the outset generalizes
his own drama into a drama of his culture. And yet it is the whole
symbolic consciousness which in the last analysis elaborates what the
child lives or does not live, suffers or does not suffer, feels or does not
feel. Consequently, there is not a single detail of his most individual
history which does not contribute something to that personal significance he will manifest when (having first thought and lived as he
thought best, and perceived according to his culture's imagery) he
finally comes to the point of reversing the relationship and slipping
into the meanings of his speech and his behavior, converting even the
most secret aspects of his experience into culture. From the casual point
of view it is unthinkable that this centripetal movement and this
centrifugal movement are compossible. These reversals, these "meta-

morphoses," this proximity and distance of the past and present (of the archaic and the "modern"), this way that cultural time and space roll up on themselves, and this perpetual overdetermination of human events which makes the social fact (no matter how singular the local or temporal conditions) always appear to us as a variant of a single life that ours is also part of, and makes every *other person another ourself* for us—all these things become conceivable or even visible to the philosophical attitude alone.

Philosophy is indeed, and always, a break with objectivism and a return from *constructa* to lived experience, from the world to ourselves. It is just that this indispensable and characteristic step no longer transports it into the rarified atmosphere of introspection or into a realm numerically distinct from that of science. It no longer makes philosophy the rival of scientific knowledge, now that we have recognized that the "interior" it brings us back to is not a "private life" but an intersubjectivity that gradually connects us ever closer to the whole of history. When I discover that the social is not simply an object but to begin with my situation, and when I awaken within myself the consciousness of this social-which-is-mine, then my whole synchrony becomes present to me, through that synchrony I become capable of really thinking about the whole past as the synchrony it has been in its time, and all the convergent and discordant action of the historical community is effectively given to me in my living present. Giving up systematic philosophy as an explanatory device does not reduce philosophy to the rank of an auxiliary or a propagandist in the service of objective knowledge; for philosophy has a dimension of its own, the dimension of coexistence—not as a *fait accompli* and an object of contemplation, but as the milieu and perpetual event of the universal *praxis*. Philosophy is irreplaceable because it reveals to us both the movement by which lives become truths, and the circularity of that singular being who in a certain sense already *is* everything he *happens to think*.

5. PHENOMENOLOGY AND PSYCHOANALYSIS: PREFACE TO HESNARD'S *L'OEUVRE DE FREUD*

Doctor Hesnard has generously asked that a philosopher be present at the beginning of this book, in which we may hear speaking forty years of experience, reading, reflection, and research in the thought of Freud. Certainly it is not for a philosopher to judge this long and militant process of thought. But, thinks Doctor Hesnard, the theory and practice of psychoanalysis presume or induce an attitude of mind and even, all unknown to Freud, a "new philosophy." As a world view psycho analysis converges with other efforts, including phenomenology. Doctor Hesnard approves of those who take care—as I did in an early work*— to separate psychoanalysis from a scientistic or objectivist ideology, who consider the Freudian unconscious as an archaic or primordial consciousness, the repressed as a zone of experience that we have not integrated, the body as a sort of natural or innate complex, and communication as a relation between incarnate beings of this sort who are well or badly integrated. Here phenomenology brings to psycho-analysis certain categories, certain means of expression that it needs in order to be completely itself. Phenomenology permits psychoanalysis to recognize "psychic reality" without equivocation, the "intra-subjective" essence of morbid formations, the fantastic operation that reconstructs a world on the margin of, and counter to, the true world, a lived history beneath the effective history—a world called illness.

Maurice Merleau-Ponty, "Preface," in A. Hesnard, *L'Oeuvre de Freud et son importance pour le Monde Moderne* (Paris: Payot, 1960), pp. 5–10. Trans. by Alden L. Fisher. Reprinted by permission.
* *Phenomenology of Perception* [TRANS.].

Freudian thought, in turn, confirms phenomenology in its description of a consciousness that is not so much knowledge or representation as investment; it brings to phenomenology a wealth of concrete examples that add weight to what it has been able to say in general of the relations of man with the world and of the interhuman bond. Phenomenology and psychoanalysis, in mutual encounter, would lead us toward a philosophy delivered from the interaction between substances, toward a "humanism of truth" without metaphysics. It is concerning this encounter that I have been called upon to testify.

I do this with great pleasure, persuaded as I am that philosophy is concrete and that psychoanalysis is informed with a thought which nevertheless is expressed only very indirectly in certain Freudian concepts. Does not the notion of libido lose all its meaning if there is a "cellular libido," if it is a property of the cells, and the notion of repression its effectiveness if it only exists as "mnemic traces" or as "unconscious representations"? For the physician or the therapist this rudimentary imagery is not so dangerous: the contact with patients and with illness always brings a surplus of meaning, of weight, of density to the meager concepts of the theory. But since psychoanalysis is also an ideology that is talked of and that is becoming an element of our culture, it cannot content itself with concepts that are simply good enough for working *in vivo;* it must formulate the treasure of experience that is hidden in psychoanalytic communication and that until now has been reserved for the initiates. Freud's genius is obviously not that of philosophical or exhaustive expression; it resides, rather, in his contact with things, his polymorphous perception of work, of acts, of dreams, of their flux and their reflux, of counter-coups, of echoes, of substitutions, of metamorphoses. Freud is sovereign in this listening to the confused noises of a life. However long we have had a world, a literature, and fathers, we had to wait for Freud's teaching to discover that in becoming a father a man can also become the child he was, place himself in another role under the oedipean constellation, and discover himself as father—with imaginable consequences for the couple, especially if, as frequently happens, the wife concurrently relates the paternity of the child she brings into the world to her own father.[1] This prodigious intuition of exchanges—exchange of roles, exchange of the soul and the body, of the imaginary and the real—this universal promiscuity, Freud has sometimes described in a language made to

[1] DeVolabrega, and also in this volume [i.e., in Hesnard's book (TRANS.)].

order ("over determination," "complexes," "instances"); but he also frequently simply makes allusions using terms from the medicine and psychologies of his time ("projections," "traces," "representations"). This leads to misunderstandings between Freud and the hurried reader (perhaps between Freud and himself).

The sexuality that is the buttress or nerve of human relations is confused with the sexuality that is a function of the organism, an objective process. The oedipus complex is spoken of as a cause, while actually it only imposes on the child certain poles, a system of references and dimensions, the child's position (or his successive positions) in this context being a matter of individual history.

Every reader of Freud, I imagine, remembers his first impressions: an incredible bias in favor of the least probable interpretations; a maniacal penchant for the sexual; and above all, on the basis of their archaic forms, signification, language, and action obscured in the interest of derisive puns. Then, to the extent that one read, that one related oneself to oneself, and that the years passed, a sort of evidence for psychoanalysis was inexplicably established and one came to live in peace with this pitiless hermeneutic. The adversaries of psychoanalysis commented that, once the barriers between good and evil are broken, a victim does not even feel his abjection. The psychoanalysts said that certain resistances had been disarmed. It was neither exactly the one nor the other. It was not that virtue had allowed itself to be tempted by vice, or bad faith by sincerity. There was really a misunderstanding, and it has been lifted. The psychoanalysis that we accept and like is not the one that we refused. We refused, as we always will, to grant to that phallus which is part of the objective body, the organ of micturition and copulation, such power of causality over so many forms of behavior. What we learned from all the material drawn from dreams, fantasies, and behaviors, and finally even in our own dreaming about the body, was to discern an imaginary phallus, a symbolic phallus, oneiric and poetic. It is not the useful, functional, prosaic body which explains man; on the contrary, it is the human body which rediscovers its symbolic or poetic weight. We refused, and always will, to see behind the dream, the humorous word, the failed act, so absurd a multiplication of associations. What we have now understood is that symbolic matrices, a language of self to self, systems of equivalences built up by the past, effect groupings, abbreviations, and distortions in a simple act and which analysis reconstitutes more and more closely. Freud never says any of this in these terms; but what is the good of allowing the misunderstanding to endure and willingly prolonging the "scandal" of psychoanalysis?

These reasons for reformulating certain Freudian concepts in the framework of a better philosophy still seem true to me. However, a philosophy that is now perhaps more mature, and also the growth of Freudian research—precisely in the direction taken by Doctor Hesnard —would today lead me to express in a different way relations of phenomenology and psychoanalysis, the implicit philosophy of psychoanalysis itself, and in the long run would make me less indulgent than Doctor Hesnard generously is toward my earlier attempts.

The more that one penetrates phenomenological thought, and the more familiar one becomes with Husserl's enterprise, thanks to the publication of his hitherto unpublished works, the better one can distinguish phenomenology from the new *philosophy of consciousness* which it took itself to be at first. A superficial reading of *Ideen I** could lead one to believe that, no matter what happens, philosophy will never have anything to describe but the transparent correlations between acts of thought and objects of thought, that it is a system of apprehensions and pure significations immersed in experience, but which imposes its style and its mode of functioning on the natural and human world. Nevertheless, given this infinite curiosity, this ambition to *see everything,* which animates the phenomenological reduction, what then is the hidden being that it seeks to surprise? As Husserl proceeded to the execution of his program, he brought to light fragments of being which disconcerted his frame of reference: neither the body, which is "subject-object"; nor the passage of interior time, which is not a system of *acts* of consciousness; nor the other person, who is born by previous deduction from me or by expansion of me, as Eve is born from the side of Adam; nor history, which is my life in others and the life of others in me, which is in principle an inexact "object" like other persons—none of these allow themselves to be brought together under the correlation of consciousness and its objects, of the noesis and the noema. Philosophy ceases to be an exact knowledge, a pure regard on pure objects; it is, says Husserl, "what is sought" by the successive generations of philosophers, and no one philosopher coincides with the

* E. Husserl, *Ideen zu einer reinen Phänomenologie und phänomenologische Philosophie,* I. [Critical edition: ed. W. Bimel (The Hague: Nijhoff), 1950]. [Trans.]

"intentional interiority" that they all invoke and that as a group they constitute.[2] All consciousness is consciousness of something or of the world, but this *something,* this world, is no longer, as "phenomenological positivism" appeared to teach, an object that is what it is, exactly adjusted to acts of consciousness. Consciousness is now the "soul of Heraclitus,"[3] and Being, which is around it rather than in front of it, is a Being of dreams, by definition hidden: Husserl sometimes uses the term "pre-being."

This phenomenology which descends into its own substratum is converging more than ever with Freudian research. To stop with intentionality as a relation of ideal objects would now seem to me disloyal to philosophy. "Phenomenological idealism" is insufficient. Furthermore, the idealistic formulation is a threat to the Freudian heritage, perhaps the gravest danger menacing it today. Biologism and objectivism reign no longer; phenomenology, so to speak, has succeeded too well. There is no longer any great risk that Freudian research will shock us by recalling what there is of the "barbarian" in us; the risk is rather that its findings will be too easily accepted in an "idealist" form. Doctor Hesnard shows in one of his chapters that today there is a race toward psychoanalysis, just as there once was a flight from it. Yesterday it was the spirit of evil; today one trims its claws and one adopts it. This is not to understand it better.

When we see what can happen to a civilization in which psychoanalysis is *too well tolerated;* in which psychoanalytic concepts, weakened and banalized, have lost their enigmas and furnish the themes of a new dogmatism; in which the doctrine, learned in elementary school and having become an institution, fashions mentalities that resemble it too much, that seem to verify it, but that actually mask, precisely under an accelerated and superficial analysis, an unconscious of the second degree; when we see all this, we must ask ourselves whether it is not essential to psychoanalysis—I mean for its existence as therapy and as verifiable knowledge—to remain, not exactly a disreputable enterprise or a secret science, but at least a paradox and an interrogation. It is psychoanalysis that has unveiled the oedipean infrastructure of science, of technology, and of "accidental" understanding. It is psychoanalysis that has returned our myths to us. What will

[2] E. Husserl, *Die Krisis Der Europäischen Wissenshaften und Die Transzendentale Phänomenologie* [Ed. W. Bimel (The Hague: Nijhoff), 1954].
[3] *Idem.*

become of all this if the tamed sphinx soberly takes its place in a new philosophy of enlightenment?

Thus there is an idealist deviation of Freudian research alongside the objectivist deviation (and perhaps they are not so opposed at that). When Doctor Lacon writes[4] that the phenomenology of hallucination, to the extent that it attempts to be rigorous, goes beyond the limits of a philosophy of consciousness, he is retracing the steps of a phenomenology which is deepening itself. On the other hand, when Freud writes that, at the time of the analytic cure, the meaning that the patient ends up by finding in his history should rejoin the "mnemic traces," or when he implies in his analyses a summary conception of the sensorium as the functioning of an objective apparatus, this is neither satisfying nor philosophically comprehensible. (These mechanistic and energic metaphors do of course protect, as against every idealization, the threshold of an intuition that is one of the most precious of Freudian thought: that of our *archeology*.)

The best parry to the two dangers we are speaking about would perhaps be to learn to read Freud the way we read a classic, that is, by understanding his words and theoretical concepts, not in their lexical and common meaning, but in the meaning they acquire from within the experience which they announce and of which we have behind our backs much more than a suspicion. Since our philosophy has given us no better way to express that *intemporal,* that *indestructible* element in us which, says Freud, is the unconscious itself, perhaps we should continue calling it the unconscious—so long as we do not forget that the word is the index of an enigma—because the term retains, like the algae or the stone that one drags up, something of the sea from which it was taken.

The accord of phenomenology and of psychoanalysis should not be understood to consist in phenomenology's saying clearly what psychoanalysis had said obscurely. On the contrary, it is by what phenomenology implies or unveils as its limits—by its *latent content* or its *unconscious*—that it is in consonance with psychoanalysis. Thus the cross validation between the two doctrines is not exactly on the subject man; their agreement is, rather, precisely in describing man as a timber yard, in order to discover, beyond the truth of immanence, that of the *Ego* and its acts, that of consciousness and its objects, of relations which a consciousness cannot sustain: man's relations to his origins and his

[4] *La psychanalyse,* 1 (Paris: Presses Universitaires de France, 1956), p. 44.

relations to his models. Freud points his finger at the *Id* and the *Superego*. Husserl, in his last writings, speaks of historical life as of a *Tiefenleben.*[5] Phenomenology and psychoanalysis are not parallel; much better, they are both aiming toward the same *latency*. This is how I would define the relationship today, if I had to take up the question again, not to attenuate what I said before, but, on the contrary, to make it more serious.

In this way I think I rejoin Doctor Hesnard's own conceptions. He who understands illness as the constitution of a world on the borders of the other certainly thinks that man could not thus pass over the true world if it were positively given, or recognizable according to "criteria." Thus these pages only bring new motives for subscribing to the *rapprochement* which Doctor Hesnard proposes, and I would like in writing them to have merited a little better the very courteous invitation which he addressed to me.

---

[5] Husserl, *Die Krisis Der Europäischen Wissenshaften und Die Transzendentale Phänomenologie, op. cit.*

PART THREE

Philosophical Anthropology

The readings in this section represent three major findings in Merleau-Ponty's philosophy of man. The first selection, a lecture he gave on September 10, 1951, at the Rencontres Internationales in Geneva, constitutes his analysis and assessment of man's situation in the middle of the twentieth century.

The second selection, the final chapter of Phenomenology of Perception, represents Merleau-Ponty's conclusions concerning the fact and the nature of human freedom. This chapter clearly shows his sharp divergence from the absolute freedom of Jean-Paul Sartre and illustrates his typical philosophical effort of finding a middle way between extremes.

The final selection is the last chapter of The Structure of Behavior. In earlier chapters the book conducted a sustained critique of objectivist physiology and psychology and attempted to disengage three levels of structure, the inanimate, the animate, and the human. In this last chapter Merleau-Ponty summarizes his findings, locates his conclusions with regard to other philosophical perspectives, and, finally, articulates his nuanced view of the relations of body and soul.

6. MAN AND ADVERSITY

It is clearly impossible to tick off in one hour the advances made in the philosophical investigation of man during the past fifty years.[1] Even if we could assume that this infinite ability existed in one single brain, we would be brought up short before the discordancy among the authors who must be taken into account. The impossibility of ever progressing in any other than an oblique fashion operates like a cultural law, each new idea becoming, after the one which instituted it, different than it was for this instituting idea. A man cannot receive a heritage of ideas without transforming it by the very fact that he comes to know it, without injecting his own and always different way of being into it. In proportion as ideas arise, a tireless volubility sets them stirring; just as a never satisfied "need for expressiveness," the linguists say, transforms languages at the very moment one would think that, having succeeded in ensuring an apparently unequivocal communication among speaking subjects, they were reaching their goal. How would we dare enumerate *acquired ideas,* since even when they have gotten themselves almost universally accepted, they have always done so by also becoming different from themselves?

Furthermore, a catalogue of acquired knowledge would not suffice. Even if we were to lay the "truths" of this half century end-to-end, in

Maurice Merleau-Ponty, "Man and Adversity," *Signs,* Part II, Ch. 11, trans. by Richard C. McCleary (Evanston, Illinois: Northwestern University Press, 1964), pp. 224–43. Reprinted by permission.

[1] Lecture given on September 10, 1951, at the *Rencontres Internationales* in Geneva.

order to restore their hidden affinity, we would still have to revive the personal and interpersonal experience they are a *response* to, and the logic of situations in reference to which they were defined. The great or valuable work is never an effect of life, but it is always a *response* to life's very particular events or most general structures. Although the writer is free to say yes or no to such circumstances, and to justify and limit his refusal or assent in different ways, he never can arrange things so that he does not have to choose his life in a certain historical landscape or state of problems which excludes certain solutions even if it imposes none, and which gives Gide, Proust, and Valéry (no matter how different they may be) the undeniable quality of contemporaries. The movement of ideas comes to discover truths only by responding to some pulsation of interpersonal life, and every change in our understanding of man is related to a new way he has of carrying on his existence. If man is the being who is not content to coincide with himself like a thing but represents himself to himself, sees himself, imagines himself, and gives himself rigorous or fanciful symbols of himself, it is quite clear that in return every change in our representation of man translates a change in man himself. Thus it is the whole history of this half century, with its projects, disappointments, wars, revolutions, audacities, panics, inventions, and failures, that we would have to evoke here. We can only refuse this unlimited task.

Yet this transformation of our understanding of man, which we cannot hope to determine by a rigorous method on the basis of works, ideas, and history, is sedimented in us. It is our substance; we have a lively, total feeling for it when we look back to the writings or the facts of the beginning of the century. What we can try to do is to mark within ourselves, according to two or three selected relationships, modifications in the human situation. We would have to present infinite explanations and commentaries, clear up a thousand misunderstandings, and translate quite different systems of concepts into one another in order to establish an objective relationship between, for example, Husserl's philosophy and Faulkner's works. And yet within us readers they are connected. The very men who (like Ingres and Delacroix) think themselves adversaries are reconciled in the eyes of a third person who witnesses them, because they are responding to a single cultural situation. We men who have lived as our problem the development of communism and the War, and who have read Gide and Valéry and Proust and Husserl and Heidegger and Freud are the same. Whatever our responses have been, there should be a way to circumscribe perceptible zones of our experience and formulate, if not ideas about man that we hold in common, at least a new experience of our condition.

With these reservations, we propose to acknowledge that our century is distinguished by a completely new association of "materialism" and "idealism," of pessimism and optimism, or rather by the fact that it has gone beyond these antitheses. Our contemporaries have no difficulty thinking both that human life is the demand for an original order and that this order could not possibly endure or even truly exist except under certain very precise and very concrete conditions which can fail to materialize, no natural arrangement of things and the world predestining them to make a human life possible.

It is true that there were philosophers and scientists in 1900 who set certain biological and material conditions for human existence. But they were ordinarily "materialists" in the sense the term had at the end of the last century. They made humanity an episode of evolution, civilizations a particular case of adaptation, and even resolved life into its physical and chemical components. For them the properly human perspective on the world was a superfluous phenomenon; and those who saw the contingency of humanity ordinarily treated values, institutions, works of art, and words as a system of signs referring in the last analysis to the elementary needs and desires of all organisms.

It is true, on the other hand, that there were "idealist" authors who assumed other motive forces than these in humanity; but when they did not derive them from some supernatural source, they related them to a human nature which guaranteed their unconditional efficacy. *Human nature* had truth and justice for attributes, as other species have fins or wings. The epoch was full of these absolutes and these divided notions. There was the absolute of the State pervading all events; and a State which did not reimburse its lenders was considered dishonest, even if it was in the midst of a revolution. The value of money was an absolute, and men scarcely dreamed of treating it as simply an aid to economic and social functioning. There was also a moral gold-standard: family and marriage were the good, even if they secreted hatred and rebellion. "Things of the spirit" were intrinsically noble, even if books (like so many works in 1900) translated only morose reveries. There were values and, on the other hand, realities, there was mind and, on the other hand, body; there was the interior and, on the other hand, the exterior. But what if it were precisely the case that the order of facts invaded that of values, if it were recognized that dichotomies are tenable only this side of a certain point of misery and danger? Even those among us today who are taking up the word "humanism" again no longer maintain the *shameless humanism* of our elders. What is perhaps proper to our time is to disassociate humanism from the idea of a humanity fully guaranteed by natural law, and not only reconcile consciousness of human values and consciousness of the infrastructures which keep them in existence, but insist upon their inseparability.

• • •

Our century has wiped out the dividing line between "body" and "mind," and sees human life as through and through mental and corporeal, always based upon the body and always (even in its most carnal modes) interested in relationships between persons. For many thinkers at the close of the nineteenth century, the body was a bit of matter, a network of mechanisms. The twentieth century has restored and deepened the notion of flesh, that is, of animate body.

In psychoanalysis for example it would be interesting to follow the development from a conception of the body which for Freud was initially that of nineteenth-century doctors to the modern notion of the experienced body. Did not psychoanalysis originally take up the tradition of mechanistic philosophies of the body—and is it not still frequently understood in this same way today? Does not the Freudian system explain the most complex and elaborate behavior of adults in terms of instinct and especially sexual instincts, that is to say physiologically, in terms of a composition of forces beyond the grasp of our consciousness or even realized once and for all in childhood prior to the age of rational control and properly human relationships to culture and to others? Perhaps things seemed this way in Freud's first works, and for a hurried reader; but as his own and his successors' psychoanalysis rectifies these initial ideas in contact with clinical experience, we see the emergence of a new idea of the body which was called for by the initial ideas.

It is not false to say that Freud wanted to base the whole of human development upon the development of instincts; but we would get farther if we said that from the start his works overturn the concept of instinct and break down the criteria by which men had previously thought they could circumscribe it. If the term instinct means anything, it means a mechanism within the organism which with a minimum of use ensures certain responses adapted to certain characteristic situations of the species. Now what is proper to Freudianism is surely to show that in this sense man has no sexual instincts, that the "polymorphous perverse" child establishes a so-called normal sexual activity (when he does so) only at the end of a difficult individual history. Unsure about its instruments as it is about its goals, the power to love wends its way through a series of investments which approach the canonical form of love, anticipates and regresses, and repeats and goes beyond itself without our ever being able to claim that what is called normal sexual love is nothing but that. The child's attachment to his parents, so powerful at the beginning as to retard that history, is not itself of the instinctual order. For Freud it is a mental attachment. It is not because the child has the same blood as his parents that he loves them; it is because he knows he is their issue or because he sees them turned toward him, and thus identifies himself with them, conceives of himself in their image, and conceives of them in his image. For Freud the ultimate psychological reality is the system of attractions and tensions which attaches the child to parental images, and then through these to all the other persons, a system within which he tries out different *positions* in turn, the last of which will be his adult attitude.

It is not simply the love-object which escapes every definition in terms of instinct, but the very way of loving itself. As we know, adult love, sustained by a trusting tenderness which does not constantly insist upon new proofs of absolute attachment but takes the other person as he is, at his distance and in his autonomy, is for psychoanalysis won from an infantile "erotic attachment" [*"aimance"*] which demands everything at all times and is responsible for whatever devouring, impossible aspects may remain in any love. And though development to the genital stage is a necessary condition of this transformation to adult love, it is never sufficient to guarantee it. Freud himself described an infantile relationship to others which is established through the intermediary of those regions and functions of the child's body which are least capable of discrimination and articulated action: the mouth, which does not know whether to suck or bite—the sphincteral apparatus, which can only hold in or let go. Now these primordial modes of relationship to others may remain predominant even in the genital life of the adult. In this case the relation to others remains trapped in the impasses of absolute immediacy, oscillating between an inhuman demand, an absolute egotism, and a voracious devotion which destroys the subject himself. Thus sexuality and, more generally, corporeality, which Freud considers the basis of our existence, is a power of investment which is absolute and universal to begin with. This power is *sexual* only in the sense that it reacts immediately to the visible differences of the body and the maternal and paternal roles. Instinct and the physiological are enveloped in a central demand for absolute possession which could not possibly be the act of a bit of matter but is of the order of what is ordinarily called consciousness.

And yet it is a mistake to speak of consciousness here, since to do so is to reintroduce the dichotomy of soul and body at the moment Freudianism is in the process of contesting it, and thus to change our idea of the body as well as our idea of the mind. "Physical facts have a meaning," Freud wrote in one of his earliest works. This meant that no human behavior is simply the result of some bodily mechanism, that in behavior there is not a mental center and a periphery of automatism, and that all our gestures in their fashion participate in that single activity of making explicit and signifying which is ourselves. At least as much as he tries to reduce superstructures to instinctive infrastructures, Freud tries to show that in human life there is no "inferior" or "lower part." Thus we could not be further from an explanation "in terms of the lower part." At least as much as he explains adult behavior by a fate inherited from childhood, Freud shows a *premature* adult life in childhood, and in the child's sphincteral behavior, for example, a first choice of his relationships of generosity or avarice to others. At least as much as he explains the psychological by the body, he shows the psychological meaning of the body, its hidden or latent logic. Thus we can no longer speak of the sexual organ taken as a localizable mechanism, or of the body taken as a mass of matter, as an ultimate cause. Neither cause nor simply instrument or means, it is the vehicle, the fulcrum, and the steadying factor of our life. None of the notions philosophy had elaborated upon—cause, effect, means, end, matter, form—suffices for thinking about the body's relationships to life as a whole, about the way it meshes into personal life or the way personal life meshes into it. The body is enigmatic: a part of the world certainly, but offered in a bizarre way, as its dwelling, to an absolute desire to draw near the other person and meet him in his body too, animated and animating, the natural face of mind. With psychoanalysis mind passes into body as, inversely, body passes into mind.

Along with our idea of the body, these investigations cannot fail to disrupt the idea we form of its partner, the mind. It must be admitted that in this respect much remains to be done to draw from psychoanalytic experience all that it contains, and that psychoanalysts, beginning with Freud himself, have been satisfied with a structure of hardly satisfactory ideas. In order to account for that osmosis between the body's anonymous life and the person's official life which is Freud's great discovery, it was necessary to introduce something *between* the organism and our selves considered as a sequence of deliberate acts and express understandings. This was Freud's *unconscious.* We have only to follow the transformations of this Protean idea in Freud's works, the diverse ways in which it is used, and the contradictions it involves to be convinced that it is not a fully developed idea, and that (as Freud himself implies in his *Essais de Psychanalyse*), we still have to find the right formulation for what he intended by this provisional designation. At first glance "the unconscious" evokes the realm of a dynamics of impulses whose results alone would presumably be given to us. And yet the unconscious cannot be a process "in third person"; since it is the unconscious which chooses what aspect of us will be admitted to official existence, which avoids the thoughts or situation we are resisting, and which is therefore not *un-knowing* but rather an un-recognized and unformulated knowing that we do not want to assume. In an approximative language, Freud is on the point of discovering what other thinkers have more appropriately named *ambiguous perception.* It is by working in this direction that we shall find a civil status for this consciousness which brushes its objects (eluding them at the moment it is going to designate them, and taking account of them as the blind man takes account of obstacles rather than recognizing them), which does not want to know about them (which does not know about them to the extent that it knows about them, and knows about them to the extent that it does not know about them), and which subtends our express acts and understandings.

Whatever their philosophical formulations may be, there is no denying that Freud had an increasingly clear view of the body's mental function and the mind's incarnation. In his mature works he speaks of the "sexual-aggressive" relationship to others as the fundamental datum of our life. As aggression does not aim at a thing but a person, the intertwining of the sexual and the aggressive signifies that sexuality has, so to speak, an interior (that it is lined throughout with a person-to-person relationship), and that the sexual is our way (since we are flesh, our carnal way) of living our relationships with others. Since sexuality is relationship to other persons, and not just to another body, it is going to weave the circular system of projections and introjections between other persons and myself, illuminating the unlimited series of reflecting reflections and reflected reflections which are the reasons why I am the other person and he is myself.

Such is this idea of the individual incarnate and (through incarnation) given to himself but also to others—incomparable yet stripped of his congenital secret and faced with his *fellows*—that Freudianism ends up offering us. At the very moment Freud was forming it, and without there being ordinarily any *influence,* writers were expressing the same experience in their own way.

It is in this way, to begin with, that the *eroticism* of writers during this half century must be understood. When in this respect we compare Proust's or Gide's works with the particular works of the preceding literary generation, the contrast is striking. Passing over the generation of writers of the 1900's, Proust and Gide pick up from the start the Sadian and Stendhalian tradition of a direct expression of the body. With Proust, with Gide, an unwearying report on the body begins. It is confirmed, consulted, listened to like a person. The intermittencies of its desire and (as they put it) its fervor are spied on. With Proust it becomes the keeper of the past; and it is the body which, in spite of the deteriorations which render it almost unrecognizable itself, maintains from one time to another a substantial relationship between us and our past. In the two inverse cases of death and awakening, Proust describes the meeting-point of mind and body, showing how, in the dispersion of the sleeping body, our gestures at awakening renew a meaning from beyond the grave; and how on the contrary meaning is undone in the tics of the death agony. He analyzes Elstir's paintings and the milkseller glimpsed in a country station with the same emotion; because in both instances there is the same queer experience, the experience of *expression,* the moment when color and flesh begin to speak to eyes or body. Gide, enumerating a few months before his death what he had loved in his life, calmly named pleasure and the Bible side by side.

As an inevitable consequence, obsession with other persons appears in their works too. When man takes an oath to exist universally, concern for himself and concern for others become indistinguishable for him; he is a person among persons, and the others are other himselves.

But if on the contrary he recognizes what is unique in incarnation lived from within, the other person necessarily appears to him in the form of torment, envy, or at least uneasiness. Cited by his incarnation to appear beneath an alien gaze and justify himself before it, yet riveted to his own situation by the same incarnation; capable of feeling the lack of and need for others, but incapable of finding his resting place in others; he is enmeshed in the to-and-fro of being for self and being for others that produces the tragic element of love in Proust's works and what is perhaps the most striking element in Gide's *Journal*.

We find admirable formulations of the same paradoxes in the writer who is perhaps least capable of being satisfied wtih the approximations of Freudian expression, that is, in Valéry. The reason is that for him the taste for rigor and the keen awareness of the fortuitous are two sides of the same coin. Otherwise he would not have spoken so well of the body as a double-edged being, responsible for many absurdities but also for our most certain accomplishments. "The artist brings along his body, withdraws, puts down and takes away something, behaves with his whole being as his eye and completely becomes an organ which makes itself at home, changes its shape, and seeks the point, the sole point, which belongs virtually to the profoundly sought *oeuvre*— which is not always the one we are seeking."[2] And for Valéry too consciousness of the body is inevitably obsession with others. "No one could think freely if his eyes could not take leave of different eyes which followed them. As soon as glances meet, we are no longer wholly two, and it is hard to remain alone. This exchange (the term is exact) realizes in a very short time a transposition or metathesis—a chiasma of two 'destinies,' two points of view. Thereby a sort of simultaneous reciprocal limitation occurs. You capture my image, my appearance; I capture yours. You are not *me*, since you see me and I do not see myself. What I lack is this me that you see. And what you lack is the you I see. And no matter how far we advance in our mutual understanding, as much as we reflect, so much will we be different. . . ."[3]

As we approach mid-century, it becomes increasingly evident that incarnation and the other person are the labyrinth of reflection and feeling—of a sort of feeling reflection— in contemporary works. Including this famous passage in which a character in *Man's Fate* in turn poses the question: if it is true that I am welded to myself, and that for

[2] *Mauvaises Pensées,* p. 200.
[3] *Tel Quel,* I, p. 42.

me there is still an absolute difference between other persons (whom I hear with my ears) and myself, the "incomparable monster" (who hears me with my throat), then which one of us will ever be able to be accepted by others as he accepts himself, beyond things said or done, praise or blame, even beyond crimes. But Malraux, like Sartre, has read Freud; and whatever they may think of him in the last analysis, it is with his help that they have learned to know themselves. And that is why, seeking as we are to establish certain traits of our times, it has seemed more significant to us to disclose an earlier experience of the body which is their starting point because their elders had prepared it for them.

· · ·

Another characteristic of this half century's investigations is the recognition of a strange relationship between consciousness and its language, as between consciousness and its body. Ordinary language thinks that it can establish, as the correlate of each word or sign, a thing or signification which can exist and be conceived of without any sign. But literature has long taken exception to ordinary language. As different as the ventures of Rimbaud and Mallarmé may well have been, they had this much in common: they freed language from the control of "obvious facts" and trusted it to invent and win new relationships of meaning. Thus language ceased to be (if it ever has been) simply a tool or means the writer uses to communicate intentions given independently of language. In our day, language is of a piece with the writer; it is the writer himself. It is no longer the servant of significations but the act of signifying itself, and the writer or man speaking no longer has to control it voluntarily any more than living man has to premeditate the means or details of his gestures. From now on there is no other way to comprehend language than to dwell in it and use it. As a professional of language, the writer is a professional of insecurity. His expressive operation is renewed from *oeuvre* to *oeuvre*. Each work, as it has been said of the painter, is a step constructed by the writer himself upon which he installs himself in order to construct (with the same risk) another step and what is called the *oeuvre*—the sequence of these attempts—which is always broken off, whether it be by the end of life or through the exhaustion of his speaking power. The writer endlessly attempts to cope with language which he is not the master of, and which is nevertheless incapable of anything without him, a language that has its own caprices and its graces, but always won through the writer's labor. Distinctions of figure and ground, sound and meaning, conception and execution are now blurred, as the limits of body and mind were previously. In going from "signifying" language to pure language, literature freed itself at the same time painting did from resemblance to things, and from the idea of a *finished* work of art. As Baudelaire already said, there are finished works which we cannot say have ever been *completed*, and unfinished works which say what they meant. What is proper to expression is to never be more than approximate.

In our century this *pathos of language* is common to writers who mutually detest one another but whose kinship is from this moment on confirmed by it. In its first stages, surrealism certainly had the air of an insurrection against language, against all meaning, and against literature itself. The fact is that Breton, after a few hesitant formulations which he quickly corrected, proposed not to destroy language to the profit of non-sense but to restore a certain profound and radical usage of speech which he realized all the writings called "automatic" were far from giving an adequate example of.[4] As Maurice Blanchot recalls, Breton already replies to the celebrated investigation, *Pourquoi Ecrivez-vous?,* by describing a task or vocation of speech which has always been expressed in the writer and which bids him enunciate and endow with a name what has never been named. To write in this sense, Breton concludes[5]—that is, in the sense of revealing or making manifest—has never been a vain or frivolous occupation. The polemic against the critical faculties or conscious controls was not carried on in order to deliver speech up to chance or chaos; it sought to recall language and literature to the whole extent of their task by freeing them from the literary world's petty formulas and fabrications of talent. It was necessary to go back to that point of innocence, youth, and unity at which speaking man is not yet man of letters, political man, or moral man—to that "sublime point" Breton speaks about elsewhere, at which literature, life, morality, and politics are equivalent and substituted for one another, because in fact each of us is the same man who loves or hates, who reads or writes, who accepts or refuses political destiny. Now that surrealism, in slipping into the past, has rid itself of its narrownesses—at the same time it has rid itself of its fine virulence—we can no longer

[4] Cf. *Le Langage automatique,* in *Point du Jour.*
[5] *Légitime Défense.*

define it in terms of what it originally rejected. For us it is one of those recalls to *spontaneous speech* which from decade to decade our century issues.

At the same time, surrealism has intermingled with these other recalls in our memory, and with them constitutes one of the constants of our time. Valéry, who was at first greatly admired and subsequently rejected by the surrealists, remains beneath his academic image very close to their experience of language. For it has not been sufficiently noticed that what he contrasts to *signifying* literature is not, as might be thought at a hasty reading, simply a literature of exercises based upon linguistic and prosodic conventions which are more efficacious to the extent they are more complicated and, in short, more absurd. What constitutes the essence of poetic language for him (he sometimes goes so far as to say the essence of all literary language) is that it does not die out in the face of what it communicates to us. It is that in poetic language meaning calls again for the very words which have served to communicate it, and no others. It is that a work cannot be summed up but must be re-read to be regained. It is that in poetic language the idea is not produced by the words as a result of the lexical significations assigned to them in the common language but as a result of more carnal relationships of meaning, the halos of signification words owe to their history and uses—as a result, in short, of the life that words lead within us, a life which from time to time ends up in those meaning-laden accidents, the great books. In his own way, Valéry calls again for the same adequation of language to its total meaning that motivates the surrealistic uses of language.

Both Valéry and the surrealists have in view what Francis Ponge was to call the "semantic thickness" and Sartre the "signifying humus" of language, that is the characteristic power that language as gesture, accent, voice, and modulation of existence has to signify in excess of what it signifies part by part according to existing conventions. It is not very far from here to what Claudel calls the word's "intelligible mouthful." And the same feeling for language is found even in contemporary definitions of prose. For Malraux too, to learn to write is "to learn to speak with one's own voice."[6] And in the works of Stendhal, who believed he was writing "like the civil laws," Jean Prévost detects a *style* in the strong sense of the term. That is, a new and very personal ordering of the words, forms, and elements of the narrative; a new

[6] *Psychologie de l'Art.*

order of correspondence between signs; an imperceptible yet character-istically Stendhalian warping of the whole language system—a system which has been constituted by years of usage and of life, which (having become Stendhal himself) finally allows him to improvise, and which should not be called a system of thought (since Stendhal was so little aware of it) but rather a system of speaking.

Thus language is that singular apparatus which, like our body, gives us more than we have put into it, either because we apprise ourselves of our thought in speaking, or because we listen to others. For when I read or listen, words do not always come touch significations already present in me. They have the extraordinary power to draw me out of my thoughts; they cut out fissures in my private universe through which *other thoughts* irrupt. "At least in that moment, I have been you," Jean Paulhan rightly says. As my body (which nevertheless is only a bit of matter) is gathered up into gestures which aim beyond it, so the words of language (which considered singly are only inert signs that only a vague or banal idea corresponds to) suddenly swell with a meaning which overflows into the other person when the act of speak-ing binds them up into a single whole. Mind is no longer set apart but springs up beside gestures and words as if by spontaneous generation.

●　　●　　●

These changes in our conception of man would not echo so deeply within us if they did not converge in a remarkable way with an ex-perience which all of us, scientists or non-scientists, have been partici-pating in, and which has therefore contributed more than any other to shaping us: I mean the experience of political relationships and history.

It seems to us that for at least thirty years our contemporaries have in this respect been living through an adventure that is much more dangerous than, but analogous to, that which we have thought to meet in the mild order of our relationships to literature or to our body. The same ambiguity that, upon analysis, leads the idea of mind into the idea of body or language has visibly invaded our political life. And in both cases it is more and more difficult to distinguish what is violence and what is idea, what is power and what is value, with the aggravating circumstance that in political life the mixture risks ending up in con-vulsion and chaos.

We grew up in a time when, *officially,* world politics were juridical. What definitively discredited juridical politics was seeing the victors of

1918 concede (and then some) to a Germany which had become powerful again what they had previously refused Weimar Germany. But six months later this new Germany took Prague as well. Thus the demonstration was complete: the victors' juridical politics was the mask for their preponderance, and vanquished's claim to "equality of rights" was the mask for a coming German preponderance. We were still faced with power relationships and death struggles; each concession was a weakness and each gain a step toward further gains. But what is important is that the decline of juridical politics has in no way involved a pure and simple return among our contemporaries to a power politics or politics of efficiency. It is a remarkable fact that political cynicism and even political hypocrisy are discredited too, that public opinion remains astonishingly sensitive about this point, that until these last months governments took care not to collide with it, and that even now there is not one of them which openly declares that it is relying on naked force, or which is effectively doing so.

The truth is that during the period immediately following the War it could almost be said that there was no world politics. Forces did not confront one another. Many questions had been left open, but just for that reason there were "no man's lands," neutral zones, provisional or transitional régimes. Europe, totally disarmed, lived through years without invasion. We know that for some years now the aspect of things has changed. From one end of the world to the other, zones which were neutral for the two rival powers no longer are; armies have appeared in a "no man's land"; economic aid has turned into military aid. Yet to us it seems remarkable that this return to power politics is nowhere lacking in reticence. Perhaps it will be said that it has always been easy to hide violence with declarations of peace, and that this is propaganda. But seeing the powers' behavior, we have come to wonder if it is only a matter of pretexts. It is possible that all the governments believe their propaganda; that in the confusion of our present they no longer know themselves what is true and what is false, because in a sense everything they say conjointly is true. It is possible that each policy is really and simultaneously peaceful and warlike.

There would be room here to analyze a whole series of curious practices which clearly seem to be becoming general in contemporary politics. For example, the twin practices of *purging* and crypto-politics, or the politics of fifth columns. Machiavelli has pointed out the recipe for it, but in passing; and it is today that these practices are tending on all sides to become institutional. Now if we really think about it, this presupposes that a government always expects to find accomplices on the side of its adversary and traitors in its own house. It is thus an admission that all causes are ambiguous. It seems to us that today's policies are distinguished from former ones by this doubt which is extended even to their own cause, coupled with expeditious measures to suppress the doubt.

The same fundamental uncertainty is expressed in the ease with which the heads of state turn aside or turn back from their policies, without of course ever recognizing that these oscillations are oscillations. After all, history has seldom seen a head of state discharge an illustrious and long-unchallenged commander-in-chief, and grant his successor more or less what he refused him a few months earlier. We have seldom seen a great power refuse to intervene in order to restrain one of its satellites in the process of invading a neighbor—and after one year of war, propose to return to the status quo.

These oscillations are understandable only if, in a world whose peoples are against war, governments cannot look it in the face and yet do not dare to make peace, which would mean admitting their weakness. Sheer power relationships are altered at each instant; governments *also* want opinion to be in their favor. Each troop movement becomes a political operation *as well*. Governments act less to obtain a certain factual result than to put their adversary in a certain moral predicament. Thus we have the strange idea of a *peace offensive;* to propose peace is to disarm the adversary, to win over opinion, and thus almost to win the war. But at the same time governments are well aware that they must not lose face, that by speaking too much of peace they would encourage their adversary. This is so true that on all sides governments alternate or, better yet, associate peaceful speeches and forceful measures, verbal threats and actual concessions. Peace overtures are made in a discouraging tone and are accompanied by new preparations for war. No one wants to reach an agreement and no one wants to break off negotiations. So we have actual armistices that are observed by everyone for weeks or months on end and that no one wants to legalize, as among irritated people who put up with one another but no longer speak. We ask a former ally to sign a treaty he disapproves of with a former enemy. But we fully expect him to refuse. If he accepts, it is a felony. This is how we have a peace that is not a peace. And also a war that—except for the combatants and the inhabitants—is not completely a war. We let our friends fight because by providing them with arms which would decide the battle we would really risk war. We withdraw before the enemy and seek to suck him into the trap of an offensive that would put him in the wrong. In addition to its manifest meaning, each political act bears a contrary and latent meaning.

It seems to us that governments get lost in these double meanings and, in the extraordinary subtlety of means-ends relationships, are no longer able to know themselves what they are actually doing. The dialectic invades our newspapers, but a fear-crazed dialectic which turns on itself and solves no problems. In all this we see less duplicity than confusion, and less wickedness than perplexity.

We are not saying that this situation itself is without risk: it is possible that we could go to war obliquely, and it could suddenly loom up before us at one of the detours of some main political highway which seemed no more likely than another to set it going. We are only saying that these characteristics of our politics prove (all things considered) that there is no profound basis for war today. Even if it comes out of all this, no one will be entitled to say that it was ineluctable. For the contemporary world's true problems are due less to the antagonism of two ideologies than to their common disarray before certain major facts that neither one controls. If war comes, it will come as a diversion or as bad luck.

The two great powers in their rivalry have accused and are accusing one another concerning Asia. Now it is not the Satanism of one government or another which has caused countries like India and China (where for centuries men have died of hunger) to come to refuse famine, debility, disorder, or corruption. It is the development of radio, a minimum of instruction, newspapers, communications with the outside, and the population increase which have suddenly made an age-old situation intolerable. It would be shameful to allow our obsessions as Europeans to hide the real problem posed there, the drama of countries to be equipped that no humanism can ignore. With the awakening of these countries, the world is closing on itself. Perhaps for the first time, the developed countries are being faced with their responsibilities toward a human community which cannot be reduced to two continents.

This fact in itself is not a mournful one. If we were not so obsessed by our own concerns, we would not find it without grandeur. But what is serious is that *all* Western doctrines are too narrow to face up to the problem of developing Asia. The classical means of the liberal economy or even those of American capitalism are not, it seems, up to operating even India's equipment. As for Marxism, it has been conceived of to assure the passage of a developed economic apparatus from the hands of a bourgeoisie which has become parasitical to those of an old and highly conscious and cultivated proletariat. It is a wholly different matter to bring an underdeveloped country up to modern forms of production, and the problem posed for Russia is posed in a far more extreme way for Asia. It is not surprising that Marxism, confronted with this task, has been profoundly modified, that it has in fact abandoned its conception of a revolution rooted in the history of the working class, substituting transferals of property managed from the top for revolutionary contagion, and putting the theory of the withering away of the State and that of the proletariat as the universal class in cold storage. But this also means that the Chinese revolution (which the U.S.S.R. has not especially encouraged) to a large extent escapes the previsions of Marxist politics.

So just when Asia is intervening as an active factor in world politics, none of the conceptions Europe has invented enables us to think about its problems. Here political thought is mired down in historical and local circumstances; it gets lost in these voluminous societies. This is undoubtedly what makes the antagonists circumspect; it is our chance for peace. It is also possible that they will be tempted to go to war, which will not solve any problems but which would allow them to put them off. So it is at the same time our risk of war. World politics is confused because the ideas it appeals to are too narrow to cover its field of action.

•   •   •

If we were asked in concluding to give our remarks a philosophical formulation, we would say that our times have experienced and are experiencing, more perhaps than any other, contingency. The contingency of evil to begin with: there is not a force at the beginning of human life which guides it toward its ruin or toward chaos. On the contrary, each gesture of our body or our language, each act of political life, as we have seen, spontaneously takes account of the other person and goes beyond itself in its singular aspects toward a universal meaning. When our initiatives get bogged down in the paste of the body, of language, or of that world beyond measure which is given to us to finish, it is not that a *malin génie* sets his will against us; it is only a matter of a sort of inertia, a passive resistance, a dying fall of meaning —an anonymous *adversity*. But good is contingent too. We do not guide the body by repressing it, nor language by putting it in thought, nor history by dint of value judgments; we must always espouse each one of these situations, and when they go beyond themselves they do so spontaneously. Progress is not necessary with a metaphysical necessity; we can only say that experience will very likely end up by eliminating false solutions and working its way out of impasses. But at what price, by how many detours? We cannot even exclude in principle the possibility that humanity, like a sentence which does not succeed in drawing to a close, will suffer shipwreck on its way.

It is true that the totality of beings known by the name of men and defined by the commonly known physical characteristics also have in common a natural light or opening to being which makes cultural acquisitions communicable to all men and to them alone. But this lightning flash we find in every glance called human is just as visible in the most cruel forms of sadism as it is in Italian painting. It is precisely this flash which makes everything possible on man's part, and right up to the end. Man is absolutely distinct from animal species, but precisely in the respect that he has no original equipment and is the place of contingency, which sometimes takes the form of a kind of miracle (in the sense in which men have spoken of the *miracle of Greece*), and sometimes the form of an unintentional adversity. Our age is as far from explaining man by the lower as it is by the higher, and for the same reasons. To explain the *Mona Lisa* by the sexual history of Leonardo da Vinci or to explain it by some divine motion Leonardo da Vinci was the instrument of or by some human nature capable of beauty still involves giving way to the retrospective illusion, realizing the valuable in advance—misunderstanding the human moment *par excellence* in which a life woven out of chance events turns back upon, regrasps, and expresses itself.

If there is a humanism today, it rids itself of the illusion Valéry designated so well in speaking of "that little man within man whom we always presuppose." Philosophers have at times thought to account for our vision by the image or reflection things form upon our retina. This was because they presupposed a second man behind the retinal image who had different eyes and a different retinal image responsible for seeing the first. But with this man within man the problem remains untouched, and we must still come to understand how a body becomes animate and how these blind organs end up bearing a perception. The "little man within man" is only the phantom of our successful expressive operations; and the admirable man is not this phantom but the man who—installed in his fragile body, in a language which has already done so much speaking, and in a reeling history—gathers himself together and begins to see, to understand, and to signify. There is no longer anything decorous or decorative about today's humanism. It no longer loves man in opposition to his body, mind in opposition to its language, values in opposition to facts. It no longer speaks of man and mind except in a sober way, with modesty: mind and man never *are;* they show through in the movement by which the body becomes gesture, language an *oeuvre,* and coexistence truth.

Between this humanism and classical doctrines there is almost an homonymous relationship. In one way or another the latter affirmed a man of divine right (for the humanism of necessary progress is a secularized theology). When the great rationalist philosophies joined battle with revealed religion, what they put in competition with divine creation was some metaphysical mechanism which evaded the idea of a fortuitous world just as much as it had. Today a humanism does not oppose religion with an explanation of the world. It begins by becoming aware of contingency. It is the continued confirmation of an astonishing junction between fact and meaning, between my body and my self, my self and others, my thought and my speech, violence and truth. It is the methodical refusal of explanations, because they destroy the mixture we are made of and make us incomprehensible to ourselves. Valéry profoundly says: "One does not see what a god could think about"—a god and, moreover (he explains in another connection), a demon as well. The Mephistopheles of *Mon Faust* quite rightly says: "I am the fleshless being who neither sleeps nor thinks. As soon as these poor fools draw away from instinct, I lose my way in caprice, in the uselessness or depth of these irritations of their brains they call 'ideas.' . . . I lose myself in this Faust who seems to me sometimes to understand me in a wholly different fashion than he should, as if there were another world than the other world! . . . It is here that he shuts himself in and amuses himself with what there is in the brain, and brews and ruminates that mixture of what he knows and does not know, which they call Thought. . . . I do not know how to think and I have no soul. . . ."[7] Thinking is man's business, if thinking always means coming back to ourselves and inserting between two distractions the thin empty space by which we see something.

A stern and (if you will excuse the word) almost vertiginous idea. We have to conceive of a labyrinth of spontaneous steps which revive one another, sometimes cut across one another, and sometimes confirm one another—but across how many detours and what tides of disorder! —and conceive of the whole undertaking as resting upon itself. It is understandable that our contemporaries, faced with this idea (which they glimpse as well as we do), retreat and turn aside toward some idol. With all reservations made concerning other modes of approaching the problem, fascism is a society's retreat in the face of a situation in which the contingency of moral and social structures is clear. It is the fear of the new which galvanizes and reaffirms precisely the very ideas that historical experience had worn out. A phenomenon which our times are far from having gone beyond. The favor an *occult* literature meets with in France today is somewhat analogous. Under the pretext that our economic, moral, or political ideas are in a state of crisis, occult thought would like to establish institutions, customs, and types of civilizations which answer our problems much less well, but which are supposed to contain a *secret* we hope to *decipher* by dreaming around the documents left for us. Whereas it is the role of art, literature, and perhaps even philosophy to create sacred things, occultism seeks them readymade (in sun cults or the religion of American Indians, for example), forgetting that ethnology shows us better each day what terrors, what dilapidation, what impotence archaic paradise is often made of.

In short, fear of contingency is everywhere, even in the doctrines which helped reveal it. Whereas Marxism is based entirely upon going beyond nature through human *praxis,* today's Marxists veil the risk such a transformation of the world implies. Whereas Catholicism, particularly in France, is being crossed by a vigorous movement of inquiry next to which the Modernism of the beginning of the century seems sentimental and vague, the heirarchy reaffirms the most worn-out forms of theological explanation with the Syllabus. Its position is understandable: it is indeed true that a man cannot seriously think about the contingency of existence and hold to the Syllabus. It is even true that religion is bound up with a minimum of explanatory thought.

[7] *Mon Faust,* p. 157.

In a recent article François Mauriac implied that atheism could receive an honorable meaning if it took issue only with the God of philosophers and scientists, God in idea. But without God in idea, without the infinite thought which created the world, Christ is a man and his birth and Passion cease to be acts of God and become symbols of the human condition. It would not be reasonable to expect a religion to conceive of humanity, according to Giraudoux's beautiful phrase, as the "caryatid of the void." But the return to an explanatory theology and the compulsive reaffirmation of the *Ens realissimum* drag back all the consequences of a massive transcendence that religious reflection was trying to escape. Once again the Church, its sacred depository, its unverifiable secret beyond the visible, separates itself from actual society. Once more the Heaven of principles and the earth of existence are sundered. Once more philosophic doubt is only a formality. Once more adversity is called Satan and the war against it is already won. Occult thought scores a point.

Once again, between Christians and non-Christians, as between Marxists and non-Marxists, conversation is becoming difficult. How could there possibly be any real exchange between the man who knows and the man who does not know? What can a man say if he sees no relationship, not even a dialectical one, between state communism and the withering away of the state, when another man says that he does? If a man sees no relationship between the Gospels and the clergy's role in Spain, when another says they are not irreconcilable? Sometimes one starts to dream about what culture, literary life, and teaching could be if all those who participate, having for once rejected idols, would give themselves up to the happiness of reflecting together. But this dream is not reasonable. The discussions of our time are so convulsive only because it is resisting a truth which is right at hand, and because in recognizing—without any intervening veil—the menace of adversity, it is closer perhaps than any other to recognizing the metamorphoses of Fortune.

7. FREEDOM

Again, it is clear that no casual relationship is conceivable between the subject and his body, his world or his society. Only at the cost of losing the basis of all my certainties can I question what is conveyed to me by my presence to myself. Now the moment I turn to myself in order to describe myself, I have a glimpse of an anonymous flux,[1] a comprehensive project in which there are so far no 'states of consciousness', nor, *a fortiori,* qualifications of any sort. For myself I am neither 'jealous', nor 'inquisitive', nor 'hunchbacked', nor 'a civil servant'. It is often a matter of surprise that the cripple or the invalid can put up with himself. The reason is that such people are not for themselves deformed or at death's door. Until the final coma, the dying man is inhabited by a consciousness, he is all that he sees, and enjoys this much of an outlet. Consciousness can never objectify itself into invalid-consciousness or cripple-consciousness, and even if the old man complains of his age or the cripple of his deformity, they can do so only by comparing themselves with others, or seeing themselves through the eyes of others, that is, by taking a statistical and objective view of themselves, so that such complaints are never absolutely genuine: when he is back in the heart of his own consciousness, each one of us feels beyond his limitations and thereupon resigns himself to them. They are the price which we automatically pay for being in the world, a

Maurice Merleau-Ponty, "Freedom," *Phenomenology of Perception,* Part III, Ch. 3, trans. by Colin Smith (New York: The Humanities Press, 1962), pp. 434–56. Reprinted by permission.

[1] In the sense in which, with Husserl, we have taken this word.

formality which we take for granted. Hence we may speak disparagingly of our looks and still not want to change our face for another. No idiosyncrasy can, seemingly, be attached to the insuperable generality of consciousness, nor can any limit be set to this immeasurable power of escape. In order to be determined (in the two senses of that word) by an external factor, it is necessary that I should be a thing. Neither my freedom nor my universality can admit of any eclipse. It is inconceivable that I should be free in certain of my actions and determined in others: how should we understand a dormant freedom that gave full scope to determinism? And if it is assumed that it is snuffed out when it is not in action, how could it be rekindled? If *per impossible* I had once succeeded in *making myself into* a thing, how should I subsequently reconvert myself to consciousness? Once I am free, I am not to be counted among things, and I must then be uninterruptedly free. Once my actions cease to be mine, I shall never recover them, and if I lose my hold on the world, it will never be restored to me. It is equally inconceivable that my liberty should be attenuated; one cannot be to some extent free, and if, as is often said, motives incline me in a certain direction, one of two things happens: either they are strong enough to force me to act, in which case there is no freedom, or else they are not strong enough, and then freedom is complete, and as great in the worst torments as in the peace of one's home. We ought, therefore, to reject not only the idea of causality, but also that of motivation.[2] The alleged motive does not burden my decision; on the contrary my decision lends the motive its force. Everything that I 'am' in virtue of nature or history—hunchbacked, handsome or Jewish—I never am completely for myself, as we have just explained: and I may well be these things for other people, nevertheless I remain free to posit another person as a consciousness whose views strike through to my very being, or on the other hand merely as an object. It is also true that this option is itself a form of constraint: if I am ugly, I have the choice between being an object of disapproval or disapproving of others. I am left free to be a masochist or a sadist, but not free to ignore others. But this dilemma, which is given as part of the human lot, is not one for me as pure consciousness: it is still I who cause the other to be for me, and who cause us both to be as members of mankind. Moreover, even if existence as a human being were imposed upon me, the manner alone being left to my choice, and considering this choice itself and ignoring the small

[2] See J. P. Sartre, *L'Être et le Néant,* pp. 508 and ff.

number of forms it might take, it would still be a free choice. If it is said that my temperament inclines me particularly to either sadism or masochism, it is still merely a manner of speaking, for my temperament exists only for the second order knowledge that I gain about myself when I see myself as others see me, and in so far as I recognize it, confer value upon it, and in that sense, choose it. What misleads us on this, is that we often look for freedom in the voluntary deliberation which examines one motive after another and seems to opt for the weightiest or most convincing. In reality the deliberation follows the decision, and it is my secret decision which brings the motives to light, for it would be difficult to conceive what the force of a motive might be in the absence of a decision which it confirms or to which it runs counter. When I have abandoned a project, the motives which I thought held me to it suddenly lose their force and collapse. In order to resuscitate them, an effort is required on my part to reopen time and set me back to the moment preceding the making of the decision. Even while I am deliberating, already I find it an effort to suspend time's flow, and to keep open a situation which I feel is closed by a decision which is already there and which I am holding off. That is why it so often happens that after giving up a plan I experience a feeling of relief: 'After all, I wasn't so very particular'; the debate was purely a matter of form, and the deliberation a mere parody, for I had decided against from the start.

We often see the weakness of the will brought forward as an argument against freedom. And indeed, although I can will myself to adopt a course of conduct and act the part of a warrior or a seducer, it is not within my power to be a warrior or seducer with ease and in a way that 'comes naturally'; really to *be* one, that is. But neither should we seek freedom in the act of will, which is, in its very meaning, something short of an act. We have recourse to an act of will only in order to go against our true decision, and, as it were, for the purpose of proving our powerlessness. If we had really and truly made the conduct of the warrior or the seducer our own, then we should *be* one or the other. Even what are called obstacles to freedom are in reality deployed by it. An unclimbable rock face, a large or small, vertical or slanting rock, are things which have no meaning for anyone who is not intending to surmount them, for a subject whose projects do not carve out such determinate forms from the uniform mass of the *in itself* and cause an orientated world to arise—a significance in things. There is, then, ultimately nothing that can set limits to freedom, except those limits that freedom itself has set in the form of its various initiatives, so that the subject has simply the external world that he gives himself. Since it is the latter who, on coming into being, brings to light significance and value in things, and since no thing can impinge upon it except through acquiring, thanks to it, significance and value, there is no action of things on the subject, but merely a signification (in the active sense), a centrifugal *Sinngebung*. The choice would seem to lie between scientism's conception of causality, which is incompatible with the consciousness which we have of ourselves, and the assertion of an absolute freedom divorced from the outside. It is impossible to decide beyond which point things cease to be ἐφ'ἡμῖν. Either they all lie within our power, or none does.

The result, however, of this first reflection on freedom would appear to be to rule it out altogether. If indeed it is the case that our freedom is the same in all our actions, and even in our passions, if it is not to be measured in terms of our conduct, and if the slave displays freedom as much by living in fear as by breaking his chains, then it cannot be held that there is such a thing as *free action,* freedom being anterior to all actions. In any case it will not be possible to declare: 'Here freedom makes its appearance', since free action, in order to be discernible, has to stand out against a background of life from which it is entirely, or almost entirely, absent. We may say in this case that it is everywhere, but equally nowhere. In the name of freedom we reject the idea of acquisition, since freedom has become a primordial acquisition and, as it were, our state of nature. Since we do not have to provide it, it is the gift granted to us of having no gift, it is the nature of consciousness which consists in having no nature, and in no case can it find external expression or a place in our life. The idea of action, therefore, disappears: nothing can pass from us to the world, since we are nothing that can be specified, and since the non-being which constitutes us could not possibly find its way into the world's plenum. There are merely intentions immediately followed by their effects, and we are very near to the Kantian idea of an intention which is tantamount to the act, which Scheler countered with the argument that the cripple who would like to be able to save a drowning man and the good swimmer who actually saves him do not have the same experience of autonomy. The very idea of choice vanishes, for to choose is to choose *something* in which freedom sees, at least for a moment, a symbol of

itself. There is free choice only if freedom comes into play in its decision, and posits the situation chosen as a situation of freedom. A freedom which has no need to be exercised because it is already acquired
could not commit itself in this way: it knows that the following instant
will find it, come what may, just as free and just as indeterminate.
The very notion of freedom demands that our decision should plunge
into the future, that something should have been *done* by it, that the
subsequent instant should benefit from its predecessor and, though not
necessitated, should be at least required by it. If freedom is doing, it
is necessary that what it does should not be immediately undone by a
new freedom. Each instant, therefore, must not be a closed world; one
instant must be able to commit its successors and, a decision once taken
and action once begun, I must have something acquired at my disposal, I must benefit from my impetus, I must be inclined to carry on,
and there must be a bent or prosperity of the mind. It was Descartes
who held that conservation demands a power as great as does creation;
a view which implies a realistic notion of the instant. It is true that the
instant is not a philosopher's fiction. It is the point at which one project
is brought to fruition and another begun[3]—the point at which my gaze
is transferred from one end to another, it is the *Augen-Blick*. But this
break in time cannot occur unless each of the two spans is of a piece.
Consciousness, it is said, is, though not atomized into instants, at least
haunted by the spectre of the instant which it is obliged continually to
exorcise by a free act. We shall soon see that we have indeed always
the power to interrupt, but it implies in any case a power to *begin*, for
there would be no severance unless freedom had taken up its abode
somewhere and were preparing to move it. Unless there are cycles of
behaviour, open situations requiring a certain completion and capable
of constituting a background to either a confirmatory or transformatory
decision, we never experience freedom. The choice of an intelligible
character is excluded, not only because there is no time anterior to time,
but because choice presupposes a prior commitment and because the
idea of an initial choice involves a contradiction. If freedom is to have
room[4] in which to move, if it is to be describable as freedom, there
must be something to hold it away from its objectives, it must have
a *field,* which means that there must be for it special possibilities, or

---

[3] J. P. Sartre, *L'Être et le Néant,* p. 544.
[4] 'avoir du champ'; in this sentence there is a play on the word 'champ'=field
(Translator's note).

realities which tend to cling to being. As J. P. Sartre himself observes, dreaming is incompatible with freedom because, in the realm of imagination, we have no sooner taken a certain significance as our goal than we already believe that we have intuitively brought it into being, in short, because there is no obstacle and nothing *to do*.[5] It is established that freedom is not to be confused with those abstract decisions of will at grips with motives or passions, for the classical conception of deliberation is relevant only to a freedom 'in bad faith' which secretly harbours antagonistic motives without being prepared to act on them, and so itself manufactures the alleged proofs of its impotence. We can see, beneath these noisy debates and these fruitless efforts to 'construct' us, the tacit decisions whereby we have marked out round ourselves the field of possibility, and it is true that nothing is done as long as we cling to these fixed points, and everything is easy as soon as we have weighed anchor. This is why our freedom is not to be sought in spurious discussion on the conflict between a style of life which we have no wish to reappraise and circumstances suggestive of another: the real choice is that between our whole character and our manner of being in the world. But either this total choice is never mentioned, since it is the silent upsurge of our being in the world, in which case it is not clear in what sense it could be said to be ours, since this freedom glides over itself and is the equivalent of a fate—or else our choice of ourselves is a genuine choice, a conversion involving our whole existence. In this case, however, there is presupposed a previous acquisition which the choice sets out to modify and it founds a new tradition: this leads us to ask whether the perpetual severance in terms of which we initially defend freedom is not simply the negative aspect of our universal commitment to a world, and whether our indifference to each determinate thing does not express merely our involvement in all; whether the ready-made freedom from which we started is not reducible to a power of initiative which cannot be transformed into *doing* without taking up the world as posited in some shape or form, and whether, in short, concrete and actual freedom is not to be found in this exchange. It is true that nothing has *significance* and value for anyone but *me* and through anyone but me, but this proposition remains indeterminate and is still indistinguishable from the Kantian idea of a consciousness which 'finds in things only what it has put into them', and from the idealist refutation of realism, as long as we fail to make

[5] J. P. Sartre, *L'Être et le Néant*, p. 562.

clear how we understand significance and the self. By defining ourselves as a universal power of *Sinn-Gebung,* we have reverted to the
method of the 'thing without which' and to the analytical reflection
of the traditional type, which seeks the conditions of possibility without
concerning itself with the conditions of reality. We must therefore
resume the analysis of the *Sinngebung* and show how it can be both
centrifugal and centripetal, since it has been established that there is no
freedom without a field.

When I say that this rock is unclimbable, it is certain that this attribute, like that of being big or little, straight and oblique, and indeed
like all attributes in general, can be conferred upon it only by the
project of climbing it, and by a human presence. It is, therefore, freedom which brings into being the obstacles to freedom, so that the latter
can be set over against it as its bounds. However, it is clear that, one
and the same project being given, one rock will appear as an obstacle,
and another, being more negotiable, as a means. My freedom, then,
does not so contrive it that this way there is an obstacle, and that way
a way through, it arranges for there to be obstacles and ways through
in general; it does not draw the particular outline of this world, but
merely lays down its general structures. It may be objected that there
is no difference; if my freedom conditions the structure of the 'there is',
that of the 'here' and the 'there', it is present wherever these structures
arise. We cannot distinguish the quality of 'obstacle' from the obstacle
itself, and relate one to freedom and the other to the world in itself
which, without freedom, would be merely an amorphous and unname-
able mass. It is not, therefore, outside myself that I am able to find a
limit to my freedom. But should I not find it in myself? We must
indeed distinguish between my express intentions, for example the
plan I now make to climb those mountains, and general intentions
which evaluate the potentialities of my environment. Whether or not
I have decided to climb them, these mountains appear high to me,
because they exceed my body's power to take them in its stride, and,
even if I have just read *Micromégas,* I cannot so contrive it that they
are small for me. Underlying myself as a thinking subject, who am able
to take my place at will on Sirius or on the earth's surface, there is,
therefore, as it were a natural self which does not budge from its terrestrial situation and which constantly adumbrates absolute valuations.
What is more, my projects as a thinking being are clearly modelled on
the latter; if I elect to see things from the point of view of Sirius, it is

still to my terrestrial experience that I must have recourse in order to do so; I may say, for example, that the Alps are *molehills*. In so far as I have hands, feet, a body, I sustain around me intentions which are not dependent upon my decisions and which affect my surroundings in a way which I do not choose. These intentions are general in a double sense: firstly in the sense that they constitute a system in which all possible objects are simultaneously included; if the mountain appears high and upright, the tree appears small and sloping; and furthermore in the sense that they are not of my own making, they originate from outside me, and I am not surprised to find them in all psycho-physical subjects organized as I am. Hence, as Gestalt psychology has shown, there are for me certain shapes which are particularly favoured, as they are for other men, and which are capable of giving rise to a psychological science and rigorous laws. The grouping of dots

•   •   •

is always perceived as six pairs of dots with two millimetres between each pair, while one figure is always perceived as a cube, and another as a plane mosaic.[6] It is as if, on the hither side of our judgement and our freedom, someone were assigning such and such a significance to such and such a given grouping. It is indeed true that perceptual structures do not always force themselves upon the observer; there are some which are ambiguous. But these reveal even more effectively the presence within us of spontaneous evaluation: for they are elusive shapes which suggest constantly changing meanings to us. Now a pure consciousness is capable of anything except being ignorant of its intentions, and an absolute freedom cannot choose itself as hesitant, since that amounts to allowing itself to be drawn in several directions, and since, the possibilities being *ex hypothesi* indebted to freedom for all the strength they have, the weight that freedom gives to one is thereby withdrawn from the rest. We *can* break up a shape by looking at it awry, but this too is because freedom uses the gaze along with its spontaneous evaluations. Without the latter, we would not have a world, that is, a collection of things which emerge from a background of formlessness, by presenting themselves to our body as 'to be touched', 'to be taken', 'to be climbed over'. We should never be aware of adjusting ourselves to things and reaching them where they are, beyond

[6] See above, p. 263.

us, but would be conscious only of restricting our thoughts to the immanent objects of our intentions, and we should not be in the world, ourselves implicated in the spectacle and, so to speak, intermingled with things, we should simply enjoy the spectacle of a universe. It is, therefore, true that there are no obstacles in themselves, but the self which qualifies them as such is not some acosmic subject; it runs ahead of itself in relation to things in order to confer upon them the form of things. There is an autochthonous significance of the world which is constituted in the dealings which our incarnate existence has with it, and which provides the ground of every deliberate *Sinngebung*.

This is true not only of an impersonal and, generally speaking, abstract function such as 'external perception'. There is something comparable present in all evaluations. It has been perceptively remarked that pain and fatigue can never be regarded as causes which 'act' upon my liberty, and that, in so far as I may experience either at any given moment, they do not have their origin outside me, but always have a significance and express my attitude towards the world. Pain makes me give way and say what I ought to have kept to myself, fatigue makes me break my journey. We all know the moment at which we decide no longer to endure pain or fatigue, and when, simultaneously, they become intolerable in fact. Tiredness does not halt my companion because he likes the clamminess of his body, the heat of the road and the sun, in short, because he likes to feel himself in the midst of things, to feel their rays converging upon him, to be the cynosure of all this light, and an object of touch for the earth's crust. My own fatigue brings me to a halt because I dislike it, because I have chosen differently my manner of being in the world, because, for instance, I endeavour, not to be in nature, but rather to win the recognition of others. I am free in relation to fatigue to precisely the extent that I am free in relation to my being in the world, free to make my way by transforming it.[7] But here once more we must recognize a sort of sedimentation of our life: an attitude towards the world, when it has received frequent confirmation, acquires a favoured status for us. Yet since freedom does not tolerate any motive in its path, my habitual being in the world is at each moment equally precarious, and the complexes which I have allowed to develop over the years always remain equally soothing, and the free act can with no difficulty blow them sky-high. However, having built our life upon an inferiority complex which has been operative for

[7] J. P. Sartre, *L'Être et le Néant,* pp. 531 and ff.

twenty years, it is not *probable* that we shall change. It is clear what a summary rationalism might say in reply to such a hybrid notion: there are no degrees of possibility; either the free act is no longer possible, or it is still possible, in which case freedom is complete. In short, 'probable' is meaningless. It is a notion belonging to statistical thought, which is not thought at all, since it does not concern any particular thing actually existing, any moment of time, any concrete event. 'It is improbable that Paul will give up writing bad books' means nothing, since Paul may well decide to write no more such books. The probable is everywhere and nowhere, a reified fiction, with only a psychological existence; it is not an ingredient of the world. And yet we have already met it a little while ago in the perceived *world*. The mountain is great or small to the extent that, as a perceived thing, it is to be found in the field of my possible actions, and in relation to a level which is not only that of my individual life, but that of 'any man'. Generality and probability are not fictions, but phenomena; we must therefore find a phenomenological basis for statistical thought. It belongs necessarily to a being which is fixed, situated and surrounded by things in the world. 'It is improbable' that I should at this moment destroy an inferiority complex in which I have been content to live for twenty years. That means that I have committed myself to inferiority, that I have made it my abode, that this past, though not a fate, has at least a specific weight and is not a set of events over there, at a distance from me, but the atmosphere of my present. The rationalist's dilemma: either the free act is possible, or it is not—either the event originates in me or is imposed on me from outside, does not apply to our relations with the world and with our past. Our freedom does not destroy our situation, but gears itself to it: as long as we are alive, our situation is open, which implies both that it calls up specially favoured modes of resolution, and also that it is powerless to bring one into being by itself.

We shall arrive at the same result by considering our relations with history. Taking myself in my absolute concreteness, as I am presented to myself in reflection, I find that I am an anonymous and pre-human flux, as yet unqualified as, for instance, 'a working man' or 'middle class'. If I subsequently think of myself as a man among men, a bourgeois among bourgeois, this can be, it would seem, no more than a second order view of myself; I am never in my heart of hearts a worker or a bourgeois, but a consciousness which freely evaluates itself as a middle class or proletarian consciousness. And indeed, it is never the case that my objective position in the production process is sufficient to awaken class consciousness. There was exploitation long before there were revolutionaries. Nor is it always in periods of economic difficulty that the working class movement makes headway. Revolt is, then, not the outcome of objective conditions, but it is rather the decision taken by the worker to will revolution that makes a proletarian of him. The evaluation of the present operates through one's free project for the future. From which we might conclude that history by itself has no significance, but only that conferred upon it by our will. Yet here again we are slipping into the method of 'the indispensable condition failing which . . .': in opposition to objective thought, which includes the subject in its deterministic system; we are setting idealist reflection which makes determinism dependent upon the constituting activity of the subject. Now, we have already seen that objective thought and analytical reflection are two aspects of the same mistake, two ways of overlooking the phenomena. Objective thought derives class consciousness from the objective condition of the proletariat. Idealist reflection reduces the proletarian condition to the awareness of it, which the proletarian arrives at. The former traces class-consciousness to the class defined in terms of objective characteristics, the latter on the other hand reduces 'being a workman' to the consciousness of being one. In each case we are in the realm of abstraction, because we remain torn between the *in itself* and the *for itself*. If we approach the question afresh with the idea of discovering, not the causes of the act of becoming aware, for there is no cause which can act from outside upon a consciousness—nor the conditions of its possibility, for we need to know the conditions which actually produce it—but class-consciousness itself, if, in short, we apply a genuinely existential method, what do we find? I am not conscious of being working class or middle class simply because, as a matter of fact, I sell my labour or, equally as a matter of fact, because my interests are bound up with capitalism, nor do I become one or the other on the day on which I elect to view history in the light of the class struggle: what happens is that 'I exist as working class' or 'I exist as middle class' in the first place, and it is this mode of dealing with the world and society which provides both the motives for my revolutionary or conservative projects and my explicit judgements of the type: 'I am working class' or 'I am middle class', without its being possible to deduce the former from the latter, or *vice versa*. What makes me a proletarian is not the economic system or society considered as systems of impersonal forces, but these institutions as I carry them within me and experience them; nor is it an intellectual operation devoid of motive, but my way of being in the world within this institutional framework.

Let us suppose that I have a certain style of living, being at the mercy of booms and slumps, not being free to do as I like, receiving a weekly wage, having no control over either the conditions or the products of my work, and consequently feeling a stranger in my factory, my nation and my life. I have acquired the habit of reckoning with a *fatum,* or appointed order, which I do not respect, but which I have to humour. Or suppose that I work as a day-labourer, having no farm of my own, no tools, going from one farm to another hiring myself out at harvest time; in that case I have the feeling that there is some anonymous power hovering over me and making a nomad of me, even though I want to settle into a regular job. Or finally suppose I am the tenant of a farm to which the owner has had no electricity laid on, though the mains are less than two hundred yards away. I have, for my family and myself, only one habitable room, although it would be easy to make other rooms available in the house. My fellow workers in factory or field, or other farmers, do the same work as I do in comparable conditions; we co-exist in the same situation and feel alike, not in virtue of some comparison, as if each one of us lived primarily within himself, but on the basis of our tasks and gestures. These situations do not imply any express evaluation, and if there is a tacit evaluation, it represents the thrust of a freedom devoid of any project against unknown obstacles; one cannot in any case talk about a choice, for in all three cases it is enough that I should be born into the world and that I exist in order to experience my life as full of difficulties and constraints—I do not choose so to experience it. But this state of affairs can persist without my becoming class-conscious, understanding that I am of the proletariat and becoming a revolutionary. How then am I to make this change? The worker learns that other workers in a different trade have, after striking, obtained a wage-increase, and notices that subsequently wages have gone up in his own factory. The appointed order with which he was at grips is beginning to take on a clearer shape. The day-labourer who has not often seen workers in regular employment, who is not like them and has little love for them, sees the price of manufactured goods and the cost of living going up, and becomes aware that he can no longer earn a livelihood. He may at this point blame town workers, in which case class-consciousness will not make its appearance. If it does, it is not because the day-labourer has decided to become a revolutionary and consequently confers a value upon his actual condition; it is because he has perceived, in a concrete way, that his life is synchronized with the life of the town labourers and that all share a common lot. The small farmer who does not associate himself with the day-labourers, still less with the town labourers, being separated from them by a whole world of customs and value judgements, nevertheless feels that he is on the same side as the journeyman when he pays them an inadequate wage, and he even feels that he has something in common with the town workers when he learns that the farm owner is chairman of the board of directors of several industrial concerns. Social space begins to acquire a magnetic field, and a region of the exploited is seen to appear. At every pressure felt from any quarter of the social horizon, the process of regrouping becomes clearly discernible beyond ideologies and various occupations. Class is coming into being, and we say that a situation is revolutionary when the connection objectively existing between the sections of the proletariat (the connection, that is, which an absolute observer would recognize as so existing) is finally experienced in perception as a common obstacle to the existence of each and every one. It is not at all necessary that at any single moment a *representation* of revolution should arise. For example, it is doubtful whether the Russian peasants of 1917 expressly envisaged revolution and the transfer of property. Revolution arises day by day from the concatenation of less remote and more remote ends. It is not necessary that each member of the proletariat should think of himself as such, in the sense that a Marxist theoretician gives to the word. It is sufficient that the journeyman or the farmer should feel that he is on the march towards a certain crossroads, to which the road trodden by the town labourers also leads. Both find their journey's end in revolution, which would perhaps have terrified them had it been described and represented to them in advance. One might say at the most that revolution is at the end of the road they have taken and in their projects in the form of 'things must change', which each one experiences concretely in his distinctive difficulties and in the depths of his particular prejudices. Neither the appointed order, nor the free act which destroys it, is represented; they are lived through in ambiguity. This does not mean that workers and peasants bring about revolution without being aware of it, and that we have here blind, 'elementary forces' cleverly exploited by a few shrewd agitators. It is possibly in this light that the prefect of police will view history. But such ways of seeing things do not help him when faced with a genuine revolutionary situation, in which the slogans of the alleged agitators are immediately understood, as if by some pre-established harmony, and meet with concurrence on all sides, because they crystallize what is latent in the life of all productive workers. The revolutionary movement, like the work of the artist, is an intention which itself creates its instruments and its means of expression. The revolutionary project is not the result of a deliberate judgement, or the explicit positing of an end. It is these things in the case of the propagandist, because the propagandist has been trained by the intellectual, or, in the case of the intellectual, because he regulates his life on the basis of his thoughts. But it does not cease to be the abstract decision of a thinker and become a historical reality until it is worked out in the dealings men have with each other, and in the relations of the man to his job. It is, therefore, true that I recognize myself as a worker or a bourgeois on the day I take my stand in relation to a possible revolution, and that this taking of a stand is not the outcome, through some mechanical causality, of my status as workman or bourgeois (which is why all classes have their traitors), but neither is it an unwarranted evaluation, instantaneous and unmotivated; it is prepared by some molecular process, it matures in co-existence before bursting forth into words and being related to objective ends. One is justified in drawing attention to the fact that it is not the greatest poverty which produces the most clear-sighted revolutionaries, but one forgets to ask why a return of prosperity frequently brings with it a more radical mood among the masses. It is because the easing of living conditions makes a fresh structure of social space possible: the horizon is not restricted to the most immediate concerns, there is economic play and room for a new project in relation to living. This phenomenon does not, then, go to prove that the worker makes himself into worker and revolutionary *ex nihilo,* but on the contrary that he does so on a certain basis of co-existence. The mistake inherent in the conception under discussion is, in general, that of disregarding all but intellectual projects, instead of considering the existential project, which is the polarization of a life towards a goal which is both determinate and indeterminate, which, to the person concerned, is entirely unrepresented, and which is recognized only on being attained. Intentionality is brought down to the particular cases of the objectifying acts, the proletarian condition is made an object of thought, and no difficulty is experienced in showing, in accordance with idealism's permanent method, that, like every other object of thought, it subsists only before and through the consciousness which constitutes it as an object. Idealism (like objective thought) passes by the side of true intentionality, of which it is true to say that it *belongs to* its object rather than that it posits it. Idealism overlooks the interrogative, the subjunctive, the aspiration, the expectation, the positive indeterminacy of these modes of consciousness, for it is acquainted only with consciousness in the present or future indicative, which is why it fails to account for class. For class is a matter neither for observation nor decree; like the appointed order of the capitalistic system, like revolution, before being thought it is lived through as an obsessive presence, as possibility, enigma and myth. To make class-consciousness the outcome of a decision and a choice is to say that problems are solved on the day they are posed, that every question already contains the reply that it awaits; it is, in short, to revert to immanence and abandon the attempt to understand history. In reality, the intellectual project and the positing of ends are merely the bringing to completion of an existential project. It is I who give a direction, significance and future to my life, but that does not mean that these are concepts; they spring from my present and past and in particular from my mode of present and past co-existence. Even in the case of the intellectual who turns revolutionary, his decision does not arise *ex nihilo;* it may follow upon a prolonged period of solitude: the intellectual is in search of a doctrine which shall make great demands on him and cure him of his subjectivity; or he may yield to the clear light thrown by a Marxist interpretation of history, in which case he has given knowledge pride of place in his life, and that in itself is understandable only in virtue of his past and his childhood. Even the decision to become a revolutionary without motive, and by an act of pure freedom would express a certain way of being in the natural and social world, which is typically that of the intellectual. He 'throws in his lot with the working class' from the starting point of his situation as an intellectual and from nowhere else (and this is why even fideism, in his case, remains rightly suspect). Now with the worker it is *a fortiori* the case that his decision is elaborated in the course of his life. This time it is through no misunderstanding that the horizon of a particular life and revolutionary aims coincide: for the worker revolution is a more immediate possibility, and one closer to his own interests than for the intellectual, since he is at grips with the economic system in his very life. For this reason there are, statistically, more workers than middle class people in a revolutionary party. Motivation, of course, does not do away with freedom. Working class parties of the most unmistakable kind have had many intellectuals among their leaders, and it is likely that a man such as Lenin identified himself with revolution and eventually transcended the distinction between intellectual and worker. But these are the virtues proper to action and commitment; at the outset, I am not an individual beyond class, I am situated in a social environment, and my freedom, though it may have the power to commit me elsewhere, has not the power to transform me instantaneously into what I decide to be. Thus to be a bourgeois or a worker is not only to be aware of being one or the other, it is to identify oneself as worker or bourgeois through an implicit or existential project which merges into our way of patterning the world and co-existing with other people. My decision draws together a spontaneous meaning of my life which it may confirm or repudiate, but not annul. Both idealism and objective thinking fail to pin down the coming into being of class consciousness, the former because it deduces actual existence from consciousness, the latter because it derives consciousness from *de facto* existence, and both because they overlook the relationship of motivation.

It will perhaps be objected, from the idealist side, that I am not, for myself, a particular project, but a pure consciousness, and that the attributes of bourgeois or worker belong to me only to the extent that I place myself among others, and see myself through their eyes, from the outside, as 'another'. Here we should have categories of For Others and not For Oneself. But if there were two sorts of categories, how could I have the experience of another, that is, of an *alter ego*? This experience presupposes that already my view of myself is half-way to having the quality of a possible 'other', and that in my view of another person is implied his quality as *ego*. It will be replied that the other person is given to me as a fact, and not as a possibility of my own being. What is meant by this? Is it that I should not have the experience of other men if there were none on the earth's surface? The proposition is self-evidently true, but does not solve our problem since, as Kant has already said, we cannot pass from 'All knowledge begins with experience' to 'All knowledge derives from experience'.

If the other people who empirically exist are to be, for me, other people, I must have a means of recognizing them, and the structures of the For Another must, therefore, already be the dimensions of the For Oneself. Moreover, it is impossible to derive from the For Another all the specifications of which we are speaking. Another person is not necessarily, is not even ever quite an object for me. And, in sympathy for example, I can perceive another person as bare existence and freedom as much or as little as myself. The-other-person-as-object is nothing but an insincere modality of others, just as absolute subjectivity is nothing but an abstract notion of myself. I must, therefore, in the most radical reflection, apprehend around my absolute individuality a kind of halo of generality or a kind of atmosphere of 'sociality'. This is necessary if subsequently the words 'a bourgeois' and 'a man' are to be able to assume meaning for me. I must apprehend myself immediately as centred in a way outside myself, and my individual existence must diffuse round itself, so to speak, an existence in quality. The For-Themselves—me for myself and the other for himself—must stand out against a background of For Others—I for the other and the other for me. My life must have a significance which I do not constitute; there must strictly speaking be an intersubjectivity; each one of us must be both anonymous in the sense of absolutely individual, and anonymous in the sense of absolutely general. Our being in the world, is the concrete bearer of this double anonymity.

Provided that this is so, there can be situations, a direction[8] of history, and a historical truth: three ways of saying the same thing. If indeed I made myself into a worker or a bourgeois by an absolute initiative, and if in general terms nothing ever courted our freedom, history would display no structure, no event would be seen to take shape in it, and anything might emerge from anything else. There would be no British Empire as a relatively stable historical form to which a name can be given, and in which certain probable properties are recognizable. There would not be, in the history of social progress, revolutionary situations or periods of set-back. A social revolution would be equally possible at any moment, and one might reasonably expect a despot to undergo conversion to anarchism. History would never move in any direction, nor would it be possible to say that even over a short period of time events were conspiring to produce any definite outcome. The statesman would always be an adventurer, that is to say, he would take

[8] 'sens' (Translator's note).

advantage of events by conferring upon them a meaning which they *did not have*. Now if it is true that history is powerless to complete anything independently of consciousnesses which assume it and thereby decide its course, and if consequently it can never be detached from us to play the part of an alien force using us for its own ends, then *precisely because it is always history lived through* we cannot withhold from it at least a fragmentary meaning. Something is being prepared which will perhaps come to nothing but which may, for the moment, conform to the adumbrations of the present. Nothing can so order it that, in the France of 1799, a military power 'above classes' should not appear as a natural product of the ebb of revolution, and that the rôle of military dictator should not here be 'a part that has to be played'. It is Bonaparte's project, known to us through its realization, which causes us to pass such a judgement. But before Bonaparte, Dumouriez, Custine and others had envisaged it, and this common tendency has to be accounted for. What is known as the significance of events is not an idea which produces them, or the fortuitous result of their occurring together. It is the concrete project of a future which is elaborated within social co-existence and in the One[9] before any personal decision is made. At the point of revolutionary history to which class dynamics had carried it by 1799, when neither the Revolution could be carried forward nor the clock put back, the situation was such that, all due reservations as to individual freedom having been made, each individual, through the functional and generalized existence which makes a historical subject of him, tended to fall back upon what had been acquired. It would have been a historical mistake at that stage to suggest to them either a resumption of the methods of revolutionary government or a reversion to the social conditions of 1789, not because there is a truth of history independent of our projects and evaluations, which are always free, but because there is an average and statistical significance of these projects. Which means that we confer upon history its significance, but not without its putting that significance forward itself. The *Sinngebung* is not merely centrifugal, which is why the subject of history is not the individual. There is an exchange between generalized and individual existence, each receiving and giving something. There is a moment at which the significance which was foreshadowed in the One, and which was merely a precarious possibility threatened by the contingency of history, is taken up by an

[9] In the sense of *Das Man*, the impersonal pronoun (Translator's note).

individual. It may well happen that now, having taken command of history, he leads it, for a time at least, far beyond what seemed to comprise its significance, and involves it in a fresh dialectic, as when Bonaparte, from being Consul, made himself Emperor and conqueror. We are not asserting that history from end to end has only one meaning, any more than has an individual life. We mean simply that in any case freedom modifies it only by taking up the meaning which history *was offering* at the moment in question, and by a kind of unobtrusive assimilation. On the strength of this proposal made by the present, the adventurer can be distinguished from the statesman, historical imposture from the truth of an epoch, with the result that our assessment of the past, though never arriving at absolute objectivity, is at the same time never entitled to be arbitrary.

We therefore recognize, around our initiatives and around that strictly individual project which is oneself, a zone of generalized existence and of projects already formed, significances which trail between ourselves and things and which confer upon us the quality of man, bourgeois or worker. Already generality intervenes, already our presence to ourselves is mediated by it and we cease to be pure consciousness, as soon as the natural or social constellation ceases to be an unformulated *this* and crystallizes into a situation, as soon as it has a meaning—in short, as soon as we exist. Every thing appears to us through a medium to which it lends its own fundamental quality; this piece of wood is neither a collection of colours and tactile data, not even their total *Gestalt,* but something from which there emanates a woody essence; these 'sense-data' modulate a certain theme or illustrate a certain style which is the wood itself, and which creates, round this piece of wood and the perception I have of it, a horizon of significance. The natural world, as we have seen, is nothing other than the place of all possible themes and styles. It is indissolubly an unmatched individual and a significance. Correspondingly, the generality and the individuality of the subject, subjectivity qualified and pure, the anonymity of the One and the anonymity of consciousness are not two conceptions of the subject between which philosophy has to choose, but two stages of a unique structure which is the concrete subject. Let us consider, for example, sense experience. I lose myself in this red which is before me, without in any way qualifying it, and it seems that this experience brings me into contact with a pre-human subject. Who perceives this red? It is nobody who can be named and placed among other perceiving subjects. For, between this experience of red which I have, and that about which other people speak to me, no direct comparison will ever be possible. I am here in my own point of view, and since all experience, in so far as it derives from impression, is in the same way strictly my own, it seems that a unique and unduplicated subject enfolds them all. Suppose I formulate a thought, the God of Spinoza, for example; this thought as it is in my living experience is a certain landscape to which no one will ever have access, even if, moreover, I manage to enter into a discussion with a friend on the subject of Spinoza's God. However, the very individuality of these experiences is not quite unadulterated. For the thickness of this red, its thisness, the power it has of reaching me and saturating me, are attributable to the fact that it requires and obtains from my gaze a certain vibration, and imply that I am familiar with a world of colours of which this one is a particular variation. The concrete colour red, therefore, stands out against a background of generality, and this is why, even without transferring myself to another's point of view, I grasp myself in perception as *a* perceiving subject, and not as unclassifiable consciousness. I feel, all round my perception of red, all the regions of my being unaffected by it, and that region set aside for colours, 'vision', through which the perception finds its way into me. Similarly my thought about the God of Spinoza is only apparently a strictly unique experience, for it is the concretion of a certain cultural world, the Spinozist philosophy, or of a certain philosophic style in which I immediately recognize a 'Spinozist' idea. There is therefore no occasion to ask ourselves why the thinking subject or consciousness perceives itself as a man, or an incarnate or historical subject, nor must we treat this apperception as a second order operation which it somehow performs starting from its absolute existence: the absolute flow takes shape beneath its own gaze as '*a* consciousness', or a man, or an incarnate subject, because it is a field of presence—to itself, to others and to the world—and because this presence throws it into the natural and cultural world from which it arrives at an understanding of itself. We must not envisage this flux as absolute contact with oneself, as an absolute density with no internal fault, but on the contrary as a being which is in pursuit of itself outside. If the subject made a constant and at all times peculiar choice of himself, one might wonder why his experience always ties up with itself and presents him with objects and definite historical phases, why we have a general notion of time valid through all times, and why finally the experience of each one of us links up with that of others. But it is the question itself which must be questioned: for what is given, is not one fragment of time followed by another, one individual flux, then another; it is the taking up of each subjectivity by itself, and of subjectivities by each other in the generality of a single nature, the cohesion of an intersubjective life and a world. The present mediates between the For Oneself and the For Others, between individuality and generality. True reflection presents me to myself not as idle and inaccessible subjectivity, but as identical with my presence in the world and to others, as I am now realizing it: I am all that I see, I am an intersubjective field, not despite my body and historical situation, but, on the contrary, by being this body and this situation, and through them, all the rest.

What, then, becomes of the freedom we spoke about at the outset, if this point of view is taken? I can no longer pretend to be a cipher, and to choose myself continually from the starting point of nothing at all. If it is through subjectivity that nothingness appears in the world, it can equally be said that it is through the world that nothingness comes into being. I am a general refusal to be anything, accompanied surreptitiously by a continual acceptance of such and such a qualified form of being. *For even this general refusal is still one manner of being, and has its place in the world.* It is true that I can at any moment interrupt my projects. But what *is* this power? It is the power to begin something else, for we never remain suspended in nothingness. We are always in a plenum, in being, just as a face, even in repose, even in death, is always doomed to express something (there are people whose faces, in death, bear expressions of surprise, or peace, or discretion), and just as silence is still a modality of the world of sound. I may defy all accepted form, and spurn everything, for there is no case in which I am utterly committed: but in this case I do not withdraw into my freedom, I commit myself elsewhere. Instead of thinking about my bereavement, I look at my nails, or have lunch, or engage in politics. Far from its being the case that my freedom is always unattended, it is never without an accomplice, and its power of perpetually tearing itself away finds its fulcrum in my universal commitment in the world. My actual freedom is not on the hither side of my being, but before me, in things. We must not say that I continually choose myself, on the excuse that I *might* continually refuse what I am. Not to refuse is not the same thing as to choose. We could identify drift and action only by depriving the implicit of all phenomenal value, and at every instant arraying the world before us in perfect transparency, that is, by destroying the world's 'worldliness'. Consciousness holds itself responsible for everything, and takes everything upon itself, but it has nothing of its own and makes its life in the world. We are led to conceive freedom as a choice continually remade as long as we do not bring in the notion of a generalized or natural time. We have seen that there is no natural time, if we understand thereby a time of things without subjectivity. There is, however, at least a generalized time, and this is what the common notion of time envisages. It is the perpetual reiteration of the sequence of past, present and future. It is, as it were, a constant disappointment and failure. This is what is expressed by saying that it is continuous: the present which it brings to us is never a present for good, since it is already over when it appears, and the future has, in it, only the appearance of a goal towards which we make our way, since it quickly comes into the present, whereupon we turn towards a fresh future. This time is the time of our bodily functions, which like it, are cyclic, and it is also that of nature with which we co-exist. It offers us only the adumbration and the abstract form of a commitment, since it continually erodes itself and undoes that which it has just done. As long as we place in opposition, with no mediator, the For Itself and the In Itself, and fail to perceive, between ourselves and the world, this natural foreshadowing of a subjectivity, this prepersonal time which rests upon itself, acts are needed to sustain the upsurge of time, and everything becomes equally a matter of choice, the respiratory reflex no less than the moral decision, conservation no less than creation. As far as we are concerned, consciousness attributes this power of universal constitution to itself only if it ignores the event which upholds it and is the occasion of its birth. A consciousness for which the world 'can be taken for granted', which finds it 'already constituted' and present even in consciousness itself, does not *absolutely* choose either its being or its manner of being.

What then is freedom? To be born is both to be born of the world and to be born into the world. The world is already constituted, but also never completely constituted; in the first case we are acted upon, in the second we are open to an infinite number of possibilities. But this analysis is still abstract, for we exist in both ways *at once*. There is, therefore, never determinism and never absolute choice, I am never a thing and never bare consciousness. In fact, even our own pieces of initiative, even the situations which we have chosen, bear us on, once they have been entered upon by virtue of a state rather than an act. The generality of the 'rôle' and of the situation comes to the aid of decision, and in this exchange between the situation and the person who takes it up, it is impossible to determine precisely the 'share contributed by the situation' and the 'share contributed by freedom'. Let us suppose that a man is tortured to make him talk. If he refuses to give the names and addresses which it is desired to extract from him, this does not arise from a solitary and unsupported decision: the man still feels himself to be with his comrades, and, being still involved in the common struggle, he is as it were incapable of talking. Or else, for months or years, he has, in his mind, faced this test and staked his whole life upon it. Or finally, he wants to prove, by coming through it, what he has always thought and said about freedom. These motives do not cancel out freedom, but at least ensure that it does not go unbuttressed in being. What withstands pain is not, in short, a bare consciousness, but the prisoner with his comrades or with those he loves and under whose gaze he lives; or else the awareness of his proudly willed solitude, which again is a certain mode of the *Mit-Sein*. And probably the individual in his prison daily reawakens these phantoms, which give back to him the strength he gave to them. But conversely, in so far as he has committed himself to this action, formed a bond with his comrades or adopted this morality, it is because the historical situation, the comrades, the world around him seemed to him to expect that conduct from him. The analysis could be pursued endlessly in this way. We choose our world and the world chooses us. What is certain, in any case, is that we can at no time set aside within ourselves a redoubt to which being does not find its way through, without seeing this freedom, immediately and by the very fact of being a living experience, take on the appearance of being and become a motive and a buttress. Taken concretely, freedom is always a meeting of the inner and the outer—even the prehuman and prehistoric freedom with which we began—and it shrinks without ever disappearing altogether in direct proportion to the lessening of the *tolerance* allowed by the bodily and institutional data of our lives. There is, as Husserl says, on the one hand a 'field of freedom' and on the other a 'conditioned freedom';[10] not that freedom is absolute within the limits of this field and non-existent outside it (like the perceptual field, this one

[10] Fink, *Vergegenwärtigung und Bild*, p. 285.

has no traceable boundaries), but because I enjoy immediate and re-mote possibilities. Our commitments sustain our power and there is no freedom without some power. Our freedom, it is said, is either total or non-existent. This dilemma belongs to objective thought and its stable-companion, analytical reflection. If indeed we place ourselves within being, it must necessarily be the case that our actions must have their origin outside us, and if we revert to constituting consciousness, they must originate within. But we have learnt precisely to recognize the order of phenomena. We are involved in the world and with others in an inextricable tangle. The idea of situation rules out absolute free-dom at the source of our commitments, and equally, indeed, at their terminus. No commitment, not even commitment in the Hegelian State, can make me leave behind all differences and free me for any-thing. This universality itself, from the mere fact of its being experi-enced, would stand out as a particularity against the world's back-ground, for existence both generalizes and particularizes everything at which it aims, and cannot ever be finally complete.

The synthesis of *in itself* and *for itself* which brings Hegelian free-dom into being has, however, its truth. In a sense, it is the very defini-tion of existence, since it is effected at every moment before our eyes in the phenomenon of presence, only to be quickly re-enacted, since it does not conjure away our finitude. By taking up a present, I draw together and transform my past, altering its significance, freeing and detaching myself from it. But I do so only by committing myself somewhere else. Psychoanalytical treatment does not bring about its cure by producing direct awareness of the past, but in the first place by binding the subject to his doctor through new existential relation-ships. It is not a matter of giving scientific assent to the psychoanalyt-ical interpretation, and discovering a notional significance for the past; it is a matter of reliving this or that as significant, and this the patient succeeds in doing only by seeing his past in the perspective of his co-existence with the doctor. The complex is not dissolved by a non-instru-mental freedom, but rather displaced by a new pulsation of time with its own supports and motives. The same applies in all cases of coming to awareness: they are real only if they are sustained by a new com-mitment. Now this commitment too is entered into in the sphere of the implicit, and is therefore valid only for a certain temporal cycle. The choice which we make of our life is always based on a certain givenness. My freedom can draw life away from its spontaneous course, but only by a series of unobtrusive deflections which necessitate first of all following its course—not by any absolute creation. All explanations of my conduct in terms of my past, my temperament and my environment are therefore true, provided that they be regarded not as separable contributions, but as moments of my total being, the significance of which I am entitled to make explicit in various ways, without its ever being possible to say whether I confer their meaning upon them or receive it from them. I am a psychological and historical structure, and have received, with existence, a manner of existing, a style. All my actions and thoughts stand in a relationship to this structure, and even a philosopher's thought is merely a way of making explicit his hold on the world, and what he is. The fact remains that I am free, not in spite of, or on the hither side of, these motivations, but by means of them. For this significant life, this certain significance of nature and history which I am, does not limit my access to the world, but on the contrary is my means of entering into communication with it. It is by being unrestrictedly and unreservedly what I am at present that I have a chance of moving forward; it is by living my time that I am able to understand other times, by plunging into the present and the world, by taking on deliberately what I am fortuitously, by willing what I will and doing what I do, that I can go further. I can pass freedom by, only if I try to get over my natural and social situation by refusing, in the first place, to take it up, instead of using it as a way into the natural and human world. Nothing determines me from outside, not because nothing acts upon me, but, on the contrary, because I am from the start outside myself and open to the world. We are *true* through and through, and have with us, by the mere fact of belonging to the world, and not merely being in the world in the way that things are, all that we need to transcend ourselves. We need have no fear that our choices or actions restrict our liberty, since choice and action alone cut us loose from our anchorage. Just as reflection borrows its wish for absolute sufficiency from the perception which causes a thing to appear, and as in this way idealism tacitly uses that 'primary opinion' which it would like to destroy as opinion, so freedom flounders in the contradictions of commitment, and fails to realize that, without the roots which it thrusts into the world, it would not be freedom at all. Shall I make this promise? Shall I risk my life for so little? Shall I give up my liberty in order to save liberty? There is no theoretical reply to these questions. But there are these *things* which stand, irrefutable, there is before you this person whom you love, there are these men whose existence around you is that of slaves, and *your* freedom cannot be willed without leaving behind its singular relevance, and without willing freedom *for all*. Whether it is a question of things or of historical situations, philosophy has no function other than to teach us once more to see them clearly, and it is true to say that it comes into being by destroying itself as separate philosophy. But what is here required is silence, for only the hero lives out his relation to men and the world. 'Your son is caught in the fire; you are the one who will save him. . . . If there is an obstacle, you would be ready to give your shoulder provided only that you can charge down that obstacle. Your abode is your act itself. Your act is you. . . . You give yourself in exchange. . . . Your significance shows itself, effulgent. It is your duty, your hatred, your love, your steadfastness, your ingenuity. . . . Man is but a network of relationships, and these alone matter to him.'[11]

---

[11] A. de Saint-Exupéry, *Pilote de Guerre,* pp. 171 and 174.

8. THE RELATIONS OF THE SOUL AND THE BODY AND THE PROBLEM OF PERCEPTUAL CONSCIOUSNESS

The Classical Solutions

That naive consciousness is realistic has been affirmed too much. Or at least the distinction should be made in this regard between the opinions of common sense, the manner in which it verbally accounts for perception,[1] and the perceptual experiences themselves; verbalized perception should be distinguished from lived perception. If we return to objects as they appear to us when we live in them without speech and without reflection and if we try to describe their mode of existence faithfully, they do not evoke any realistic metaphor. If I adhere to what immediate consciousness tells me, the desk which I see in front of me and on which I am writing, the room in which I am and whose walls enclose me beyond the sensible field, the garden, the street, the city and, finally, the whole of my spatial horizon do not appear to me to be causes of the perception which I have of them, causes which would impress their mark on me and produce an image of themselves by a transitive action. It seems to me rather that my perception is like a beam of light which reveals the objects there where they are and mani-

Maurice Merleau-Ponty, "The Relations of the Soul and the Body and the Problem of Perceptual Consciousness," *The Structure of Behavior,* Ch. IV, trans. by Alden L. Fisher (Boston: Beacon Press, 1963), pp. 185–224, 246–49. Reprinted by permission.

[1] This distinction between direct perception and verbal account remains valid even if linguistic consciousness is primary (cf. the preceding chapter) and even in regard to the latter.

fests their presence, latent until then. Whether I myself perceive or consider another subject perceiving, it seems to me that the gaze "is posed" on objects and reaches them from a distance—as is well expressed by the use of the Latin *lumina* for designating the gaze. Doubtless I know that my present experience of this desk is not complete, that it shows me only some of its aspects: be it the color, the form or the size, I know very well that they would vary under another lighting, from another point of view and standing in another place; I know that "the desk" is not reducible to the determinations with which it is presently clothed. But in immediate consciousness this perspectival character of my knowledge is not conceived as an accident in its regard, as an imperfection relative to the existence of my body and its proper point of view; and knowledge by "profiles"[2] is not treated as the degradation of a true knowledge which would grasp the totality of the possible aspects of the object all at once.

Perspective does not appear to me to be a subjective deformation of things but, on the contrary, to be one of their properties, perhaps their essential property. It is precisely because of it that the perceived possesses in itself a hidden and inexhaustible richness, that it is a "thing." In other words, when one speaks of the perspectival character of knowledge, the expression is equivocal. It can signify that only the perspectival projection of objects would be given to primitive knowledge; and in this sense the expression is inexact since the first reactions of an infant are adapted, for example, to the distance of objects[3]—a fact which excludes the idea of a phenomenal world originally without depth. From the beginning the perspectival character of knowledge is known as such and not something to which we are subjected. Far from introducing a coefficient of subjectivity into perception, it provides it on the contrary with the assurance of communicating with a world which is richer than what we know of it, that is, of communicating with a real world. The profiles of my desk are not given to direct knowledge as appearances without value, but as "manifestations" of the desk.

Although naive consciousness never confuses the thing with the

[2] *Abschattungen.* Cf. E. Husserl, "Ideen zu einer reinen Phänomenologie und phänomenologische Philosophie," in *Jahrbuch für Philosophie und phänomenologische Forschung,* Halle, M. Niemayer, 1913, I, *passim.*
[3] Cf. P. Guillaume, "Le problème de la perception de l'espace et la psychologie de l'enfant," *Journal de Psychologie,* XXI, 1924.

manner which it has of appearing to us, and precisely because it does not make this confusion, it is the thing itself which naive consciousness thinks it is reaching, and not some inner double, some subjective reproduction. It does not imagine that the body or that mental "representations" function as a screen between itself and reality. The perceived is grasped in an indivisible manner as "in-itself" (*en soi*), that is, as gifted with an interior which I will never have finished exploring; and as "for-me" (*pour moi*), that is, as given "in person" through its momentary aspects. Neither this metallic spot which moves while I glance toward it, nor even the geometric and shiny mass which emerges from it when I look at it, nor finally, the ensemble of perspectival images which I have been able to have of it *are* the ashtray; they do not exhaust the meaning of the "this" by which I designate it; and, nevertheless, it is the ashtray which appears in all of them.

This is not the place to analyze further the parodoxical relation of the "aspects" to the thing, of the "manifestations"[4] to that which is manifested by them and beyond them. But what we have said is sufficient to show that this relation is original and founds a consciousness of reality in a specific manner. The perspectival appearance of the ashtray is not to the "ashtray itself" what one event is to another event which it announces, or what a sign is to that which it signifies. Neither the sequence of "states of consciousness" nor the logical organization of thought accounts for perception: the first, because it is an external relation while the perspectival appearances of the ashtray are representative of each other; the second, because it presupposes a mind in possession of its object while my will is without direct action on the unfolding of the perceived perspectives and because their concordant multiplicity is organized of itself. A "cube" is not what I see of it since I see only three sides at a time; but no more is it a judgment by which I link together the successive appearances. A judgment, that is, a coordination conscious of itself, would be necessary only if the isolated appearances were given beforehand, which is counter to the hypothesis of intellectualism. Something of the empiricism which it surmounts always remains in intellectualism—something like a repressed empiricism. Thus, to do justice to our direct experience of things it would be necessary to maintain at the same time, against empiricism, that they are beyond their sensible manifestations and,

4 We are trying to translate the German *Erscheinung*.

against intellectualism, that they are not unities in the order of judgment, that they are embodied in their apparitions. The "things" in naive experience are evident as *perspectival beings:* it is essential to them, both to offer themselves without interposed milieu and to reveal themselves only gradually and never completely; they are mediated by their perspectival appearances; but it is not a question of a logical mediation since it introduces us to their bodily reality; I grasp *in* a perspectival appearance, which I know is only one of its possible aspects, the thing itself which transcends it. A transcendence which is nevertheless open to my knowledge—this is the very definition of a thing as it is intended (*visée*) by naive consciousness.

Whatever difficulty one may find in conceptualizing perception described in this way, it is for us to accommodate ourselves to it; this is the way that we perceive and that consciousness lives in things. Nothing is more foreign to perception therefore than the idea of a universe which would produce in us representations which are distinct from it by means of a causal action. To speak Kantian language, the realism of naive consciousness is an empirical realism—the assurance of an external experience in which there is no doubt about escaping "states of consciousness" and acceding to solid objects—and not a transcendental realism which, as a philosophical thesis, would posit these objects as the ungraspable causes of "representations" which alone are given.

The bodily mediation most frequently escapes me: when I witness events that interest me, I am scarcely aware of the perpetual breaks which the blinking of the eyelids imposes on the scene, and they do not figure in my memory. But after all, I know very well that I am able to interrupt the view by closing my eyes, that I see by the intermediary of my eyes. This knowledge does not prevent my believing that I see things themselves when I look at them. This is because the body proper and its organs remain the bases or vehicles of my intentions and are not yet grasped as "physiological realities." The body is *present* to the soul as external things are present; in neither case is it a question of a causal relation between the two terms. The unity of man has not yet been broken; the body has not been stripped of human predicates; it has not yet become a machine; and the soul has not yet been defined as existence for-itself (*pour soi*). Naive consciousness does not see in the soul the *cause* of the movements of the body nor does it put the soul in the body as the pilot in his ship. This way of thinking belongs to philosophy; it is not implied in immediate experience.

Since the body itself is not grasped as a material and inert mass or as an external instrument but as the living envelope of our actions, the principle of these actions has no need of being a quasi-physical force. Our intentions find their natural clothing or their embodiment in movements and are expressed in them as the thing is expressed in its perspectival aspects. Thus, thinking can be "in the throat," as the children questioned by Piaget say it is,[5] without any contradiction or confusion of the extended and the non-extended, because the throat is not yet an ensemble of vibrating cords capable of producing the sonorous phenomena of language, because it remains that privileged region of a qualitative space where my signifying intentions manifest themselves in words. Since the soul remains coextensive with nature, since the perceiving subject does not grasp himself as a microcosm into which messages of external events would make their way mediately and since his gaze extends over the things themselves, to act upon them is not for him to get outside the self and provoke a local movement in a fragment of extension; it is to make an intention explode in the phenomenal field in a cycle of significative gestures, or to join to the things in which he lives the actions which they solicit by an attraction comparable to that of the first unmoved mover.

One can say, if you like, that the relation of the thing perceived to perception, or of the intention to the gestures which realize it, is a magical relation in naive consciousness; but it would still be necessary to understand magical consciousness as it understands itself and not to reconstruct it from subsequent categories. The subject does not live in a world of states of consciousness or representations from which he would believe himself able to act on and know external things by a sort of miracle. He lives in a universe of experience, in a milieu which is neutral with regard to the substantial distinctions between the organism, thought and extension; he lives in a direct commerce with beings, things and his own body. The ego as a center from which his intentions radiate, the body which carries them and the beings and things to which they are addressed are not confused: but they are only three sectors of a unique field. Things are things,

---

[5] J. Piaget, *Le Représentation du monde chez l'enfant,* Paris, Presses Universitaires de France. 1948.

that is, transcendent with respect to all that I know of them and accessible to other perceiving subjects, but intended precisely as things; as such they are the indispensable moment of the lived dialectic which embraces them.

But on the other hand consciousness discovers, particularly in illness, a resistance of the body proper. Since an injury to the eyes is sufficient to eliminate vision, we must then see through the body. Since an illness is sufficient to modify the phenomenal world, it must be then that the body forms a screen between us and things. In order to understand this strange power of the body to upset the entire view of the world, we are obliged to renounce the image of it which direct experience gives us. The phenomenal body, with the human determinations which permitted consciousness not to be distinguished from it, is going to take on the status of appearance; the "real body" will be the one which we know through anatomy or, more generally, through the isolating methods of analysis: an ensemble of organs of which we have no notion in immediate experience and which interpose their mechanisms, their unknown powers, between ourselves and things. One could still conserve the favorite metaphor of naive consciousness and admit that the subject perceives *in conformity with* his body—as a colored glass modifies what the beam illuminates—without denying him access to the things themselves or putting them outside him.

But the body appears capable of fabricating the pseudo-perception. Thus certain phenomena of which it is the seat must be the necessary and sufficient condition for perception; the body must be the necessary intermediary between the real world and perception which are henceforth disassociated from each other. Perception can no longer be a taking-possession of things which finds them in their proper place; it must be an event internal to the body and one which results from their action on it. The world is doubled: there will be the real world as it is outside my body and the world as it is for me, numerically distinct from the first; the external cause of perception and the internal object which it contemplates will have to be separated. The body proper has become a material mass and, correlatively, the subject withdraws from it to contemplate its representations within himself.

Instead of the three inseparable terms bound together in the living unity of an experience which a pure *description* reveals, one finds oneself in the presence of three orders of events which are external to each other: the events of nature, the organic events and those of thought, which will explain each other. Perception will result from an action of the thing on the body and of the body on the soul. First it is the sensible, the perceived itself, to which the functions of extramental things are attributed; then the problem is to understand how a duplicate or an imitation of the real is aroused in the body, then in thought. Since a picture makes us think of what it represents, it will be supposed—based on the privileged case of the visual apparatus— that the senses receive "little pictures" of real things which excite the soul to perceive them.[6] The Epicurean "simulacra" or the "intentional species," "all those little images fluttering through the air"[7] which bring the sensible appearance of things into the body, only transpose the ideal presence of the thing to the perceiving subject into terms of causal explanation and real operations. It is the former, as we have seen, which is an evidence for naive consciousness. In default of a numerical identity the philosopher seeks to maintain a specific identity between the perceived and the real, to have the distinctive characteristic of the perceived come from the things themselves; this is why perception is understood as an imitation or a duplication in us of sensible things, or as the actualization in the soul of something which was in potency in an external sensible thing.

The difficulties which this explanatory mythology encounters would not have to be mentioned if they issued only from the realism of the sensible which has been abandoned since Descartes. In fact they are the permanent difficulties of any causal explanation applied to perception. The Descartes of the *Dioptrics* rejects the transitive action by means of which sensible things, identical with perceived objects, would impress their image in the body, where the soul would find it. Since light is only a movement, there is no need to suppose any resemblance between the things external to the body, the physiological phenomena and what the soul perceives. And, moreover, even if the perceived object resembled the bodily phenomena which condition perception or their external causes, perception would still not have been explained. "Even if this painting, by passing into the interior of our head in this way, still retains something of a resemblance to the objects from which it proceeds, one must still not be persuaded . . . that it is by means of this resemblance that it causes us to sense them, as if

---

[6] Descartes, *Dioptrique,* "Discours quatrième," édition Cousin, Paris, 1824–1826, pp. 39–40.
[7] *Ibid.,* "Discours premier," pp. 7–8.

there were other eyes over again in our brain with which we could apperceive; one should hold rather that it is the movements which compose it which, acting immediately on the soul inasmuch as it is united to our body, are constituted by nature to cause the soul to have such feelings."[8]

The external thing and the bodily impression do not act therefore as exemplar causes; they are the occasional causes[9] of the feelings of the soul. But all the difficulties are not removed; if the cerebral impressions are only the occasional causes of perception there must still be a regulated correspondence between certain cerebral impressions and certain perceptions. One has indeed gotten rid of the myths which made the idea of a real transference of sensible things into the mind inevitable; but one is obliged to construct physiological schemata which make comprehensible how sensory impressions are prepared in the brain to become the adequate occasions of our perceptions. Since we perceive only one object in spite of the two images which it forms on our retina, only one space in which the givens of the different senses are distributed, it will be necessary to imagine a bodily operation which combines these multiple elements and provides the soul with the occasion of forming a single perception.[10] Thus the substitution of occasional causes for exemplar causes does not eliminate the necessity of placing some physiological representation of the perceived object in the brain. This necessity is inherent in the realist attitude in general.

It is found again in the pseudo-Cartesianism of scientists and psychologists. Both consider perception and its proper objects as "internal" or "mental phenomena," as functions of certain physiological and mental variables. If by nature one means a group of events bound by laws, perception would be a part of nature, the perceived world a function of the real world of primary qualities. Then the problem is to designate in the body the adequate conditions of perception. Just as Descartes is obliged to reserve the mediation of the body and perception to the pineal gland[11] as seat of the common sense, so physiologists have had to give up designating fixed spatial and chromatic values in the periphery of the nervous system and to make those which

[8] *Ibid.*, "Discours sixième," p. 54.
[9] ". . . ce qui donne occasion à son âme de sentir tout autant de diverses qualités en ces corps qu'il se trouve de variétés dans les mouvements qui sont causés par eux en son cerveau" (*ibid.*, "Discours quatrième," p. 40).
[10] *Traité des passions*, art. 32 and 35; *Dioptrique*, "Discours quatrième," p. 53.
[11] *Traité des passions*, art. 34.

in perception are distributed over the different points of the visual field depend on the assimilation of the corresponding excitations into variable associative circuits. Descartes' pineal gland plays the role of the association zone of modern physiologists.

As soon as one accepts as given, as realism wants it, that the soul "sees immediately only by the interposition of the brain,"[12] this mediation, even if it is not a transitive action, necessitates looking in the body for a physiological equivalent of the perceived. But the nerve functioning which distributes their spatial or chromatic values to the different points of the sensory field, and which in normal cases, for example, renders diplopia impossible, is not itself conceivable without reference to the phenomenal field and its laws of internal equilibrium; it is a process of form, the notion of which is borrowed in the final analysis from the perceived world.

"It is the soul that sees and not the eyes," Descartes said[13] in order to get rid of the "little images fluttering through the air." The evolution of modern physiology shows that this expression must be taken absolutely literally and turned back against Descartes himself. It is the soul which sees and not the brain; it is by means of the perceived world and its proper structures that one can explain the spatial value assigned to a point of the visual field in each particular case. The coordinate axes of the phenomenal field, the direction which at each moment receives the value of "vertical" or "horizontal" and "frontal" or "lateral," the ensembles to which are assigned the index "immobile" and with respect to which the remainder of the field appears "in movement," the colored stimuli which are seen as "neutral" and determine the distribution of the apparent colors in the rest of the field, and the contexts of our spatial and chromatic perception—none of these result as effects from an intersection of mechanical actions; they are not a function of certain physical variables. Gestalt theory believed that a causal explanation, and even a physical one, remained possible on the condition that one recognized processes of structuration in physics in addition to mechanical actions.

But, as we have seen, physical laws do not furnish an explanation *of* the structures, they represent an explanation *within* the structures. They express the least integrated structures, those in which the simple

---

[12] *Dioptrique,* "Discours sixième," p. 64.
[13] *Idem.*

relations of function to variable can be established. They are already becoming inadequate in the "acausal" domain of modern physics. In the functioning of the organism, the structuration is constituted according to new dimensions—the typical activity of the species or the individual—and the preferred forms of action and perception can be treated even less as the summative effect of partial interactions. Thus the properties of the phenomenal field are not expressible in a language which would owe nothing to them. The structure of the "thing perceived" now offers a new support to this conclusion.

The relation of the perspectival aspects to the thing which they present to us is not reducible to any of the relations which exist within nature. As we have seen, it is neither the relation of effect to cause, nor that of function to corresponding variable. All the difficulties of realism arise precisely from having tried to convert this original relation into a causal action and to integrate perception into nature. As soon as the presence or the presentation of a "thing" to consciousness— instead of remaining an ideal relation, as in naive experiences—is interpreted as a real operation of the thing on the body and on the perceiving subject, it becomes impossible to reconstitute the descriptive content of perception, the actual view of the world, as an effect. The difficulty was evident in the theory of "simulacra" or in that of "intentional species" since, as copies of the thing itself, these "little pictures" which were transported into the body could not assume the variable perspectival aspects through which we nevertheless perceive things. Perspectival variation becomes understandable, on the contrary, once optics and the theory of light have excluded the idea of a resemblance between the real thing and the perceived.

But, inversely, it is the constancy of perceived things under their variable perspectival aspect which is going to become a problem. How are retinal images—so different depending on the points of view—going "to provide the soul with a means" of perceiving the same thing under several profiles? It would be necessary to suppose some association of present cerebral impressions with traces left by past impressions. But modern physiology has precisely given up the supposition of stores of cerebral traces, of "image centers" distinct from "perception centers"; and the physiological substrate of our perception is conceived as an indecomposable coordinating process in which the influence of prior excitations is not separately assignable. Most often one tries to "explain" the constancy of the phenomenal thing by a psychological process, by some "projection"[14] of memories which will complete or correct the present lacunary givens. To the extent that this "psychological explanation" is only a new kind of causal thinking we can reject it as we can every "explanation." Whether it is a question of memories or of cerebral traces, only a real transformation of sensible givens can be obtained by the real operations of a psychological or physiological causality: it will be shown how the "mental image" of an object does not follow exactly the perspectival variations of its "retinal image," how its phenomenal size when it is at some distance represents a mean between the size of the retinal image for a short distance and the size of the retinal image for a long one. But even if it could be established (which is false) that the mental image remains constant for variable distances, one would still not have explained the presentation of an identical thing under variable aspects since one would have purely and simply eliminated the perspectival variation by replacing it with the inertia of a constant "conscious content," with an immutable "mental image." The view of a thing seen through its "profiles," this original structure, is nothing which can be "explained" by some real physiological or psychological process. When I see an object at a distance I do not contemplate a *mental image of a determinate size,* as a sensitive plate can receive a physical image. I grasp in and by the perspectival aspect a constant thing which it mediates. The phenomenal object is not spread out on a plane, as it were; it involves two layers: the layer of perspectival aspects and that of the thing which they present. This ideal reference, this ambiguous mode of organization, can be described or understood, but not explained—with the help of a psycho-physiological law, for example—as if the "mental image" were another retinal image the size of which could be measured and related to certain variables.

But until now we have spoken only of a pseudo-Cartesianism. The *Dioptrics,* the *Treatise on Man,* and the *Treatise on the Passions* are situated in a ready-made world in which they delineate the human body and into which the soul is finally introduced. This is evidently not the principal undertaking of Cartesianism. Descartes' first step was to abandon the extra-mental things which philosophical realism had introduced in order to return to an inventory, to a description, of

[14] Bergson still employs this language.

human experience without presupposing anything at first which explains it from the outside. With regard to perception, the radical originality of Cartesianism is to situate itself within perception itself, not to analyze vision and touch as functions of our body, but "only the thought of seeing and touching."[15] Beyond causal explanations which constitute the appearance of perception as an effect of nature, Descartes, in search of the internal structure, makes its meaning explicit and disengages the grounds which assure naive consciousness that it is acceding to "things"; that, beyond the transitory appearances, it is grasping a solid being in a piece of wax, for example. If, as is always said, methodic doubt concerning sensible things is distinguished from sceptical doubt—the one finding in itself that which brings it to an end, the other being a state of uncertitude which does not admit of a solution —this difference in the results should stem from a difference in the operations which lead to them. Sceptical doubt is insurmountable because it is not radical; it presupposes extra-mental things as the ideal term of knowledge and it is in relation to this inaccessible reality that dreams and perception take on the character of equivalent appearances.

The Cartesian doubt necessarily carries its solution within itself precisely because it presupposes nothing—no realist idea of knowledge and because bringing attention back in this way from the vision or touch which lives in things to the "thought of seeing and touching" and laying bare the internal meaning of perception and of acts of knowledge in general—it reveals to thought the indubitable domain of significations. Even if I see and touch nothing which exists outside my thought, it is still a fact that I think I am seeing and touching something and that certain judgments are possible concerning the meaning of this thought considered as such. The *cogito* not only discloses to me the certitude of my existence, but more generally it provides me with access to a whole field of knowledges by giving me a general method: the method of searching, by reflection, for the pure thought in each domain which defines it; with regard to perception, for example, of analyzing the thought of perceiving and the meaning of the perceived which are immanent in the sight of a piece of wax, which animate it and sustain it internally.

One can say that here Descartes was very close to the modern notion

[15] Descartes, *Réponses aux Cinquièmes objections,* Bridoux (ed)., *Œuvres et Lettres,* Paris, Bibliothèque de la Piéiade, N.R.F., p. 376.

of consciousness understood as the center in which all the objects about which man can speak and all the mental acts which intend them take on an indubitable clarity. With the help of this notion Kant was able to go definitively beyond scepticism and realism by recognizing the descriptive and irreducible characteristics of external and internal experience as the sufficient foundation of the world. From this point of view perception could no longer appear to be the effect in us of the action of an external thing, nor the body as the intermediary of this causal action; the external thing and the body, defined as the "thought of" the thing and the "thought of" the body, as the "signification thing" and the "signification body," became indubitable as they presented themselves to us in a lucid experience at the same time that they lost the occult powers that philosophical realism had given them.

But Descartes does not follow this path to the end. The analysis of the piece of wax gives us only the essence of the thing, only the intelligible structure of dream objects or of perceived objects.[16] The imagination already contains something which this analysis does not take into account: it gives us the pentagon as "present."[17] In perception, the object "presents" itself without having been willed.[18] There is an existential index which distinguishes the perceived or imaginary object from the idea and which manifests "something" in them "which differs from my mind,"[19] whatever this "other" may be in the other respects.[20] Thus the experience of a sensible presence is explained by a real presence; the soul, when it perceives, is "excited" to think such and such an existing object by means of a bodily event to which it "applies itself" and which "represents" to it an event from the real extension.[21] The body ceases to be what it was vis-à-vis the understanding—a fragment of extension in which there are no real parts and in which the soul could not have a special seat[22]—to become, like the cubic foot of

16 ". . . il ne s'agissait pas ici de la vue et du toucher qui se font par l'entremise des organes corporels, mais de la seule pensée de voir et de toucher qui n'a pas besoin de ces organes comme nous expérimentons toutes les nuits dans nos songes." *Réponses aux Cinquièmes objections*, p. 376.
17 *Méditations touchant la Philosophie Première* in Adam and Tannery (eds.), *Œuvres de Descartes*, Paris, Cerf, 1897–1910, 12 vols., IX ("Sixième Méditation"), pp. 57–58.
18 *Ibid.*, p. 59.
19 *Ibid.*, p. 58.
20 *Ibid.*, p. 63.
21 *Traité des passions*, Part I.
22 *Ibid.*, art. 30.

which Malebranche will speak,[23] a real individual. As such, it could be the occasional cause of perceptions and it could even be so in only one of its parts to which the soul is immediately connected.[24] The experience of my body as "mine"[25]—which discredits the Aristotelian metaphor of the soul as a pilot of his ship[26]—is explained in turn by a real "mixture" of "the mind with the body."

Thus the universe of consciousness revealed by the *cogito* and in the unity of which even perception itself seemed to be necessarily enclosed was only a universe of thought in the restricted sense: it accounts for the thought of seeing, but the fact of vision and the ensemble of existential knowledges remain outside of it. The intellection which the *cogito* had found in the heart of perception does not exhaust its content; to the extent that perception opens out on an "other," to the extent that it is the experience of an existence, it arises from a primary and original notion which "can only be understood in its own terms,"[27] from an order of "life" in which the distinctions of the understanding are purely and simply annulled.[28] Thus Descartes did not attempt to integrate the knowledge of truth and the experience of reality, intellection and sensation.[29] It is not in the soul, it is in God that they are

[23] "Je sais bien qu'un pied-cube est de même nature que toute autre étendue, mais ce qui fait qu'un pied cube est distingué de tout autre, c'est son existence." (Malebranche, *Correspondance avec Mairan, édition nouvelle,* J. Moreau (ed.), Paris, Vrin, 1947, p. 139).

[24] *Traité des passions,* art. 31.

[25] "Ce corps lequel par un certain droit particulier, j'appelais mien. . . ." "Sixième Méditation," ed. Adam and Tannery, IX, p. 60.

[26] *Ibid.,* p. 64.

[27] Letter: A. Élisabeth, 21 mai 1643," ed. Adam and Tannery, III, p. 666.

[28] "Bien qu'on veuille concevoir l'âme comme matérielle (ce qui est proprement concevoir son union avec le corps) . . ." ("A Élisabeth, 28 juin 1643," *ibid.,* p. 691).

[29] The *Réponses aux Sixièmes objections* speaks, concerning the perception of size, distance and shape, of explicit reasoning in childhood and refers in this connection to the *Dioptrique.* But though it is true that the *Dioptrique* describes, with respect to the situation of objects, an "action de la pensée qui, n'etant qu'une imagination toute simple, ne laisse pas d'envelopper en soi un raisonnement" ("Discours Sixième," ed. Cousin, p. 62), Descartes accepts the fact that the soul knows directly the situation of objects without passing through that of the members, and this by an "institution de la nature" ("Discours Sixième," ed. Cousin, p. 60) which brings it about that such and such a situation is "vue" (*ibid.,* p. 63) when this or that disposition of the parts of the brain is realized. It is only when Descartes analyzes perception from within, as happens in the *Méditations,* that the "géométrie naturelle" (*Traité de l'homme,* ed. Cousin, IV, p. 380) of perception becomes a reasoning of the soul itself and perception an inspection of the mind (cf. "Sixième Méditation," ed. Adam and Tannery,

linked with each other. But after Descartes this integration was to appear to be the solution of the problems posed by philosophical realism. It would permit abandoning the action of the body or of things on the mind and allow them to be defined as the indubitable objects of a consciousness; it would permit surpassing the alternatives of realism and scepticism by associating, following Kant's terms, a transcendental idealism and an empirical realism.

The conception of sensible knowledge which was taught by Descartes is taken up again by a philosophy in the critical tradition. To know something is not only to find oneself in the presence of a compact ensemble of givens and to live in it as it were; this "co-nascence,"[30] this blind contact with a singular object and this participation in its existence would be as nothing in the history of a mind and would leave no more acquisitions and available memories in the mind than would a physical pain or a fainting spell if the contrary movement by which I detach myself from the thing in order to apprehend the meaning were not already contained in them. Red, as sensation, and red, as *quale,* must be distinguished; the quality already includes two moments: the pure impression of red and its function, which for example is to cover a certain extension of space and of time.[31] To know therefore is always to grasp a given in a certain function, in a certain relation, "in as much" as it signifies to me or presents to me such or such a structure.

Psychologists often speak as if the whole question were to know where the signification of the perceived *comes from;* they treat it as an aggregate of additional givens and explain it by means of a projection of images over the brute givens of the senses. They do not see

---

IX, p. 66). The *Dioptrique* enunciates the "jugements naturels," that is, the "naturized" thought, of Malebranche ("L'âme ne fait point tous les jugements que je lui attribue: ces jugements naturels ne sont que des sensations . . ." [*Recherche de la vérité,* I, chapter IX]; "Dieu les fait en nous pour nous . . . tels que nous les pourrions former nous-mêmes si nous savions divinement l'optique et la géométrie [*ibid.*]). The implicit reasonings of perception arise from God, not as word and place of ideas, but as creative will and legislator of occasional causes. On the other hand, the *Méditations* enunciates the "naturizing" thought of Spinoza.

[30] P. Claudel, *Art poétique: Traité de la co-naissance au monde et de soi-même,* Paris, Mercure de France.

[31] E. Husserl, "Vorlesungen zur Phänomenologie des inneren Zeitbewusztseins," in *Jahrbuch für Phänomenologie und phänomenologische Philosophie,* IX (1928), p. 5.

that the same problem poses itself with respect to the images introduced. If they are the simple copy of old perceptions, "little pictures"
which are less clear, the becoming aware of these new "things" will
still have to be analyzed once they have been brought back under
the gaze of the mind by some psychological or physiological mechanism. And even if a "dynamic plan" presides over the evocation of
memories, it remains an operation in the third person as long as *I* do
not recognize an illustration of the plan in the memory evoked.

One does not construct perception as one does a house: by assembling
the material gotten from the senses and the material gotten from
memory; one does not explain it as an event of nature by situating it
at the confluence of several causal series—sensory mechanisms and
mnemonic mechanisms. Even if the search for physiological and psychological determinants were to make possible the establishment of
a relation of function to variable between them and the view perceived
—we have seen that this is not at all the case—this explanation would
give us only the conditions of existence of the view; since it connects
the view with bodily and mental events situated in space and time,
this explanation would make it a mental event also. But there is something else. If I look steadily at an object in front of me, the psychologist
will say that external conditions remaining the same—the mental image of the object has remained the same. But it would still be necessary
to analyze the act by which at each instant I recognize this image as
identical in its meaning to that of the preceding instant.

The mental image of the psychologist is one thing; what the consciousness of that thing is must still be understood. The act of knowing
is not of the order of events; it is a taking-possession of events, even internal ones, which is not mingled with them; it is always an internal
"re-creation" of the mental image and, as Kant and Plato have said,
a recognizance, a recognition. It is not the eye, not the brain, but no
more is it the "psychism" of the psychologist which can accomplish the
act of vision. It is a question of an inspection of the mind in which
events are known in their meaning at the same time as they are lived
in their reality. No matter how evident the determination of the perceived contents by natural conditions may be in each particular case,
perception, by its general structure at least, eludes natural explanation
and admits of only an internal analysis.

It follows from this that the moments of knowledge in which I
grasp myself as determined to perceive a thing by that thing itself

should be considered as derived modes of consciousness, founded in the final analysis on a more original mode of consciousness. Since the grounds for our affirmations can only be sought within their proper sphere (*sens*), the experience of a real thing cannot be explained by the action of that thing on my mind: the only way for a thing to act on a mind is to offer it a meaning, to manifest itself to it, to *constitute* itself vis-à-vis the mind in its intelligible articulations. The analysis of the act of knowing leads to the idea of a constituting or naturizing thought which internally subtends the characteristic structure of objects. In order to indicate both the intimacy of objects to the subject and the presence in them of solid structures which distinguish them from appearances, they will be called "phenomena"; and philosophy, to the extent that it adheres to this theme, becomes a phenomenology, that is, an inventory of consciousness as milieu of the universe.

Thus philosophy returns to the evidences of naive consciousness. Transcendental idealism, by making the subject and the object inseparable correlatives, guarantees the validity of perceptual experience in which the world appears in person and nonetheless as distinct from the subject. If knowledge, instead of being the presentation to the subject of an inert tableau, is the apprehension of the meaning of this tableau, the distinction of the objective world and subjective appearances is no longer that of two sorts of beings, but of two significations; as such, it is unchallengeable. It is the thing itself which I reach in perception since everything of which one can think is a "signification of thing" and since the act in which this signification is revealed to me is precisely called perception. One must go back, not to Bergson, but to Kant for this idea that the perception of point "o" is at point "o."[32] It follows immediately from a notion of consciousness as universal life in which every affirmation of object finds its grounds.

The body becomes one of the objects which is constituted vis-à-vis consciousness; it is integrated into the objective world; and, since any nature is conceivable only as the correlate of a naturizing knowledge, there is no longer any question of treating knowledge as a fact of nature. Doubtless consciousness itself recognizes that natural laws determine the order of its perceptual events in terms of the position of the body and of bodily phenomena. In this sense it manifests itself as a part of the world, since it can be integrated into the relations

[32] M. Wahl seems to see in it a discovery of contemporary philosophy (*Vers le concret,* Paris, Vrin, 1932, preface).

which constitute it. It seems to include two aspects: on the one hand it is milieu of the universe, presupposed by every affirmation of a world; on the other hand it is conditioned by it. Thus, the first moment of critical philosophy will be to distinguish, on the one hand, a general form of consciousness which cannot be derived from any bodily or psychological event, in order to do justice to its analysis of knowledge; and, on the other, the empirical contents whose actual existence could be related to such and such external events or to this or that particularity of our psycho-physical constitution, in order to account for the external conditions which govern perception as well as the passivity which we grasp in it. Such is approximately the meaning of the *Transcendental Esthetic*.[33] But this attitude can be only provisional, as is shown by the second edition of the *Critique of Pure Reason*.

How, as a matter of fact, are we to conceive the relations of the "given" and "thought," the operation of consciousness on inert "things" which pure sensations would be, the connection of "affection" and knowledge and the connection of sensible and intellectual consciousness? In the final analysis, then, there will be no sensible consciousness, no hiatus between the esthetic and the analytic, and no naturized consciousness.[34] An analysis which would try to isolate the perceived content would find nothing; for all consciousness of something, as soon as this thing ceases to be an indeterminate existence, as soon as it is identifiable and recognizable, for example, *as* "a color" or even as "this unique red," presupposes the apprehension of a meaning through the lived impression which is not *contained* in consciousness and is not a real part of it. The matter of knowledge becomes a borderline-notion posed by consciousness in its reflection upon itself, and not a component of the act of knowing. But from then on perception is a variety of intellection and, in all its positive aspects, a judgment.

Critical philosophy would resolve the problems posed by the relations

[33] The *Esthétique transcendental* (tr. Barni, I, pp. 64, 68, 70, 80; cf. "The Transcendental Esthetic" in *Critique of Pure Reason,* tr. N. K. Smith, London, Macmillan, 1933, pp. 65–91) goes so far as to relate, besides the empirical contents, the form of space itself to the contingencies of the human constitution.

[34] It is known how the second edition of the *Critique of Pure Reason* withdraws "formal intuition" from the sensibility—the "Transcendental Esthetic" spoke of the "manner in which we are affected"—and gives it to the understanding, how it abandons the three syntheses of transcendental imagination—which, even if each one presupposed the following one, gave the appearance of a structure of the mind—in order to manifest better the presence of the "I think" at all the levels of consciousness which an abstract analysis could distinguish.

of form and matter, given and thought, and soul and body by ter-
minating in an intellectualist theory of perception.[35] If as a matter of
fact an incipient science, a first organization of experience which is
completed only by scientific coordination, could be shown in perception, the alleged sensible consciousness would no longer pose any problem, since the "original" characteristics of perceptual experience would
be nothing but privation and negation: "The universe of immediate
experience contains, not *more* than what is required by science, but
less; for it is a superficial and mutilated world; it is, as Spinoza says,
the world of *conclusions without premises.*"[36] The problem of the relations of the soul and the body would be posed only at the level of
a confused thought which adheres to the products of consciousness
instead of rediscovering in them the intellectual activity which produces them. Put back into the intellectual context which alone gives
it a meaning, "sensible consciousness" is eliminated as a problem. The
body rejoins the extension whose action it undergoes and of which it
is only a part; perception rejoins judgment, which subtends it. Every
form of consciousness presupposes its completed form: the dialectic
of the epistemological subject and the scientific object.

Is There Not a Truth of Naturalism?

Are we compelled in this direction by the preceding analyses? At
least they lead to the transcendental attitude, that is, to a philosophy
which treats all conceivable reality as an object of consciousness. It
has seemed to us that matter, life, and mind could not be defined as
three orders of reality or three sorts of beings, but as three planes of
signification or three forms of unity. In particular, life would not be
a force which is added to physico-chemical processes; its originality
would be that of modes of connection without equivalent in the physical
domain, that of phenomena gifted with a proper structure and which
bind each other together according to a special dialectic. In a living
being, bodily movements and moments of behavior can be described
and understood only in a specially tailored language and in accordance
with the categories of an original experience. And it is in this same
sense that we have recognized a psychological order and a mental

---

[35] Brunschvicg, *L'Expérience humaine et la causalité physique,* Paris, Alcan, 1922,
p. 466.
[36] *Ibid.,* p. 73.

order. But these distinctions then are those of different regions of experience. We have been moved from the idea of a *nature* as *omnitudo realitatis* to the idea of objects which could not be conceived in-themselves (*en soi*), *partes extra partes,* and which are defined only by an idea in which they participate, by a signification which is realized in them. Since the relations of the physical system and the forces which act upon it and those of the living being and its milieu are not the external and blind relations of juxtaposed realities, but dialectical relations in which the effect of each partial action is determined by its signification for the whole, the human order of consciousness does not appear as a third order superimposed on the two others, but as their condition of possibility and their foundation.

The problem of the relations of the soul and the body seems to disappear from the point of view of this absolute consciousness, milieu of the universe, as it did from the critical point of view. There can be no question of a causal operation between three planes of signification. One says that the soul "acts" on the body when it happens that our conduct has a rational signification, that is, when it cannot be understood by any play of physical forces or by any of the attitudes which are characteristic of the vital dialectic. In reality the expression is improper: we have seen that the body is not a self-enclosed mechanism on which the soul could act from the outside. It is defined only by its functioning, which can present all degrees of integration. To say that the soul acts on the body is wrongly to suppose a univocal notion of the body and to add to it a second force which accounts for the rational signification of certain conducts. In this case it would be better to say that bodily functioning is integrated with a level which is higher than that of life and that the body has truly become a human body. Inversely one will say that the body has acted on the soul if the behavior can be understood without residue in terms of the vital dialectic or by known psychological mechanisms.

Here again one does not, properly speaking, have the right to imagine a transitive action from substance to substance, as if the soul were a constantly present force whose activity would be held in check by a more powerful force. It would be more exact to say that the behavior had become disorganized, leaving room for less integrated structures. In brief, the alleged reciprocal action is reducible to an alternation or a substitution of dialectics. Since the physical, the vital and the mental individual are distinguished only as different degrees of integration, to the extent that man is completely identified with the third dialectic, that is, to the extent that he no longer allows systems of isolated conduct to function in him, his soul and his body are no longer distinguished.

If one supposes an anomaly of vision in El Greco, as has sometimes been done, it does not follow that the form of the body in his paintings, and consequently the style of the attitudes, admit of a "physiological explanation." When irremedial bodily peculiarities are integrated with the whole of our experience, they cease to have the dignity of a cause in us. A visual anomaly can receive a universal signification by the mediation of the artist and become for him the occasion of perceiving one of the "profiles" of human existence. The accidents of our bodily constitution can always play this revealing role on the condition that they become a means of extending our knowledge by the consciousness which we have of them, instead of being submitted to as pure facts which dominate us. Ultimately, El Greco's supposed visual disorder was conquered by him and so profoundly integrated into his manner of thinking and being that it appears finally as the necessary expression of his being much more than as a peculiarity imposed from the outside. It is no longer a paradox to say that "El Greco was astigmatic because he produced elongated bodies."[37] Everything which was accidental in the individual, that is, everything which revealed partial and independent dialectics without relationship to the total signification of his life, has been assimilated and centered in his deeper life. Bodily events have ceased to constitute autonomous cycles, to follow the abstract patterns of biology and psychology, and have received a new meaning. It is nevertheless the body, it will be said, which in the final analysis explains El Greco's vision; his liberty consisted only in justifying this accident of nature by infusing it with a metaphysical meaning. Unity does not furnish an adequate criterion of the liberty which has been won, since a man dominated by a complex, for example, and subject to the same psychological mechanism in all his undertakings, realizes unity in slavery. But here it is only a question of an apparent unity, of a stereotyped unity, which will not withstand an unexpected experience. It can be maintained only in a chosen milieu which the sick person has constructed for himself precisely by avoiding all situations in which the apparent coherence of his conduct would be disorganized. True unity on the contrary is recognized from the

[37] J. Cassou, *Le Greco,* Paris, Rieder, 1931, p. 35.

fact that it is not obtained by a restriction of the milieu. The same sensory or constitutional infirmity can be a cause of slavery if it imposes on man a type of vision and monotonous action from which he can no longer escape, or the occasion of a greater liberty if he makes use of it as an instrument. This supposes that he knows it instead of obeys it. For a being who lives at the simply biological level, it is a fatality.

For a being who has acquired the consciousness of self and his body, who has reached the dialectic of subject and object, the body is no longer the cause of the structure of consciousness; it has become the object of consciousness. Then one can no longer speak of a psycho-physiological parallelism: only a disintegrated consciousness can be paralleled with physiological processes, that is, with a partial functioning of the organism. By acceding to true knowledge, by going beyond the dialectic of the living or the social being and its circumscribed milieu, by becoming the pure subject who knows the world objectively, man ultimately realizes that absolute consciousness with respect to which the body and individual existence are no longer anything but objects; death is deprived of meaning. Reduced to the status of object of consciousness, the body could not be conceived as an intermediary between "things" and the consciousness which knows them; and since consciousness, having left the obscurity of instinct, no longer expresses the vital properties of objects but their *true* properties, the parallelism here is between consciousness and the true world which it knows directly. All the problems seem to be eliminated: the relations of the soul and the body—obscure as long as the body is treated in abstraction as a fragment of matter—are clarified when one sees in the body the bearer of a dialectic. Since the physical world and the organism can be conceptualized only as objects of consciousness or as significations, the problem of the relations of consciousness and its physical or organic "conditions" would exist only at the level of a confused thought which adheres to abstractions; it would disappear in the domain of truth in which the relation of the epistemological subject and its object alone subsists as original. This would constitute the only legitimate theme of philosophical reflection.

Let us consider a subject who turns his eyes toward a sensible object placed in front of him. Our preceding remarks permit us to say that the consecutive modification of his perceptual field is not an "effect" of the physical phenomenon of excitation or of the corresponding physiological phenomenon. We have shown that the most remarkable characteristics of the perceived object—its distance, its size, its apparent color—cannot be deducted from the physiological antecedents of perception. The modern theory of nerve functioning relates them to "transverse phenomena" of which there is neither a physical nor a physiological definition and which are conceived precisely by borrowing from the perceived world and the image of its descriptive properties. It becomes impossible to assign a *somatic* substrate of perception. The elaboration of stimuli and the distribution of motor influxes are accomplished according to articulations proper to the phenomenal field; what is introduced under the name of "transverse phenomena" is in reality the perceived field itself. For us this signifies that the living body and the nervous system, instead of being like annexes of the physical world in which the occasional causes of perception would be prepared, are "phenomena" emerging from among those which consciousness knows. Perceptual behavior, as science studies it, is not defined in terms of nerve cells and synapses; it is not in the brain or even in the body; science has not been able to construct the "central sectors" of behavior from the outside like something which is enclosed within a cranial box; it can understand it only as a dialectic, the moments of which are not stimuli and movements but phenomenal objects and actions. The illusion of a transitive operation of stimuli on the sensory apparatus and of the latter "against" consciousness comes from the fact that we actualize separately the physical body, the body of the anatomists or even the organism of the physiologists, all of which are abstractions, snapshots taken from the functional body.

When its existence is accepted, the hallucinatory image is no longer treated in recent works as an isolated phenomenon which could be explained by some irritation of centers: it is connected with the whole of organic-vegetative functioning;[38] which is to say that, rather than a perception without object, hallucination is a global conduct related to a global alteration of nerve functioning. It supposes a complete structure the description of which, like that of normal functioning, cannot be given in somatic terms. The somatic events do not act directly. Section of the optic nerve can be called the cause of blindness only in the sense in which Beethoven's deafness "explains" his last works. It provokes a change of the phenomenal field only by rendering impossible the functioning of the whole of the cortex under the action

[38] R. Mourgue, *Neurobiologie de l'hallucination*, Brussels, Lamertin, 1932.

of luminous excitants. Is it this functioning itself which can be considered as a cause? No, if it is understood as the sum of the nerve events which are produced in each point of the cortex. This whole can be only the *condition of existence* of such and such a sensible scene; it accounts for the *fact that* I perceive but not for *that which* I perceive,[39] not for the scene as such since this latter is presupposed in a complete definition of the nerve process. Everything takes place as if my perception opened out on a network of original significations. The passage of nerve influx in such and such conductors does not produce the visible scene; it does not even determine its structure in a univocal manner since it is organized according to laws of equilibrium which are neither those of a physical system nor those of the body considered as such. The somatic substrate is the passage point, the base of a dialectic. In the same way, nobody thinks of explaining the content of a delirium by its physiological conditions even though this form of consciousness presupposes *in existendo* some alteration of the brain.

Speaking generally, it seems that we are rejoining the critical idea. Whatever the external conditions may be—bodily, psychological, social—upon which the development of consciousness depends and even if it is only gradually constituted in history, the history itself out of which it comes is only a view which consciousness gives itself with regard to the acquired consciousness of self. A reversal of perspective is produced vis-à-vis adult consciousness: the historical becoming which prepared it was not *before* it, it is only *for* it; the time during which it progressed is no longer the time *of* its constitution, but a time which it constitutes; and the series of events is subordinated to its eternity. Such is the perpetual reply of critical thought to psychologism, sociologism and historicism.

This discussion of causal thinking has seemed valid to us and we have pursued it at all levels of behavior. It leads, as we have just said, to the transcendental attitude.[40] This is the first conclusion which we have to draw from the preceding chapters. It is not the only one, and it would even be necessary to say that this first conclusion stands in

[39] M. Scheler, *Die Wissensformen und die Gesellschaft,* Leipzig, Der Neue Geist, 1926, p. 394.
[40] "Without leaving the natural attitude one could show how the problems of totality *(Ganzheitsprobleme)* of the natural world, pursued to their root, end up instigating the passage to the transcendental attitude." E. Fink, "Vergegenwärtigung und Bild," *Jahrbuch für Philosophie und phänomenologische Forschung,* 1930, XI, p. 279.

a relation of simple homonymy with a philosophy in the critical tradition.[41] What is profound in the notion of "Gestalt" from which we started is not the idea of signification but that of *structure,* the joining of an idea and an existence which are indiscernible, the contingent arrangement by which materials begin to have meaning in our presence, intelligibility in the nascent state. The study of the reflex has shown us that the nervous system is the place in which an order without anatomical guarantee is realized by means of a continuing organization. It already permitted us to establish a rigorously reciprocal relation between function and substrate; there was not an area which was not linked in its functioning to the global activity of the nervous system, but also not a function which was not profoundly altered by the subtraction of a single one of these areas; and function was nothing outside the process which is delineated at each instant and which, based on the nerve mass, organizes itself.[42]

The study of the "central sector" of behavior confirmed this ambiguity of bodily nature. On the one hand it appeared that absolutely no function could be localized, since each region plays a role only in the context of a global activity and since the diverse movements which it governs correspond to several modes of qualitatively distinct functioning rather than to several locally differentiated devices. On the other hand, it was equally clear that certain parts of the nerve substance are indispensable for the reception of certain stimuli, that the execution of certain movements is assigned to certain receptive regions or to some muscular ensemble, and that, even when nerve substance is not the depository of any special power of this kind, there can be no substitution for the nerve substance in each place. Thus, we were dealing less with two types of localization than with an inextricable intersecting of "horizontal" and "vertical" localizations—without the body being anywhere pure thing, *but also without it being anywhere pure idea.*[43] It is not possible to designate separate contributions of the visual and auditive regions of the brain; both function only with the center; and integral thinking transfigures the hypothetical "visual contents" and "auditive contents" to the point of rendering them unrecognizable; but also the alteration of one of these regions is mani-

---

[41] We are thinking of a philosophy like that of L. Brunschvicg and not of Kantian philosophy, which, particularly in the *Critique of the Judgment,* contains essential indications concerning the problems of which it is a question here.
[42] Cf. Chapter I.
[43] Cf. Chapter I, p. 227, n. 31, and Chapter II.

fested in thought by a determinate deficit: it is the intuition of simultaneous wholes or that of successive wholes which becomes impossible.[44]
Thus the integration of the optic or auditive regions in a functional
whole, although it infuses the corresponding "contents" with a new
signification, does not annul their specificity; it uses and sublimates it.

For life, as for the mind, there is no past which is absolutely past;
"the moments which the mind seems to have behind it are also borne
in its present depths."[45] Higher behavior retains the subordinated
dialectics in the present depths of its existence, from that of the physical
system and its topographical conditions to that of the organism and
its "milieu." They are not recognizable in the whole when it functions
correctly, but the disintegration in case of partial lesion attests to their
imminence. There is no essence of thinking which would receive the
particular forms of "visual thought" and "auditive thought" by a contingency of our nerve organization and as a condition of existence.
The alleged conditions of existence are indiscernible in the whole with
which they collaborate *and reciprocally the essence of the whole cannot be concretely conceptualized without them and without its constitutive history.* Consequently, the relations of matter and form in the
object-organism and the relations of the soul and body were found to
be conceived differently than in critical thought.

While critical philosophy, having step by step repressed quality and
existence—residues of its ideal analysis—to place them finally in a matter about which nothing can be thought and which is for us therefore
as if it were not, deploys a homogeneous activity of the understanding
from one end of knowledge to the other; each "formation" (*mise
en forme*) appears to us on the contrary to be an event in the world
of ideas, the institution of a new dialectic, the opening of a new region
of phenomena, and the establishment of a new constitutive layer which
eliminates the preceding one as isolated moment, but conserves and
integrates it. While critical thought pushed the problem of the relations of the soul and body back step by step by showing that we never
deal with a body in-itself (*en soi*) but with a body for-a-consciousness
and that thus we never have to put consciousness in contact with an
opaque and foreign reality, for us consciousness experiences its inherence in an organism at each moment; for it is not a question of an

[44] Cf. *supra.*
[45] Hegel, *Vorlesungen über die Philosophie der Geschichte,* in G. Lasson (ed.),
Hegels Sämmtliche Werke kritische Ausgabe, Leipzig, Meiner, 1905—.

inherence in material apparatuses, which as a matter of fact can be only *objects* for consciousness, but of a presence to consciousness of its proper history and of the dialectical stages which it has traversed.

Therefore, we could not accept any of the materialistic models to represent the relations of the soul and body—but neither could we accept the mentalistic models, for example, the Cartesian metaphor of the artisan and his tool.[46] An organ cannot be compared to an instrument, as if it existed and could be conceived apart from integral functioning, nor the mind to an artisan who uses it: this would be to return to a wholly external relation like that of the pilot and his ship which was rightly rejected by Descartes. The mind does not use the body, but realizes itself through it while at the same time transferring the body outside of physical space. When we were describing the structures of behavior[47] it was indeed to show that they are irreducible to the dialectic of physical stimulus and muscular contraction and that in this sense behavior, far from being a thing which exists in-itself (*en soi*), is a whole significative for a consciousness which considers it; but it was at the same time and reciprocally to make manifest in "expressive conduct" the *view of a consciousness* under our eyes, to show a mind which *comes into the world*.

Doubtless it is understood why we cannot even accept without reservations a relation of expression between the soul and the body comparable to that of the concept and the word, nor define the soul as the "meaning of the body," the body as the "manifestation of the

---

[46] ". . . on ne vous croit pas quand vous avancez si hardiant et san aucune preuve que l'esprit croît et s'affaiblit avec le corps; car de ce qu'il n'agit pas si parfaitement dans le corps d'un enfant que dans celui d'un homme parfait, et que souvent ses actions peuvent être empêchées par le vin et par d'autres choses corporelles, il s'ensuit seulement que tandis qu'il est uni au corps il s'en sert comme d'un instrument pour faire ces sortes d'opérations auxquelles il est pour l'ordinaire occupé, mais non pas que le corps le rende plus ou moins parfait qu'il est en soi; et la conséquence que vous tirez de là n'est pas meilleure que si, de ce qu'un artisan ne travaille pas bien toutes les fois qu'il se sert d'un mauvais outil, vous inferiez qu'il emprunte son adresse et la science de son art de la bonté de son instrument." ("Réponses aux Cinquièmes objections," Bridoux (ed.) *Œuvres et Lettres,* p. 371.) It is not a question of approving Gassendi, who attributed to the biological body what belongs to the phenomenal body—but this is not a reason for speaking of a perfection of the mind in-itself (*en soi*). If the body plays a role in preventing the actualization of the mind, it is because the body is involved with the mind when this actualization is achieved.

[47] Cf. Chapter II, Section III.

soul."[48] These formulae have the inconvenience of evoking two terms, solidary perhaps, but external to each other and the relation of which would be invariable. But sometimes our body manifests externally an intention arising from a dialectic which is higher than biology; sometimes, by a play of mechanisms which its past life has built up, it limits itself to mimicking intentions which it *does not have* any longer, as do the movements of a dying person for example;[49] from one case to the other the relation of the soul and the body and even the terms themselves are modified depending on whether the "formation" succeeds or fails and whether the inertia of the subordinated dialectics allows itself to be surmounted or not. Our body does not always have meaning, and our thoughts, on the other hand—in timidity for example—do not always find in it the plenitude of their vital expression. In these cases of disintegration, the soul and the body are apparently distinct; and this is the truth of dualism. But the soul, if it possesses no means of expression—one should say rather, no means of actualizing itself—soon ceases to be *anything whatsoever* and in particular ceases to be the soul, as the thought of the aphasic weakens and becomes dissolved; the body which loses its meaning soon ceases to be a living body and falls back into the state of a physico-chemical mass; it arrives at non-meaning only by dying. The two terms can never be distinguished absolutely without ceasing to be; thus their

---

[48] "The soul is the meaning of the body and the body is the manifestation of the soul; neither of the two acts on the other because neither of the two belongs to the world of things. . . . The soul is inherent in the body as the concept is inherent in speech: the former is the meaning of the word, the latter is the meaning of the body; the word is the clothing of thought and the body the manifestation of the soul. And there are no souls without manifestations any more than there are concepts without speech" (L. Klages, *Vom Wesen des Bewusztseins,* Leipzig, Barth, 1921).

[49] ". . . sa main qui écartait les couvertures d'un geste qui eût autrefois signifié que ces couvertures la gênaient et qui maintenant ne signifiait rien" (Proust, *Le Côté des Guermantes,* II, p. 27). "Dégagé par la double action de la morphine et de l'oxygène, le souffle de ma grandmère ne peinait plus, ne geignait plus, mais vif, léger, glissait, patineur, vers le fluide délicieux. Peu-être à l'haleine, insensible comme celle du vent dans la flûte d'un roseau, se mêlait-il dans ce chant quelques-uns de ces soupirs plus humains qui, libérés à l'approche de la mort, font croire à des impressions de souffrance ou de bonheur chez ceux qui déjà ne sentent plus, et venaient ajouter un accent plus mélodieux, mais sans changer son rythme, à cette longue phrase qui s'élevait, montait encore puis retombait, pour s'élancer de nouveau, de la poitrine allégée, à la poursuite de l'oxygène" (*ibid.,* p. 31).

empirical connection is based on the original operation which establishes a meaning in a fragment of matter and makes it live, appear and be in it. In returning to this *structure* as the fundamental reality, we are rendering comprehensible both the distinction and the union of the soul and the body.

There is always a duality which reappears at one level or another: hunger or thirst prevents thought or feelings; the properly sexual dialectic ordinarily reveals itself through a passion; integration is never absolute and it always fails—at a higher level in the writer, at a lower level in the aphasic. There always comes a moment when we divest ourselves of a passion because of fatigue or self-respect. This duality is not a simple fact; it is founded in principle—all integration presupposing the normal functioning of subordinated formations, which always demand their own due.

But it is not a duality of substances; or, in other words, the notions of soul and body must be relativized: there is the body as mass of chemical components in interaction, the body as dialectic of living being and its biological milieu, and the body as dialectic of social subject and his group; even all our habits are an impalpable body for the ego of each moment. Each of these degrees is soul with respect to the preceding one, body with respect to the following one. The body in general is an ensemble of paths already traced, of powers already constituted; the body is the acquired dialectical soil upon which a higher "formation" is accomplished, and the soul is the meaning which is then established.[50] The relations of the soul and the body can indeed be compared to those of concept and word, but on the condition of perceiving, beneath the separated products, the constituting operation which joins them and of rediscovering, beneath the empirical languages—the external accompaniment or contingent clothing of thought—the living *word* which is its unique actualization, in which the meaning is formulated for the first time and thus establishes itself as meaning and becomes available for later operations.

In this way our analyses have indeed led us to the ideality of the

[50] Nevertheless there would be a place for investigating more thoroughly the distinction of our "natural body," which is always already there, already constituted for consciousness, and our "cultural body," which is the sedimentation of its spontaneous acts. The problem is posed by Husserl when he distinguishes "original passivity" and "secondary passivity." Cf. in particular "Formale and transzendentale Logik," in *Jahrbuch für Philosophie und phänomenologische Forschung,* X (1929), p. 287.

body, but it was a question of an idea which proffers itself and even constitutes itself in the contingency of existence. By a natural development the notion of "Gestalt" led us back to its Hegelian meaning, that is, to the concept before it has become consciousness of self. Nature, we said, is the exterior of a concept.[51] But precisely the concept as concept has no exterior and the Gestalt still had to be conceptualized as unity of the interior and exterior, of nature and idea.[52] Correlatively the consciousness *for* which the Gestalt exists was not intellectual consciousness but perceptual experience.[53] Thus, it is perceptual consciousness which must be interrogated in order to find in it a definitive clarification. Let us limit ourselves here to indicating how the status of the object, the relations of form and matter, those of soul and body, and the individuality and plurality of consciousness are founded in it.

I cannot simply identify what I perceive and the thing itself. The real color of the object which I look at is and will always remain known to myself alone. I have no means whatsoever of knowing if the colored impression which it gives to others is identical to my own. Our intersubjective confrontations bear only upon the intelligible structure of the perceived world: I can assure myself that another viewer employs the same word as I to designate the color of this object and the same word, on the other hand, to qualify a series of other objects which I also call red objects. But, the relationships being conserved, it could happen that the scale of colors which he sees is completely different from mine. However, it is when objects give me the unique impression of the "sensed," when they have that direct manner of taking hold of me, that I say they are existing. It follows from this that perception, as knowledge of existing things, is an individual consciousness and not the consciousness in general of which we were speaking above. This sensible mass in which I live when I stare at a sector of the field without trying to recognize it, the "this" which my consciousness wordlessly intends, is not a signification or an idea, although subsequently it can serve as base for acts of logical explicitation and verbal expression. Already when I name the perceived or when I recognize it *as* a chair or tree, I substitute the subsumption under a concept for the experience of a fleeting reality; even when I pronounce the word

[51] Cf. p. 162.
[52] Cf. p. 136.
[53] Cf. p. 144.

"this," I already relate a singular and lived existence to the essence of lived existence. But these acts of expression or reflection intend an original text which cannot be deprived of meaning.

The signification which I find in a sensible whole was already adherent in it. When I "see" a triangle, my experience would be very poorly described by saying that I conceive or comprehend the triangle with respect to certain sensible givens. The signification is embodied. It is here and now that I perceive this triangle as such, while conception gives it to me as an eternal being whose meaning and properties, as Descartes said, owe nothing to the fact that I perceive it. It is not only the matter of perception which comes off the thing as it were and becomes a content of my individual consciousness. In a certain manner, the form also makes up a part of the psychological individual, or rather is related to it; and *this reference is included in its very meaning,* since it is the form *of* this or that thing which presents itself to me here and now and since this encounter, which is revealed to me by perception, does not in the least concern the proper nature of the thing and is, on the contrary, an episode of my life. If two subjects placed near each other look at a wooden cube, the total structure of the cube is the same for both; it has the value of intersubjective truth and this is what they both express in saying that there is a cube there. But it is not the same sides of the cube which, in each of them, are strictly seen and sensed.

We have said that this "perspectivism" of perception is not an indifferent fact, since without it the two subjects would not be aware of perceiving an existent cube subsisting beyond the sensible contents. If all the sides of the cube could be known at once, I would no longer be dealing with a thing which offers itself for inspection little by little, but with an idea which my mind would truly possess. This is what happens when I think of objects which I hold to be existent without actually perceiving them. In affirming that they continue to exist, I mean that a properly placed psycho-physical subject would see this or that sensible sight, articulated in this or that way and connected with the view which I perceive here and now by such and such objective transitions.

But this *knowing about* the world must not be confused with my *perception of* this or that segment of the world and its immediate horizon. The objects which do not belong to the circle of the perceived exist in the sense in which truths do not cease to be true when I am not thinking about them: their mode of being is one of logical necessity and not of "reality." For I certainly suppose a "perspectivism" in them also, and it is essential to them to present themselves to a viewer through a multiplicity of "profiles." But since I do not perceive them, it is a question of a perspectivism in idea and of an essence of the viewer; the relation of the one to the other is itself a relation of significations. These objects belong therefore to the order of significations and not to that of existences.[54] A perception which would be coextensive with sensible things is inconceivable; and it is not physically but logically that it is impossible. For there to be perception, that is, apprehension of an existence, it is absolutely necessary that the object not be completely given to the look which rests on it, that aspects intended but not possessed in the present perception be kept in reserve. A seeing which would not take place from a certain point of view and which would give us, for example, all the sides of a cube at once is a pure contradiction in terms; for, in order to be visible all together, the sides of a wooden cube would have to be transparent, that is, would cease to be the sides of a wooden cube. And if each of the six sides of a transparent cube were visible as square, it is not a cube which we would be seeing. Thus the Bergsonian idea of a "pure perception," that is, adequate to the object or identical with it, is inconsistent. It is the cube as signification or geometrical idea which is made of six equal sides. The relation—unique and characteristic of existing things—of the "aspects" to the total object is not a logical relation like that of sign to signification: the sides of the chair are not its "signs," but precisely the sides.

In the same way the phenomena of my body should be distinguished from purely logical significations. What differentiates it from external things even as they are presented in lived perception is the fact that it is not, like them, accessible to an unlimited inspection. When it is a question of an external thing, I know that by changing place I could see the sides which are hidden from me; by occupying the

---

[54] We reserve the question of whether there is not, as Heidegger suggests, a perception of the *world,* that is, a manner of acceding to an indefinite field of objects which gives them in their reality. What is certain is that the perceived is not limited to that which strikes my eyes. When I am sitting at my desk, the space is closed behind me not only in idea but also in reality. Even if the horizon of the perceived can be expanded to the limits of the world, the perceptual consciousness of the world as existing remains distinct from the intellectual consciousness of the world as object of an infinity of true judgments.

position which was that of my neighbor a moment ago, I could obtain a new perspectival view and give a verbal account which would concur with the description of the object which my neighbor gave a moment ago. I do not have the same liberty with my body. I know very well that I will never see my eyes directly and that, even in a mirror, I cannot grasp their movement and their living expression. For me, my retinas are an absolute unknowable. This is, after all, only a particular case of the perspectival character of perception.

To say that I have a body is simply another way of saying that my knowledge is an individual dialectic in which intersubjective objects appear, that these objects, when they are given to knowledge in the mode of actual existence, present themselves to it by successive aspects which cannot coexist; finally, it is a way of saying that one of them offers itself obstinately "from the same side" without my being able to go around it. Reservation made for its image which mirrors give me (but *this image moves* as soon as I try to see it from different points of view, by leaning the head to the right and left; it is not a true "thing"), my body as given to me by sight is broken at the height of the shoulders and terminates in a tactile-muscular object. I am told that an object is visible for others in this lacuna in which my head is located; science teaches that organs, a brain and—each time that I perceive an external thing—"nerve influxes" in this visible object would be found by means of analyses. I will never see anything of all that. I could never make an actually present experience of my body adequately correspond to the signification, "human body," as it is given to me by science and witnesses. There are entities which will always remain pure significations for me under some of their aspects and which will never be offered to other than lacunary perception. In itself, this structure is not much more mysterious than that of external objects with which, moreover, it is one: how could I receive an object "in a certain direction" if I, the perceiving subject, were not in some way hidden in one of my phenomena, one which envelops me since I cannot go around it? Two points are necessary for determining a direction.

We have not completely described the structure of the body proper, which also includes an affective perspective, the importance of which is evident. But the preceding is sufficient to show that there is no enigma of "my body," nothing inexpressible in its relation to myself. It is true that, by describing it, we are transforming into signification the lived perspective which by definition is not one. But this alogical essence of perceived beings can be clearly designated: one will say, for example, that to offer themselves through profiles which I do not possess as I possess an idea is included in the idea of perceived being and of the body.

Reduced to its positive meaning, the connection of the soul and body signifies nothing other than the *ecceitas* of knowledge by profiles; it appears to be a marvel only if, by a dogmatic prejudice, it is posited that all entities which we experience should be given to us "completely," as significations pretend to be. Thus the obscure causality of the body is reducible to the original structure of a phenomenon; and we do not dream of explaining perception as an event of an individual consciousness "by means of the body" and in terms of causal thinking. But if it is still not a question of externally connecting my consciousness to a body whose point of view it would adopt in an explicable manner, and if, in order to remain faithful to this phenomenon, it all comes back in brief to accepting the fact that some *men see things which I do not see,* the zone of individual perspectives and that of intersubjective significations must be distinguished in my knowledge. This is not the classical distinction between sensibility and intelligence, since the horizon of the perceived extends beyond the perimeter of vision and encloses, in addition to the objects which make an impression on my retina, the walls of the room which are behind me, the house and perhaps the town in which I am, arranged perspectively around the "sensible" nucleus. Nor are we returning to the distinction of matter and form since, on the one hand, the very form of perception participates in the *ecceitas* and since, inversely, I can bring acts of recognition and denomination to bear on the sensible content which will convert it into signification.

The distinction which we are introducing is rather that of the lived and the known. The problem of the relations of the soul and body is thus transformed instead of disappearing: now it will be the problem of the relations of consciousness as flux of individual events, of concrete and resistant structures, and that of consciousness as tissue of ideal significations. The idea of a transcendental philosophy, that is, the idea of consciousness as constituting the universe before it and grasping the objects themselves in an indubitable external experience, seems to us to be a definitive acquisition as the first phase of reflection. But is one not obliged to re-establish a duality within consciousness which is no longer accepted between it and external realities? The objects as ideal unities and as significations are grasped through individual perspectives. When I look at a book placed in front of me, its rectangular form is a concrete and embodied structure. What is the relation between this rectangular "physiognomy" and the signification, "rectangle," which I can make explicit by a logical act?

Every theory of perception tries to surmount a well-known contradiction: on the one hand, consciousness is a function of the body—thus it is an "internal" event dependent upon certain external events; on the other hand, these external events themselves are known only by consciousness. In another language, consciousness appears on one hand to be part of the world and on the other to be co-extensive with the world. In the development of methodical knowledge, of science, that is, the first observation seems initially to be confirmed: the subjectivity of the secondary qualities seems to have as a counterpart the reality of the primary qualities. But a deeper reflection on the objects of science and on physical causality finds relations in them which cannot be posited in-themselves (*en soi*) and which have meaning only before the inspection of mind.

The antinomy of which we are speaking disappears along with its realistic thesis at the level of reflexive thought (*la pensée réfléchie*); it is in perceptual knowledge that it has its proper location. Until now critical thought seemed to us to be incontestable. It shows marvelously that the problem of perception does not exist for a consciousness which adheres to objects of reflexive thought, that is, to significations. It is subsequently that it seems necessary to leave it. Having in this way referred the antinomy of perception to the order of life, as Descartes says, or to the order of confused thought, one pretends to show that it has no consistency there: if perception conceptualizes itself ever so little and knows what it is saying, it reveals that the experience of passivity is also a construction of the mind. Realism is not even based on a coherent appearance, it is an *error*. One wonders then what can provide consciousness with the very notion of passivity and why this notion is confused with its body if these natural errors rest on no authentic experience and *possess strictly no meaning whatsoever*. We have tried to show that, as a matter of fact, to the extent that the scientific knowledge of the organism becomes more precise, it becomes impossible to give a coherent meaning to the alleged action of the world on the body and of the body on the soul. The body and the soul are significations and have meaning, then, only with regard to a consciousness.

From our point of view also, the realistic thesis of common sense disappears at the level of reflexive thought, which encounters only significations in front of it. The experience of passivity *is not explained* by an actual passivity. But it should have a meaning and be able *to be understood*. As philosophy, realism is an error because it transposes into dogmatic thesis an experience which it deforms or renders impossible by that very fact. But it is a motivated error; it rests on an authentic phenomenon which philosophy has the function of making explicit. The proper structure of perceptual experience, the reference of partial "profiles" to the total signification which they "present," would be this phenomenon. Indeed, the alleged bodily conditioning of perception, taken in its actual meaning, requires nothing more—and nothing less—than this phenomenon in order to be understood. We have seen that excitations and nerve influxes are abstractions and that science links them to a total functioning of the nervous system in the definition of which the phenomenal is implied. The perceived is not an effect of cerebral functioning; it is its signification.

All the consciousnesses which we know present themselves in this way through a body which is their perspectival aspect. But, after all, each individual dialectic has cerebral stages, as it were, of which it itself knows nothing; the signification of nerve functioning has organic bases which do not figure in it. Philosophically, this fact admits of the following translation: each time that certain sensible phenomena are actualized in my field of consciousness, a properly placed observer would see certain other phenomena in my brain which cannot be given to me myself in the mode of actuality. In order to understand these phenomena, he would be led to grant them (as we did in Chapter II) a signification which would concur with the content of my perception. Inversely, I can represent for myself in the virtual mode, that is, as pure significations, certain retinal and cerebral phenomena which I localize in a virtual image of my body on the basis of the actual view which is given to me. The fact that the spectator and myself are both bound to our bodies comes down in sum to this: that that which can be given to me in the mode of actuality, as a concrete perspective, is given to him only in the mode of virtuality, as a signification, and conversely. In sum, my total psycho-physical being (that is, the experience which I have of myself, that which others

have of me, and the scientific knowledge which they and I apply to
the knowledge of myself) is an interlacing of significations such that,
when certain among them are perceived and pass into actuality, the
others are only virtually intended. But this structure of experience is
similar to that of external objects. Even more, they mutually presuppose each other. If there are things for me, that is, perspectival beings,
reference to a point from which I see them is included in their perspectival character itself.

But to be situated within a certain point of view necessarily involves not seeing that point of view itself, not possessing it as a visual
object except in a virtual signification. Therefore, the existence of an
external perception, that of my body and, "in" this body, the existence
of phenomena which are imperceptible for me are rigorously synony-
mous. There is no relation of causality between them. They are *concordant phenomena*. One often speaks as if the perspectival character
of perception were explained by the projection of objects on my retina:
I see only three sides of a cube *because* I see with my eyes, where a
projection of only these three sides is possible; I do not see objects
which are behind me *because they* are not projected on my retina. But
the converse could be said just as well. Indeed, what are "my eyes,"
"my retina," "the external cube" in itself, and "the objects which I do
not see"? They are logical significations which are bound up with my
actual perception on valid "grounds"[55] and which explicitate its meaning, but which get *the index of real existence from it*. These significations do not have in themselves therefore the means to explain the
actual existence of my perception. The language which one habitually
uses is nevertheless understandable: my perception of the cube presents
it to me as a complete and real cube, my perception of space, as a
space which is complete and real beyond the aspects which are given
to me. Thus it is natural that I have a tendency to detach the space
and the cube from the concrete perspectives and to posit them in-
themselves (*en soi*).

The same operation takes place with respect to the body. And as a
consequence I am naturally inclined to engender perception by an
operation of the cube or of objective space on my objective body. This
attempt is natural, but its failure is no less inevitable: as we have
seen, one cannot reconstitute the structure of perceptual experience by

[55] Husserl, "Ideen zu einer reinen Phänomenologie und phänomenologische Philosophie," p. 89.

combining ideal significations (stimuli, receptors, associative circuits). But if physiology does not explain perception, optics and geometry do not explain it either. To imagine that I see my image in the mirror *because* the light waves form a certain angle in reaching my eyes and because I situate their origin at their point of coincidence is to make the use of mirrors during so many centuries when optics was not yet invented mysterious indeed. The truth is that man first sees his image "through" the mirror, without the word yet having the signification which it will take on vis-à-vis the geometrical mind. Then he constructs a geometrical representation of this phenomenon which is *founded* on the concrete articulations of the perceived field, which makes them explicit and accounts for them—without the representation ever being able to be the cause of the concrete articulations, as realism wants to do, and without our being able to substitute it for them, as critical idealism does.

Access to the proper domain of perception has been rendered difficult for all philosophies which, because of a retrospective illusion, actualized a natural geometry in perception on the pretext that it has been possible to construct a geometry of perceived objects. The perception of a distance or a size is not the same as the quantitative estimations by which science makes distance and size precise.

All the sciences situate themselves in a "complete" and real world without realizing that perceptual experience is constituting with respect to this world. Thus we find ourselves in the presence of a field of lived perception which is prior to number, measure, space and causality and which is nonetheless given only as a perspectival view of objects gifted with stable properties, a perspectival view of an objective world and an objective space. The problem of perception consists in trying to discover how the intersubjective world, the determinations of which science is gradually making precise, is grasped through this field. The antinomy of which we spoke above is based upon this ambiguous structure of perceptual experience. The thesis and the antithesis express the two aspects of it: it is true to say that my perception is always a flux of individual events and that what is radically contingent in the lived perspectivism of perception accounts for the realistic appearance. But it is also true to say that my perception accedes to things themselves, for these perspectives are articulated in a way which makes access to inter-individual significations possible; they "present" a world.

Thus there are things *exactly in the sense in which I see them,* in my history and outside it, and inseparable from this double relation. I perceive things directly without my body forming a screen between them and me; it is a phenomenon just as they are, a phenomenon (gifted, it is true, with an original structure) which precisely presents the body to me as an intermediary between the world and myself although it *is not* as a matter of fact. I see with my eyes, which are not an ensemble of transparent or opaque tissues and organs, but the instruments of my looking. The retinal image, to the extent that I know it, is not yet produced by the light waves issuing from the object; but these two phenomena resemble and correspond to each other in a magical way across an interval which is not yet space.

We are returning to the givens of naive consciousness which we were analyzing at the beginning of this chapter. The philosophy of perception is not ready made in life: we have just seen that it is natural for consciousness to misunderstand itself precisely because it is consciousness of things. The classical discussions centering around perception are a sufficient testimony to this natural error. The constituted world is confronted with the perceptual experience of the world and one either tries to engender perception from the world, as realism does, or else to see in it only a commencement of the science of the world, as critical thought does. To return to perception as to a type of original experience in which the real world is constituted in its specificity is to impose upon oneself an inversion of the natural movement of consciousness;[56] on the other hand every question has not been eliminated: it is a question of understanding, without confusing it with a logical relation, the lived relation of the "profiles" to the "things" which they present, of the perspectives to the ideal significations which are intended through them.[57] The problem which Malebranche tried to resolve by occasionalism or Leibnitz by pre-established harmony is carried over into human consciousness.

Conclusion

Yet until now we have considered only the perspectivism of true perception. Instances in which lived experience appears clothed with a signification which breaks apart, so to speak, in the course of sub-

[56] We are defining here the "phenomenological reduction" in the sense which is given to it in Husserl's final philosophy.
[57] The notion of intentionality will be of help in this regard.

sequent experience and is not verified by concordant syntheses would still have to be analyzed. We have not accepted the causal explanation which naturalism provides in order to account for this subjectivity in the second degree. What is called bodily, psychological or social determinism in hallucination and error has appeared to us to be reducible to the emergence of imperfect dialectics, of partial structures. But why, *in existendo,* does such a dialectic at the organic-vegetative level break up a more integrated dialectic, as happens in hallucination? Consciousness is not only and not always consciousness of truth; how are we to understand the inertia and the resistance of the inferior dialectics which stand in the way of the advent of the pure relations of impersonal subject and true object and which affect my knowledge with a coefficient of subjectivity? How are we to understand the adherence of a fallacious signification to the lived, which is constitutive of illusion?

We have rejected Freud's causal categories and replaced his energic metaphors with structural metaphors. But although the complex is not a thing outside of consciousness which would produce its effects in it, although it is only a structure of consciousness, at least this structure tends as it were to conserve itself. It has been said that what is called unconsciousness[58] is only an inapperceived signification: it may happen that we ourselves do not grasp the true meaning of our life, not because an unconscious personality is deep within us and governs our actions, but because we understand our lived states only through an idea which is not adequate for them.

But, even unknown to us, the efficacious law of our life is constituted by its true signification. Everything happens as if this signification directed the flux of mental events. Thus it will be necessary to distinguish their ideal signification, which can be true or false, and their immanent signification, or—to employ a clearer language which we will use from now on—their ideal *signification* and their actual *structure.* Correlatively, it will be necessary to distinguish in development an ideal liberation, on the one hand, which does not transform us in our being and changes only the consciousness which we have of ourselves, and, on the other, a real liberation which is the *Umgestaltung* of which we spoke, along with Goldstein. We are not reducible to the ideal consciousness which we have of ourselves any more than the existent thing is reducible to the signification by which we express it.

[58] J. P. Sartre, "La Transcendance de l'Ego," *Recherches philosophiques,* 1936–1937.

It is easy to argue in the same way, in opposition to the sociologist, that the structures of consciousness which he relates to a certain economic structure are in reality the consciousness of certain structures. This argument hints at a liberty very close to mind, capable by reflection of grasping itself as spontaneous source, and naturizing from below the contingent forms with which it has clothed itself in a certain milieu. Like Freud's complex, the economic structure is only one of the objects of a transcendental consciousness. But "transcendental consciousness," the full consciousness of self, is not ready made; it is to be achieved, that is, realized in existence. In opposition to Durkheim's "collective consciousness" and his attempts at sociological explanation of knowledge, it is rightly argued that consciousness cannot be treated as an effect since it is that which constitutes the relation of cause and effect. But beyond a causal thinking which can be all too easily challenged, there is a truth of sociologism. Collective consciousness does not produce categories, but neither can one say that collective representations are only the objects of a consciousness which is always free in their regard, only the consciousness in a "we" of an object of consciousness in an "I."

The mental, we have said,[59] is reducible to the structure of behavior. Since this structure is visible from the outside and for the spectator at the same time as from within and for the actor, another person is in principle accessible to me as I am to myself; and we are both objects laid out before an impersonal consciousness.[60] But just as I can be mistaken concerning myself and grasp only the apparent or ideal signification of my conduct, so can I be mistaken concerning another and know only the envelope of his behavior. The perception which I have of him is never, in the case of suffering or mourning, for example, the equivalent of the perception which he has of himself unless I am sufficiently close to him that our feelings constitute together a single "form" and that our lives cease to flow separately. It is by this rare and difficult consent that I can be truly united with him, just as I can grasp my natural movements and know myself sincerely only by the decision to belong to myself. Thus I do not know myself because of my special position, but neither do I have the innate power of truly knowing another. I communicate with him by the signification of his conduct; but it is a question of attaining its structure, that is of attain-

[59] Cf. *supra,* p. 184.
[60] This is the thesis of J. P. Sartre, "La Transcendance de l'Ego."

ing, beyond his words or even his actions, the region where they are prepared.

As we have seen,[61] the behavior of another expresses a certain manner of existing before signifying a certain manner of thinking. And when this behavior is addressed to me, as may happen in dialogue, and seizes upon my thoughts in order to respond to them—or more simply, when the "cultural objects" which fall under my regard suddenly adapt themselves to my powers, awaken my intentions and make themselves "understood" by me—I am then drawn into a *coexistence* of which I am not the unique constituent and which founds the phenomenon of social nature as perceptual experience founds that of physical nature. Consciousness can *live* in existing things without reflection, can abandon itself to their concrete structure, which has not yet been converted into expressible signification; certain episodes of its life, before having been reduced to the condition of available memories and inoffensive objects, can imprison its liberty by their proper inertia, shrink its perception of the world, and impose stereotypes on behavior; likewise, before having conceptualized our class or our milieu, we *are* that class or that milieu.

Thus, the "I think" can be as if hallucinated by its objects. It will be replied (which is true) that it "should be able" to accompany all our representations and that it is presupposed by them, if not as term of an act of actual consciousness at least as a possibility in principle. But this response of critical philosophy poses a problem. The conversion of seeing which transforms the life of consciousness into a pure dialectic of subject and object, which reduces the thing in its sensible density to a bundle of significations, the traumatic reminiscence into an indifferent memory, and submits the class structure of my consciousness to examination—does this conversion make explicit an eternal "condition of possibility" or does it bring about the appearance of a new structure of consciousness? It is a problem to know what happens, for example, when consciousness disassociates itself from time, from this uninterrupted gushing forth at the center of itself, in order to apprehend it as an intellectual and manipulable signification. Does it lay bare only what was implicit? Or, on the contrary, does it not enter as into a lucid dream in which indeed it encounters no opaqueness, not because it has clarified the existence of things and its own existence, but because it lives at the surface of itself and on the envelope of

[61] Cf. *supra*, p. 126.

things? Is the reflexive passage to intellectual consciousness an adequation of our knowing to our being or only a way for consciousness to create for itself a separated existence—a quietism? These questions express no empiricist demand, no complaisance for "experiences" which would not have to account for themselves. On the contrary, we want to make consciousness equal with the whole of experience, to gather into consciousness for-itself (*pour soi*) all the life of consciousness in-itself (*en soi*).

A philosophy in the critical tradition founds moral theory on a reflection which discovers the thinking subject in its liberty behind all objects. If, however, one acknowledges—be it in the status of phenomenon—an existence of consciousness and of its resistant structures, our knowledge depends upon what we are; moral theory begins with a psychological and sociological critique of oneself; man is not assured ahead of time of possessing a source of morality; consciousness of self is not given in man by right; it is acquired only by the elucidation of his concrete being and is verified only by the active integration of isolated dialectics—body and soul—between which it is initially broken up. And finally, death is not *deprived of meaning,* since the contingency of the lived is a perpetual menace for the eternal significations in which it is believed to be completely expressed. It will be necessary to assure oneself that the experience of eternity is not the unconsciousness of death, that it is not on this side but beyond; similarly, moreover, it will be necessary to distinguish the love of life from the attachment to biological existence. The sacrifice of life will be philosophically impossible; it will be a question only of "staking" one's life, which is a deeper way of living.

If one understands by perception the act which makes us know existences, all the problems which we have just touched on are reducible to the problem of perception. It resides in the duality of the notions of structure and signification. A "form," such as the structure of "figure and ground," for example, is a whole which has a meaning and which provides therefore a base for intellectual analysis. But at the same time it is not an idea: it constitutes, alters and reorganizes itself before us like a spectacle. The alleged bodily, social and psychological "causalities" are reducible to this contingency of lived perspectives which limit our access to eternal significations. The "horizontal localizations" of cerebral functioning, the adhesive structures of animal behavior and those of pathological behavior are only particularly striking examples of this. "Structure" is the philosophical truth of naturalism and realism. What are the relations of this naturized consciousness and the pure consciousness of self? Can one conceptualize perceptual consciousness without eliminating it as an original mode; can one maintain its specificity without rendering inconceivable its relation to intellectual consciousness? If the essence of the critical solution consists in driving existence back to the limits of knowledge and of discovering intellectual signification in concrete structure, and if, as has been said, the fate of critical thought is bound up with this intellectualist theory of perception, in the event that this were not acceptable, it would be necessary to define transcendental philosophy anew in such a way as to integrate with it the very phenomenon of the real. The natural "thing," the organism, the behavior of others and my own behavior exist only by their meaning; but this meaning which springs forth in them is not yet a Kantian object; the intentional life which constitutes them is not yet a representation; and the "comprehension" which gives access to them is not yet an intellection.

PART FOUR

The Philosophy of Language

"The Body as Expression and Speech," the first selection in Part Four, is one of the central chapters of Phenomenology of Perception; *in it Merleau-Ponty locates the phenomenon of language in the more general context of his philosophy of the body, which holds that bodily behavior is through and through expressive of meaning. Language is only the most central means of expression.*

This central means, language, is given a separate analysis in the second selection, a paper Merleau-Ponty presented at the first Colloque international de phénoménologie, *which took place in Brussels in 1951. It is a major statement of his philosophy of language.*

9. THE BODY AS EXPRESSION AND SPEECH

We have seen in the body a unity distinct from that of the scientific object. We have just discovered, even in its "sexual function," intentionality and sense-giving powers. In trying to describe the phenomenon of speech and the specific act of meaning, we shall have the opportunity to leave behind us, once and for all, the traditional subject—object dichotomy.

The realization that speech is an originating realm naturally comes late. Here as everywhere, the relation of *having,* which can be seen in the very etymology of the word habit, is at first concealed by relations belonging to the domain of *being,* or, as we may equally say, by ontic relations obtaining within the world.[1] The possession of language is in the first place understood as no more than the actual existence of 'verbal images', or traces left in us by words spoken or heard.

Maurice Merleau-Ponty, "The Body as Expression, and Speech," *Phenomenology of Perception,* Part I, Ch. 6, trans. by Colin Smith (New York: The Humanities Press, 1962), pp. 174–99. Reprinted by permission.

[1] This distinction of having and being does not coincide with M. G. Marcel's (*Être et Avoir*), although not incompatible with it. M. Marcel takes having in the weak sense which the word has when it designates a proprietary relationship (I have a house, I have a hat) and immediately takes being in the existential sense of belonging to . . . , or taking up (I am my body, I am my life). We prefer to take account of the usage which gives to the term 'being' the weak sense of existence as a thing, or that of predication (the table is, or is big), and which reserves 'having' for the relation which the subject bears to the term into which it projects itself (I have an idea, I have a desire, I have fears). Hence our 'having' corresponds roughly to M. Marcel's being, and our being to his 'having'.

Whether these traces are physical, or whether they are imprinted on an 'unconscious psychic life', is of little importance, and in both cases the conception of language is the same in that there is no 'speaking subject'. Whether the stimuli, in accordance with the laws of neurological mechanics, touch off excitations capable of bringing about the articulation of the word, or whether the states of consciousness cause, by virtue of acquired associations, the appearance of the appropriate verbal image, in both cases speech occurs in a circuit of third person phenomena. There is no speaker, there is a flow of words set in motion independently of any intention to speak. The meaning of words is considered to be given with the stimuli or with the states of consciousness which it is simply a matter of naming; the shape of the word, as heard or phonetically formed, is given with the cerebral or mental tracks; speech is not an action and does not show up the internal possibilities of the subject: man can speak as the electric lamp can become incandescent. Since there are elective disturbances which attack the spoken language to the exclusion of the written one, or *vice versa,* and since language can disintegrate into fragments, we have to conclude that it is built up by a set of independent contributions, and that speech in the general sense is an entity of rational origin.

The theory of aphasia and of language seemed to be undergoing complete transformation when it became necessary to distinguish from anarthria,[2] which affects the articulation of the word, true aphasia which is inseparable from disturbances affecting intelligence —and from automatic language, which is in effect a third person motor phenomenon, an intentional language which is alone relevant to the majority of cases of aphasia. The individuality of the 'verbal image' was, indeed, dissociated: what the patient has lost, and what the normal person possesses, is not a certain stock of words, but a certain way of using them. The same word which remains at the disposal of the patient in the context of automatic languages escapes him in that of language unrelated to a purpose—the patient who has no difficulty in finding the word 'no' in answer to the doctor's questions, that is when he intends to furnish a denial arising from his present experience, cannot do so when it is a question of an exercise having no emotional and vital bearing. There is thus revealed, underlying the word, an attitude, a function of speech which condition it. The word

[2] *Anarthria:* loss of power of articulate speech (Translator's note).

could be identified as an instrument of action and as a means of disinterested designation. Though 'concrete' language remained a third person process, gratuitous language, or authentic denomination, became a phenomenon of thought, and it is in some disturbance of thinking that the origin of certain forms of aphasia must be sought. For example, amnesia concerning names of colours, when related to the general behaviour of the patient, appeared as a special manifestation of a more general trouble. The same patients who cannot name colours set before them, are equally incapable of classifying them in the performance of a set task. If, for example, they are asked to sort out samples according to basic colour, it is immediately noticed that they do it more slowly and painstakingly than a normal subject: they slowly place together the samples to be compared and fail to see at a glance which ones 'go together'. Moreover, having correctly assembled several blue ribbons, they make unaccountable mistakes: if for example the last blue ribbon was of a pale shade, they carry on by adding to the collection of 'blues' a pale green or pale pink—as if it were beyond them to stick to the proposed principle of classification, and to consider the samples from the point of view of basic colour from start to finish of the operation. They have thus become unable to subsume sense-data under a category, to see immediately the samples as representatives of the *eidos* blue. Even when, at the beginning of the test, they proceed correctly, it is not the conformity of the samples to an idea which guides them, but the experience of an immediate resemblance, and hence it comes about that they can classify the samples only when they have placed them side by side. The sorting test brings to light in these subjects a fundamental disorder, of which forgetting names of colours is simply another manifestation. For to name a thing is to tear oneself away from its individual and unique characteristics to see it as representative of an essence or a category, and the fact that the patient cannot identify the samples is a sign, not that he has lost the verbal image of the words red or blue, but that he has lost the general ability to subsume a sense-datum under a category, that he has lapsed back from the categorical to the concrete attitude.[3] These analyses and other similar ones lead us, it would seem, to the antithesis of the theory of the verbal image, since language now appears as conditioned by thought.

In fact we shall once again see that there is a kinship between the

[3] Gelb and Goldstein, *Über Farbennamenamnesie.*

empiricist or mechanistic psychologies and the intellectualist ones, and the problem of language is not solved by going from one extreme to the other. A short time ago the reproduction of the word, the revival of the verbal image, was the essential thing. Now it is no more than what envelops true denomination and authentic speech, which is an inner process. And yet these two conceptions are at one in holding that the word *has* no significance. In the first case this is obvious since the word is not summoned up through the medium of any concept, and since the given stimuli or 'states of mind' call it up in accordance with the laws of neurological mechanics or those of association, and that thus the word is not the bearer of its own meaning, has no inner power, and is merely a psychic, physiological or even physical phenomenon set alongside others, and thrown up by the working of an objective causality. It is just the same when we duplicate denomination with a categorial operation. The word is still bereft of any effectiveness of its own, this time because it is only the external sign of an internal recognition, which could take place without it, and to which it makes no contribution. It is not without meaning, since behind it there is a categorial operation, but this meaning is something which it does not *have,* does not possess, since it is thought which has a meaning, the word remaining an empty container. It is merely a phenomenon of articulation, of sound, or the consciousness of such a phenomenon, but in any case language is but an external accompaniment of thought. In the first case, we are on this side of the word as meaningful; in the second we are beyond it. In the first there is nobody to speak; in the second, there is certainly a subject, but a thinking one, not a speaking one. As far as speech itself is concerned, intellectualism is hardly any different from empiricism, and is no better able than the latter to dispense with an explanation in terms of involuntary action. Once the categorial operation is performed, the appearance of the word which completes the process still has to be explained, and this will still be done by recourse to a physiological or psychic mechanism, since the word is a passive shell. Thus we refute both intellectualism and empiricism by simply saying that *the word has a meaning*.

If speech presupposed thought, if talking were primarily a matter of meeting the object through a cognitive intention or through a representation, we could not understand why thought tends towards expression as towards its completion, why the most familiar thing

.

appears indeterminate as long as we have not recalled its name, why the thinking subject himself is in a kind of ignorance of his thoughts so long as he has not formulated them for himself, or even spoken and written them, as is shown by the example of so many writers who begin a book without knowing exactly what they are going to put into it. A thought limited to existing for itself, independently of the constraints of speech and communication, would no sooner appear than it would sink into the unconscious, which means that it would not exist even for itself. To Kant's celebrated question, we can reply that it is indeed part of the experience of thinking, in the sense that we present our thought to ourselves through internal or external speech. It does indeed move forward with the instant and, as it were, in flashes, but we are then left to lay hands on it, and it is through expression that we make it our own. The denomination of objects does not follow upon recognition; it is itself recognition. When I fix my eyes on an object in the half-light, and say: 'It is a brush', there is not in my mind the concept of a brush, under which I subsume the object, and which moreover is linked by frequent association with the word 'brush', but the word bears the meaning, and, by imposing it on the object, I am conscious of reaching that object. As has often been said,[4] for the child the thing is not known until it is named, the name is the essence of the thing and resides in it on the same footing as its colour and its form. For pre-scientific thinking, naming an object is causing it to exist or changing it: God creates beings by naming them and magic operates upon them by speaking of them. These 'mistakes' would be unexplainable if speech rested on the concept, for the latter ought always to know itself as distinct from the former, and to know the former as an external accompaniment. If it is pointed out in reply that the child learns to know objects through the designations of language, that thus, given in the first place as linguistic entities, objects receive only secondarily their natural existence, and that finally the actual existence of a linguistic community accounts for childish beliefs, this explanation leaves the problem untouched, since, if the child can know himself as a member of a linguistic community before knowing himself as thinking about some Nature, it is conditional upon the subject's being able to overlook himself as universal thought and apprehend himself as speech, and on the fact that the word, far from being the mere sign of objects and meanings, inhabits things and is

[4] E.g. Piaget, *La Représentation du Monde chez l'Enfant*, pp. 60 and ff.

the vehicle of meanings. Thus speech, in the speaker, does not translate ready-made thought, but accomplishes it.[5] *A fortiori* must it be recognized that the listener receives thought from speech itself. At first sight, it might appear that speech heard can bring him nothing: it is he who gives to words and sentences their meaning, and the very combination of words and sentences is not an alien import, since it would not be understood if it did not encounter in the listener the ability spontaneously to effect it. Here, as everywhere, it seems at first sight true that consciousness can find in its experience only what it has itself put there. Thus the experience of communication would appear to be an illusion. A consciousness constructs—for x—that linguistic mechanism which will provide another consciousness with the chance of having the same thoughts, but nothing really passes between them. Yet, the problem being how, to all appearances, consciousness learns something, the solution cannot consist in saying that it knows everything in advance. The fact is that we have the power to understand over and above what we may have spontaneously thought. People can speak to us only a language which we already understand, each word of a difficult text awakens in us thoughts which were ours beforehand, but these meanings sometimes combine to form new thought which recasts them all, and we are transported to the heart of the matter, we find the source. Here there is nothing comparable to the solution of a problem, where we discover an unknown quantity through its relationship with known ones. For the problem can be solved only if it is determinate, that is, if the cross-checking of the data provides the unknown quantity with one or more definite values. In understanding others, the problem is always indeterminate[6] because only the solution will bring the data retrospectively to light as convergent, only the central theme of a philosophy, once understood, endows the philosopher's writings with the value of adequate signs. There is, then, a taking up of others' thought through speech, a re-

---

[5] There is, of course, every reason to distinguish between an authentic speech, which formulates for the first time, and second-order expression, speech about speech, which makes up the general run of empirical language. Only the first is identical with thought.

[6] Again, what we say here applies only to first-hand speech—that of the child uttering its first word, of the lover revealing his feelings, of the 'first man who spoke', or of the writer and philosopher who reawaken primordial experience anterior to all traditions.

flection in others, an ability to think *according to others*[7] which enriches our own thoughts. Here the meaning of words must be finally induced by the words themselves, or more exactly, their conceptual meaning must be formed by a kind of deduction from a *gestural meaning,* which is immanent in speech. And as, in a foreign country, I begin to understand the meaning of words through their place in a context of action, and by taking part in a communal life—in the same way an as yet imperfectly understood piece of philosophical writing discloses to me at least a certain 'style'—either a Spinozist, criticist or phenomenological one—which is the first draft of its meaning. I begin to understand a philosophy by feeling my way into its existential manner, by reproducing the tone and accent of the philosopher. In fact, every language conveys its own teaching and carries its meaning into the listener's mind. A school of music or painting which is at first not understood, eventually, by its own action, creates its own public, if it really *says* something; that is, it does so by secreting its own meaning. In the case of prose or poetry, the power of the spoken word is less obvious, because we have the illusion of already possessing within ourselves, in the shape of the common property meaning of words, what is required for the understanding of any text whatsoever. The obvious fact is, however, that the colours of the palette or the crude sounds of instruments, as presented to us in natural perception, are insufficient to provide the musical sense of music, or the pictorial sense of a painting. But, in fact, it is less the case that the sense of a literary work is provided by the common property meaning of words, than that it contributes to changing that accepted meaning. There is thus, either in the man who listens or reads, or in the one who speaks or writes, a *thought in speech* the existence of which is unsuspected by intellectualism.

To realize this, we must turn back to the phenomenon of speech and reconsider ordinary descriptions which immobilize thought and speech, and make anything other than external relations between them inconceivable. We must recognize first of all that thought, in the speaking subject, is not a representation, that is, that it does not expressly posit objects or relations. The orator does not think before speaking, nor even while speaking; his speech is his thought. In the

---

[7] *Nachdenken, nachvollziehen* of Husserl, *Ursprung der Geometrie,* pp. 212 and ff.

same way the listener does not form concepts on the basis of signs. The orator's 'thought' is empty while he is speaking and, when a text is read to us, provided that it is read with expression, we have no thought marginal to the text itself, for the words fully occupy our mind and exactly fulfil our expectations, and we feel the necessity of the speech. Although we are unable to predict its course, we are possessed by it. The end of the speech or text will be the lifting of a spell. It is at this stage that thoughts on the speech or text will be able to arise. Previously the speech was improvised and the text understood without the intervention of a single thought; the sense was everywhere present, and nowhere posited for its own sake. The speaking subject does not think of the sense of what he is saying, nor does he visualize the words which he is using. To know a word or a language is, as we have said, not to be able to bring into play any pre-established nervous network. But neither is it to retain some 'pure recollection' of the word, some faded perception. The Bergsonian dualism of habit-memory and pure recollection does not account for the near-presence of the words I know: they are behind me, like things behind my back, or like the city's horizon round my house, I reckon with them or rely on them, but without having any 'verbal image'. In so far as they persist within me, it is rather as does the Freudian Imago which is much less the representation of a former perception than a highly specific emotional essence, which is yet generalized, and detached from its empirical origins. What remains to me of the word once learnt is its style as constituted by its formation and sound. What we have said earlier about the 'representation of movement' must be repeated concerning the verbal image: I do not need to visualize external space and my own body in order to move one within the other. It is enough that they exist for me, and that they form a certain field of action spread around me. In the same way I do not need to visualize the word in order to know and pronounce it. It is enough that I possess its articulatory and acoustic style as one of the modulations, one of the possible uses of my body. I reach back for the word as my hand reaches towards the part of my body which is being pricked; the word has a certain location in my linguistic world, and is part of my equipment. I have only one means of representing it, which is uttering it, just as the artist has only one means of representing the work on which he is engaged: by doing it. When I imagine Peter absent, I am not aware of contemplating an image of Peter numerically distinct from Peter himself.

However far away he is, I visualize him in the world, and my power of imagining is nothing but the persistence of my world around me.[8] To say that I imagine Peter is to say that I bring about the pseudo-presence of Peter by putting into operation the 'Peter-behaviour-pattern'. Just as Peter in imagination is only one of the modalities of my being in the world, so the verbal image is only one of the modalities of my phonetic gesticulation, presented with many others in the all-embracing consciousness of my body. This is obviously what Bergson means when he talks about a 'motor framework' of recollection, but if pure representations of the past take their place in this framework, it is not clear why they should need it to become actual once more. The part played by the body in memory is comprehensible only if memory is, not only the constituting consciousness of the past, but an effort to reopen time on the basis of the implications contained in the present, and if the body, as our permanent means of 'taking up attitudes' and thus constructing pseudo-presents, is the medium of our communication with time as well as with space.[9] The body's function in remembering is that same function of projection which we have already met in starting to move: the body converts a certain motor essence into vocal form, spreads out the articulatory style of a word into audible phenomena, and arrays the former attitude, which is resumed, into the panorama of the past, projecting an intention to move into actual movement, because the body is a power of natural expression.

[8] Sartre, *L'Imagination,* p. 148.

[9] '. . . when I awoke like this, and my mind struggled in an unsuccessful attempt to discover where I was, everything would be moving round me through the darkness, things, places, years. My body, still too heavy with sleep to move, would make an effort to construe the form which its tiredness took as an orientation of its various members, so as to induce from that where the wall lay and the furniture stood, to piece together and to give a name to the house in which it must be living. Its memory, the composite memory of its ribs, knees, and shoulder-blades offered it a whole series of rooms in which it had at one time or another slept; while the unseen walls kept changing, adapting themselves to the shape of each successive room that it remembered, whirling madly through the darkness. . . . My body, the side upon which I was lying, loyally preserving from the past an impression which my mind should never have forgotten, brought back before my eyes the glimmering flame of the night-light in its bowl of Bohemian glass, shaped like an urn and hung by chains from the ceiling, and the chimney-piece of Sienna marble in my bedroom at Combray, in my great-aunt's house, in those far-distant days which, at the moment of waking, seemed present without being clearly defined.' (Proust, *Swann's Way,* I, trans. C. K. Scott Moncrieff, Chatto and Windus, pp. 5–6.)

These considerations enable us to restore to the act of speaking its true physiognomy. In the first place speech is not the 'sign' of thought, if by this we understand a phenomenon which heralds another as smoke betrays fire. Speech and thought would admit of this external relation only if they were both thematically given, whereas in fact they are intervolved, the sense being held within the word, and the word being the external existence of the sense. Nor can we concede, as is commonly done, that speech is a mere means of fixation, nor yet that it is the envelope and clothing of thought. Why should it be easier to recall words or phrases than thoughts, if the alleged verbal images need to be reconstructed on every occasion? And why should thought seek to duplicate itself or clothe itself in a succession of utterances, if the latter do not carry and contain within themselves their own meaning? Words cannot be 'strongholds of thought', nor can thought seek expression, unless words are in themselves a comprehensible text, and unless speech possesses a power of significance entirely its own. The word and speech must somehow cease to be a way of designating things or thoughts, and become the presence of that thought in the phenomenal world, and, moreover, not its clothing but its token or its body. There must be, as psychologists say, a 'linguistic concept' (*Sprachbegriff*)[10] or a word concept (*Wortbegriff*), a 'central inner experience, specifically verbal, thanks to which the sound, heard, uttered, read or written, becomes a linguistic fact'.[11] Certain patients can read a text, 'putting expression into it', without, however, understanding it. This is because the spoken or written words carry a top coating of meaning which sticks to them and which presents the thought as a style, an affective value, a piece of existential mimicry, rather than as a conceptual statement. We find here, beneath the conceptual meaning of the words, an existential meaning which is not only rendered by them, but which inhabits them, and is inseparable from them. The greatest service done by expression is not to commit to writing ideas which might be lost. A writer hardly ever re-reads his own works, and great works leave in us at a first reading all that we shall ever subsequently get out of them. The process of expression, when it is successful, does not merely leave for the reader and the writer himself a kind of reminder, it brings the meaning into existence as a thing at the very heart of the text, it brings it to life in an organism of words,

---

[10] Cassirer, *Philosophie der symbolischen Formen*, III, p. 383.
[11] Goldstein, *L'Analyse de l'aphasie et l'essence du langage*, p. 459.

establishing it in the writer or the reader as a new sense organ, opening a new field or a new dimension to our experience. This power of expression is well known in the arts, for example in music. The musical meaning of a sonata is inseparable from the sounds which are its vehicle: before we have heard it no analysis enables us to anticipate it; once the performance is over, we shall, in our intellectual analyses of the music, be unable to do anything but carry ourselves back to the moment of experiencing it. During the performance, the notes are not only the 'signs' of the sonata, but it is there through them, it enters into them.[12] In the same way the actress becomes invisible, and it is Phaedra who appears. The meaning swallows up the signs, and Phaedra has so completely taken possession of Berma that her passion as Phaedra appears the apotheosis of ease and naturalness.[13] Aesthetic expression confers on what it expresses an existence in itself, installs it in nature as a thing perceived and accessible to all, or conversely plucks the signs themselves—the person of the actor, or the colours and canvas of the painter—from their empirical existence and bears them off into another world. No one will deny that here the process of expression brings the meaning into being or makes it effective, and does not merely translate it. It is no different, despite what may appear to be the case, with the expression of thoughts in speech. Thought is no 'internal' thing, and does not exist independently of the world and of words. What misleads us in this connection, and causes us to believe in a thought which exists for itself prior to expression, is thought already constituted and expressed, which we can silently recall to ourselves, and through which we acquire the illusion of an inner life. But in reality this supposed silence is alive with words, this inner life is an inner language. 'Pure' thought reduces itself to a certain void of consciousness, to a momentary desire. The new sense-giving intention knows itself only by donning already available meanings, the outcome of previous acts of expression. The available meanings suddenly link up in accordance with an unknown law, and once and for all a fresh cultural entity has taken on an existence. Thought and expression, then, are simultaneously constituted, when our cultural store is put at the service of this unknown law, as our body suddenly lends itself to some new gesture in the formation of habit. The spoken word is a genuine gesture, and it contains its meaning in the same way as the

---

[12] Proust, *Swann's Way*, II, trans. C. K. Scott Moncrieff, p. 185.
[13] Proust, *The Guermantes Way*, I, pp. 55 and ff.

gesture contains its. This is what makes communication possible. In order that I may understand the words of another person, it is clear that his vocabulary and syntax must be 'already known' to me. But that does not mean that words do their work by arousing in me 'representations' associated with them, and which in aggregate eventually reproduce in me the original 'representation' of the speaker. What I communicate with primarily is not 'representations' or thought, but a speaking subject, with a certain style of being and with the 'world' at which he directs his aim. Just as the sense-giving intention which has set in motion the other person's speech is not an explicit thought, but a certain lack which is asking to be made good, so my taking up of this intention is not a process of thinking on my part, but a synchronizing change of my own existence, a transformation of my being. We live in a world where speech is an *institution*. For all these many commonplace utterances, we possess within ourselves ready-made meanings. They arouse in us only second order thoughts; these in turn are translated into other words which demand from us no real effort of expression and will demand from our hearers no effort of comprehension. Thus language and the understanding of language apparently raise no problems. The linguistic and intersubjective world no longer surprises us, we no longer distinguish it from the world itself, and it is within a world already spoken and speaking that we think. We become unaware of the contingent element in expression and communication, whether it be in the child learning to speak, or in the writer saying and thinking something for the first time, in short, in all who transform a certain kind of silence into speech. It is, however, quite clear that constituted speech, as it operates in daily life, assumes that the decisive step of expression has been taken. Our view of man will remain superficial so long as we fail to go back to that origin, so long as we fail to find, beneath the chatter of words, the primordial silence, and as long as we do not describe the action which breaks this silence. The spoken word is a gesture, and its meaning, a world.

Modern psychology[14] has demonstrated that the spectator does not look within himself into his personal experience for the meaning of the gestures which he is witnessing. Faced with an angry or threatening gesture, I have no need, in order to understand it, to recall the feelings which I myself experienced when I used these gestures on my own account. I am not well able to visualize, in my mind's eye, the

[14] For example, M. Scheler, *Nature et Formes de la Sympathie,* pp. 347 and ff.

outward signs of anger, so that a decisive factor is missing for any association by resemblance or reasoning by analogy, and what is more, I do not see anger or a threatening attitude as a psychic fact hidden behind the gesture, I read anger into it. The gesture *does not make me think* of anger, it is anger itself. However, the meaning of the gesture is not perceived as the colour of the carpet, for example, is perceived. If it were given to me as a thing, it is not clear why my understanding of gestures should for the most part be confined to human ones. I do not 'understand' the sexual pantomime of the dog, still less of the cockchafer or the praying mantis. I do not even understand the expression of the emotions in primitive people or in circles too unlike the ones in which I move. If a child happens to witness sexual intercourse, it may understand it although it has no experience of desire and of the bodily attitudes which translate it. The sexual scene will be merely an unfamiliar and disturbing spectacle, without meaning unless the child has reached the stage of sexual maturity at which this behaviour becomes possible for it. It is true that often knowledge of other people lights up the way to self-knowledge: the spectacle outside him reveals to the child the meaning of its own impulses, by providing them with an aim. The example would pass unnoticed if it did not coincide with the inner possibilities of the child. The sense of the gestures is not given, but understood, that is, seized upon by an act on the spectator's part. The whole difficulty is to conceive this act clearly without confusing it with a cognitive operation. The communication or comprehension of gestures comes about through the reciprocity of my intentions and the gestures of others, of my gestures and intentions discernible in the conduct of other people. It is as if the other person's intention inhabited my body and mine his. The gesture which I witness outlines an intentional object. This object is genuinely present and fully comprehended when the powers of my body adjust themselves to it and overlap it. The gesture presents itself to me as a question, bringing certain perceptible bits of the world to my notice, and inviting my concurrence in them. Communication is achieved when my conduct identifies this path with its own. There is mutual confirmation between myself and others. Here we must rehabilitate the experience of others which has been distorted by intellectualist analyses, as we shall have to rehabilitate the perceptual experience of the thing. When I perceive a thing, a fireplace for example, it is not the concordance of its various aspects which leads me to believe in the existence of the fireplace as the flat projection and collective significance of all these perspectives. On the contrary I perceive the thing in its own self-evident completeness and this is what gives me the assurance that, in the course of perceptual experience, I shall be presented with an indefinite set of concordant views. The identity of the thing through perceptual experience is only another aspect of the identity of one's own body throughout exploratory movements; thus they are the same in kind as each other. Like the body image, the fireplace is a system of equivalents not founded on the recognition of some law, but on the experience of a bodily presence. I become involved in things with my body, they co-exist with me as an incarnate subject, and this life among things has nothing in common with the elaboration of scientifically conceived objects. In the same way, I do not understand the gestures of others by some act of intellectual interpretation; communication between consciousness is not based on the common meaning of their respective experiences, for it is equally the basis of that meaning. The act by which I lend myself to the spectacle must be recognized as irreducible to anything else. I join it in a kind of blind recognition which precedes the intellectual working out and clarification of the meaning. Successive generations 'understand' and perform sexual gestures, such as the caress, before the philosopher[15] makes its intellectual significance clear, which is that we lock within itself a passive body, enwrap it in a pleasurable lethargy, thus imposing a temporary respite upon the continual drive which projects it into things and towards others. It is through my body that I understand other people, just as it is through my body that I perceive 'things'. The meaning of a gesture thus 'understood' is not behind it, it is intermingled with the structure of the world outlined by the gesture, and which I take up on my own account. It is arrayed all over the gesture itself—as, in perceptual experience, the significance of the fireplace does not lie beyond the perceptible spectacle, namely the fireplace itself as my eyes and movements discover it in the world.

The linguistic gesture, like all the rest, delineates its own meaning. This idea seems surprising at first, yet one is forced to accept it if one wishes to understand the origin of language, always an insistent problem, although psychologists and linguistics both question its validity in the name of positive knowledge. It seems in the first place impossible to concede to either words or gestures an immanent meaning,

[15] Here J. P. Sartre, *L'Être et le Néant*, pp. 453 and ff.

because the gesture is limited to showing a certain relationship between man and the perceptible world, because this world is presented to the spectator by natural perception, and because in this way the intentional object is offered to the spectator at the same time as the gesture itself. Verbal 'gesticulation', on the other hand, aims at a mental setting which is not given to everybody, and which it is its task to communicate. But here what nature does not provide, cultural background does. Available meanings, in other words former acts of expression, establish between speaking subjects a common world, to which the words being actually uttered in their novelty refer as does the gesture to the perceptible world. And the meaning of speech is nothing other than the way in which it handles this linguistic world or in which it plays modulations on the keyboard of acquired meanings. I seize it in an undivided act which is as short as a cry. It is true that the problem has been merely shifted one stage further back: how did the available meanings themselves come to be constituted? Once language is formed, it is conceivable that speech may have meaning, like the gesture, against the mental background held in common. But do syntactical forms and vocabulary, which are here presupposed, carry their meaning within themselves? One can see what there is in common between the gesture and its meaning, for example in the case of emotional expression and the emotions themselves: the smile, the relaxed face, gaiety of gesture really have in them the rhythm of action, the mode of being in the world which are joy itself. On the other hand, is not the link between the word sign and its meaning quite accidental, a fact demonstrated by the existence of a number of languages? And was not the communication of the elements of language between the 'first man to speak' and the second necessarily of an entirely different kind from communication through gesture? This is what is commonly expressed by saying that gesture or emotional pantomime are 'natural signs', and the word a 'natural convention'. But conventions are a late form of relationship between men; they presuppose an earlier means of communication, and language must be put back into this current of intercourse. If we consider only the conceptual and delimiting meaning of words, it is true that the verbal form—with the exception of endings—appears arbitrary. But it would no longer appear so if we took into account the emotional content of the word, which we have called above its 'gestural' sense, which is all-important in poetry, for example. It would then be found that the words, vowels and phonemes are so many ways of 'singing' the world, and that their function is to represent things not, as the naïve onomatopoeic theory had it, by reason of an objective resemblance, but because they extract, and literally express, their emotional essence. If it were possible, in any vocabulary, to disregard what is attributable to the mechanical laws of phonetics, to the influences of other languages, the rationalization of grammarians, and assimilatory processes, we should probably discover in the original form of each language a somewhat restricted system of expression, but such as would make it not entirely arbitrary, if we designate night by the word 'nuit', to use 'lumière' for light. The predominance of vowels in one language, or of consonants in another, and constructional and syntactical systems, do not represent so many arbitrary conventions for the expression of one and the same idea, but several ways for the human body to sing the world's praises and in the last resort to live it. Hence the *full* meaning of a language is never translatable into another. We may speak several languages, but one of them always remains the one in which we live. In order completely to assimilate a language, it would be necessary to make the world which it expresses one's own, and one never does belong to two worlds at once.[16] If there is such a thing as universal thought, it is achieved by taking up the effort towards expression and communication in *one* single language, and accepting all its ambiguities, all the suggestions and overtones of meaning of which a linguistic tradition is made up, and which are the exact measure of its power of expression. A conventional algorism—which moreover is meaningful only in relation to language—will never express anything but nature without man. Strictly speaking, therefore, there are no conventional signs, standing as the simple notation of a thought pure and clear in itself, there are only

[16] 'In my case, the effort for these years to live in the dress of Arabs, and to imitate their mental foundation, quitted me of my English self, and let me look at the West and its conventions with new eyes: they destroyed it all for me. At the same time I could not sincerely take on the Arab skin: it was an affectation only. Easily was a man made an infidel, but hardly might he be converted to another faith. I had dropped one form and not taken on the other, and was become like Mohammed's coffin in our legend. . . . Such detachment came at times to a man exhausted by prolonged physical effort and isolation. His body plodded on mechanically, while his reasonable mind left him, and from without looked down critically on him, wondering what that futile lumber did and why. Sometimes these selves would converse in the void; and then madness was very near, as I believe it would be near the man who could see things through the veils at once of two customs, two educations, two environments.' T. E. Lawrence, *The Seven Pillars of Wisdom,* Jonathan Cape, pp. 31–2.

words into which the history of a whole language is compressed, and which effect communication with no absolute guarantee, dogged as they are by incredible linguistic hazards. We think that language is more transparent than music because most of the time we remain within the bounds of constituted language, we provide ourselves with available meanings, and in our definitions we are content, like the dictionary, to explain meanings in terms of each other. The meaning of a sentence appears intelligible throughout, detachable from the sentence and finitely self-subsistent in an intelligible world, because we presuppose as given all those exchanges, owed to the history of the language, which contribute to determining its sense. In music, on the other hand, no vocabulary is presupposed, the meaning appears as linked to the empirical presence of the sounds, and that is why music strikes us as dumb. But in fact, as we have said, the clearness of language stands out from an obscure background, and if we carry our research far enough we shall eventually find that language is equally uncommunicative of anything other than itself, that its meaning is inseparable from it. We need, then, to seek the first attempts at language in the emotional gesticulation whereby man superimposes on the given world the world according to man. There is here nothing resembling the famous naturalistic conceptions which equate the artificial sign with the natural one, and try to reduce language to emotional expression. The artificial sign is not reducible to the natural one, because in man there is no natural sign, and in assimilating language to emotional expressions, we leave untouched its specific quality, if it is true that emotion, viewed as a variation of our being in the world, is contingent in relation to the mechanical resources contained in our body, and shows the same power of giving shape to stimuli and situations which is at its most striking at the level of language. It would be legitimate to speak of 'natural signs' only if the anatomical organization of our body produced a correspondence between specific gestures and given 'states of mind'. The fact is that the behaviour associated with anger or love is not the same in a Japanese and an Occidental. Or, to be more precise, the difference of behaviour corresponds to a difference in the emotions themselves. It is not only the gesture which is contingent in relation to the body's organization, it is the manner itself in which we meet the situation and live it. The angry Japanese smiles, the westerner goes red and stamps his foot or else goes pale and hisses his words. It is not enough for two conscious subjects to have the same organs and nervous system for the same emotions to produce in both the same signs. What is important is how they use their bodies, the simultaneous patterning of body and world in emotion. The psycho-physiological equipment leaves a great variety of possibilities open, and there is no more here than in the realm of instinct a human nature finally and immutably given. The use a man is to make of his body is transcendent in relation to that body as a mere biological entity. It is no more natural, and no less conventional, to shout in anger or to kiss in love[17] than to call a table 'a table'. Feelings and passional conduct are invented like words. Even those which, like paternity, seem to be part and parcel of the human make-up are in reality institutions.[18] It is impossible to superimpose on man a lower layer of behaviour which one chooses to call 'natural', followed by a manufactured cultural or spiritual world. Everything is both manufactured and natural in man, as it were, in the sense that there is not a word, not a form of behaviour which does not owe something to purely biological being —and which at the same time does not elude the simplicity of animal life, and cause forms of vital behaviour to deviate from their pre-ordained direction, through a sort of *leakage* and through a genius for ambiguity which might serve to define man. Already the mere presence of a living being transforms the physical world, bringing to view here 'food', there a 'hiding place', and giving to 'stimuli' a sense which they have not hitherto possessed. *A fortiori* does this apply to the presence of a man in the animal world. Behaviour creates meanings which are transcendent in relation to the anatomical apparatus, and yet immanent to the behaviour as such, since it communicates itself and is understood. It is impossible to draw up an inventory of this irrational power which creates meanings and conveys them. Speech is merely one particular case of it.

What is true, however—and justifies the view that we ordinarily take of language, as being in a peculiar category—is that, alone of all expressive processes, speech is able to settle into a sediment and constitute an acquisition for use in human relationships. This fact

[17] It is well known that the kiss is not one of the traditional customs of Japan.
[18] Paternity is unknown to the Trobriand Islanders. Children are brought up under the authority of the maternal uncle. A husband, on his return from a long journey, is delighted to find new children in his home. He looks after them, watches over them and cherishes them as if they were his own children. Malinowski, *The Father in Primitive Psychology,* quoted by Bertrand Russell, *Marriage and Morals,* Allen and Unwin, pp. 20 and ff.

cannot be explained by pointing out that speech can be recorded on paper, whereas gestures or forms of behaviour are transmitted only by direct imitation. For music too can be written down, and, although there is in music something in the nature of an initiation into the tradition, although that is, it would probably be impossible to graduate to atonal music without passing through classical music, yet every composer starts his task at the beginning, having a new world to deliver, whereas in the realm of speech, each writer is conscious of taking as his objective the same world as has already been dealt with by other writers. The worlds of Balzac and Stendhal are not like planets without communication with each other, for speech implants the idea of truth in us as the presumptive limit of its effort. It loses sight of itself as a contingent fact, and takes to resting upon itself; this is, as we have seen, what provides us with the ideal of thought without words, whereas the idea of music without sounds is ridiculous. Even if this is pushing the principle beyond its limits and reducing things to the absurd, even if a linguistic meaning can never be delivered of its inherence in some word or other, the fact remains that the expressive process in the case of speech can be indefinitely reiterated, that it is possible to speak about speech whereas it is impossible to paint about painting, and finally that every philosopher has dreamed of a form of discourse which would supersede all others, whereas the painter or the musician does not hope to exhaust all possible painting or music. Thus there is a privileged position accorded to Reason. But if we want to understand it clearly, we must begin by putting thought back among the phenomena of expression.

This conception of language carries further the best and most recent analysis of aphasia, of which we have so far made use of only a part. We have seen, to start with, that after an empiricist phase, the theory of aphasia, since Pierre Marie, seemed to move ever to intellectualism, and that, in linguistic disturbances, it invoked the 'representative function' (*Darstellungsfunktion*) or 'categorial' activity[19] and that it based speech on thought. In reality, it is not towards a new intellectualism that the theory moves. Whether its authors are aware of it or not, they are trying to formulate what we shall call an existential theory of aphasia, that is, a theory which treats thought and objective language as two manifestations of that fundamental activity whereby man pro-

[19] Notions of this kind appear in the works of Head, van Woerkom, Bouman and Grünbaum, and Goldstein.

jects himself towards a 'world'.[20] Take, for example, amnesia relating to names of colours. It is demonstrated, by sorting tests, that the sufferer from amnesia has lost the general ability to subsume colours under a category, and to this same cause is attributed the verbal deficiency. But if we go back to concrete descriptions we notice that the categorial activity, before being a thought or a form of knowledge, is a certain manner of relating oneself to the world, and, correspondingly, a style or shape of experience. In a normal subject, the perception of a heap of samples is organized in virtue of the task set: 'The colours belonging to the same category as the model sample stand out against the background of the rest',[21] all the reds, for example, forming a group, and the subject has now only to split up this group in order to bring together all the samples which belong to it. For the patient, on the other hand, each of the samples is confined within its individual existence. Against the formation of any group according to a given principle, they bring a sort of viscosity or inertia. When two objectively similar colours are presented to the patient, they do not necessarily appear similar: it may happen that in one the basic shade is dominant, in the other the degree of lightness or warmth.[22] We can ourselves experience something similar by taking up, before a pile of samples, an attitude of passive perception: the identical colours group themselves before our eyes, but those colours which are merely rather alike establish only vague mutual relations, 'the heap seems unstable, shifting, and we observe an incessant alteration in it, a kind of contest between several possible groupings of colours according to different points of view'.[23] We are reduced to the immediate experience of relationships (*Kohärenzerlebnis, Erlebnis des Passens*) and such is probably the experience of the patient. We were wrong to say that he cannot abide by a given principle of classification, but goes from one to the other: in reality he never adopts any.[24] The disturbance touches 'the way in which the colours group themselves for the observer, the way in which the visual field is put together from the point of view

[20] Grünbaum, for example (*Aphasie und Motorik*) shows both that aphasic disturbances are *general* and that they are *motor,* in other words he makes motility into an original mode of intentionality or meaning (cf. above, pp. 227–28), which amounts to conceiving man, no longer in terms of consciousness, but in terms of existence.

[21] Gelb and Goldstein, *Über Farbennamenamnesie,* p. 151.

[22] *Ibid.,* p. 149.

[23] *Ibid.,* pp. 151–52.

[24] *Ibid.,* p. 150.

of colours'.[25] It is not only the thought or knowledge, but the very experience of colours which is in question. We might say with another author that normal experience involves 'circles' or 'vortices' within which each element is representative of all others and carries, as it were, 'vectors' which link it to them. In the patient, 'this life is enclosed in narrower limits, and, compared to the normal subject's perceived world, it moves in smaller and more restricted circles. A movement which has its origin on the periphery of the vortex no longer spreads immediately as far as its centre, but remains, so to speak, within the stimulated area or may be transmitted to its immediate surrounding, but no further. More comprehensive units of meaning can no longer be built up within the perceived world. . . . Here again, each sense impression is provided with a "sense-vector", but these vectors have no common direction, for, being no longer directed towards main determinate centres, they diverge much more than in the normal person.'[26] Such is the disturbance of 'thought' discoverable at the root of amnesia; it can be seen that it concerns not so much the judgement as the setting of experience in which the judgement has its source, not so much spontaneity as the footing which spontaneity has in the perceptible world, and our ability to discern in it any intention whatsoever. In Kantian terms: it affects not so much the understanding as the productive imagination. The categorial act is therefore not an ultimate fact, it builds itself up into a certain 'attitude' (*Einstellung*). It is on this attitude, moreover, that speech is based, so that there can be no question of making language rest upon pure thought. 'Categorial behaviour and the possession of meaningful language express one and the same fundamental form of behaviour. Neither can be a cause or effect of the other.'[27] In the first place, thought is not an effect of language. It is true that certain patients,[28] being unable to group colours by comparing them to a given sample, succeed through the intermediary of language: they name the colour of the exemplar and subsequently collect together all the samples which that name fits without looking back at the exemplar. It is true also that abnormal children[29] classify even different colours together if they have been taught to call them by the same name. But these are precisely abnormal

---

[25] *Ibid.*, p. 162.
[26] E. Cassirer, *Philosophie der symbolischen Formen*, T. III, p. 258.
[27] Gelb and Goldstein, *Über Farbennamenamnesie*, p. 158.
[28] *Ibid.*
[29] *Ibid.*

procedures; they do not express the essential relationship between language and thought, but the pathological or accidental relationship of language and thought both cut off from their living significance. Indeed, many patients are able to repeat the names of the colours without being any more capable of classifying them. In cases of amnesic aphasia, 'it cannot, therefore, be the lack of the word taken in itself which makes categorial behaviour difficult or impossible. Words must have lost something which normally belongs to them and which fits them for use in relation to categorial behaviour.'[30] What have they lost? Their notional significance? Must we say that the concept has been withdrawn from them, thus making thought the cause of language? But clearly, when the word loses its meaning, it is modified down to its sensible aspect, *it is emptied*.[31] The patient suffering from amnesia, to whom a colour name is given, and who is asked to choose a corresponding sample, repeats the name as if he expected something to come of it. But the name is now useless to him, it *tells* him nothing more, it is alien and absurd, as are for us names which we go on repeating for too long a time.[32] Patients for whom words have lost their meaning sometimes retain in the highest degree the ability to associate ideas.[33] The name, therefore, has not become separated from former 'associations', it has suffered deterioration, like some inanimate body. The link between the word and its living meaning is not an external link of association, the meaning inhabits the word, and language 'is not an external accompaniment to intellectual processes'.[34] We are therefore led to recognize a gestural or existential significance in speech, as we have already said. Language certainly has an inner content, but this is not self-subsistent and self-conscious thought. What then does language express, if it does not express thoughts? It presents or rather it *is* the subject's taking up of a position in the world of his meanings. The term 'world' here is not a manner of speaking: it means that the 'mental' or cultural life borrows its structures from natural life and that the thinking subject must have its basis in the subject incarnate.

[30] *Ibid.*
[31] Gelb and Goldstein, *Über Farbennamenamnesie,* p. 158.
[32] *Ibid.*
[33] One sees them faced with a given sample (red), recalling some object of the same colour (strawberry), and from there rediscovering the name of the colour (red strawberry, red). *Ibid.,* p. 177.
[34] *Ibid.,* p. 158.

The phonetic 'gesture' brings about, both for the speaking subject and for his hearers, a certain structural co-ordination of experience, a certain modulation of existence, exactly as a pattern of my bodily behaviour endows the objects around me with a certain significance both for me and for others. The meaning of the gesture is not contained in it like some physical or physiological phenomenon. The meaning of the word is not contained in the word as a sound. But the human body is defined in terms of its property of appropriating, in an indefinite series of discontinuous acts, significant cores which transcend and transfigure its natural powers. This act of transcendence is first encountered in the acquisition of a pattern of behaviour, then in the mute communication of gesture: it is through the same power that the body opens itself to some new kind of conduct and makes it understood to external witnesses. Here and there a system of definite powers is suddenly decentralized, broken up and reorganized under a fresh law unknown to the subject or to the external witness, and one which reveals itself to them at the very moment at which the process occurs. For example, the knitting of the brows intended, according to Darwin, to protect the eye from the sun, or the narrowing of the eyes to enable one to see sharply, become component parts of the human act of meditation, and convey this to an observer. Language, in its turn, presents no different a problem: a contraction of the throat, a sibilant emission of air between the tongue and teeth, a certain way of bringing the body into play suddenly allows itself to be invested with a *figurative significance* which is conveyed outside us. This is neither more nor less miraculous than the emergence of love from desire, or that of gesture from the unco-ordinated movements of infancy. For the miracle to come about, phonetic 'gesticulation' must use an alphabet of already acquired meanings, the word-gesture must be performed in a certain setting common to the speakers, just as the comprehension of other gestures presupposes a perceived world common to all, in which each one develops and spreads out its meaning. But this condition is not sufficient: speech puts up a new sense, if it is authentic speech, just as gesture endows the object for the first time with human significance, if it is an initiating gesture. Moreover significances now acquired must necessarily have been new once. We must therefore recognize as an ultimate fact this open and indefinite power of giving significance— that is, both of apprehending and conveying a meaning—by which man transcends himself towards a new form of behaviour, or towards other people, or towards his own thought, through his body and his speech.

When authors try to bring the analysis of aphasia to its conclusion in some general conception of language[35] they can more clearly be seen forsaking the intellectualist language which they adopted after Pierre Marie and in reaction against the conceptions of Broca. It cannot be said of speech either that it is an 'operation of intelligence', or that it is a 'motor phenomenon': it is wholly motility and wholly intelligence. What establishes its inherence in the body is the fact that linguistic deficiencies cannot be reduced to a unity, and that the primary disturbances affect sometimes the body of the word, the material instrument of verbal expression—sometimes the word's physiognomy, the verbal intention, the kind of group image on the basis of which we succeed in saying or writing down a word exactly—sometimes the immediate meaning of the word, what German writers call the verbal concept—and sometimes the structure of the whole experience, not merely the linguistic experience, as in the case of amnesic aphasia examined above. Speech, then, rests upon a stratification of powers relatively capable of being isolated. But at the same time it is impossible to find anywhere a linguistic disturbance which is 'purely motor' and which does not to some extent impinge upon the significance of language. In pure alexia,[36] if the subject can no longer recognize the letters of a word, it is through inability to pattern the visual data, or constitute the word's structure, or apprehend its visual significance. In motor aphasia, the list of words lost and preserved does not correspond to their objective characteristics (length or complexity), but to their value from the subject's point of view: the patient is unable to pronounce, in isolation, a letter or word within a familiar motor series, through being incapable of differentiating between the 'figure' and 'background' and freely conferring upon a certain word or letter the value of a figure. Articulatory and syntactical accuracy always stand in inverse ratio to each other, which shows that the articulation of a word is not a merely motor phenomenon, but that it draws upon the same energies which organize the syntactical order. When disturbances of verbal

[35] Cf. Goldstein, *L'Analyse de l'aphasie et l'essence du langage*.
[36] *Alexia:* Loss of power to grasp meaning of written or printed words and sentences: word-blindness (Translator's note).

intention are present, as in the case of literal paraphasia[37] in which letters are omitted, displaced, or added, and in which the rhythm of the word is changed, it is, *a fortiori,* clearly not a question of a destruction of engrams,[38] but of the reduction to a common level of figure and background, of a powerlessness to structurize the word and grasp its articulatory physiognomy.[39]

If we are to summarize these two sets of observations, we shall have to say that any linguistic operation presupposes the apprehension of a significance, but that the significance in both cases is, as it were, specialized: there are different layers of significance, from the visual to the conceptual by way of the verbal concept. These two ideas will never be simultaneously understood unless we cease to vacillate between the notions of 'motility' and 'intelligence', and unless we discover a third notion which enables us to integrate them, a function which shall be the same at all levels, which shall be equally at work in the hidden preliminaries to speech and in articulatory phenomena, which shall support the whole edifice of language, and which nevertheless shall be stabilized in relatively autonomous processes. We shall have the opportunity of seeing this power, essential to speech, in cases in which neither thought nor 'motility' is noticeably affected, and yet in which the 'life' of language is impaired. It does happen that vocabulary, syntax and the body of language appear intact, the only peculiarity being that main clauses predominate. But the patient does not make the same use as the normal subject of these materials. He speaks practically only when he is questioned, or, if he himself takes the initiative in asking a question, it is never other than of a stereotyped kind, such as he asks daily of his children when

[37] *Paraphasia:* jargon; form of aphasia in which patient has lost power of speaking correctly, though words are heard and comprehended: he substitutes one word for another, and jumbles his words and sentences in such a way as to make his speech unintelligible (Translator's note).
[38] *Engram:* traces left by stimuli on protoplasm of animal or plant (Translator's note).
[39] Goldstein, *L'Analyse de l'aphasie et l'essence du langage,* p. 460. Goldstein here agrees with Grünbaum (*Aphasie und Motorik*) in going beyond the situation in which one is faced with the choice between the traditional conception (Broca) and the modern works (Head). Grünbaum's complaint against the moderns is that they do not 'give absolute priority to motor exteriorization, and the psychophysical structures on which it rests, as a fundamental field which dominates the picture of aphasia' (p. 386).

they come home from school. He never uses language to convey a merely possible situation, and false statements (e.g. the sky is black) are meaningless to him. He can speak only if he has prepared his sentences.[40] It cannot be held that language in his case has become automatic; there is no sign of a decline of general intelligence, and it is still the case that words are organized through their meaning. But the meaning is, as it were, ossified. Schneider never feels the need to speak; his experience never tends towards speech, it never suggests a question to him, it never ceases to have that kind of self-evidence and self-sufficiency of reality which stifles any interrogation, any reference to the possible, any wonder, any improvisation. We can perceive, in contrast with this, the essence of normal language: the intention to speak can reside only in an open experience. It makes its appearance like the boiling point of a liquid, when, in the density of being, volumes of empty space are built up and move outwards. 'As soon as man uses language to establish a living relation with himself or with his fellows, language is no longer an instrument, *no longer a means; it is a manifestation, a revelation of intimate being and of the psychic link which unites us to the world and our fellow men.* The patient's language may display great knowledge, it may be capable of being turned to account for specific activities, but it is totally lacking in that productivity which is man's deepest essence and which is perhaps revealed nowhere so clearly, among civilisation's creations, as in the creation of language itself.'[41] It might be said, restating a celebrated distinction, that *languages* or constituted systems of vocabulary and syntax, empirically existing 'means of expression', are both the repository and residue of acts of *speech,* in which unformulated significance not only finds the means of being conveyed outwardly, but moreover acquires existence for itself, and is genuinely created as significance. Or again one might draw a distinction between the *word in the speaking* and the *spoken word.* The former is the one in which the significant intention is at the stage of coming into being. Here existence is polarized into a certain 'significance'[42] which cannot be defined in terms of any natural object. It is somewhere at a point

---

[40] Benary, *Analyse eines Seelenbildes von der Sprache aus.* This is again Schneider's case, which we have analysed in connection with motility and sexuality.
[41] Goldstein, *L'Analyse de l'aphasie et l'essence du langage,* p. 496. Our italics.
[42] 'sens' in French means 'direction' and 'significance' (Translator's note).

beyond being that it aims to catch up with itself again, and that is why it creates speech as an empirical support for its own not-being. Speech is the surplus of our existence over natural being. But the act of expression constitutes a linguistic world and a cultural world, and allows that to fall back into being which was striving to outstrip it. Hence the spoken word, which enjoys available significances as one might enjoy an acquired fortune. From these gains other acts of authentic expression—the writer's, artist's or philosopher's—are made possible. This ever-recreated opening in the plenitude of being is what conditions the child's first use of speech and the language of the writer, as it does the construction of the word and that of concepts. Such is the function which we intuit through language, which reiterates itself, which is its own foundation, or which, like a wave, gathers and poises itself to hurtle beyond its own limits.

The analysis of speech and expression brings home to us the enigmatic nature of our own body even more effectively than did our remarks on bodily space and unity. It is not a collection of particles, each one remaining in itself, nor yet a network of processes defined once and for all—it is not where it is, nor what it is—since we see it secreting in itself a 'significance' which comes to it from nowhere, projecting that significance upon its material surrounding, and communicating it to other embodied subjects. It has always been observed that speech or gesture transfigure the body, but no more was said on the subject than that they develop or disclose another power, that of thought or soul. The fact was overlooked that, in order to express it, the body must in the last analysis become the thought or intention that it signifies for us. It is the body which points out, and which speaks; so much we have learnt in this chapter. Cézanne used to say of a portrait: 'If I paint in all the little blue and brown touches, I make him gaze as he does gaze. . . . Never mind if they suspect how, by bringing together a green of various shades and a red, we sadden a mouth or bring a smile to a cheek.'[43] This disclosure of an immanent or incipient significance in the living body extends, as we shall see, to the whole sensible world, and our gaze, prompted by the experience of our own body, will discover in all other 'objects' the miracle of expression. In his *Peau de Chagrin* Balzac describes a 'white tablecloth, like a covering of snow newly fallen, from which rose symmetrically the plates and napkins crowned with light-coloured rolls'. 'Throughout

[43] J. Gasquet, *Cézanne*, p. 117.

my youth,' Cézanne said, 'I wanted to paint that table-cloth like freshly fallen snow. . . . I know now that one must try to paint only: "the plates and napkins rose symmetrically", and "the light-coloured rolls". If I paint: "crowned", I'm finished, you see. And if I really balance and shade my napkins and rolls as they really are, you may be sure that the crowning, the snow and all the rest of it will be there.'[44] The problem of the world, and, to begin with, that of one's own body, consists in the fact that *it is all there.*

We have become accustomed, through the influence of the Cartesian tradition, to jettison the subject: the reflective attitude simultaneously purifies the common notions of body and soul by defining the body as the sum of its parts with no interior, and the soul as a being wholly present to itself without distance. These definitions make matters perfectly clear both within and outside ourselves: we have the transparency of an object with no secret recesses, the transparency of a subject which is nothing but what it thinks it is. The object is an object through and through, and consciousness a consciousness through and through. There are two senses, and two only, of the word 'exist': one exists as a thing or else one exists as a consciousness. The experience of our own body, on the other hand, reveals to us an ambiguous mode of existing. If I try to think of it as a cluster of third person processes—'sight', 'motility', 'sexuality'—I observe that these 'functions' cannot be interrelated, and related to the external world, by causal connections, they are all obscurely drawn together and mutually implied in a unique drama. Therefore the body is not an object. For the same reason, my awareness of it is not a thought, that is to say, I cannot take it to pieces and reform it to make a clear idea. Its unity is always implicit and vague. It is always something other than what it is, always sexuality and at the same time freedom, rooted in nature at the very moment when it is transformed by cultural influences, never hermetically sealed and never left behind. Whether it is a question of another's body or my own, I have no means of knowing the human body other than that of living it, which means taking up on my own account the drama which is being played out in it, and losing myself in it. I am my body, at least wholly to the extent that I possess experience, and yet at the same time my body is as it were a 'natural' subject, a provisional sketch of my total being. Thus experience of one's own body runs counter to the reflec-

[44] J. Gasquet, *Cézanne,* pp. 123 and ff.

tive procedure which detaches subject and object from each other, and which gives us only the thought about the body, or the body as an idea, and not the experience of the body or the body in reality. Descartes was well aware of this, since a famous letter of his to Elizabeth draws the distinction between the body as it is conceived through use in living and the body as it is conceived by the understanding.[45] But in Descartes this peculiar knowledge of our body, which we enjoy from the mere fact that we are a body, remains subordinated to our knowledge of it through the medium of ideas, because, behind man as he in fact is, stands God as the rational author of our *de facto* situation. On the basis of this transcendent guarantee, Descartes can blandly accept our irrational condition: it is not we who are required to bear the responsibility for reason and, once we have recognized it at the basis of things, it remains for us only to act and think in the world.[46] But if our union with the body is substantial, how is it possible for us to experience in ourselves a pure soul from which to accede to an absolute Spirit? Before asking this question, let us look closely at what is implied in the rediscovery of our own body. It is not merely one object among the rest which has the peculiarity of resisting reflection and remaining, so to speak, stuck to the subject. Obscurity spreads to the perceived world in its entirety.

[45] To Elizabeth, 28th June 1643, AT, T. III, p. 690.
[46] 'Finally, as I consider that it is very necessary to have understood, once in one's lifetime, the principles of metaphysics, since they are what provide us with knowledge of God and our soul, I think too, however, that it would be extremely harmful to occupy our mind often in meditating upon them, since it could not then attend so effectively to the work of imagination and the senses; but that the best course is merely to retain in memory and belief conclusions once arrived at, and thenceforth to employ the rest of the time one can devote to study to thoughts in which the understanding acts along with the imagination and the senses.' *Ibid*.

I0. ON THE PHENOMENOLOGY OF LANGUAGE

Husserl and the Problem of Language[1]

In the philosophical tradition, the problem of language does not pertain to "first philosophy," and that is just why Husserl approaches it more freely than the problems of perception or knowledge. He moves it into a central position, and what little he says about it is both original and enigmatic. Consequently, this problem provides us with our best basis for questioning phenomenology and recommencing Husserl's efforts instead of simply repeating what he said. It allows us to resume, instead of his theses, the very movement of his thought.

The contrast between certain early and late texts is striking. In the fourth of the *Logische Untersuchungen,* Husserl sets forth the concept of an eidetic of language and a universal grammar which would establish the forms of signification indispensable to every language if it is to be a language, and which would allow us to think with complete clarity about empirical languages as "confused" realizations of the essential language. This project assumes that language is one of the objects supremely constituted by consciousness, and that actual languages are very special cases of a possible language which consciousness holds the key to—that they are systems of signs linked to *their* meaning by

Maurice Merleau-Ponty, "On the Phenomenology of Language," *Signs,* Part II, Ch. 2, trans. by Richard C. McCleary (Evanston, Illinois: Northwestern University Press, 1964), pp. 84–97. Reprinted by permission.

[1] A paper presented at the first *Colloque international de phénoménologie,* Brussels, 1951.

univPHENOMENOLOGY OF LANGUAGE 215

univocal relationships which, in their structure as in their function, are susceptible to a total explication. Posited in this way as an object before thought, language could not possibly play any other role in respect to thought than that of an accompaniment, substitute, memorandum, or secondary means of communication.

In more recent writings, on the other hand, language appears as an original way of intending certain objects, as thought's body (*Formale und transzendentale Logik*[2]), or even as the operation through which thoughts that without it would remain private phenomena acquire intersubjective value and, ultimately, ideal existence (*Ursprung der Geometrie*[3]). According to this conception, philosophical thinking which reflects upon language would be its beneficiary, enveloped and situated in it. Pos ("Phénoménologie et linguistique," *Revue Internationale de philosophie,* 1939) defines the phenomenology of language not as an attempt to fit existing languages into the framework of an eidetic of all possible languages (that is, to objectify them before a universal and timeless constituting consciousness), but as a return to the speaking subject, to my contact with the language I am speaking. The scientist and the observer see language in the past. They consider the long history of a language, with all the random factors and all the shifts of meaning that have finally made it what it is today. It becomes incomprehensible that a language which is the result of so many accidents can signify anything whatsoever unequivocally. Taking language as a *fait accompli*—as the residue of past acts of signification

[2] "Diese aber (sc.: die Meinung) liegt nicht äusserlich neben den Worten; sondern redend vollziehen wir fortlaufend ein inneres, sich mit den Worten verschmelzendes, sie gleichsam beseelendes Meinen. Der Erfolg dieser Beseelung ist dass die Worte und die ganzen Reden in sich eine Meinung gleichsam verleiblichen und verleiblicht in sich als Sinn tragen." (p. 20).

[3] "Objektives Dasein 'in der Welt' das als solches zugänglich ist für jedermann kann aber die geistige Objektivität des Sinngebildes letzlich nur haben vermöge der doppelschichtigen Wiederholungen und vornehmlich der sinnlich verkörpernden. In der sinnlichen Verkörperung geschiet die 'Lokalisation' und 'Temporalisation' von Solchem das seinen Seinssinn nach nicht-lokal und nicht-temporal ist . . . Wir fragen nun: . . . Wie macht die sprachliche Verleiblichung aus dem bloss innersubjektiven Gebilde, dem Gedanke, das *objektive,* das etwa als geometrischer Begriff oder Satz in der Tat für jedermann und in aller Zukunft verständlich da ist? Auf das Problem des Ursprunges der Sprache in ihrer idealen und durch Ausserung und Dokumentierung begründeten Existenz in der realen Welt wollen wir hier nicht eingehen, obschon wir uns bewusst sind, dass eine radikale Aufklärung der Seinsart der 'idealen Sinngebilde' hier ihren tiefsten Problemgrund haben muss." (*Revue Internationale de philosophie,* 1939, p. 210).

and the record of already acquired meanings—the scientist inevitably misses the peculiar clarity of speaking, the fecundity of expression. From the phenomenological point of view (that is, for the speaking subject who makes use of his language as a means of communicating with a living community), a language regains its unity. It is no longer the result of a chaotic past of independent linguistic facts but a system all of whose elements cooperate in a single attempt to express which is turned toward the present or the future and thus governed by a present logic.

Such being Husserl's points of departure and arrival as far as language is concerned, we would like to submit for discussion a few propositions concerning first the phenomenon of language and next the conception of intersubjectivity, rationality, and philosophy implied by this phenomenology.

The Phenomenon of Language

LANGUAGE AND SPEECH

Can we simply juxtapose the two perspectives on language we have just distinguished—language as object of thought and language as mine? This is what Saussure did, for example, when he made a distinction between a synchronic linguistics of speech and a diachronic linguistics of a language, which are irreducible to one another because a panchronic view would inevitably blot out the originality of the present. Pos similarly limits himself to describing the objective and the phenomenological attitude by turns without saying anything about their relationship. But then we might think that phenomenology is distinguished from linguistics only as psychology is distinguished from the science of language. Phenomenology would add our inner experience of a language to our linguistic knowledge of it as pedagogy adds to our knowledge of mathematical concepts the experience of what they become in the minds of those who learn them. Our experience of speech would then have nothing to teach us about the being of language; it would have no ontological bearing.

But this is impossible. As soon as we distinguish, alongside of the objective science of language, a phenomenology of speech, we set in motion a dialectic through which the two disciplines open communications.

At first the "subjective" point of view envelops the "objective" point of view; synchrony envelops diachrony. The past of language began by being present. The series of fortuitous linguistic facts brought out by the objective perspective has been incorporated in a language which was at every moment a system endowed with an inner logic. Thus if language is a system when it is considered according to a cross-section, it must be in its development too. No matter how strongly Saussure insisted upon the duality of the two perspectives, his successors have had to conceive of a mediating principle in the form of the *sublinguistic schema* (Gustave Guillaume).[4]

In another connection, diachrony envelops synchrony. If language allows random elements when it is considered according to a longitudinal section, the system of synchrony must at every moment allow fissures where brute events can insert themselves.

Thus a double brute task is imposed upon us:

a) We have to find a meaning in the development of language, and conceive of language as a moving equilibrium. For example, certain forms of expression having become decadent by the sole fact that they have been used and have lost their "expressiveness," we shall show how the gaps or zones of weakness thus created elicit from speaking subjects who want to communicate a recovery and a utilization, in terms of a new principle, of linguistic débris left by the system in process of regression. It is in this way that a new means of expression is conceived of in a language, and a persistent logic runs through the effects of wear and tear upon the language and its volubility itself. It is in this way that the French system of expression, based upon the preposition, was substituted for the Latin system, which was based upon declension and inflectional changes.

b) But correlatively, we must understand that since synchrony is only a cross-section of diachrony, the system realized in it never exists wholly in act but always involves latent or incubating changes. It is never composed of absolutely univocal meanings which can be made completely explicit beneath the gaze of a transparent constituting consciousness. It will be a question not of a system of forms of signification clearly articulated in terms of one another—not of a structure of linguistic ideas built according to a strict plan—but of a cohesive whole of convergent linguistic gestures, each of which will be defined less by a signification than by a use value. Far from particular lan-

---

[4] Gustave Guillaume, contemporary French linguist.—Trans.

guages appearing as the "confused" realization of certain ideal and universal forms of signification, the possibility of such a synthesis becomes problematical. If universality is attained, it will not be through a universal language which would go back prior to the diversity of languages to provide us with the foundations of all possible languages. It will be through an oblique passage from a given language that I speak and that initiates me into the phenomenon of expression, to another given language that I learn to speak and that effects the act of expression according to a completely different style—the two languages (and ultimately all given languages) being contingently comparable only at the outcome of this passage and only as signifying wholes, without our being able to recognize in them the common elements of one single categorial structure.

Far from our being able to juxtapose a psychology of language and a science of language by reserving language in the present for the first and language in the past for the second, we must recognize that the present diffuses into the past to the extent that the past has been present. History is the history of successive synchronies, and the contingency of the linguistic past invades even the synchronic system. What the phenomenology of language teaches me is not just a psychological curiosity—the language observed by linguistics experienced in me and bearing my particular additions to it. It teaches me a new conception of the being of language, which is now logic in contingency—an oriented system which nevertheless always elaborates random factors, taking what was fortuitous up again into a meaningful whole—incarnate logic.

THE QUASI-CORPOREALITY OF THE SIGNIFYING

By coming back to spoken or living language we shall find that its expressive value is not the sum of the expressive values which allegedly belong individually to each element of the "verbal chain." On the contrary, these elements form a system in synchrony in the sense that each of them signifies only its difference in respect to the others (as Saussure says, signs are essentially "diacritical"); and as this is true of them all, there are only differences of signification in a language. The reason why a language finally intends to say and does say [*veut dire et dit*] something is not that each sign is the vehicle for a signification which allegedly belongs to it, but that all the signs together allude to a signification which is always in abeyance when they are considered singly, and which I go beyond them toward without their ever containing it. Each of them expresses only by reference to a certain mental equipment, to a certain arrangement of our cultural implements, and as a whole they are like a blank form we have not yet filled out, or like the gestures of others, which intend and circumscribe an object of the world that I do not see.

The speaking power the child assimilates in learning his language is not the sum of morphological, syntactical, and lexical meanings. These attainments are neither necessary nor sufficient to acquire a language, and once the act of speaking is acquired it presupposes no comparison between what I want to express and the conceptual arrangement of the means of expression I make use of. The words and turns of phrase needed to bring my significative intention to expression recommend themselves to me, when I am speaking, only by what Humboldt called *innere Sprachform* (and our contemporaries call *Wortbegriff*), that is, only by a certain style of speaking from which they arise and according to which they are organized without my having to represent them to myself. There is a "languagely" [*"langagière"*] meaning of language which effects the mediation between my as yet unspeaking intention and words, and in such a way that my spoken words surprise me myself and teach me my thought. Organized signs have their immanent meaning, which does not arise from the "I think" but from the "I am able to."

This action at a distance by language, which brings significations together without touching them, and this eloquence which designates them in a peremptory fashion without ever changing them into words or breaking the silence of consciousness, are eminent cases of corporeal intentionality. I have a rigorous awareness of the bearing of my gestures or of the spatiality of my body which allows me to maintain relationships with the world without thematically representing to myself the objects I am going to grasp or the relationships of size between my body and the avenues offered to me by the world. On the condition that I do not reflect expressly upon it, my consciousness of my body immediately signifies a certain landscape about me, that of my fingers a certain fibrous or grainy style of the object. It is in the same fashion that the spoken word (the one I utter or the one I hear) is pregnant with a meaning which can be read in the very texture of the linguistic gesture (to the point that a hesitation, an alteration of the voice, or the choice of a certain syntax suffices to modify it), and yet is never contained in that gesture, every expression always appearing to me as a trace, no idea being given to me except in transparency, and every attempt to close our hand on the thought which dwells in the spoken word leaving only a bit of verbal material in our fingers.

THE RELATIONSHIP OF THE SIGNIFYING AND THE SIGNIFIED. SEDIMENTATION

Speech is comparable to a gesture because what it is charged with expressing will be in the same relation to it as the goal is to the gesture which intends it, and our remarks about the functioning of the signifying apparatus will already involve a certain theory of the significations expressed by speech. My corporeal intending of the objects of my surroundings is implicit and presupposes no thematization or "representation" of my body or milieu. Signification arouses speech as the world arouses my body—by a mute presence which awakens my intentions without deploying itself before them. In me as well as in the listener who finds it in hearing me, the significative intention (even if it is subsequently to fructify in "thoughts") is at the moment no more than a *determinate gap* to be filled by words—the excess of what I intend to say over what is being said or has already been said.

This means three things: (a) The significations of speech are already ideas in the Kantian sense, the poles of a certain number of convergent acts of expression which magnetize discourse without being in the strict sense given for their own account. Consequently, (b) expression is never total. As Saussure points out, we have the feeling that our language expresses totally. But it is not because it expresses totally that it is ours; it is because it is ours that we believe it expresses totally. For an Englishman, "the man I love" is just as complete an expression as "l'homme *que* j'aime" is for a Frenchman. And for a German who by declension can expressly indicate the function of the direct object, "j'aime cet homme" is a wholly allusive way of expressing oneself. Thus there are always things understood in expression; or rather the idea of things understood is to be rejected. It is meaningful only if we take as the model and absolute norm of expression a language (ordinarily our own) which, like all the others, can never in fact lead us "as if by the hand" to the signification, to the things themselves. So let us not say that every expression is imperfect because it leaves things understood. Let us say that every expression is perfect to the extent it is unequivocally understood, and admit as a fundamental fact of expression *a surpassing of the signifying by the signified which it is the very virtue of the signifying to make possible.* The fact that the significative intention is only a determinate gap means, finally, that (c) this act of expression—this joining through transcendence of the linguistic meaning of speech and the signification it intends—is not for us speaking subjects a second-order operation we supposedly have recourse to only in order to communicate our thoughts to others, but our own taking possession or acquisition of significations which otherwise are present to us only in a muffled way. The reason why the thematization of the signified does not precede speech is that it is the result of it. Let us stress this third consequence.

For the speaking subject, to express is to become aware of; he does not express just for others, but also to know himself what he intends. Speech does not seek to embody a significative intention which is only *a certain gap* simply in order to recreate the same lack or privation in others, but also to know *what* there is a lack or privation of. How does it succeed in doing so? The significative intention gives itself a body and knows itself by looking for an equivalent in the system of available significations represented by the language I speak and the whole of the writings and culture I inherit. For that speechless want, the significative intention, it is a matter of realizing a certain arrangement of already signifying instruments or already speaking significations (morphological, syntactical, and lexical instruments, literary *genres,* types of narrative, modes of presenting events, etc.) which arouses in the hearer the presentiment of a new and different signification, and which inversely (in the speaker or the writer) manages to anchor this original signification in the already available ones. But why, how, and in what sense are they available? They became such when, in their time, they were *established* as significations I can have recourse to—that I *have*—through the same sort of expressive operation. It is this operation which must be described if I want to comprehend the peculiar power of speech.

I understand or think I understand the words and forms of French; I have a certain experience of the literary and philosophical modes of expression offered me by the given culture. I express when, utilizing all these already speaking instruments, I make them say something they have never said. We begin reading a philosopher by giving the words he makes use of their "common" meaning; and little by little, through what is at first an imperceptible reversal, his speech comes to dominate his language, and it is his use of words which ends up assigning them a new and characteristic signification. At this moment he has made himself understood and his signification has come to dwell in me. We say that a thought is expressed when the converging words intending it are numerous and eloquent enough to designate it unequivocally for me, its author, or for others, and in such a manner that we all have the experience of its presence in the flesh in speech. Even though only *Abschattungen* of the signification are given thematically, the fact is that once a certain point in discourse has been passed the *Abschattungen,* caught up in the movement of discourse outside of which they are nothing, suddenly contract into a single signification. And then we feel that *something has been said*—just as we perceive a thing once a minimum of sensory messages has been exceeded, even though the explanation of the thing extends as a matter of principle to infinity; or, as beholders of a certain number of actions, we come to *perceive someone* even though in the eyes of reflection no one other than myself can really and in the same sense be an *ego.*

The consequences of speech, like those of perception (and particularly the perception of others), always exceed its premises. Even we who speak do not necessarily know better than those who listen to us what we are expressing. I say that I *know an idea* when the power to organize discourses which make coherent sense around it has been established in me; and this power itself does not depend upon my alleged possession and face-to-face contemplation of it, but upon my having acquired a certain style of thinking. I say that a signification is acquired and henceforth available when I have succeeded in making it dwell in a speech apparatus which was not originally destined for it. Of course the elements of this expressive apparatus did not really contain it—the French language did not, from the moment it was established, contain French literature; I had to throw them off center and recenter them in order to make them signifiy what I intended. It is just this "coherent deformation" (Malraux) of available significations which arranges them in a new sense and takes not only the hearers *but the speaking subject as well* through a decisive *step.*

For from this point on the preparatory stages of expression—the first pages of the book—are taken up again into the final meaning of the whole and are directly given as derivatives of that meaning, which is now installed in the culture. The way will be open for the speaking subject (and for others) to go straight to the whole. He will not need to reactivate the whole process; he will possess it eminently in its result. A personal and interpersonal tradition will have been founded. The *Nachvollzug*, freed from the cautious gropings of the *Vollzug*, contracts the steps of the process into a single view. Sedimentation occurs, and I shall be able to think farther. Speech, as distinguished from language, is that moment when the significative intention (still silent and wholly in act) proves itself capable of incorporating itself into my culture and the culture of others—of shaping me and others by transforming the meaning of cultural instruments. It becomes "available" in turn because in retrospect it gives us the illusion that it was contained in the already available significations, whereas by a sort of *ruse* it espoused them only in order to infuse them with a new life.

CONSEQUENCES FOR PHENOMENOLOGICAL PHILOSOPHY

What philosophical bearing must we grant these descriptions? The relation of phenomenological analyses to philosophy proper is not clear. They are often considered *preparatory*, and Husserl himself always distinguished "phenomenological investigations" in the broad sense from the "philosophy" which was supposed to crown them. Yet it is hard to maintain that the philosophical problem remains untouched after the phenomenological exploration of the *Lebenswelt*. The reason why the return to the "life-world" is considered an absolutely indispensable first step in Husserl's last writings is undoubtedly that it is not without consequence for the work of universal constitution which should follow, that in some respects something of the first step remains in the second, that it is in some fashion preserved in it, that it is thus never gone beyond completely, and that phenomenology is already philosophy. If the philosophical subject were a transparent constituting consciousness before which the world and language were wholly explicit as its significations and its objects, any experience whatsoever—phenomenological or no—would suffice to motivate our passing to philosophy, and the systematic exploration of the *Lebenswelt* would not be necessary. The reason why the return to the *Lebenswelt* (and particularly the return from objectified language to speech) is considered absolutely necessary is that philosophy must reflect upon the object's mode of presence to the subject—upon the conception of the object and of the subject as they appear to the phenomenological revelation—instead of replacing them by the object's relationship to the subject as an idealistic philosophy of total reflection conceives of it. From this point on, phenomenology envelops philosophy, which cannot be purely and simply added on to it.

This is particularly clear in the case of the phenomenology of language. More clearly than any other, this problem requires us to make a decision concerning the relationships between phenomenology and philosophy or metaphysics. For more clearly than any other it takes the form of both a special problem and a problem which contains all the others, including the problem of philosophy. If speech is what we have said it is, how could there possibly be an ideation which allows us to dominate this *praxis?* How could the phenomenology of speech possibly help being a philosophy of speech as well? And how could there possibly be any place for a subsequent elucidation of a higher degree? It is absolutely necessary to underline the *philosophical* import of the return to speech.

The description we have given of the signifying power of speech, and in general of the body as mediator of our relation to the object, would provide no philosophical information at all if it could be considered a matter of mere psychological depiction. In this case we would admit that in effect the body, such as it is in our living experience of it, seems to us to involve the world, and speech a landscape of thought. But this would be only an appearance. In the light of serious thinking, my body would still be an object, my consciousness pure consciousness, and their coexistence the object of an *apperception* which (as pure consciousness) I would still be the subject of (in Husserl's early writings, things are set forth in more or less this way). Similarly, since the relationship according to which my speech or the speech I hear points beyond itself toward a signification could (like every other relationship) only be posited by me *qua* consciousness, thought's radical autonomy would be restored at the very moment it seemed to be in doubt.

Yet in neither case can I classify the phenomenon of incarnation simply as psychological appearance; and if I were tempted to do so, I would be blocked by my perception of others. For more clearly (*but not differently*) in my experience of others than in my experience of speech or the perceived world, I inevitably grasp my body as a *spontaneity which teaches me what I could not know in any other way except through* it. Positing another person as an other myself is not as a matter of fact possible if it is *consciousness* which must do it. To be conscious is to constitute, so that I cannot be conscious of another person, since that would involve constituting him as constituting, and as constituting in respect to the very act through which I constitute him. This difficulty of principle, posited as a limit at the beginning of the fifth *Cartesian Meditation,* is nowhere eliminated. Husserl *disregards* it: since I have the idea of others, it follows that in some way the difficulty mentioned *has in fact been overcome*. But I have been able to overcome it only because he within me who perceives others is capable of ignoring the radical contradiction which makes theoretical conception of others impossible. Or rather (since if he ignored it he would no longer be dealing with others), only because he is able to live that contradiction as the very definition of the presence of others.

This subject which experiences itself as constituted at the moment it functions as constituting is my body. We remember that Husserl ended up basing my perception of a way of behaving (*Gebaren*) which appears in the space surrounding me upon what he calls the "mating phenomenon" and "intentional transgression." It happens that my gaze stumbles against certain sights (those of other human and, by extension, animal bodies) and is thwarted by them. I am invested by them just when I thought I was investing them, and I see a form sketched out in space that arouses and convokes the possibilities of my own body as if it were a matter of my own gestures or behavior. Everything happens as if the functions of intentionality and the intentional object were paradoxically interchanged. The scene invites me to become its adequate viewer, as if a different mind than my own suddenly came to dwell in my body, or rather as if my mind were drawn out there and emigrated into the scene it was in the process of setting for itself. I am snapped up by a second myself outside me; I perceive an other.

Now speech is evidently an eminent case of these "ways of behaving" [*"conduites"*] which reverse my ordinary relationship to objects and give certain ones of them the value of subjects. And if objectification makes no sense in respect to the living body (mine or another's), the incarnation of what I call its thinking in its total speech must also be considered an ultimate phenomenon. If phenomenology did not really already involve our conception of being and our philosophy, when we arrived at the philosophical problem we would find ourselves confronted again with the very difficulties which gave rise to phenomenology to begin with.

In a sense, phenomenology is all or nothing. That order of instructive spontaneity—the body's "I am able to," the "intentional transgression" which gives us others, the "speech" which gives us the idea of an ideal or absolute signification—cannot be subsequently placed under the jurisdiction of an acosmic and a pancosmic consciousness without becoming meaningless again. It must teach me to comprehend what no constituting consciousness can know—my involvement in a "pre-constituted" world. But how, people will object, can the body and speech give me more than I have put into them? It is clearly not my body as organism which teaches me to see the emergence of *another myself* in a way of behaving [*conduite*] that I witness; as such it could at best only be reflected and recognize itself in *another organism*. In order for the alter ego and the thought of others to appear to me, I must be the *I* of *this* body of mine, *this* incarnate life's thought. The subject who effects the intentional transgression could not possibly do so except insofar as he is situated. The experience of others is possible to the exact degree that the situation is part of the Cogito.

But then we must take with equal strictness what phenomenology has taught us about the relationship between the signifying and the signified. If the central phenomenon of language is in fact *the common act of the signifying and the signified,* we would deprive it of its distinctive characteristic by realizing the result of expressive operations in advance in a heaven of ideas; we would lose sight of the *leap* these operations take from already available significations to those we are in the process of constructing and acquiring. And the intelligible substitute we would try to base them on would not exempt us from understanding how our knowing apparatus expands to the point of understanding what it does not contain. We would not husband our transcendence by prescribing it to a factual transcendent. In any case the place of truth would still be that anticipation (*Vorhabe*) through which each spoken word or acquired truth opens a field of understanding, and the symmetrical recovery (*Nachvollzug*) through which we bring this advent of understanding or this commerce with others to a conclusion and contract them into a new view.

Our present expressive operations, instead of driving the preceding ones away—simply succeeding and annulling them—salvage, preserve, and (insofar as they contain some truth) take them up again;

and the same phenomenon is produced in respect to others' expressive operations, whether they be past or contemporary. Our present keeps the promises of our past; we keep others' promises. Each act of philosophical or literary expression contributes to fulfilling the vow to retrieve the world taken with the first appearance of a language, that is, with the first appearance of a finite system of signs which claimed to be capable in principle of winning by a sort of ruse any being which might present itself. Each act of expression realizes for its own part a portion of this project, and by opening a new field of truths, further extends the contract which has just expired. This is possible only through the same "intentional transgression" which gives us others; and like it the phenomenon of truth, which is theoretically impossible, is known only through the praxis which *creates* it.

To say there is a truth is to say that when my renewal meets the old or alien project, and successful expression frees what has always been held captive in being, an inner communication is established in the density of personal and interpersonal time through which our present becomes the *truth* of all the other knowing events. It is like a wedge we drive into the present, a milestone bearing witness that in this moment something has taken place which being was always waiting for or "intending to say" [*voulait dire*], and which will never stop if not being true at least signifying and stimulating our thinking apparatus, if need be by drawing from it truths more comprehensive than the present one. At this moment something has been founded in signification; an experience has been transformed into its meaning, has become truth. Truth is another name for sedimentation, which is itself the presence of all presents in our own. That is to say that even and especially for the ultimate philosophical subject, there is no objectivity which accounts for our super-objective relationship to all times, no light that shines more brightly than the living present's light.

In the late text we cited to begin with, Husserl writes that speech realizes a "localization" and "temporalization" of an ideal meaning which, "according to the meaning of its being," is neither local nor temporal. And later on he adds that speech also objectifies, as concept or proposition, what was heretofore only a formation internal to a single subject, thereby opening it up to the plurality of subjects. So there would seem to be a movement through which ideal existence descends into locality and temporality, and an inverse movement through which the act of speaking here and now establishes the ideality of what is true. These two movements would be contradictory if they took place between the same extreme terms; and it seems to us that their relationship must be conceived of in terms of a circuit of reflection. In a first approximation, reflection recognizes ideal existence as neither local nor temporal. It then becomes aware of a locality and temporality of speech that can neither be derived from those of the objective world nor suspended from a world of ideas. And finally, it makes the mode of being of ideal formations rest upon speech. Ideal existence is based upon the document. Not, undoubtedly, upon the document as a physical object, or even as the vehicle of one-to-one significations assigned to it by the language it is written in. But ideal existence is based upon the document insofar as (still through an "intentional transgression") the document solicits and brings together all knowing lives—and as such establishes and re-establishes a "Logos" of the cultural world.

Thus the proper function of a phenomenological philosophy seems to us to be to establish itself definitively in the order of instructive spontaneity that is inaccessible to psychologism and historicism no less than to dogmatic metaphysics. The phenomenology of speech is among all others best suited to reveal this order to us. When I speak or understand, I experience that presence of others in myself or of myself in others which is the stumbling-block of the theory of intersubjectivity, I experience that presence of what is represented which is the stumbling-block of the theory of time, and I finally understand what is meant by Husserl's enigmatic statement, "Transcendental subjectivity is intersubjectivity." To the extent that what I say has meaning, I am a different "other" for myself when I am speaking; and to the extent that I understand, I no longer know who is speaking and who is listening.

The ultimate philosophical step is to recognize what Kant calls the "transcendental affinity" of moments of time and temporalities. This is undoubtedly what Husserl is trying to do when he takes up the finalist vocabulary of various metaphysics again, speaking of "monads," "entelechies," and "teleology." But these words are often put in quotations in order to indicate that he does not intend to introduce along with them some agent who would then assure externally the connection of related terms. Finality in a dogmatic sense would be a compromise; it would leave the terms to be connected and their connecting principle unconnected. Now it is at the heart of my present that I find the meaning of those presents which preceded it, and that I find the means of understanding others' presence at the same world; and it is in the actual practice of speaking that I learn to understand. There is finality only in the sense in which Heidegger defined it when he said approximately that finality is the trembling of a unity exposed to contingency and tirelessly recreating itself. And it is to the same undeliberated and inexhaustible spontaneity that Sartre was alluding when he said that we are "condemned to freedom."

PART FIVE

Philosophical Esthetics

Of all the arts Merleau-Ponty was probably most interested in painting, perhaps because of his overriding interest in human perception. In "Cézanne's Doubt" he dismisses the effort to understand Cézanne's art simply through psychological or historical facts about the man. The meaning of a work of art always goes beyond such "accidents" in the life of the artist. What he sees in Cézanne's paintings is an original mode of perception analogous to man's own primordial way of perceiving things. He also sees confirmed in Cézanne his thesis that art is an original mode of human expression.

In "Eye and Mind" (his last published work), Merleau-Ponty again engages in philosophical reflection on the nature of painting and the artist, and contrasts the activity of painting with that of science and philosophy. Once again painting is seen to involve a special kind of perception on the part of the artist and art is seen as providing a special mode of access to being. Thus, in this essay Merleau-Ponty's esthetic concern is situated in a much broader context.

I I. CÉZANNE'S DOUBT

He needed one hundred working sessions for a still life, five hundred sittings for a portrait. What we call his work was, for him, only an essay, an approach to painting. In September, 1906, at the age of 67— one month before his death—he wrote: "I was in such a state of mental agitation, in such great confusion that for a time I feared my weak reason would not survive. . . . Now it seems I am better and that I see more clearly the direction my studies are taking. Will I ever arrive at the goal, so intensely sought and so long pursued? I am still learning from nature, and it seems to me I am making slow progress." Painting was his world and his way of life. He worked alone, without students, without admiration from his family, without encouragement from the critics. He painted on the afternoon of the day his mother died. In 1870 he was painting at l'Estaque while the police were after him for dodging the draft. And still he had moments of doubt about his vocation. As he grew old, he wondered whether the novelty of his painting might not come from trouble with his eyes, whether his whole life had not been based upon an accident of his body. The uncertainty or stupidity of his contemporaries correspond to this effort and this doubt. "The painting of a drunken privy cleaner," said a critic in 1905. Even today, C. Mauclair finds Cézanne's admissions of powerlessness an argument against him. Meanwhile, Cézanne's paintings have spread throughout the world. Why so much uncertainty, so

Maurice Merleau-Ponty, "Cézanne's Doubt," *Sense and Non-Sense,* Part I, Ch. 1, trans. by Hubert L. Dreyfus and Patricia Allen Dreyfus (Evanston, Illinois: Northwestern University Press, 1964), pp. 9–25. Reprinted by permission.

much labor, so many failures, and, suddenly, the greatest success?

Zola, Cézanne's friend from childhood, was the first to find genius in him and the first to speak of him as a "genius gone wrong." An observer of Cézanne's life such as Zola, more concerned with his character than with the meaning of his painting, might well consider it a manifestation of ill-health.

For as far back as 1852, upon entering the Collège Bourbon at Aix, Cézanne worried his friends with his fits of temper and depression. Seven years later, having decided to become an artist, he doubted his talent and did not dare to ask his father—a hatter and later a banker —to send him to Paris. Zola's letters reproach him for his instability, his weakness, and his indecision. When finally he came to Paris, he wrote: "The only thing I have changed is my location: my ennui has followed me." He could not tolerate discussions, because they wore him out and because he could never give arguments. His nature was basically anxious. Thinking that he would die young, he made his will at the age of 42; at 46 he was for six months the victim of a violent, tormented, overwhelming passion of which no one knows the outcome and to which he would never refer. At 51 he withdrew to Aix, where he found landscape best suited to his genius but where also he returned to the world of his childhood, his mother and his sister. After the death of his mother, Cézanne turned to his son for support. "Life is terrifying," he would often say. Religion, which he then set about practicing for the first time, began for him in the fear of life and the fear of death. "It is fear," he explained to a friend; "I feel I will be on earth for another four days—what then? I believe in life after death, and I don't want to risk roasting *in aeternum*." Although his religion later deepened, its original motivation was the need to put his life in order and to be relieved of it. He became more and more timid, mistrustful, and sensitive: on his occasional visits to Paris he motioned his friends, when still far away, not to approach him. In 1903, after his pictures had begun to sell in Paris at twice the price of Monet's and when young men like Joachim Gasquet and Emile Bernard came to see him and ask him questions, he unbent a little. But his fits of anger continued. (In Aix a child once hit him as he passed by; after that he could not bear any contact.) One day when Cézanne was quite old, Emile Bernard supported him as he stumbled. Cézanne flew into a rage. He could be heard striding around his studio and shouting that he wouldn't let anybody "get his hooks into me." Because of these "hooks" he pushed women who could have modeled for him out of his studio, priests, whom he called "sticky," out of his life, and Emile Bernard's theories out of his mind, when they became too insistent.

This loss of flexible human contact; this inability to master new situations; this flight into established habits, in at atmosphere which presented no problems; this rigid opposition in theory and practice of the "hook" versus the freedom of a recluse—all these symptoms permit one to speak of a morbid constitution and more precisely, as, for example, in the case of El Greco, of schizophrenia. The notion of painting "from nature" could be said to arise from the same weakness. His extremely close attention to nature and to color, the inhuman character of his paintings (he said that a face should be painted as an object), his devotion to the visible world: all of these would then only represent a flight from the human world, the alienation of his humanity.

The conjectures nevertheless do not give any idea of the positive side of his work; one cannot thereby conclude that his painting is a phenomenon of decadence and what Nietzsche called "impoverished" life or that it has nothing to say to the educated man. Zola's and Emile Bernard's belief in Cézanne's failure probably arises from their having put too much emphasis on psychology and their personal knowledge of Cézanne. It is quite possible that, on the basis of his nervous weaknesses, Cézanne conceived a form of art which is valid for everyone. Left to himself, he could look at nature as only a human being can. The meaning of his work cannot be determined from his life.

This meaning will not become any clearer in the light of art history —that is, by bringing in the influences on Cézanne's methods (the Italian school and Tintoretto, Delacroix, Courbet and the Impressionists)—or even by drawing on his own judgment of his work.

His first pictures—up to about 1870—are painted fantasies: a rape, a murder. They are therefore almost always executed in broad strokes and present the moral physiognomy of the actions rather than their visible aspect. It is thanks to the Impressionists, and particularly to Pissarro, that Cézanne later conceived painting not as the incarnation of imagined scenes, the projection of dreams outward, but as the exact study of appearances: less a work of the studio than a working from nature. Thanks to the Impressionists, he abandoned the baroque technique, whose primary aim is to capture movement, for small dabs placed close together and for patient hatchings.

He quickly parted ways with the Impressionists, however. Impressionism tries to capture, in the painting, the very way in which objects strike our eyes and attack our senses. Objects are depicted as they appear to instantaneous perception, without fixed contours, bound together by light and air. To capture this envelope of light, one had to exclude siennas, ochres, and black and use only the seven colors of the spectrum. The color of objects could not be represented simply by putting on the canvas their local tone, that is, the color they take on isolated from their surroundings; one also had to pay attention to the phenomena of contrast which modify local colors in nature. Furthermore, by a sort of reversal, every color we perceive in nature elicits the appearance of its complement; and these complementaries heighten one another. To achieve sunlit colors in a picture which will be seen in the dim light of apartments, not only must there be a green—if you are painting grass—but also the complementary red which will make it vibrate. Finally, the Impressionists break down the local tone itself. One can generally obtain any color by juxtaposing rather than mixing the colors which make it up, thereby achieving a more vibrant hue. The result of these procedures is that the canvas—which no longer corresponds point by point to nature—affords a generally true impression through the action of the separate parts upon one another. But at the same time, depicting the atmosphere and breaking up the tones submerges the object and causes it to lose its proper weight. The composition of Cézanne's palette leads one to suppose that he had another aim. Instead of the seven colors of the spectrum, one finds eighteen colors—six reds, five yellows, three blues, three greens, and black. The use of warm colors and black shows that Cézanne wants to represent the object, to find it again behind the atmosphere. Likewise, he does not break up the tone; rather, he replaces his technique with graduated colors, a progression of chromatic nuances across the object, a modulation of colors which stays close to the object's form and to the light it receives. Doing away with exact contours in certain cases, giving color priority over the outline—these obviously mean different things for Cézanne and for the Impressionists. The object is no longer covered by reflections and lost in its relationships to the atmosphere and to other objects: it seems subtly illuminated from within, light emanates from it, and the result is an impression of solidity and material substance. Moreover, Cézanne does not give up making the warm colors vibrate but achieves this chromatic sensation through the use of blue.

One must therefore say that Cézanne wished to return to the object without abandoning the Impressionist aesthetic which takes nature as its model. Emile Bernard reminded him that, for the classical artists, painting demanded outline, composition, and distribution of light. Cézanne replied: "They created pictures; we are attempting a piece of nature." He said of the old masters that they "replaced reality by imagination and by the abstraction which accompanies it." Of nature, he said that "the artist must conform to this perfect work of art. Everything comes to us from nature; we exist through it; nothing else is worth remembering." He stated that he wanted to make of Impressionism "something solid, like the art in the museums." His painting was paradoxical: he was pursuing reality without giving up the sensuous surface, with no other guide than the immediate impression of nature, without following the contours, with no outline to enclose the color, with no perspectival or pictorial arrangement. This is what Bernard called Cézanne's suicide: aiming for reality while denying himself the means to attain it. This is the reason for his difficulties and for the distortions one finds in his pictures between 1870 and 1890. Cups and saucers on a table seen from the side should be elliptical, but Cézanne paints the two ends of the ellipse swollen and expanded. The work table in his portrait of Gustave Geoffrey stretches, contrary to the laws of perspective, into the lower part of the picture. In giving up the outline Cézanne was abandoning himself to the chaos of sensations, which would upset the objects and constantly suggest illusions, as, for example, the illusion we have when we move our head that objects themselves are moving—if our judgment did not constantly set these appearances straight. According to Bernard, Cézanne "submerged his painting in ignorance and his mind in shadows." But one cannot really judge his painting in this way except by closing one's mind to half of what he said and one's eyes to what he painted.

It is clear from his conversations with Emile Bernard that Cézanne was always seeking to avoid the ready-made alternatives suggested to him: sensation versus judgment; the painter who sees against the painter who thinks; nature versus composition; primitivism as opposed to tradition. "We have to develop an optics," said Cézanne, "by which I mean a logical vision—that is, one with no element of the absurd." "Are you speaking of our nature?" asked Bernard. Cézanne: "It has to do with both." "But aren't nature and art different?" "I want to make them the same. Art is a personal apperception, which I embody in sen-

sations and which I ask the understanding to organize into a painting."[1] But even these formulas put too much emphasis on the ordinary
notions of "sensitivity" or "sensations" and "understanding"—which is
why Cézanne could not convince by his arguments and preferred to
paint instead. Rather than apply to his work dichotomies more appropriate to those who sustain traditions than to those men, philosophers
or painters, who initiate these traditions, he preferred to search for the
true meaning of painting, which is continually to question tradition.
Cézanne did not think he had to choose between feeling and thought,
between order and chaos. He did not want to separate the stable things
which we see and the shifting way in which they appear; he wanted to
depict matter as it takes on form, the birth of order through spontaneous organization. He makes a basic distinction not between "the
senses" and "the understanding" but rather between the spontaneous
organization of the things we perceive and the human organization of
ideas and sciences. We see things; we agree about them; we are an-
chored in them; and it is with "nature" as our base that we construct
our sciences. Cézanne wanted to paint this primordial world, and his
pictures therefore seem to show nature pure, while photographs of
the same landscapes suggest man's works, conveniences, and imminent
presence. Cézanne never wished to "paint like a savage." He wanted
to put intelligence, ideas, sciences, perspective, and tradition back in
touch with the world of nature which they must comprehend. He
wished, as he said, to confront the sciences with the nature "from
which they came."

By remaining faithful to the phenomena in his investigations of
perspective, Cézanne discovered what recent psychologists have come
to formulate: the lived perspective, that which we actually perceive,
is not a geometric or photographic one. The objects we see close at
hand appear smaller, those far away seem larger than they do in a
photograph. (This can be seen in a movie, where a train approaches
and gets bigger much faster than a real train would under the same
circumstances.) To say that a circle seen obliquely is seen as an ellipse
is to substitute for our actual perception what we would see if we were
cameras: in reality we see a form which oscillates around the ellipse
without being an ellipse. In a portrait of Mme Cézanne, the border of
the wallpaper on one side of her body does not form a straight line with

[1] Cézanne's conversations with Bernard are recorded in *Souvenirs sur Paul
Cézanne* (Paris, 1912).—Trans.

that on the other: and indeed it is known that if a line passes beneath a wide strip of paper, the two visible segments appear dislocated. Gustave Geoffrey's table stretches into the bottom of the picture, and indeed, when our eye runs over a large surface, the images it successively receives are taken from different points of view, and the whole surface is warped. It is true that I freeze these distortions in repainting them on the canvas; I stop the spontaneous movement in which they pile up in perception and in which they tend toward the geometric perspective. This is also what happens with colors. Pink upon gray paper colors the background green. Academic painting shows the background as gray, assuming that the picture will produce the same effect of contrast as the real object. Impressionist painting uses green in the background in order to achieve a contrast as brilliant as that of objects in nature. Doesn't this falsify the color relationship? It would if it stopped there, but the painter's task is to modify all the other colors in the picture so that they take away from the green background its characteristics of a real color. Similarly, it is Cézanne's genius that when the over-all composition of the picture is seen globally, perspectival distortions are no longer visible in their own right but rather contribute, as they do in natural vision, to the impression of an emerging order, of an object in the act of appearing, organizing itself before our eyes. In the same way, the contour of an object conceived as a line encircling the object belongs not to the visible world but to geometry. If one outlines the shape of an apple with a continuous line, one makes an object of the shape, whereas the contour is rather the ideal limit toward which the sides of the apple recede in depth. Not to indicate any shape would be to deprive the objects of their identity. To trace just a single outline sacrifices depth—that is, the dimension in which the thing is presented not as spread out before us but as an inexhaustible reality full of reserves. That is why Cézanne follows the swelling of the object in modulated colors and indicates *several* outlines in blue. Rebounding among these, one's glance captures a shape that emerges from among them all, just as it does in perception. Nothing could be less arbitrary than these famous distortions which, moreover, Cézanne abandoned in his last period, after 1890, when he no longer filled his canvases with colors and when he gave up the closely-woven texture of his still lifes.

The outline should therefore be a result of the colors if the world is to be given in its true density. For the world is a mass without gaps, a system of colors across which the receding perspective, the outlines, angles, and curves are inscribed like lines of force; the spatial structure vibrates as it is formed. "The outline and the colors are no longer distinct from each other. To the extent that one paints, one outlines; the more the colors harmonize, the more the outline becomes precise. . . . When the color is at its richest, the form has reached plenitude." Cézanne does not try to use color to *suggest* the tactile sensations which would give shape and depth. These distinctions between touch and sight are unknown in primordial perception. It is only as a result of a science of the human body that we finally learn to distinguish between our senses. The lived object is not rediscovered or constructed on the basis of the contributions of the senses; rather, it presents itself to us from the start as the center from which these contributions radiate. We *see* the depth, the smoothness, the softness, the hardness of objects; Cézanne even claimed that we see their odor. If the painter is to express the world, the arrangement of his colors must carry with it this indivisible whole, or else his picture will only hint at things and will not give them in the imperious unity, the presence, the insurpassable plenitude which is for us the definition of the real. That is why each brushstroke must satisfy an infinite number of conditions. Cézanne sometimes pondered hours at a time before putting down a certain stroke, for, as Bernard said, each stroke must "contain the air, the light, the object, the composition, the character, the outline, and the style." Expressing what *exists* is an endless task.

Nor did Cézanne neglect the physiognomy of objects and faces: he simply wanted to capture it emerging from the color. Painting a face "as an object" is not to strip it of its "thought." "I realize that the painter interprets it," said Cézanne. "The painter is not an imbecile." But this interpretation should not be a reflection distinct from the act of seeing. "If I paint all the little blues and all the little maroons, I capture and convey his glance. Who gives a damn if they want to dispute how one can sadden a mouth or make a cheek smile by wedding a shaded green to a red." One's personality is seen and grasped in one's glance, which is, however, no more than a combination of colors. Other minds are given to us only as incarnate, as belonging to faces and gestures. Countering with the distinctions of soul and body, thought and vision is of no use here, for Cézanne returns to just that primordial experience from which these notions are derived and in which they are inseparable. The painter who conceptualizes and seeks the expression first misses the mystery—renewed every time we look at someone—of a person's appearing in nature. In *La Peau de chagrin* Balzac describes a "tablecloth white as a layer of newly fallen snow, upon which the place-settings rise symmetrically, crowned with blond rolls." "All through youth," said Cézanne, "I wanted to paint that, that tablecloth of new snow. . . . Now I know that one must will only to paint the place-settings rising symmetrically and the blond rolls. If I paint 'crowned' I've had it, you understand? But if I really balance and shade my place-settings and rolls as they are in nature, then you can be sure that the crowns, the snow, and all the excitement will be there too."

We live in the midst of man-made objects, among tools, in houses, streets, cities, and most of the time we see them only through the human actions which put them to use. We become used to thinking that all of this exists necessarily and unshakeably. Cézanne's painting suspends these habits of thought and reveals the base of inhuman nature upon which man has installed himself. This is why Cézanne's people are strange, as if viewed by a creature of another species. Nature itself is stripped of the attributes which make it ready for animistic communions: there is no wind in the landscape, no movement on the Lac d'Annecy; the frozen objects hesitate as at the beginning of the world. It is an unfamiliar world in which one is uncomfortable and which forbids all human effusiveness. If one looks at the work of other painters after seeing Cézanne's paintings, one feels somehow relaxed, just as conversations resumed after a period of mourning mask the absolute change and give back to the survivors their solidity. But indeed only a human being is capable of such a vision which penetrates right to the root of things beneath the imposed order of humanity. Everything indicates that animals cannot *look at* things, cannot penetrate them in expectation of nothing but the truth. Emile Bernard's statement that a realistic painter is only an ape is therefore precisely the opposite of the truth, and one sees how Cézanne was able to revive the classical definition of art: man added to nature.

Cézanne's painting denies neither science nor tradition. He went to the Louvre every day when he was in Paris. He believed that one must learn how to paint and that the geometric study of planes and forms is a necessary part of this learning process. He inquired about the geological structure of his landscapes, convinced that these abstract relationships, expressed, however, in terms of the visible world, should affect the act of painting. The rules of anatomy and design are present in each stroke of his brush just as the rules of the game underlie each stroke of a tennis match. But what motivates the painter's movement can never be simply perspective or geometry or the laws governing color, or, for that matter, particular knowledge. Motivating all the movements from which a picture gradually emerges there can be only one thing: the landscape in its totality and in its absolute fullness, precisely what Cézanne called a "motif." He would start by discovering the geological foundations of the landscape; then, according to Mme Cézanne, he would halt and look at everything with widened eyes, "germinating" with the countryside. The task before him was, first to forget all he had ever learned from science and, second *through* these sciences to recapture the structure of the landscape as an emerging organism. To do this, all the partial views one catches sight of must be welded together; all that the eye's versatility disperses must be reunited; one must, as Gasquet put it, "join the wandering hands of nature." "A minute of the world is going by which must be painted in its full reality." His meditation would suddenly be consummated: "I have my *motif,*" Cézanne would say, and he would explain that the land-scape had to be centered neither too high nor too low, caught alive in a net which would let nothing escape. Then he began to paint all parts of the painting at the same time, using patches of color to sur-round his original charcoal sketch of the geological skeleton. The picture took on fullness and density; it grew in structure and balance; it came to maturity all at once. "The landscape thinks itself in me," he said, "and I am its consciousness." Nothing could be farther from naturalism than this intuitive science. Art is not imitation, nor is it something manufactured according to the wishes of instinct or good taste. It is a process of expressing. Just as the function of words is to name—that is, to grasp the nature of what appears to us in a confused way and to place it before us as a recognizable object—so it is up to the painter, said Gasquet, to "objectify," "project," and "arrest." Words do not *look like* the things they designate; and a picture is not a *trompe-l'oeil.* Cézanne, in his own words, "wrote in painting what had never yet been painted, and turned it into painting once and for all." Forgetting the viscous, equivocal appearances, we go through them straight to the things they present. The painter recaptures and converts into visible objects what would, without him, remain walled up in the separate life of each consciousness: the vibration of appearances which is the cradle of things. Only one emotion is possible for this painter—the feeling of strangeness—and only one lyricism—that of the continual rebirth of existence.

Leonardo da Vinci's motto was persistent rigor, and all the classical works on the art of poetry tell us that the creation of art is no easy matter. Cézanne's difficulties—like those of Balzac or Mallarmé—are of a different nature. Balzac (probably taking Delacroix for his model) imagined a painter who wants to express life through the use of color alone and who keeps his masterpiece hidden. When Frenhofer dies, his friends find nothing but a chaos of colors and elusive lines, a wall of painting. Cézanne was moved to tears when he read *Le Chef-d'oeuvre inconnu* and declared that he himself was Frenhofer. The effort made by Balzac, himself obsessed with "realization," sheds light on Cézanne's. In *La Peau de chagrin* Balzac speaks of "a thought to be expressed," "a system to be built," "a science to be explained." He makes Louis Lambert, one of the abortive geniuses of the Comédie Humaine, say: "I am heading toward certain discoveries . . . , but how shall I describe the power which binds my hands, stops my mouth, and drags me in the opposite direction from my vocation?" To say that Balzac set himself to understand the society of his time is not sufficient. It is no superhuman task to describe the typical traveling salesman, to "dissect the teaching profession," or even to lay the foundations of a sociology. Once he had named the visible forces such as money and passion, once he had described the way they evidently work, Balzac wondered where it all led, what was the impetus behind it, what was the *meaning* of, for example, a Europe "whose efforts tend toward some unknown mystery of civilization." In short, he wanted to understand what interior force holds the world together and causes the proliferation of visible forms. Frenhofer had the same idea about the meaning of painting: "A hand is not simply part of the body, but the expression and continuation of a thought which must be captured and conveyed. . . . That is the real struggle! Many painters triumph instinctively, unaware of this theme of art. You draw a woman, but you do not see her." The artist is the one who arrests the spectacle in which most men take part without really seeing it and who makes it visible to the most "human" among them.

There is thus no art for pleasure's sake alone. One can invent pleasurable objects by linking old ideas in a new way and by presenting forms that have been seen before. This way of painting or speaking at second hand is what is generally meant by culture. Cézanne's or Balzac's artist is not satisfied to be a cultured animal but assimilates the culture down to its very foundations and gives it a new structure: he speaks as the first man spoke and paints as if no one had ever painted before. What he expresses cannot, therefore, be the translation of a clearly defined thought, since such clear thoughts are those which have already been uttered by ourselves or by others. "Conception" cannot precede "execution." There is nothing but a vague fever before the act of artistic expression, and only the work itself, completed and understood, is proof that there was *something* rather than *nothing* to be said. Because he returns to the source of silent and solitary experience on which culture and the exchange of ideas have been built in order to know it, the artist launches his work just as a man once launched the first word, not knowing whether it will be anything more than a shout, whether it can detach itself from the flow of individual life in which it originates and give the independent existence of an identifiable *meaning* either to the future of that same individual life or to the monads coexisting with it or to the open community of future monads. The meaning of what the artist is going to say *does not exist* anywhere—not in things, which as yet have no meaning, nor in the artist himself, in his unformulated life. It summons one away from the already constituted reason in which "cultured men" are content to shut themselves, toward a reason which contains its own origins.

To Bernard's attempt to bring him back to human intelligence, Cézanne replied: "I am oriented toward the intelligence of the *Pater Omnipotens*." He was, in any case, oriented toward the idea or the project of an infinite Logos. Cézanne's uncertainty and solitude are not essentially explained by his nervous temperament but by the purpose of his work. Heredity may well have given him rich sensations, strong emotions, and a vague feeling of anguish or mystery which upset the life he might have wished for himself and which cut him off from men; but these qualities cannot create a work of art without the expressive act, and they can no more account for the difficulties than for the virtues of that act. Cézanne's difficulties are those of the first word. He considered himself powerless because he was not omnipotent, because he was not God and wanted nevertheless to portray the world, to change it completely into a spectacle, to make *visible* how the world *touches* us. A new theory of physics can be proven because calculations connect the idea or meaning of it with standards of measurement already common to all men. It is not enough for a painter like Cézanne, an artist, or a philosopher, to create and express an idea; they must also awaken the experiences which will make their idea take root in the consciousness of others. A successful work has the strange power to teach its own lesson. The reader or spectator who follows the clues of the book or painting, by setting up stepping stones and rebounding from side to side guided by the obscure clarity of a particular style, will end by discovering what the artist wanted to communicate. The painter can do no more than construct an image; he must wait for this image to come to life for other people. When it does, the work of art will have united these separate lives; it will no longer exist in only one of them like a stubborn dream or a persistent delirium, nor will it exist only in space as a colored piece of canvas. It will dwell undivided in several minds, with a claim on every possible mind like a perennial acquisition.

Thus, the "hereditary traits," the "influences"—the accidents in Cézanne's life—are the text which nature and history gave him to decipher. They give only the literal meaning of his work. But an artist's creations, like a man's free decisions, impose on this given a figurative sense which did not pre-exist them. If Cézanne's life seems to us to carry the seeds of his work within it, it is because we get to know his work first and see the circumstances of his life through it, charging them with a meaning borrowed from that work. If the givens for Cézanne which we have been enumerating, and which we spoke of as pressing conditions, were to figure in the web of projects which he was, they could have done so only by presenting themselves to him as *what* he had to live, leaving *how* to live it undetermined. An imposed theme at the start, they become, when replaced in the existence of which they are part, the monogram and the symbol of a life which freely interpreted itself.

But let us make no mistake about this freedom. Let us not imagine an abstract force which could superimpose its effects on life's "givens" or which cause breaches in life's development. Although it is certain that a man's life does not *explain* his work, it is equally certain that the two are connected. The truth is that *this work to be done called for this life*. From the very start, the only equilibrium in Cézanne's life came from the support of his future work. His life was the projection of his future work. The work to come is hinted at, but it would be wrong to take these hints for causes, although they do make a single adventure of his life and work. Here we are beyond causes and effects; both come together in the simultaneity of an eternal Cézanne who is at the same time the formula of what he wanted to be and what he wanted to do. There is a rapport between Cézanne's schizoid temperament and his work because the work reveals a metaphysical sense of the disease: a way of seeing the world reduced to the totality of frozen appearances, with all expressive values suspended. Thus the illness ceases to be an absurd fact and a fate and becomes a general possibility of human existence. It becomes so when this existence bravely faces one of its paradoxes, the phenomenon of expression. In this sense to be schizoid and to be Cézanne come to the same thing. It is therefore impossible to separate creative liberty from that behavior, as far as possible from deliberate, already evident in Cézanne's first gestures as a child and in the way he reacted to things. The meaning Cézanne gave to objects and faces in his paintings presented itself to him in the world as it appeared to him. Cézanne simply released this meaning: it was the objects and the faces themselves as he saw them which demanded to be painted, and Cézanne simply expressed what they *wanted* to say. How, then, can any freedom be involved? True, the conditions of existence can only affect consciousness by way of a detour through the *raisons d'être* and the justifications consciousness offers to itself. We can only see what we are by looking ahead of ourselves, through the lens of our aims, and so our life always has the form of a project or of a choice and therefore seems spontaneous. But to say that we are from the start our way of aiming at a particular future would be to say that our project has already stopped with our first ways of being, that the choice has already been made for us with our first breath. If we experience no external constraints, it is because we are our whole exterior. That eternal Cézanne whom we first saw emerge and who then brought upon the human Cézanne the events and influences which seemed *exterior* to him, and who planned all that happened to him—that attitude toward men and toward the world which was not chosen through deliberation—free as it is from external causes, is it free in respect to itself? Is the choice not pushed back beyond life, and can a choice exist where there is as yet no clearly articulated field of possibilities, only one probability and, as it were, only one temptation? If I am a certain project from birth, the given and the created are indistinguishable in me, and it is therefore impossible to name a single gesture which is merely hereditary or innate, a single gesture which is not spontaneous—but also impossible to name a single gesture which is absolutely new in regard to that way of being in the world which, from the very beginning, is myself. There is no difference between saying that our life is completely constructed and that it is completely given. If there is a true liberty, it can only come about in the course of our life by our going beyond our original situation and yet not ceasing to be the same: this is the problem. Two things are certain about freedom: that we are never determined and yet that we never change, since, looking back on what we were, we can always find hints of what we have become. It is up to us to understand both these things simultaneously, as well as the way freedom dawns in us without breaking our bonds with the world.

Such bonds are always there, even and above all when we refuse to admit they exist. Inspired by the paintings of Da Vinci, Valéry described a monster of pure freedom, without mistresses, creditors, anecdotes, or adventures. No dream intervenes between himself and the things themselves; nothing taken for granted supports his certainties; and he does not read his fate in any favorite image, such as Pascal's abyss. Instead of struggling against the monsters he has understood what makes them tick, has disarmed them by his attention, and has reduced them to the state of known things. "Nothing could be more free, that is, less human, than his judgments on love and death. He hints at them in a few fragments from his notebooks: 'In the full force of its passion,' he says more or less explicitly, 'love is something so ugly that the human race would die out (*la natura si perderebbe*) if lovers could see what they were doing.' This contempt is brought out in various sketches, since the leisurely examination of certain things is, after all, the height of scorn. Thus, he now and again draws anatomical unions, frightful cross-sections of love's very act."[2] He has complete mastery of his means, he does what he wants, going at will from knowledge to life with a superior elegance. Everything he did was done knowingly, and the artistic process, like the act of breathing or living, does not go beyond his knowledge. He has discovered the "central attitude," on the basis of which it is equally possible to know, to act, and to create

[2] "Introduction à la méthode de Léonard de Vinci," *Variété,* p. 185. [English translation by Thomas McGreevy, *Introduction to the Method of Leonardo da Vinci* (London, 1929).]

because action and life, when turned into exercises, are not contrary to detached knowledge. He is an "intellectual power"; he is a "man of the mind."

Let us look more closely. For Leonardo there was no revelation; as Valéry said, no abyss yawned at his right hand. Undoubtedly true. But in "Saint Anne, the Virgin, and Child," the Virgin's cloak suggests a vulture where it touches the face of the Child. There is that fragment on the flight of birds where Da Vinci suddenly interrupts himself to pursue a childhood memory: "I seem to have been destined to be especially concerned with the vulture, for one of the first things I remember about my childhood is how a vulture came to me when I was still in the cradle, forced open my mouth with its tail, and struck me several times between the lips with it."[3] So even this transparent consciousness has its enigma, whether truly a child's memory or a fantasy of the grown man. It does not come out of nowhere, nor does it sustain itself alone. We are caught in a secret history, in a forest of symbols. One would surely protest if Freud were to decipher the riddle from what we know about the meaning of the flight of birds and about *fellatio* fantasies and their relation to the period of nursing. But it is still a fact that to the ancient Egyptians the vulture was the symbol of maternity because they believed all vultures were female and that they were impregnated by the wind. It is also a fact that the Church Fathers used this legend to refute, on the grounds of natural history, those who were unwilling to believe in a virgin birth, and it is probable that Leonardo came across the legend in the course of his endless reading. He found in it the symbol of his own fate: he was the illegitimate son of a rich notary who married the noble Donna Albiera the very year Leonardo was born. Having no children by her, he took Leonardo into his home when the boy was five. Thus Leonardo spent the first four years of his life with his mother, the deserted peasant girl; he was a child without a father, and he got to know the world in the sole company of that unhappy mother who seemed to have miraculously created him. If we now recall that he was never known to have a mistress or even to have felt anything like passion; that he was accused—but acquitted—of homosexuality; that his diary, which tells us nothing about many other, larger expenses, notes with meticulous detail the costs of

---

[3] Sigmund Freud, *Un souvenir d'enfance de Léonard de Vinci*, p. 65. [English translation by A. A. Brill, *Leonardo da Vinci: A Study in Psychosexuality* (New York, 1947).]

his mother's burial, as well as the cost of linen and clothing for two of his students—then we are on the verge of saying that Leonardo loved only one woman, his mother, and that this love left no room for anything but the platonic tenderness he felt for the young boys surrounding him. In the four decisive years of his childhood he formed a basic attachment which he had to give up when he was recalled to his father's home and into which he had poured all his resources of love and all his power of abandon. His thirst for life could only be turned toward the investigation and knowledge of the world, and, since he himself had been *"detached,"* he had to become that intellectual power, that man who was all mind, that stranger among men. Indifferent, incapable of any strong indignation, love or hate, he left his paintings unfinished to devote his time to bizarre experiments; he became a person in whom his contemporaries sensed a mystery. It was as if Leonardo had never quite grown up, as if all the places in his heart had already been spoken for, as if the spirit of investigation was a way for him to escape from life, as if he had invested all his power of assent in the first years of his life and had remained true to his childhood right to the end. His games were those of a child. Vasari tells how "he made up a wax paste and, during his walks, he would model from it very delicate animals, hollow and filled with air; when he breathed into them, they would float; when the air had escaped, they would fall to the ground. When the wine-grower from Belvedere found a very unusual lizard, Leonardo made wings for it out of the skin of other lizards and filled these wings with mercury so that they waved and quivered whenever the lizard moved; he likewise made eyes, a beard, and horns for it in the same way, tamed it, put it in a box, and used this lizard to terrify his friends."[4] He left his work unfinished, just as his father had abandoned him. He paid no heed to authority and trusted only nature and his own judgment in matters of knowledge, as is often the case with people who have not been raised in the shadow of a father's intimidating and protective power. Thus even this pure power of examination, this solitude, this curiosity—which are the essence of mind—became Leonardo's only in reference to his history. At the height of his freedom he was, *in that very freedom*, the child he had been; he was detached in one way only because he was attached in another. Becoming a pure consciousness is just another way of taking a stand about the world and other people; Leonardo learned this attitude

[4] *Ibid.,* p. 189.

in assimilating the situation which his birth and childhood had made for him. There can be no consciousness that is not sustained by its primordial involvement in life and by the manner of this involvement.

Whatever is arbitrary in Freud's *explanations* cannot in this context discredit *psychoanalytical intuition.* True, the reader is stopped more than once by the lack of evidence. Why this and not something else? The question seems all the more pressing since Freud often offers several interpretations, each symptom being "over-determined" according to him. Finally, it is obvious that a doctrine which brings in sexuality everywhere cannot, by the rules of inductive logic, establish its effectiveness anywhere, since, excluding all differential cases beforehand, it deprives itself of any counter-evidence. This is how one triumphs over psychoanalysis, but only on paper. For if the suggestions of the analyst can never be proven, neither can they be eliminated: how would it be possible to credit chance with the complex correspondences which the psychoanalyst discovers between the child and the adult? How can we deny that psychoanalysis has taught us to notice echoes, allusions, repetitions from one moment of life to another—a concatenation we would not dream of doubting if Freud had stated the theory behind it correctly? Unlike the natural sciences, psychoanalysis was not meant to give us necessary relations of cause and effect but to point to motivational relationships which are in principle simply possible. We should ot take Leonardo's fantasy of the vulture, or the infantile past which it masks, for a force which determined his future. Rather, it is like the words of the oracle, an ambiguous symbol which applies in advance to several possible chains of events. To be more precise: in every life, one's birth and one's past define categories or basic dimensions which do not impose any particular act but which can be found in all. Whether Leonardo yielded to his childhood or whether he wished to flee from it, he could never have been other than he was. The very decisions which transform us are always made in reference to a factual situation; such a situation can of course be accepted or refused, but it cannot fail to give us our impetus nor to be for us, as a situation "to be accepted" or "to be refused," the incarnation for us of the value we give to it. If it is the aim of psychoanalysis to describe this exchange between future and past and to show how each life muses over riddles whose final meaning is nowhere written down, then we have no right to demand inductive rigor from it. The psychoanalyst's hermeneutic musing, which multiplies the communications between us and ourselves, which takes sexuality as the symbol of existence and existence as symbol of sexuality, and which looks in the past for the meaning of the future and in the future for the meaning of the past, is better suited than rigorous induction to the circular movement of our lives, where the future rests on the past, the past on the future, and where everything symbolizes everything else. Psychoanalysis does not make freedom impossible; it teaches us to think of this freedom concretely, as a creative repetition of ourselves, always, in retrospect, faithful to ourselves.

Thus it is true both that the life of an author can teach us nothing and that—if we know how to interpret it—we can find everything in it, since it opens onto his work. Just as we may observe the movements of an unknown animal without understanding the law which inhabits and controls them, so Cézanne's observers did not guess the transmutations which he imposed on events and experiences; they were blind to *his* significance, to that glow from out of nowhere which surrounded him from time to time. But he himself was never at the center of himself: nine days out of ten all he saw around him was the wretchedness of his empirical life and of his unsuccessful attempts, the leftovers of an unknown party. Yet it was in the world that he had to realize his freedom, with colors upon a canvas. It was on the approval of others that he had to wait for the proof of his worth. That is the reason he questioned the picture emerging beneath his hand, why he hung on the glances other people directed toward his canvas. That is the reason he never finished working. We never get away from our life. We never see our ideas or our freedom face to face.

12. EYE AND MIND

> "What I am trying to translate to you is more mysterious; it is entwined in the very roots of being, in the impalpable source of sensations." J. Gasquet, *Cézanne*

[*1*] [1]

Science manipulates things and gives up living in them. It makes its own limited models of things; operating upon these indices or variables to effect whatever transformations are permitted by their definition, it comes face to face with the real world only at rare intervals. Science is and always has been that admirably active, ingenious, and bold way of thinking whose fundamental bias is to treat everything as though it were an object-in-general—as though it meant nothing to us and yet was predestined for our own use.

But classical science clung to a feeling for the opaqueness of the world, and it expected through its constructions to get back into the

Maurice Merleau-Ponty, "Eye and Mind," *The Primacy of Perception and Other Essays,* Part II, Ch. 5, ed. by James M. Edie, trans. by Carleton Dallery (Evanston, Illinois: Northwestern University Press, 1964), pp. 159–90. Reprinted by permission.

[1] "L'Oeil et l'esprit" was the last work Merleau-Ponty saw published. It appeared in the inaugural issue of *Art de France,* vol. I, no 1 (January, 1961). After his death it was reprinted in *Les Temps Modernes,* no. 184–85, along with seven articles devoted to him. It has now been published, in book form, by Editions Gallimard (1964). Both the *Art de France* article and the book contain illustrations chosen by Merleau-Ponty. According to Professor Claude Lefort, "L'Oeil et l'esprit" is a preliminary statement of ideas that were to be developed in the second part of the book Merleau-Ponty was writing at the time of his death—*Le visible et l'invisible* (part of which was published posthumously by Gallimard in February, 1964). The translator wishes to acknowledge his immense debt to George Downing, who spent many long hours working over the final revisions of the translation. Also, thanks are due to Michel Beaujour, Arleen B. Dallery, and Robert Reitter for their advice and encouragement.—*Trans.*

world. For this reason classical science felt obliged to seek a transcendent or transcendental foundation for its operations. Today we find—not in science but in a widely prevalent philosophy of the sciences—an entirely new approach. Constructive scientific activities see themselves and represent themselves to be autonomous, and their thinking deliberately reduces itself to a set of data-collecting techniques which it has invented. To think is thus to test out, to operate, to transform—on the condition that this activity is regulated by an experimental control that admits only the most "worked-out" phenomena, more likely produced by the apparatus than recorded by it. From this state of affairs arise all sorts of vagabond endeavors.

Today more than ever, science is sensitive to intellectual fads and fashions. When a model has succeeded in one order of problems, it is tried out everywhere else. At the present time, for example, our embryology and biology are full of "gradients." Just how these differ from what tradition called "order" or "totality" is not at all clear. This question, however, is not raised; it is not even permitted. The gradient is a net we throw out to sea, without knowing what we will haul back in it. Or again, it is the slender twig upon which unforeseeable crystallizations will form. Certainly this freedom of operation will serve well to overcome many a pointless dilemma—provided only that we ask from time to time why the apparatus works in one place and fails in others. For all its fluency, science must nevertheless understand itself; it must see itself as a construction based on a brute, existent world and not claim for its blind operations that constituting value which "concepts of nature" were able to have in an idealist philosophy. To say that the world is, by nominal definition, the object x of our operations is to treat the scientist's knowledge as if it were absolute, as if everything that is and has been was meant only to enter the laboratory. Thinking "operationally" has become a sort of absolute artificialism, such as we see in the ideology of cybernetics, where human creations are derived from a natural information process, itself conceived on the model of human machines. If this kind of thinking were to extend its reign to man and history; if, pretending to ignore what we know of them through our own situations, it were to set out to construct man and history on the basis of a few abstract indices (as a decadent psychoanalysis and a decadent culturalism have done in the United States)—then, since man really becomes the *manipulandum* he takes himself to be, we enter into a cultural regimen where there is neither truth nor falsity concerning man and history, into a sleep, or a nightmare, from which there is no awakening.

Scientific thinking, a thinking which looks on from above, and thinks of the object-in-general, must return to the "there is" which underlies it; to the site, the soil of the sensible and opened world such as it is in our life and for our body—not that possible body which we may legitimately think of as an information machine but that actual body I call mine, this sentinel standing quietly at the command of my words and my acts. Further, *associated bodies* must be brought forward along with my body—the "others," not merely as my congeners, as the zoologist says, but the others who haunt me and whom I haunt; the "others" along *with* whom I haunt a single, present, and actual Being as no animal ever haunted those beings of his own species, locale, or habitat. In this primordial historicity, science's agile and improvisatory thought will learn to ground itself upon things themselves and upon itself, and will once more become philosophy. . . .

But art, especially painting, draws upon this fabric of brute meaning which activism [or operationalism—*Trans.*] would prefer to ignore. Art and only art does so in full innocence. From the writer and the philosopher, in contrast, we want opinions and advice. We will not allow them to hold the world suspended. We want them to take a stand; they cannot waive the responsibilities of men who speak. Music, at the other extreme, is too far beyond the world and the designatable to depict anything but certain outlines of Being—its ebb and flow, its growth, its upheavals, its turbulence.

Only the painter is entitled to look at everything without being obliged to appraise what he sees. For the painter, we might say, the watchwords of knowledge and action lose their meaning and force. Political regimes which denounce "degenerate" painting rarely destroy paintings. They hide them, and one senses here an element of "one never knows" amounting almost to a recognition. The reproach of escapism is seldom aimed at the painter; we do not hold it against Cézanne that he lived hidden away at Estaque during the war of 1870. And we recall with respect his "C'est effrayant, la vie," even when the lowliest student, ever since Nietzsche, would flatly reject philosophy if it did not teach how to live fully [*à être de grands vivants*]. It is as if in the painter's calling there were some urgency above all other claims on him. Strong or frail in life, he is incontestably sovereign in his own rumination of the world. With no other technique than what his eyes and hands discover in seeing and painting, he persists in drawing from this world, with its din of history's glories and scandals, *canvases* which will hardly add to the angers or the hopes of man—and no one complains.[2]

What, then, is this secret science which he has or which he seeks? That dimension which lets Van Gogh say he must go "further on"? What is this fundamental of painting, perhaps of all culture?

[2]

The painter "takes his body with him," says Valéry. Indeed we cannot imagine how a *mind* could paint. It is by lending his body to the world that the artist changes the world into paintings. To understand these transubstantiations we must go back to the working, actual body—not the body as a chunk of space or a bundle of functions but that body which is an intertwining of vision and movement.

I have only to see something to know how to reach it and deal with it, even if I do not know how this happens in the nervous machine. My mobile body makes a difference in the visible world, being a part of it; that is why I can steer it through the visible. Conversely, it is just as true that vision is attached to movement. We see only what we look at. What would vision be without eye movement? And how could the movement of the eyes bring things together if the movement were blind? If it were only a reflex? If it did not have its antennae, its clairvoyance? If vision were not prefigured in it?

In principle all my changes of place figure in a corner of my landscape; they are recorded on the map of the visible. Everything I see is in principle within my reach, at least within reach of my sight, and is marked upon the map of the "I can." Each of the two maps is complete. The visible world and the world of my motor projects are each total parts of the same Being.

This extraordinary overlapping, which we never think about sufficiently, forbids us to conceive of vision as an operation of thought that would set up before the mind a picture or a representation of the world, a world of immanence and of ideality. Immersed in the visible by his

[2] Il est là, fort ou faible dans la vie, mais souverain sans conteste dans sa rumination du monde, sans autre "technique" que celle que ses yeux et ses mains se donnent à force de voir, à force de peindre, acharné à tirer de ce monde où sonnent les scandales et les gloires de l'histoire des *toiles* qui n'ajouteront guère aux colères ni aux espoirs des hommes, et personne ne murmure.

body, itself visible, the see-er does not appropriate what he sees; he merely approaches it by looking, he opens himself to the world. And on its side, this world of which he is a part is not *in itself,* or matter. My movement is not a decision made by the mind, an absolute doing which would decree, from the depths of a subjective retreat, some change of place miraculously executed in extended space. It is the natural consequence and the maturation of my vision. I say of a thing that it is moved; but my body moves itself, my movement deploys itself. It is not ignorant of itself; it is not blind for itself; it radiates from a self. . . .

The enigma is that my body simultaneously sees and is seen. That which looks at all things can also look at itself and recognize, in what it sees, the "other side" of its power of looking. It sees itself seeing; it touches itself touching; it is visible and sensitive for itself. It is not a self through transparence, like thought, which only thinks its object by assimilating it, by constituting it, by transforming it into thought. It is a self through confusion, narcissism, through inherence of the one who sees in that which he sees, and through inherence of sensing in the sensed—a self, therefore, that is caught up in things, that has a front and a back, a past and a future. . . .

This initial paradox cannot but produce others. Visible and mobile, my body is a thing among things; it is caught in the fabric of the world, and its cohesion is that of a thing. But because it moves itself and sees, it holds things in a circle around itself.[3] Things are an annex or prolongation of itself; they are incrusted into its flesh, they are part of its full definition; the world is made of the same stuff as the body. This way of turning things around [*ces renversements*], these antinomies,[4] are different ways of saying that vision happens among, or is caught in, things—in that place where something visible undertakes to see, becomes visible for itself by virtue of the sight of things; in that place where there persists, like the mother water in crystal, the undividedness [*l'indivision*] of the sensing and the sensed.

This interiority no more precedes the material arrangement of the human body than it results from it. What if our eyes were made in such a way as to prevent our seeing any part of our body, or if some baneful arrangement of the body were to let us move our hands over things, while preventing us from touching our own body? Or what if,

---

[3] Cf. *Le visible et l'invisible* (Paris, 1964), pp. 273, 308–11.—*Trans.*
[4] See *Signes* (Paris, 1960), pp. 210, 222–23, especially the footnotes, for a clarification of the "circularity" at issue here.—*Trans.*

like certain animals, we had lateral eyes with no cross blending of visual fields? Such a body would not reflect itself; it would be an almost adamantine body, not really flesh, not really the body of a human being. There would be no humanity.

But humanity is not produced as the effect of our articulations or by the way our eyes are implanted in us (still less by the existence of mirrors which could make our entire body visible to us). These contingencies and others like them, without which mankind would not exist, do not by simple summation bring it about that there *is* a single man.

The body's animation is not the assemblage or juxtaposition of its parts. Nor is it a question of a mind or spirit coming down from somewhere else into an automaton; this would still suppose that the body itself is without an inside and without a "self." There is a human body when, between the seeing and the seen, between touching and the touched, between one eye and the other, between hand and hand, a blending of some sort takes place—when the spark is lit between sensing and sensible, lighting the fire that will not stop burning until some accident of the body will undo what no accident would have sufficed to do. . . .

Once this strange system of exchanges is given, we find before us all the problems of painting. These exchanges illustrate the enigma of the body, and this enigma justifies them. Since things and my body are made of the same stuff, vision must somehow take place in them; their manifest visibility must be repeated in the body by a secret visibility. "Nature is on the inside," says Cézanne. Quality, light, color, depth, which are there before us, are there only because they awaken an echo in our body and because the body welcomes them.

Things have an internal equivalent in me; they arouse in me a carnal formula of their presence. Why shouldn't these [correspondences] in their turn give rise to some [external] visible shape in which anyone else would recognize those motifs which support his own inspection of the world?[5] Thus there appears a "visible" of the second power, a carnal essence or icon of the first. It is not a faded copy, a *trompe-l'oeil,* or another *thing.* The animals painted on the walls of Lascaux

[5] Cet équivalent interne, cette formule charnelle de leur présence que les choses suscitent en moi, pourquoi à leur tour ne susciteraient-ils pas un tracé, visible encore, où tout autre regard retrouvera les motifs qui soutiennent son inspection du monde?

are not there in the same way as the fissures and limestone formations. But they are not *elsewhere*. Pushed forward here, held back there, held up by the wall's mass they use so adroitly, they spread around the wall without ever breaking from their elusive moorings in it. I would be at great pains to say *where* is the painting I am looking at. For I do not look at it as I do at a thing; I do not fix it in its place. My gaze wanders in it as in the halos of Being. It is more accurate to say that I see according to it, or with it, than that I *see it*.

The word "image" is in bad repute because we have thoughtlessly believed that a design was a tracing, a copy, a second thing, and that the mental image was such a design, belonging among our private bric-a-brac. But if in fact it is nothing of the kind, then neither the design nor the painting belongs to the in-itself any more than the image does. They are the inside of the outside and the outside of the inside, which the duplicity of feeling [*le sentir*] makes possible and without which we would never understand the quasi presence and imminent visibility which make up the whole problem of the imaginary. The picture and the actor's mimicry are not devices to be borrowed from the real world in order to signify prosaic things which are absent. For the imaginary is much nearer to, and much farther away from, the actual—nearer because it is in my body as a diagram of the life of the actual, with all its pulp and carnal obverse [*son envers charnel*] exposed to view for the first time. In this sense, Giacometti[6] says energetically, "What interests me in all paintings is resemblance— that is, what is resemblance for me: something which makes me discover more of the world." And the imaginary is much farther away from the actual because the painting is an analogue or likeness only according to the body; because it does *not* present the *mind* with an occasion to rethink the constitutive relations of things; because, rather, it offers to our *sight* [*regard*], so that it might join with them, the inward traces of vision, and because it offers to vision its inward tapestries, the imaginary texture of the real.[7]

Shall we say, then, that we look out from the inside, that there is a third eye which sees the paintings and even the mental images, as we used to speak of a third ear which grasped messages from the outside

[6] G. Charbonnier, *Le monologue du peintre* (Paris, 1959), p. 172.
[7] Beaucoup plus loin, puisque le tableau n'est un analogue que selon le corps, qu'il n'offre pas à l'esprit une occasion de repenser les rapports constitutifs des choses, mais au regard, pour qu'il les épouse, les traces de la vision du dedans, à la vision ce qui la tapissee intérieurement, la texture imaginaire du réel.

through the noises they caused inside us? But how would this help us when the real problem is to understand how it happens that our fleshly eyes are already much more than receptors for light rays, colors, and lines? They are computers of the world, which have the gift of the visible as it was once said that the inspired man had the gift of tongues. Of course this gift is earned by exercise; it is not in a few months, or in solitude, that a painter comes into full possession of his vision. But that is not the question; precocious or belated, spontaneous or cultivated in museums, his vision in any event learns only by seeing and learns only from itself. The eye sees the world, sees what inade-quacies [*manques*] keep the world from being a painting, sees what keeps a painting from being itself, sees—on the palette—the colors awaited by the painting, and sees, once it is done, the painting that answers to all these inadequacies just as it sees the paintings of others as other answers to other inadequacies.

It is no more possible to make a restrictive inventory of the visible than it is to catalogue the possible usages of a language or even its vocabulary and devices. The eye is an instrument that moves itself, a means which invents its own ends; it is *that which* has been moved by some impact of the world, which it then restores to the visible through the offices of an agile hand.

In whatever civilization it is born, from whatever beliefs, motives, or thoughts, no matter what ceremonies surround it—and even when it appears devoted to something else—from Lascaux to our time, pure or impure, figurative or not, painting celebrates no other enigma but that of visibility.

What we have just said amounts to a truism. The painter's world is a visible world, nothing but visible: a world almost demented because it is complete when it is yet only partial. Painting awakens and carries to its highest pitch a delirium which is vision itself, for to see is *to have at a distance;* painting spreads this strange possession to all aspects of Being, which must in some fashion become visible in order to enter into the work of art. When, apropos of Italian painting, the young Berenson spoke of an evocation of tactile values, he could hardly have been more mistaken; painting evokes nothing, least of all the tactile. What it does is much different, almost the inverse. It gives visible existence to what profane vision believes to be invisible; thanks to it we do not need a "muscular sense" in order to possess the voluminosity of the world. This voracious vision, reaching beyond the "visual givens," opens upon a texture of Being of which the discrete sensorial messages are only the punctuations or the caesurae. The eye lives in this texture as a man lives in his house.

Let us remain within the visible in the narrow and prosaic sense. The painter, whatever he is, *while he is painting* practices a magical theory of vision. He is obliged to admit that objects before him pass into him or else that, according to Malebranche's sarcastic dilemma, the mind goes out through the eyes to wander among objects; for the painter never ceases adjusting his clairvoyance to them. (It makes no difference if he does not paint from "nature"; he paints, in any case, because he has seen, because the world has at least once emblazoned in him the ciphers of the visible.) He must affirm, as one philosopher has said, that vision is a mirror or concentration of the universe or that, in another's words, the *idios kosmos* opens by virtue of vision upon a *koinos kosmos;* in short, that the same thing is both out there in the world and here in the heart of vision—the same or, if one prefers, a *similar* thing, but according to an efficacious similarity which is the parent, the genesis, the metamorphosis of Being in his vision. It is the mountain itself which from out there makes itself seen by the painter; it is the mountain that he interrogates with his gaze.

What exactly does he ask of it? To unveil the means, visible and not otherwise, by which it makes itself a mountain before our eyes. Light, lighting, shadows, reflections, color, all the objects of his quest are not altogether real objects; like ghosts, they have only visual existence. In fact they exist only at the threshold of profane vision; they are not seen by everyone. The painter's gaze asks them what they do to suddenly cause something to be and to be *this* thing, what they do to compose this worldly talisman and to make us see the visible.

We see that the hand pointing to us in *The Nightwatch* is truly there only when we see that its shadow on the captain's body presents it simultaneously in profile. The spatiality of the captain lies at the meeting place of two lines of sight which are incompossible and yet together. Everyone with eyes has at some time or other witnessed this play of shadows, or something like it, and has been made by it to see a space and the things included therein. But it works in us without us; it hides itself in making the object visible. To see the object, it is necessary *not* to see the play of shadows and light around it. The visible in the profane sense forgets its premises; it rests upon a total visibility which is to be re-created and which liberates the phantoms captive in it. The moderns, as we know, have liberated many others; they have added many a blank note [*note sourde*] to the official gamut of our means of seeing. But the interrogation of painting in any case looks toward this secret and feverish genesis of things in our body.

And so it is not a question asked of someone who doesn't know by someone who does—the schoolmaster's question. The question comes from one who does not know, and it is addressed to a vision, a seeing, which knows everything and which we do not make, for it makes itself in us. Max Ernst (with the surrealists) says rightly, "Just as the role of the poet since [Rimbaud's] famous *Lettre du voyant* consists in writing under the dictation of what is being thought, of what articulates itself in him, the role of the painter is to grasp and project what is seen in him."[8] The painter lives in fascination. The actions most proper to him—those gestures, those paths which he alone can trace and which will be revelations to others (because the others do not lack what he lacks or in the same way)—to him they seem to emanate from the things themselves, like the patterns of the constellations.

Inevitably the roles between him and the visible are reversed. That is why so many painters have said that things look at them. As André Marchand says, after Klee: "In a forest, I have felt many times over that it was not I who looked at the forest. Some days I felt that the trees were looking at me, were speaking to me. . . . I was there, listening. . . . I think that the painter must be penetrated by the universe and not want to penetrate it. . . . I expect to be inwardly submerged, buried. Perhaps I paint to break out."[9]

We speak of "inspiration," and the word should be taken literally. There really is inspiration and expiration of Being, action and passion so slightly discernible that it becomes impossible to distinguish between what sees and what is seen, what paints and what is painted.

It can be said that a human is born at the instant when something that was only virtually visible, inside the mother's body, becomes at one and the same time visible for itself and for us. The painter's vision is a continued birth.

In paintings themselves we could seek a figured philosophy[10] of vision—its iconography, perhaps. It is no accident, for example, that

[8] Charbonnier, *op. cit.,* p. 34.
[9] *Ibid.,* pp. 143–45.
[10] ". . . une philosophie figurée . . ." Cf. Bergson (Ravaisson), note 46 below.—*Trans.*

frequently in Dutch paintings (as in many others) an empty interior is
"digested" by the "round eye of the mirror."[11] This prehuman way of
seeing things is the painter's way. More completely than lights, shadows, and reflections, the mirror image anticipates, within things, the
labor of vision. Like all other technical objects, such as signs and tools,
the mirror arises upon the open circuit [that goes] from seeing body to
visible body. Every technique is a "technique of the body." A technique
outlines and amplifies the metaphysical structure of our flesh. The
mirror appears because I am seeing-visible [*voyant-visible*], because
there is a reflexivity of the sensible; the mirror translates and repro-
duces that reflexivity. My outside completes itself in and through the
sensible. Everything I have that is most secret goes into this *visage*,
this face, this flat and closed entity about which my reflection in the
water has already made me puzzle. Schilder[12] observes that, smoking a
pipe before a mirror, I feel the sleek, burning surface of the wood not
only where my fingers are but also in those ghostlike fingers, those
merely visible fingers inside the mirror. The mirror's ghost lies outside
my body, and by the same token my own body's "invisibility" can invest
the other bodies I see.[13] Hence my body can assume segments derived
from the body of another, just as my substance passes into them;
man is mirror for man. The mirror itself is the instrument of a universal magic that changes things into a spectacle, spectacles into things,
myself into another, and another into myself. Artists have often
mused upon mirrors because beneath this "mechanical trick," they
recognized, just as they did in the case of the trick of perspective,[14] the
metamorphosis of seeing and seen which defines both our flesh and
the painter's vocation. This explains why they have so often liked to
draw themselves in the act of painting (they still do—witness Matisse's

[11] P. Claudel, *Introduction à la peinture hollandaise* (Paris, 1935).
[12] P. Schilder, *The Image and Appearance of the Human Body* (London, 1935;
New York, 1950), pp. 223–24. [". . . the body-image is not confined to the
borderlines of one's own body. It transgresses them in the mirror. There is a
body-image outside ourselves, and it is remarkable that primitive peoples even
ascribe a substantial existence to the picture in the mirror" (p. 278). Schilder's
earlier, shorter study, *Das Körperschema* (Berlin, 1923), is cited several times in
The Structure of Behavior and in *Phenomenology of Perception*. Schilder's later
work is of especial interest with regard to Merleau-Ponty's own elaborations of
the meaning of the human body; it is worth examining for that reason, as well as
for the chance it provides to discern some fundamental coincidences between
Merleau-Ponty and certain American pragmatists.]
[13] Cf. Schilder, *Image*, pp. 281–82.—*Trans.*
[14] Robert Delaunay, *Du cubisme à l'art abstrait* (Paris, 1957).

drawings), adding to what *they* saw then, what *things* saw of them. It is as if they were claiming that there is a total or absolute vision, outside of which there is nothing and which closes itself over them. Where in the realm of the understanding can we place these occult operations, together with the potions and idols they concoct? What can we call them? Consider, as Sartre did in *Nausea,* the smile of a long-dead king which continues to exist and to reproduce itself [*de se produire et de se reproduire*] on the surface of a canvas. It is too little to say that it is there as an image or essence; it is there as itself, as that which was always most alive about it, even now as I look at the painting. The "world's instant" that Cézanne wanted to paint, an instant long since passed away, is still thrown at us by his paintings.[15] His Mount Saint Victor is made and remade from one end of the world to the other in a way that is different from, but no less energetic than, that of the hard rock above Aix. Essence and existence, imaginary and real, visible and invisible—a painting mixes up all our categories in laying out its oneiric universe of carnal essences, of effective likenesses, of mute meanings.

[3]

How crystal clear everything would be in our philosophy if only we could exorcise these specters, make illusions or object-less perceptions out of them, keep them on the edge of a world that doesn't equivocate! Descartes' *Dioptric* is an attempt to do just that. It is the breviary of a thought that wants no longer to abide in the visible and so decides to construct the visible according to a model-in-thought. It is worthwhile to remember this attempt and its failure.

Here there is no concern to cling to vision. The problem is to know "how it happens," but only so far as it is necessary to invent, whenever the need arises, certain "artificial organs"[16] which correct it. We are to reason not so much upon the light we see as upon the light which, from outside, enters our eyes and commands our vision. And for that we are to rely upon "two or three comparisons which help us to conceive it

---

[15] "A minute in the world's life passes! to paint it in its reality! and forget everything for that. To become that minute, be the sensitive plate, . . . give the image of what we see, forgetting everything that has appeared before our time. . . ." Cézanne, quoted in B. Dorival, *Paul Cézanne,* trans. H. H. A. Thackthwaite (London, 1948), p. 101.—*Trans.*

[16] Descartes, *La Dioptrique,* Discours VII [conclusion]. Édition Adam et Tannery, VI, p. 165.

[light]" in such a way as to explain its known properties and to deduce others.[17] The question being so formulated, it is best to think of light as an action by contact—not unlike the action of things upon the blind man's cane. The blind, says Descartes, "see with their hands."[18] The Cartesian concept of vision is modeled after the sense of touch.

At one swoop, then, he removes action at a distance and relieves us of that ubiquity which is the whole problem of vision (as well as its peculiar virtue). Why should we henceforth puzzle over reflections and mirrors? These unreal duplications are a class of things; they are real effects like a ball's bouncing. If the reflection resembles the thing itself, it is because this reflection acts upon the eyes more or less as a thing would. It deceives the eye by engendering a perception which has no object but which does not affect our idea of the world. In the world there is the thing itself, and outside this thing itself there is that other thing which is only reflected light rays and which happens to have an ordered correspondence with the real thing; there are two individuals, then, bound together externally by causality. As far as the thing and its mirror image are concerned, their resemblance is only an external denomination; the resemblance belongs to thought. [What for us is] the "cross-eyed" [louche] relationship of resemblance is—in the things —a clear relationship of projection.

A Cartesian does not see *himself* in the mirror; he sees a dummy, an "outside," which, he has every reason to believe, other people see in the very same way but which, no more for himself than for others, is not a body in the flesh. His "image" in the mirror is an effect of the mechanics of things. If he recognizes himself in it, if he thinks it "looks like him," it is his thought that weaves this connection. The mirror image is nothing that belongs to him.

Icons lose their powers.[19] As vividly as an etching "represents" forests, towns, men, battles, storms, it does not resemble them. It is only a bit of ink put down here and there on the paper. A figure flattened down onto a plane surface scarcely retains the forms of things; it is a deformed figure that *ought* to be deformed—the square becomes a lozenge, the circle an oval—in order to represent the object. It is an

[17] *Ibid.*, Discours I. Adam et Tannery, p. 83. [*Oeuvres et lettres de Descartes,* ed. André Bridoux, Edition Pléiade, p. 181. Page references from the Bridoux selections have been added in the belief that this volume is more widely accessible today than the Adam and Tannery complete edition.]
[18] *Ibid.*, Adam et Tannery, p. 84. [Bridoux, p. 182.]
[19] This paragraph continues the exposition of the *Dioptric.—Trans.*

image only as long as it does not resemble its object. If not through resemblance, how, then, does it act? It "excites our thought" to "conceive," as do signs and words "which in no way resemble the things they signify."[20] The etching gives us sufficient indices, unequivocal means for forming an idea of the thing represented that does not come from the icon itself; rather, it arises in us as it is "occasioned." The magic of intentional species—the old idea of effective resemblance as suggested by mirrors and paintings—loses its final argument if the entire potency of a painting is that of a text to be read, a text totally free of promiscuity between the seeing and the seen. We need no longer understand how a painting of things in the body could make them felt in the soul—an impossible task, since the very resemblance between this painting and those things would have to be seen in turn, since we would "have to have other eyes in our head with which to apperceive it,"[21] and since the problem of vision remains whole even when we have given ourselves these likenesses which wander between us and the real things. What the light designs upon our eyes, and thence upon our brain, does not resemble the visible world any more than etchings do. There is nothing more going on between the things and the eyes, and the eyes and vision, than between the things and the blind man's hands, and between his hands and thoughts.

Vision is not the metamorphosis of things themselves into the sight of them; it is not a matter of things' belonging simultaneously to the huge, real world and the small, private world. It is a thinking that deciphers strictly the signs given within the body. Resemblance is the result of perception, not its mainspring. More surely still, the mental image, the clairvoyance which renders present to us what is absent, is nothing like an insight penetrating into the heart of Being. It is still a thought relying upon bodily indices, this time insufficient, which are made to say more than they mean. Nothing is left of the oneiric world of analogy. . . .

What interests us in these famous analyses is that they make us aware of the fact that any theory of painting is a metaphysics. Descartes does not say much about painting, and one might think it unfair on our part to make an issue out of a few pages on copper engravings.

---

[20] *Ibid.,* Discours IV. Adam et Tannery, pp. 112–14. [Bridoux, pp. 203–4; in English, *Descartes: Philosophical Writings,* ed. and trans. N. Kemp Smith, Modern Library Edition, pp. 145–47.]
[21] *Ibid.,* p. 130. [Bridoux, p. 217; Smith, p. 148.]

And yet even if he speaks of them only in passing, that in itself is significant. Painting for him is not a central operation contributing to the definition of our access to Being; it is a mode or a variant of thinking, where thinking is canonically defined according to intellectual possession and evidence. It is this option that is expressed within the little he does say, and a closer study of painting would lead to another philosophy. It is significant too that when he speaks of "pictures" he takes line drawings as typical. We shall see that all painting is present in each of its modes of expression; one drawing, even a single line, can embrace all its bold potential.

But what Descartes likes most in copper engravings is that they preserve the forms of objects, or at least give us sufficient signs of their forms. They present the object by its outside, or its envelope. If he had examined that other, deeper opening upon things given us by secondary qualities, especially color, then—since there is no ordered or projective relationship between them and the true properties of things and since we understand their message all the same—he would have found himself faced with the problem of a conceptless universality and a conceptless opening upon things. He would have been obliged to find out how the indecisive murmur of colors can present us with things, forests, storms—in short the world; obliged, perhaps, to integrate perspective, as a particular case, with a more ample ontological power. But for him it goes without saying that color is an ornament, mere coloring [*coloriage*], and that the real power of painting lies in design, whose power in turn rests upon the ordered relationship existing between it and space-in-itself as taught to us by perspective-projection. Pascal is remembered for speaking of the frivolity of paintings which attach us to images whose originals would not touch us; this is a Cartesian opinion. For Descartes it is unarguably evident that one can paint only existing things, that their existence consists in being extended, and that design, or line drawing, alone makes painting possible by making the representation of extension possible. Thus painting is only an artifice which presents to our eyes a projection similar to that which the things themselves in ordinary perception would and do inscribe in our eyes. A painting makes us see in the same way in which we actually see the thing itself, even though the thing is absent. Especially it makes us see a *space* where there is none.[22]

[22] The system of means by which painting makes us see is a scientific matter. Why, then, do we not methodically produce perfect images of the world, arriving

The picture is a flat thing contriving to give us what we would see in the [actual] presence of "diversely contoured" things, by offering sufficient diacritical signs of the missing dimension, according to height and width.[23] Depth is a *third dimension* derived from the other two.

It will pay us to dwell for a moment upon this third dimension. It has, first of all, something paradoxical about it. I see objects which hide each other and which consequently I do not see; each one stands behind the other. I see it [the third dimension] and it is not visible, since it goes toward things from, as starting point, this body to which I myself am fastened. But the mystery here is a false one. I don't really see it [the third dimension], or if I do, it is only another *size* [measured by height and width]. On the line which lies between my eyes and the horizon, the first [vertical] plane forever hides all the others, and if from side to side I think I see things spread out in order before me, it is because they do not completely hide each other. Thus I see each thing to be outside the others, according to some measure otherwise reckoned [*autrement compté*].[24] We are always on this side of space or beyond it entirely. It is never the case that things really *are* one behind the other. The fact that things overlap or are hidden does not enter into their definition, and expresses only my incomprehensible solidarity with one of them—my body. And whatever might be positive in these facts, they are only thoughts that I formulate and not attributes of the things. I know that at this very moment another man, situated elsewhere—or better, God, who is everywhere—could penetrate their "hiding place" and see them openly deployed. Either what I call depth is nothing, or else it is my participation in a Being without restriction, a participation primarily in the being of space beyond every [particular] point of view. Things encroach upon one another *because each is outside of the others*. The proof of this is that I can see depth in a painting which everyone agrees has none and which organizes for me an illusion of an illusion. . . . This two-dimensional being,[25] which makes me see another [dimension], is a being that is opened up [*troué*] —as the men of the Renaissance said, a window. . . .

---

at a universal art purged of personal art, just as the universal language would free us of all the confused relationships that lurk in existent languages?
[23] *Dioptrique,* Discours IV, *loc. cit.* [Note 20 above.]
[24] Discours V of the *Dioptrique,* especially Descartes' diagrams, helps considerably to clarify this compressed passage.—*Trans.*
[25] That is, the painting.—*Trans.*

But in the last analysis the window opens only upon those *partes extra partes,* upon height and width seen merely from another angle—upon the absolute positivity of Being.

It is this identity of Being, or this space without hiding places which in each of its points is only what it is, neither more nor less, that underlies the analysis of copper engravings. Space is in-itself; rather, it is the in-itself *par excellence.* Its definition is *to be* in itself. Every point of space is and is thought to be right where it is—one here, another there; space is the evidence of the "where." Orientation, polarity, envelopment are, in space, derived phenomena inextricably bound to my presence. *Space* remains absolutely in itself, everywhere equal to itself, homogeneous; its dimensions, for example, are interchangeable.

Like all classical ontologies, this one builds certain properties of beings into a structure of Being. Reversing Leibniz's remark, we might say that in doing this, it is true and false: true in what it denies and false in what it affirms. Descartes' space is true over against a too empirical thought which dares not construct. It was necessary first to idealize space, to conceive of that being—perfect in its genus, clear, manageable, and homogeneous—which our thinking glides over without a vantage point of its own: a being which thought reports entirely in terms of three rectangular dimensions. This done, we were enabled eventually to find the limits of construction, to understand that space does not have three dimensions or more or fewer, as an animal has either four or two feet, and to understand that the three dimensions are taken by different systems of measurement from a single dimensionality, a polymorphous Being, which justifies all without being fully expressed by any. Descartes was right in setting space free. His mistake was to erect it into a positive being, outside all points of view, beyond all latency and all depth, having no true thickness [*épaisseur*].

He was right also in taking his inspiration from the perspectival techniques of the Renaissance; they encouraged painting to freely produce experiences of depth and, in general, presentations of Being. These techniques were false only in so far as they pretended to bring an end to painting's quest and history, to found once and for all an exact and infallible art of painting. As Panofsky has shown concerning the men of the Renaissance,[26] this enthusiasm was not without bad faith. The theoreticians tried to forget the spherical visual field of the ancients,

---

[26] E. Panofsky, *Die Perspektive als symbolische Form,* in *Vorträge der Bibliotek Warburg,* IV (1924–25).

their angular perspective which relates the apparent size not to distance but to the angle from which we see the object. They wanted to forget what they disdainfully called the *perspectiva naturalis,* or *communis,* in favor of a *perspectiva artificialis* capable in principle of founding an exact construction. To accredit this myth, they went so far as to expurgate Euclid, omitting from their translations that eighth theorem which bothered them so much. But the painters, on the other hand, knew from experience that no technique of perspective is an exact solution and that there is no projection of the existing world which respects it in all aspects and deserves to become the fundamental law of painting. They knew too that linear perspective was so far from being an ultimate breakthrough that, on the contrary, it opens several pathways for painting. For example, the Italians took the way of representing the object, but the northern painters discovered and worked out the formal technique of *Hochraum, Nahraum,* and *Schrägraum.* Thus plane projection does not always provoke our thought to reach the true form of things, as Descartes believed. Beyond a certain degree of deformation, it refers back, on the contrary, to our own vantage point. And the painted objects are left to retreat into a remoteness out of reach of all thought. Something in space escapes our attempts to look at it from "above."

The truth is that no means of expression, once mastered, resolves the problems of painting or transforms it into a technique. For no symbolic form ever functions as a stimulus. Wherever it has been put to work and has acted, has *gone* to work, it has been put to work and has acted with the entire context of the *oeuvre,* and not in the slightest by means of a *trompe-l'oeil.* The *Stilmoment* never gets rid of the *Wermoment.*[27] The language of painting is never "instituted by nature"; it is to be made and remade over and over again. The perspective of the Renaissance is no infallible "gimmick." It is only a particular case, a date, a moment in a poetic information of the world which continues after it.

Yet Descartes would not have been Descartes if he had thought to *eliminate* the enigma of vision. There is no vision without thought. But *it is not enough* to think in order to see. Vision is a conditioned thought; it is born "as occasioned" by what happens in the body; it is "incited" to think by the body. It does not *choose* either to be or not to be or to think this thing or that. It has to carry in its heart that heavi-

[27] *Ibid.*

ness, that dependence which cannot come to it by some intrusion from outside. Such bodily events are "instituted by nature" in order to bring us to see this thing or that. The thinking that belongs to vision functions according to a program and a law which it has not given itself. It does not possess its own premises; it is not a thought altogether present and actual; there is in its center a mystery of passivity.

As things stand, then, everything we say and think of vision has to make a *thought* of it. When, for example, we wish to understand how we see the way objects are situated, we have no other recourse than to suppose the soul to be capable, knowing where the parts of its body are, of "transferring its attention from there" to all the points of space that lie in the prolongation of [i.e., beyond] the bodily members.[28] But so far this is only a "model" of the event. For the question is, how does the soul know this space, its own body's, which it extends toward things, this primary *here* from which all the *there's* will come? This space is not, like them, just another mode or specimen of the extended; it is the place of the body the soul calls "mine," a place the soul inhabits. The body it animates is not, for it, an object among objects, and it does not derive from the body all the rest of space as an implied premise. The soul thinks with reference to the body, not with reference to itself, and space, or exterior distance, is stipulated as well within the natural pact that unites them. If for a certain degree of accommodation and eye convergence the soul takes note of a certain distance, the thought which draws the second relationship from the first is as if immemorially enrolled in our internal "works" [*fabrique*]. "Usually this comes about without our reflecting upon it—just as, when we clasp a body with our hand, we conform the hand to the size and shape of the body and thereby sense the body, without having need to think of those movements of the hand."[29] For the soul, the body is both natal space

[28] Descartes *op. cit.,* Adam et Tannery, VI, p. 135 [Bridoux, p. 220; Smith, p. 154. Here is Smith's translation of the passage under discussion: "Our knowledge of it (the situation of an object) does not depend on any image or action which comes to us from the object, but solely on the situation of the small parts of the brain whence the nerves take their origin. For this situation—a situation which changes with every change however small in the points at which these nerve-fibers are located—is instituted by nature in order to secure, not only that the mind be aware of the location of each part of the body which it animates, relatively to all the others, but also that it be able to transfer its attention to all the positions contained in the straight line that can be imaged as drawn from the extremity of each of these parts, and as prolonged to infinity."]

[29] *Ibid.,* Adam et Tannery, p. 137. [Bridoux, p. 222; Smith, p. 155. Smith's translation is given here.]

and matrix of every other existing space. Thus vision divides itself. There is the vision upon which I reflect; I cannot think it except *as* thought, the mind's inspection, judgment, a reading of signs. And then there is the vision that really takes place, an honorary or instituted thought, squeezed into a body—its own body, of which we can have no idea except in the exercise of it and which introduces, between space and thought, the autonomous order of the compound of soul and body. The enigma of vision is not done away with; it is relegated from the "thought of seeing" to vision in act.

Still this *de facto* vision and the "there is" which it contains do not upset Descartes' philosophy. Being thought united with a body, it cannot, by definition, really be thought [conceived]. One can practice it, exercise it, and, so to speak, exist it; yet one can draw nothing from it which deserves to be called true. If, like Queen Elizabeth,[30] we want at all costs to think *something* about it, all we can do is go back to Aristotle and scholasticism, to conceive thought as a corporeal something which cannot be conceived but which is the only way to formulate, for our understanding, the union of soul and body. The truth is that it is absurd to submit to pure understanding the mixture of understanding and body. These would-be thoughts are the hallmarks of "ordinary usage," mere verbalizations of this union, and can be allowed only if they are not taken to be thoughts. They are indices of an order of existence—of man and world as existing—about which we do not have to think. For this order there is no *terra incognita* on our map of Being. It does not confine the reach of our thoughts, because it, just as much as they, is sustained by a truth which grounds its obscurity as well as our own lights.[31]

We have to push Descartes this far to find in him something like a metaphysics of depth [*de la profondeur*]. For we do not attend the birth of this truth; God's being for us is an abyss. An anxious trembling quickly mastered; for Descartes it is just as vain to plumb that abyss as it is to think the space of the soul and the depth of the visible. Our very position, he would say, disqualifies us from looking into such things. Here is the Cartesian secret of equilibrium: a metaphysics which gives

30 No doubt Merleau-Ponty is speaking of Princess Elizabeth, Descartes' correspondent. Cf. *Phénoménologie de la perception,* pp. 230–32 (C. Smith translation, pp. 198–99), and Descartes' letter to Elizabeth of June 28, 1643 (Bridoux, pp. 1157–61).—*Trans.*
31 That is, the obscurity of the "existential" order is just as necessary, just as grounded in God, as is the clarity of true thoughts ("nos lumières").—*Trans.*

us decisive reasons to be no longer involved with metaphysics, which validates our evidences while limiting them, which opens up our thinking without rending it.

The secret has been lost for good, it seems. If we ever again find a balance between science and philosophy, between our models and the obscurity of the "there is," it must be of a new kind. Our science has rejected the justifications as well as the restrictions which Descartes assigned to its domain. It no longer pretends to deduce its invented models from the attributes of God. The depth of the existing world and that of the unfathomable God come no longer to stand over against the platitudes [and flatness] of "technicized" thinking. Science gets along without the excursion into metaphysics which Descartes had to make at least once in his life; it takes off from the point he ultimately reached. Operational thought claims for itself, in the name of psychology, that domain of contact with oneself and with the world which Descartes reserved for a blind but irreducible experience. It is fundamentally hostile to philosophy as thought-in-contact, and if operational thought rediscovers the sense of philosophy it will be through the very excess of its ingenuousness [*sa désinvolture*]. It will happen when, having introduced all sorts of notions which for Descartes would have arisen from confused thought—quality, scalar structures, solidarity of observer and observed—it will suddenly become aware that one cannot summarily speak of all these beings as *constructs*. As we await this moment, philosophy maintains itself against such thinking, entrenching itself in that dimension of the compound of soul and body, that dimension of the existent world, of the abyssal Being that Descartes opened up and so quickly closed again. Our science and our philosophy are two faithful and unfaithful consequences of Cartesianism, two monsters born from its dismemberment.

Nothing is left for our philosophy but to set out toward the prospection of the actual world. We *are* the compound of soul and body, and so there must be a thought of it. To this knowledge of position or situation Descartes owes what he himself says of it [this compound] or what he says sometimes of the presence of the body "against the soul," or the exterior world "at the end" of our hands. Here the body is not the means of vision and touch but their depository.

Our organs are no longer instruments; on the contrary, our instruments are detachable organs. Space is no longer what it was in the *Dioptric,* a network of relations between objects such as would be seen by a witness to my vision or by a geometer looking over it and reconstructing it from outside. It is, rather, a space reckoned starting from me as the zero point or degree zero of spatiality. I do not see it according to its exterior envelope; I live in it from the inside; I am immersed in it. After all, the world is all around me, not in front of me. Light is viewed once more as action at a distance. It is no longer reduced to the action of contact or, in other words, conceived as it might be by those who do not see in it.[32] Vision reassumes its fundamental power of showing forth more than itself. And since we are told that a bit of ink suffices to make us see forests and storms, light must have its *imaginaire*. Light's transcendence is not delegated to a reading mind which deciphers the impacts of the light-thing upon the brain and which could do this quite as well if it had never lived in a body. No more is it a question of speaking of space and light; the question is to make space and light, which are *there,* speak to us. There is no end to this question, since the vision to which it addresses itself is itself a question. The inquiries we believed closed have been reopened.

What is depth, what is light, τί τὸ ὄν? What are they—not for the mind that cuts itself off from the body but for the mind Descartes says is suffused throughout the body? And what are they, finally, not only for the mind but for themselves, since they pass through us and surround us?

Yet this philosophy still to be done is that which animates the painter—not when he expresses his opinions about the world but in that instant when his vision becomes gesture, when, in Cézanne's words, he "thinks in painting."[33]

[4]

The entire modern history of painting, with its efforts to detach itself from illusionism and to acquire its own dimensions, has a metaphysical significance. This is not something to be demonstrated. Not for reasons drawn from the limits of objectivity in history and from the inevitable plurality of interpretations, which would prevent the linking of a philosophy and an event; the metaphysics we have in mind is not a body of detached ideas [*idées séparées*] for which inductive justifica-

[32] "those who do not see in it," i.e., the blind (note 18, above).—*Trans.*
[33] B. Dorival, *Paul Cézanne* (Paris, 1948), p. 103 *et seq.* [*trans.* Thackthwaite, *op. cit.,* pp. 101–3].

tions could be sought in the experiential realm. There are, in the flesh of contingency, a structure of the event and a virtue peculiar to the scenario. These do not prevent the plurality of interpretations but in fact are the deepest reasons for this plurality. They make the event into a durable theme of historical life and have a right to philosophical status. In a sense everything that could have been said and that will be said about the French Revolution has always been and is henceforth within it, in that wave which arched itself out of a roil of discrete facts, with its froth of the past and its crest of the future. And it is always by looking more deeply into *how it came about* that we give and will go on giving new representations of it. As for the history of art works, if they are great, the sense we give to them later on has issued from them. It is the work itself that has opened the field from which it appears in another light. It changes *itself* and *becomes* what follows; the interminable reinterpretations to which it is *legitimately* susceptible change it only in itself. And if the historian unearths beneath its manifest content the surplus and thickness of meaning, the texture which held the promise of a long history, this active manner of being, then, this possibility he unveils in the work, this monogram he finds there—all are grounds for a philosophical meditation. But such a labor demands a long familiarity with history. We lack everything for its execution, both the competence and the place. Just the same, since the power or the fecundity of art works exceeds every positive causal or filial relation, there is nothing wrong with letting a layman, speaking from his memory of a few paintings and books, tell us how painting enters into his reflections; how painting deposits in him a feeling of profound discordance, a feeling of mutation within the relations of man and Being. Such feelings arise in him when he holds a universe of classical thought, en bloc, up against the explorations [*recherches*] of modern painting. This is a sort of history by contact, perhaps, never extending beyond the limits of one person, owing everything nevertheless to his frequentation of others. . . .

"I believe Cézanne was seeking depth all his life," says Giacometti.[34] Says Robert Delaunay, "Depth is the new inspiration."[35] Four centuries after the "solutions" of the Renaissance and three centuries after Descartes, depth is still new, and it insists on being sought, not "once in a lifetime" but all through life. It cannot be merely a question

[34] Charbonnier, *op. cit.,* p. 176.
[35] Delaunay, *op. cit.,* p. 109.

of an unmysterious interval, as seen from an airplane, between these trees nearby and those farther away. Nor is it a matter of the way things are conjured away, one by another, as we see happen so vividly in a perspective drawing. These two views are very explicit and raise no problems. The enigma, though, lies in their bond, in what is between them. The enigma consists in the fact that I see things, each one in its place, precisely because they eclipse one another, and that they are rivals before my sight precisely because each one is in its own place. Their exteriority is known in their envelopment and their mutual dependence in their autonomy. Once depth is understood in this way, we can no longer call it a third dimension. In the first place, if it were a dimension, it would be the *first* one; there are forms and definite planes only if it is stipulated how far from me their different parts are. But a *first* dimension that contains all the others is no longer a dimension, at least in the ordinary sense of a *certain relationship* according to which we make measurements. Depth thus understood is, rather, the experience of the reversibility of dimensions, of a global "locality"— everything in the same place at the same time, a locality from which height, width, and depth are abstracted, of a voluminosity we express in a word when we say that a thing is *there*. In search of depth Cézanne seeks this deflagration of Being, and it is all in the modes of space, in form as much as anything. Cézanne knows already what cubism will repeat: that the external form, the envelope, is secondary and derived, that it is not that which causes a thing to take form, that this shell of space must be shattered, this fruit bowl broken—and what is there to paint, then? Cubes, spheres, and cones (as he said once)? Pure forms which have the solidity of what could be defined by an internal law of construction, forms which all together, as traces or slices of the thing, let it appear between them like a face in the reeds? This would be to put Being's solidity on one side and its variety on the other. Cézanne made an experiment of this kind in his middle period. He opted for the solid, for space—and came to find that inside this space, a box or container too large for them, the things began to move, color against color; they began to modulate in instability.[36] Thus we must seek space and its content *as* together. The problem is generalized; it is no longer that of distance, of line, of form; it is also, and equally, the problem of color.

[36] F. Novotny, *Cézanne und das Ende der wissenschaftlichen Perspective* (Vienna, 1938).

Color is the "place where our brain and the universe meet," he says in that admirable idiom of the artisan of Being which Klee liked to cite.[37] It is for the benefit of color that we must break up the form-spectacle. Thus the question is not of colors, "simulacra of the colors of nature."[38] The question, rather, concerns the dimension of color, that dimension which creates identities, differences, a texture, a materiality, a something—creates them from itself, for itself. . . .

Yet (and this must be emphasized) there is no one master key of the visible, and color alone is no closer to being such a key than space is. The return to color has the merit of getting somewhat nearer to "the heart of things,"[39] but this heart is beyond the color envelope just as it is beyond the space envelope. The *Portrait of Vallier* sets between the colors white spaces which take on the function of giving shape to, and setting off, a being more general than the yellow-being or green-being or blue-being. Also in the water colors of Cézanne's last years, for example, space (which had been taken to be evidence itself and of which it was believed that the question of *where* was not to be asked) radiates around planes that cannot be assigned to any place at all: "a superimposing of transparent surfaces," "a flowing movement of planes of color which overlap, which advance and retreat."[40]

Obviously it is not a matter of adding one more dimension to those of the flat canvas, of organizing an illusion or an objectless perception whose perfection consists in simulating an empirical vision to the maximum degree. Pictorial depth (as well as painted height and width) comes "I know not whence" to alight upon, and take root in, the sustaining support. The painter's vision is not a view upon the *outside,* a merely "physical-optical"[41] relation with the world. The world no longer stands before him through representation: rather, it is the painter to whom the things of the world give birth by a sort of concentration or coming-to-itself of the visible. Ultimately the painting relates to nothing at all among experienced things unless it is first of all "autofigurative."[42] It is a spectacle of something only by being a

---

[37] W. Grohmann, *Paul Klee* (Paris, 1954), p. 141 [New York, 1956].
[38] Delaunay, *op. cit.,* p. 118.
[39] Klee, *Journal* . . . , French trans. P. Klossowski (Paris, 1959).
[40] George Schmidt, *Les aquarelles de Cézanne,* p. 21. [*The Watercolors of Cézanne* (New York, 1953).]
[41] Klee, *op. cit.*
[42] "The spectacle is first of all a spectacle of itself before it is a spectacle of something outside of it."—*Translator's note from Merleau-Ponty's 1961 lectures.*

"spectacle of nothing," [43] by breaking the "skin of things" [44] to show how the things become things, how the world becomes world. Apollinaire said that in a poem there are phrases which do not appear to have been *created,* which seem to have *formed themselves.* And Henri Michaux said that sometimes Klee's colors seem to have been born slowly upon the canvas, to have emanated from some primordial ground, "exhaled at the right place"[45] like a patina or a mold. Art is not construction, artifice, meticulous relationship to a space and a world existing outside. It is truly the "inarticulate cry," as Hermes Trismegistus said, "which seemed to be the voice of the light." And once it is present it awakens powers dormant in ordinary vision, a secret of preexistence. When through the water's thickness I see the tiling at the bottom of a pool, I do not see it *despite* the water and the reflections there; I see it through them and because of them. If there were no distortions, no ripples of sunlight, if it were without this flesh that I saw the geometry of the tiles, then I would cease to see it *as* it is and where it is—which is to say, beyond any identical, specific place. I cannot say that the water itself—the aqueous power, the sirupy and shimmering element—is *in* space; all this is not somewhere else either, but it is not in the pool. It inhabits it, it materializes itself there, yet it is not contained there; and if I raise my eyes toward the screen of cypresses where the web of reflections is playing, I cannot gainsay the fact that the water visits it, too, or at least sends into it, upon it, its active and living essence. This internal animation, this radiation of the visible is what the painter seeks under the name of depth, of space, of color.

Anyone who thinks about the matter finds it astonishing that very often a good painter can also make good drawings or good sculpture. Since neither the means of expression nor the creative gestures are comparable, this fact [of competence in several media] is proof that there is a system of equivalences, a Logos of lines, of lighting, of colors, of reliefs, of masses—a conceptless presentation of universal Being. The effort of modern painting has been directed not so much toward choosing between line and color, or even between the figuration of things and the creation of signs, as it has been toward multiplying the systems of equivalences, toward severing their adherence to the en-

[43] C. P. Bru, *Esthétique de l'abstraction* (Paris, 1959), pp. 99, 86.
[44] Henri Michaux, *Aventures de lignes.*
[45] *Ibid.*

velope of things. This effort might force us to create new materials or
new means of expression, but it could well be realized at times by the
reexamination and reinvestment of those which existed already.

There has been, for example, a prosaic conception of the line as a
positive attribute and a property of the object in itself. Thus, it is the
outer contour of the apple or the border between the plowed field and
the meadow, considered as present in the world, such that, guided by
points taken from the real world, the pencil or brush would only have
to pass over them. But this line has been contested by all modern
painting, and probably by all painting, as we are led to think by da
Vinci's comment in his *Treatise on Painting:* "The secret of the art of
drawing is to discover in each object the particular way in which a
certain flexuous line, which is, so to speak, its generating axis, is directed through its whole extent. . . ."[46] Both Ravaisson and Bergson
sensed something important in this, without daring to decipher the
oracle all the way. Bergson scarcely looked for the "sinuous outline"
[*serpentement*] outside living beings, and he rather timidly advanced
the idea that the undulating line "could be no one of the visible lines of
the figure," that it is "no more here than there," and yet "gives the key
to the whole."[47] He was on the threshold of that gripping discovery,
already familiar to the painters, that there are no lines visible in themselves, that neither the contour of the apple nor the border between
field and meadow is in *this* place or that, that they are always on the
near or the far side of the point we look at. They are always between or
behind whatever we fix our eyes upon; they are indicated, implicated,
and even very imperiously demanded by the things, but they themselves are not things. They were supposed to circumscribe the apple or
the meadow, but the apple and the meadow "form themselves" from
themselves, and come into the visible as if they had come from a pre-
spatial world behind the scenes.

Yet this contestation of the prosaic line is far from ruling out all
lines in painting, as the impressionists may have thought. It is simply a
matter of freeing the line, of revivifying its constituting power; and we
are not faced with a contradiction when we see it reappear and triumph
in painters like Klee or Matisse, who more than anyone believed in

[46] Ravaisson, cited by Bergson, "La vie et l'oeuvre de Ravaisson," in *La pensée
et le mouvant* (Paris, 1934), pp. 264–65. [The passage quoted here is from M. L.
Andison's translation of that work, *The Creative Mind* (New York, 1946), p.
229. It remains moot whether these are Ravaisson's or da Vinci's words.]
[47] Bergson, *ibid.*

color. For henceforth, as Klee said, the line no longer imitates the visible; it "renders visible"; it is the blueprint of a genesis of things. Perhaps no one before Klee had "let a line muse."[48] The beginning of the line's path establishes or installs a certain level or mode of the linear, a certain manner for the line to be and to make itself a line, "to go line."[49] Relative to it, every subsequent inflection will have a diacritical value, will be another aspect of the line's relationship to itself, will form an adventure, a history, a meaning of the line—all this according as it slants more or less, more or less rapidly, more or less subtly. Making its way in space, it nevertheless corrodes prosaic space and the *partes extra partes;* it develops a way of extending itself actively into that space which sub tends the spatiality of a thing quite as much as that of a man or an apple tree. This is so simply because, as Klee said, to give the generating axis of a man the painter "would have to have a network of lines so entangled that it could no longer be a question of a truly elementary representation."[50]

In view of this situation two alternatives are open, and it makes little difference which one is chosen. First, the painter may, like Klee, decide to hold rigorously to the principle of the genesis of the visible, the principle of fundamental, indirect, or—as Klee used to say—absolute painting, and then leave it up to the *title* to designate by its prosaic name the entity thus constituted, in order to leave the painting free to function more purely as a painting. Or alternatively he may choose with Matisse (in his drawings) to put into a single line both the prosaic definition [*signalement*] of the entity and the hidden [*sourde*] operation which composes in it such softness or inertia and such force as are required to constitute it as *nude,* as *face,* as *flower.*

There is a painting by Klee of two holly leaves, done in the most figurative manner. At first glance the leaves are thoroughly indecipherable, and they remain to the end monstrous, unbelievable, ghostly, *on account of their exactness [à force d' exactitude].* And Matisse's women (let us keep in mind his contemporaries' sarcasm) were not immediately women; they became women. It is Matisse who taught us to see their contours not in a "physical-optical" way but rather as structural filaments [*des nervures*], as the axes of a corporeal system of activity and passivity. Figurative or not, the line is no longer a thing or an

---

[48] Michaux, *op. cit.* ["l'aisse rêver une ligne"]
[49] *Ibid.* ["d'aller ligne"]
[50] Grohmann, *op. cit.,* p. 192.

imitation of a thing. It is a certain disequilibrium kept up within the indifference of the white paper; it is a certain process of gouging within the in-itself, a certain constitutive emptiness—an emptiness which, as Moore's statues show decisively, upholds the pretended positivity of the things. The line is no longer the apparition of an entity upon a vacant background, as it was in classical geometry. It is, as in modern geometries, the restriction, segregation, or modulation of a pre-given spatiality.

Just as it has created the latent line, painting has made itself a movement without displacement, a movement by vibration or radiation. And well it should, since, as we say, painting is an art of space and since it comes about upon a canvas or sheet or paper and so lacks the wherewithal to devise things that actually move. But the immobile canvas could suggest a change of place in the same way that a shooting star's track on my retina suggests a transition, a motion not contained in it. The painting itself would offer to my eyes almost the same thing offered them by real movements: a series of appropriately mixed, instantaneous glimpses along with, if a living thing is involved, attitudes unstably suspended between a before and an after—in short, the outsides of a change of place which the spectator would read from the imprint it leaves. Here Rodin's well-known remark reveals its full weight: the instantaneous glimpses, the unstable attitudes, petrify the movement, as is shown by so many photographs in which an athlete-in-motion is forever frozen. We could not thaw him out by multiplying the glimpses. Marey's photographs, the cubists' analyses, Duchamp's *La Mariée* do not move; they give a Zenonian reverie on movement. We see a rigid body as if it were a piece of armor going through its motions; it is here and it is there, magically, but it does not *go* from here to there. Cinema portrays movement, but *how*? Is it, as we are inclined to believe, by copying more closely the changes of place? We may presume not, since slow-motion shows a body floating among objects like an alga but not moving *itself*.

Movement is given, says Rodin,[51] by an image in which the arms, the legs, the trunk, and the head are each taken at a different instant, an image which therefore portrays the body in an attitude which it never at any instant really held and which imposes fictive linkages between the parts, as if this mutual confrontation of incompossibles could, and could alone, cause transition and duration to arise in bronze

[51] Rodin, *L'art*. Interviews collected by Paul Gsell (Paris, 1911).

and on canvas. The only successful instantaneous glimpses of movement are those which approach this paradoxical arrangement—when, for example, a walking man is taken at the moment when both his feet are touching the ground; for then we almost have the temporal ubiquity of the body which brings it about that the man *bestrides* space. The picture makes movement visible by its internal discordance. Each member's position, precisely by virtue of its incompatibility with the others' (according to the body's logic), is otherwise dated or is not "in time" with the others; and since all of them remain visibly within the unity of a body, it is the body which comes to bestride time [*la durée*]. Its movement is something premeditated between legs, trunk, arms, and head in some virtual "control center," and it breaks forth only with a subsequent change of place. When a horse is photographed at that instant when he is completely off the ground, with his legs almost folded under him—an instant, therefore, when he must be moving—why does he look as if he were leaping in place? Then why do Géricault's horses really *run* on canvas, in a posture impossible for a real horse at the gallop? It is just that the horses in *Epsom Derby* bring me to see the body's grip upon the soil and that, according to a logic of body and world I know well, these "grips" upon space are also ways of taking hold of time [*la durée*]. Rodin said very wisely, "It is the artist who is truthful, while the photograph is mendacious; for, in reality, time never stops cold."[52] The photograph keeps open the instants which the onrush of time closes up forthwith; it destroys the overtaking, the overlapping, the "metamorphosis" [Rodin] of time. But this is what painting, in contrast, makes visible, because the horses have in them that "leaving here, going there,"[53] because they have a foot in each instant. Painting searches not for the outside of movement but for its secret ciphers, of which there are some still more subtle than those of which Rodin spoke. All flesh, and even that of the world, radiates beyond itself. But whether or not one is, depending on the times and the "school," attached more to manifest movement or to the monumental, the art of painting is never altogether outside time, because it is always within the carnal [*dans le charnel*].

Now perhaps we have a better sense of what is meant by that little verb "to see." Vision is not a certain mode of thought or presence to self; it is the means given me for being absent from myself, for being

52 *Ibid.,* p. 86.
53 Michaux, *op. cit.*

present at the fission of Being from the inside—the fission at whose termination, and not before, I come back to myself.

Painters always knew this. Da Vinci[54] invoked a "pictorial science" which does not speak with words (and still less with numbers) but with *oeuvres* which exist in the visible just as natural things do and which nevertheless communicate through those things "to all the generations of the universe." This silent science, says Rilke (apropos of Rodin), brings into the *oeuvre* the forms of things "whose seal has not been broken";[55] it comes from the eye and addresses itself to the eye. We must understand the eye as the "window of the soul." "The eye . . . through which the beauty of the universe is revealed to our contemplation is of such excellence that whoever should resign himself to losing it would deprive himself of the knowledge of all the works of nature, the sight of which makes the soul live happily in its body's prison, thanks to the eyes which show him the infinite variety of creation: whoever loses them abandons his soul in a dark prison where all hope of once more seeing the sun, the light of the universe, must vanish." The eye accomplishes the prodigious work of opening the soul to what is not soul—the joyous realm of things and their god, the sun.

A Cartesian can believe that the existing world is not visible, that the only light is that of the mind, and that all vision takes place in God. A painter cannot grant that our openness to the world is illusory or indirect, that what we see is not the world itself, or that the mind has to do only with its thoughts or with another mind. He accepts with all its difficulties the myth of the windows of the soul; it must be that what has no place is subjected to a body—even more, that what has no place be initiated *by* the body to all the others and to nature. We must take literally what vision teaches us: namely, that through it we come in contact with the sun and the stars, that we are everywhere all at once, and that even our power to imagine ourselves elsewhere—"I am in Petersburg in my bed, in Paris, my eyes see the sun"—or to intend [*viser*] real beings wherever they are, borrows from vision and employs means we owe to it. Vision alone makes us learn that beings that are different, "exterior," foreign to one another, are yet absolutely *together,*

---

[54] Cited by Delaunay, *op. cit.,* p. 175.
[55] Rilke, *Auguste Rodin,* French translation by Maurice Betz (Paris, 1928), p. 150. [English translation by Jessie Lamont and Hans Trausil (New York, 1919; republished 1945).]

are "simultaneity"; this is a mystery psychologists handle the way a child handles explosives. Robert Delaunay says succinctly, "The railroad track is the image of succession which comes closest to the parallel: the parity of the rails." The rails converge and do not converge; they converge *in order to* remain equidistant down below. The world is in accordance with my perspective *in order to* be independent of me, is for me in *order to be* without me, and to be the world. The "visual quale"[56] gives me, and alone gives me, the presence of what is not me, of what *is* simply and fully. It does so because, like texture, it is the concretion of a universal visibility, of a unique space which separates and reunites, which sustains every cohesion (and even that of past and future, since there would be no such cohesion if they were not essentially relevant to the same space). Every visual something, as individual as it is, functions also as a dimension, because it gives itself as the result of a dehiscence of Being. What this ultimately means is that the proper essence [*le propre*] of the visible is to have a layer [*doublure*] of invisibility in the strict sense, which it makes present as a certain absence. "In their time, our bygone antipodes, the impressionists, were perfectly right in making their abode with the castaways and the undergrowth of daily life. As for us, our heart throbs to bring us closer to the depths. . . . These oddities will become . . . realities . . . because instead of being held to the diversely intense restoration of the visible, they will annex to it the proper share [*la part*] of the invisible, occultly apperceived."[57] There is that which reaches the eye directly [*de face*], the frontal properties of the visible; but there is also that which reaches it from below—the profound postural latency where the body raises itself to see—and that which reaches vision from above like the phenomena of flight, of swimming, of movement, where it participates no longer in the heaviness of origins but in free accomplishments.[58] Through it, then, the painter touches the two extremities. In the immemorial depth of the visible, something moved, caught fire, and engulfed his body; everything he paints is in answer to this incitement, and his hand is "nothing but the instrument of a distant will." Vision encounters, as at a crossroads, all the aspects of Being. "[A] certain fire pretends to be alive; it awakens. Working its way along the hand as conductor, it reaches the support and engulfs it;

---

[56] Delaunay, *op. cit.,* pp. 115, 110.
[57] Klee, *Conférence d'Iena* (1924), according to Grohmann, *op. cit.,* p. 365.
[58] Klee, *Wege des Naturstudiums* (1923), as found in G. di San Lazzaro, *Klee.*

then a leaping spark closes the circle it was to trace, coming back to the eye, and beyond."[59]

There is no break at all in this circuit; it is impossible to say that nature ends here and that man or expression starts here. It is, therefore, mute Being which itself comes to show forth its own meaning. Herein lies the reason why the dilemma between figurative and nonfigurative art is badly posed; it is true and uncontradictory that no grape was ever what it is in the most figurative painting and that no painting, no matter how abstract, can get away from Being, that even Caravaggio's grape is the grape itself.[60] This precession of what is upon what one sees and makes seen, of what one sees and makes seen upon what is—this is vision itself. And to give the ontological formula of painting we hardly need to force the painter's own words, Klee's words written at the age of thirty-seven and ultimately inscribed on his tomb: "I cannot be caught in immanence."[61]

[5]

Because depth, color, form, line, movement, contour, physiognomy are all branches of Being and because each one can sway all the rest, there are no separated, distinct "problems" in painting, no really opposed paths, no partial "solutions," no cumulative progress, no irretrievable options. There is nothing to prevent a painter from going back to one of the devices he has shied away from—making it, of course, speak differently. Rouault's contours are not those of Ingres. Light is the "old sultana," says Georges Limbour, "whose charms withered away at the beginning of this century."[62] Expelled first by the painters of materials [*les peintres de le matière*], it reappears finally in Dubuffet as a certain texture of matter. One is never immune to this kind of turning back or to the least expected convergences; some of Rodin's fragments are almost statues by Germain Richier *because they were both sculptors*—that is to say, enmeshed in a single, identical network of Being. For the same reason nothing is ever finally acquired and possessed for good.

[59] Klee, cited by Grohmann, *op. cit.,* p. 99.
[60] A. Berne-Joffroy, *Le dossier Caravage* (Paris, 1959), and Michel Butor, "La Corbeille de l'Ambrosienne," *Nouvelle Revue Française,* pp. 969–89.
[61] Klee, *Journal, op. cit.* ["Je suis insaissable dans l'immanence."]
[62] G. Limbour, *Tableau bon levain à vous de cuire la pâte: l'art brut de Jean Dubuffet* (Paris, 1953), pp. 54–55.

In "working over" a favorite problem, even if it is just the problem of velvet or wool, the true painter unknowingly upsets the givens of all the other problems. His quest is total even where it looks partial. Just when he has reached proficiency in some area, he finds that he has reopened another one where everything he said before must be said again in a different way. The upshot is that what he has found he does not yet have. It remains to be sought out; the discovery itself calls forth still further quests. The idea of a universal painting, of a totalization of painting, of a fully and definitively achieved painting is an idea bereft of sense. For painters the world will always be yet to be painted, even if it lasts millions of years . . . it will end without having been conquered in painting.

Panofsky shows that the "problems" of painting which magnetize its history are often solved obliquely, not in the course of inquiries instigated to solve them but, on the contrary, at some point when the painters, having reached an impasse, apparently forget those problems and permit themselves to be attracted by other things. Then suddenly, altogether off guard, they turn up the old problems and surmount the obstacle. This unhearing [sourde] historicity, advancing through the labyrinth by detours, transgression, slow encroachments and sudden drives, does not imply that the painter does not know what he wants. It does imply that what he wants is beyond the means and goals at hand and commands from afar all our *useful* activity.

We are so fascinated by the classical idea of intellectual adequation that painting's mute "thinking" sometimes leaves us with the impression of a vain swirl of significations, a paralyzed or miscarried utterance. Suppose, then, that one answers that no thought ever detaches itself completely from a sustaining support; that the only privilege of speaking-thought is to have rendered its own support manageable; that the figurations of literature and philosophy are no more settled than those of painting and are no more capable of being accumulated into a stable treasure; that even science learns to recognize a zone of the "fundamental," peopled with dense, open, rent [déchirés] beings of which an exhaustive treatment is out of the question—like the cyberneticians' "aesthetic information" or mathematical-physical "groups of operations"; that, in the end, we are never in a position to take stock of everything objectively or to think of progress in itself; and that the whole of human history is, in a certain sense, stationary. *What,* says the understanding, like [Stendhal's] Lamiel, *is it only that?*

Is this the highest point of reason, to realize that the soil beneath our feet is shifting, to pompously name "interrogation" what is only a persistent state of stupor, to call "research" or "quest" what is only trudging in a circle, to call "Being" that which never fully *is?*

But this disappointment issues from that spurious fantasy[63] which claims for itself a positivity capable of making up for its own emptiness. It is the regret of not being everything, and a rather groundless regret at that. For if we cannot establish a hierarchy of civilizations or speak of progress—neither in painting nor in anything else that matters—it is not because some fate holds us back; it is, rather, because the very first painting in some sense went to the farthest reach of the future. If no painting comes to be *the* painting, if no work is ever absolutely completed and done with, still each creation changes, alters, enlightens, deepens, confirms, exalts, re-creates, or creates in advance all the others. If creations are not a possession, it is not only that, like all things, they pass away; it is also that they have almost all their life still before them.

Le Tholonet, July–August 1960

---

[63] "Mais cette deception est celle du faux imaginaire, qui . . ."

PART SIX

History and Politics:
Moral Dimensions

Merleau-Ponty's moral philosophy and moral concerns are to be found primarily in his writings on the nature of history and politics. His thought in this context was shaped by his experiences before, during, and after the Second World War. France's humiliating defeat in 1940 seemed to reveal the bankruptcy of bourgeois capitalist institutions and caused many French intellectuals to become sympathetic to Marxism if not communism.

The first of these essays was published in 1946, not long after the war and a time when Merleau-Ponty was closer to Marxism and communism than at any other point in his career. The second essay, taken from Les aventures de la dialectique, *was written at a time when Merleau-Ponty was breaking with Sartre and is much less sympathetic to French communism. The first essay centers around the nature of fascism and Marxism and is a running commentary on a book by the fascist writer, Thierry Maulnier. The second is more concerned with the philosophy of history and centers around the writings of Max Weber.*

I3. CONCERNING MARXISM

Thierry Maulnier began writing about politics in the period of fascism's ascendancy. He has thought about it and written about it a great deal, sometimes fervently and sometimes with reserve. There is no doubt that he helped make fascism respected, precisely because he took it seriously and submitted it to sober examination, accepting this and rejecting that. As he himself wrote, the sincerity of a few men is a necessary auxiliary of historical mystifications.[1] Once that has been said, one must immediately add that our author comported himself in such a way as to escape polemics and tendentiousness and find a place on the level of political philosophy where opinions may be true or false but none deserve to be condemned. Let us remember that in May, 1940, when chance circumstances left him sole editor of a weekly paper, Thierry Maulnier brought out several resolutely "warmongering" issues which two years later earned him the same paper's denunciation as a British agent. Between 1940 and 1944 he limited himself to the role of military critic in the newspapers on which he collaborated in the unoccupied zone and never permitted the interest he had shown in the Fascist phenomenon to be utilized by the propaganda of foreign fascisms. He thereby not only gave proof of his independence and sincerity—private virtues which are not decisive in politics—but he showed that he had a sense of historical responsibility, and he understood that a writer in an even partially occupied country,

Maurice Merleau-Ponty, "Concerning Marxism," *Sense and Non-Sense,* Part II, Ch. 9, trans. by Hubert L. Dreyfus and Patricia Allen Dreyfus (Evanston, Illinois: Northwestern University Press, 1964), pp. 99–124. Reprinted by permission.

[1] *Violence et conscience,* p. 128.

especially if he had been interested in fascism, could no longer put his name to a political chronicle. This is what gives him the complete right to publish his reflections today and gives us complete liberty to discuss them without any mental reservations.

His interest in fascism was conditional. For Thierry Maulnier the problem of our time was to unite two forces which had up to this time been separate: the proletarian forces heading toward a classless society by means of economic and social revolution, and the forces which tended to preserve the nation, the form of Western European civilization. Looking at fascism in its first stages—and perhaps giving too much credit to the declarations of its theoreticians—he believed that the significance of the phenomenon lay in bringing about this union. This, he thought, was the historical *truth* of fascism, no matter how the different existing fascisms—which might or might not remain true to their mission—conducted themselves. On this point, Thierry Maulnier multiplied his reservations: "The recourse to Action, Race, Blood, the predestined Leader, the superior mission of one people—all the suspicious instruments of modern nationalism are nothing but the substitutes of faltering intelligence, man's appeal to shadows in order to regain control of a world in which knowledge is powerless to guide him."[2] His only hope was that "the confused instincts and contradictory tendencies associated with fragments of old doctrines, with resentments that are sometimes vulgar and interests that are sometimes sordid," would introduce into history a *true* fascism, one without racial persecutions, oppression, or war, wholly dedicated to solving the proletarian problem within the limits of the nation.[3]

It was therefore necessary to help fascism become aware of its true historical destination and in some way to transform it into itself. Fascism thus far had appealed to "moral relics, vague claims, to myths as vague as those of heroism, duty, and sacrifice, to the easiest and sometimes the most suspicious sources of exaltation."[4] The gold buried in that mud had to be mined. The question was whether restricted social reforms, racism, and the exaltation of the national community were not merely instruments designed to conjure away the social and proletarian problem according to the tested formulas of traditional nationalism or whether, on the contrary, one was to witness the

[2] *Au-dela du nationalisme,* p. 19.
[3] *Ibid.,* p. 29.
[4] *Ibid.,* p. 25.

emergence of a new type of society in Germany and Italy. We can understand how Munich, the occupation of Prague six months later, the war on Poland, and all the rest definitively enlightened Thierry Maulnier about fascism's relation to its historical "essence" and how he unhesitatingly refused the existing fascism the sympathy he had shown for a certain "possible" fascism.

The important thing is to draw from this historical experience all the lessons which it entails. We mean: Was Thierry Maulnier's fascism really a *possible* fascism? Was it by chance or through an unforeseeable choice of certain individuals that naziism and fascism resorted in the end to war and conquest? Was it reasonable to expect it to solve the problems of our time? Are we free to give a regime the meaning we are pleased to find in it, or isn't there a way to grasp the concrete logic of the system, which leads it necessarily—or at least probably—to its ultimate decisions? Wasn't it possible, from 1938 on, to tell which of fascism's different aspects (innovating or traditional) would finally prevail? Abandoning the naïve method of intellectualism and looking for the latent content of fascism beneath its manifest content was all that would have been necessary. Thierry Maulnier drew up a finished design for fascism by putting together a few ideas he liked: the idea of a social revolution and the idea of a national civilization. He strove to show that these ideas are compatible. But political criticism is not concerned solely with ideas, for it must take account of the modes of behavior for which these ideas are more masks than expressions. Even if the nation and the revolution are not incompatible on the level of ideas, on the level of action and in the dynamics of history if a socialism is "national," it ceases to be a socialism; the bourgeois of all countries have understood very well that the addition of this prefix eliminates all that is disturbing about socialism. We must know how to decipher this language which the powers can read at a single glance. For now, let us only say that if you put the national problem and the proletarian problem on the same level, you are in reality corrupting the socialist consciousness: by making it fall from humanism to empiricism, or, if you like, from "open" to "closed" politics; because it will be qualitatively modified from that moment on; and because, by a vital logic against which good will is helpless, it ceases in fact to choose the revolution because it ceases to choose it absolutely. Marxism is well aware of this law of all or nothing, and its criticism of opportunism or social democracy contains a psychoanalysis of political life which will have to be developed one day. Six years of grief and mourning will be as nothing for political experience if we go on thinking that fascism *might have* made socialism a reality, if we do not understand that fascism chose the "solutions" (which were, moreover, illusory) of war and conquest from the very start when it shrank before the proletarian problem, if we have not learned to connect exterior and interior politics as two aspects of an undivided choice, if we have not learned to consider a regime or a political movement as a living organism in which everything is related to everything else.

It will be seen that *Violence et conscience* does not go that far. Thierry Maulnier's solutions are today still what they were seven years ago. He undertook to criticize fascism "from the inside." The young people who read the magazine *Combat* were obviously Fascist sympathizers, and this magazine taught them to severely criticize fascism's inadequacies in matters of social politics. As Thierry Maulnier so excellently puts it today, each fascism has an "avant-garde" which, unknown to itself, fulfills the double function of reassuring the Leftist elements which rally to the regime in the hope of a social revolution and of disquieting the Rightist elements which would pull the system in a reactionary direction were it not for this threat.[5] One cannot avoid the thought that Thierry Maulnier is reflecting on his own past conduct in writing these lines. His claim to go beyond both nationalism and Marxism is precisely what put him in the avant-garde of Fascist ideology. Even today, when he has long since (and as flatly as possible) withdrawn any sort of support for certain Fascist milieus, his position is scarcely different. He teaches that the proletarian problem is the problem of problems and that capitalism must be destroyed. But he usually addresses himself to the readers of *Figaro* and the *Carrefour*— and we will not step on anyone's toes if we say that they are not wholeheartedly dedicated to social revolution. Which paper devoted two front-page columns to *Violence et conscience* this summer? *Epoque*. What did it get out of the book? Precisely those quite timid conclusions which we shall have to discuss. In such a setting, Thierry Maulnier's ideas can only serve once more as a moral guaranty for reactionary politics, and in the end it is with good reason that Thierry Maulnier has remained sociologically a Rightist critic.

Such great lucidity, honesty, and vigor in his thought, such timidity in his choice of a public and in his conclusions: the only way to

[5] *Violence et conscience,* pp. 112 ff.

explain their co-existence within the author is in terms of some political complex. Thierry Maulnier's problem is the problem of the French intellectual Right, and men of thirty-five are all the more aware of that problem because at some moment it was theirs in one way or another. Around 1930 *Action Française* enjoyed such credit among the students as is unimaginable to the young people of today, and the reasons for this must be sought. It is fascinating in any case to see Thierry Maulnier gradually rejecting all that was hasty in his first views without, for all that, completely getting rid of them and to see how such a rigorous thought process sometimes is held back and falls short of Marxism and sometimes touches on Marxism's basic problems.

•   •   •

There was a healthy reaction against Kantian illusions of democracy in the Maurrasianism of 1900. Democratic optimism allows that, in a State where the rights of man are guaranteed, no liberty any longer encroaches on any other, and the co-existence of men as autonomous and reasonable subjects is assured. This is to suppose that violence appears only episodically in human history, that economic relationships in particular tend of themselves to effect harmony and justice, and, finally, that the structure of the human and natural world is rational. We know today that formal equality of rights and political liberty mask rather than eliminate relationships based on force. And the political problem is then to institute social structures and real relationships among men such that liberty, equality, and right become effective. The weakness of democratic thinking is that it is less political than moral, since it poses no problem of social structure and considers the conditions for the exercise of justice to be given with humanity. In opposition to that particular moralism we all rallied to realism, if by that one means a politics concerned with realizing the conditions of existence for its chosen values. Maurrasian immoralism is something else again: it renounces equality and liberty instead of concluding that, since they have not been given, they must be created. Having acknowledged that the view of man which we get through consciousness is abstract and that a society is not a collection of pure, free, and equal consciousnesses but is first of all a system of institutions to which consciousnesses owe whatever effective reason and liberty they might have, Maurras definitively rejects the judgment of consciousnesses and makes politics a technique for order with no place for value judgments. Maurrasianism is in large part a criticism of the interior to the profit of the exterior. Justice and truth, whose source men think they possess insofar as they are consciousnesses, are in reality based upon law-courts, books, and traditions and are therefore fragile like these and, like them, are threatened by individual judgment. The individual's evaluations and his ability to think correctly depend upon his external supports, and it is essential that these be maintained. The political man is he who has recognized the price of existing things and defends them against private fantasy. The problem is to save historically constituted man from nature which, within us and outside of us, always threatens him because it is pure transition. We should therefore place no faith in the course of events and should revere the admirable happenstance which permitted the appearance of humanity; there can be no question of abandoning an inheritance to heirs who will squander it or of consulting them about how it should be used. There are those who know because they have understood history, and there are those who foolishly make their consciousness their only guide. This results in a pessimistic, cynical, and authoritarian *pathos* of which traces are to be found in all of Thierry Maulnier's works, as, for example, when he says that hatred and the passions catch fire more readily than good will or that "a large part of true politics doubtless consists in making what are conventionally called men's vices serve the general good and in keeping what one calls their virtues from harming them—insofar as this is possible."[6] Or when he evokes "the effective power of stupidity."[7] Or when he defines liberty as "the benefit demanded by those who aspire to power as long as they still are weak."[8] Or each time he speaks of democracy, and even today when he stresses the hazards of history.[9] Barrès and Maurras thought that the world and our life were a senseless confusion in which a few fragile and precious *forms* appear. Their ideas are rooted in the despair of 1900. Thierry Maulnier owes this sense of a possible chaos, this respect for man and scorn for men, to his earliest political awakening.

[6] *Au-dela du nationalisme,* p. 84.
[7] *Ibid.,* p. 23.
[8] *Ibid.,* p. 106.
[9] *Violence et conscience,* p. 10.

Yet as far back as his book of 1938 appears another idea which leads somewhere else. He rejects the idea of necessary progress but rejects as well the Maurrasian idea of an immutable human nature which reduces political problems to those of an immutable sociology of order. "It is ridiculous to deny that man is capable of progress; it is no less ridiculous to believe that such progress will set him free. . . . Every time man introduces a new element into the system of known relationships which constitute an old civilization, he transforms this whole system of relationships to an inestimable extent and can plant in it the seed of an immense disorganization; thus certain steps forward can be paid for by much greater setbacks. . . . Let us at least realize that we create nothing which must not later be faced. It is only on this condition that we will be able to tackle the problems posed by the modern world without the stupid disdain, the imbecile terror, and the inane optimism which are the masks of impotent thought."[10] Thus Thierry Maulnier introduced the idea of a social dynamics and a movement of history. Politics could therefore no longer restrict itself to the tested formulas of an art of governing and a happy use of chance. It required an analysis of the present situation and acknowledged a certain meaning in history which it had to take into account on pain of being ineffectual. One was led to make a distinction among empirical events between those which make history take a step it will not retrace, because they respond to the problems of the time, and those which are merely adventitious, since they are based on a conjunction of circumstances which they will not outlive.[11] There is no guarantee that power will return to the men and the forces best able to dominate the difficulties of the moment. The course of history is contingent, and it is not always the best or the truest which carries the day. "History is full of lost chances, of squandered wealth, of blind paths embarked upon."[12] Success can crown the least rigorous ideologies—at least for a while. There are true doctrines which, as Péguy said, do not get written into history, and, inversely, there are conspicuous events which do not carry history one step further. But history is at least rational in that a movement which fails to perceive its historical destination and to pose the problems of its origin has every likelihood of getting off the track, of

[10] *Au-dela du nationalisme,* pp. 5–16.
[11] *Ibid.,* pp. 20–21.
[12] *Ibid.,* p. 21.

miscarrying, of being deleted from the course of things or of leaving only an "ephemeral rent" in the web of history.[13] The movement which is successful at one moment is not always the truest or the most valuable, but such it must be if it is to last. If, for example, fascism only overcomes class antagonism by the ephemeral exaltation of national feeling and by resorting anew to the good will of the oppressed, if it continues to ignore problems instead of resolving them, it will disappear for failing to rejoin, by an act of conscious will, the deep-lying motives which gave it birth and for not assuming responsibility for its own truth.

Thus one witnessed the emergence of the idea of a politics which is not created *ex nihilo* in the minds of individuals but is prepared and worked out in history—and not in the Maurrasian sense of a history which repeats itself but in the sense of a history which goes beyond itself and presents men with new situations to dominate. History contains vectors; it has a meaning—not that all things fall into place in terms of one end, but because it rejects the men and the institutions which do not respond to existing problems; not that everything which occurs deserves to happen, but because everything that disappears deserves to disappear. If, then, one grants that there are certain *effective problems* present at the core of history, the analysis of our present situation should not be concerned solely with men's wishes and ideas but should be total. Analysis should tackle the very arrangement of things and the economic situation which, like everything else, henceforth takes on a historical significance. The inevitable consequence of the idea of a logic of history is a certain historical materialism. Thierry Maulnier encountered Marxism from these two angles. What did he think of it?

First, he criticized it for having underestimated man's role in effecting history. For him, if history poses problems, it does not of itself offer any solution to them. The breakdown of capitalism does not carry within itself the seeds of the regime which is to replace it. It is up to man freely to conceive the institutions which will extract a new order from chaos and preserve history on the brink of nothingness. On our view Thierry Maulnier was here just disagreeing with a superficial Marxism. Indeed, how can one deny the role of human initiative if a class is effective only insofar as it has become aware of itself? Since Marxism has always said that the revolution is not inevitable, for it as

[13] *Ibid.,* p. 31.

for Thierry Maulnier history is only "half-determined."[14] For Marxism as for Thierry Maulnier, the historical determination of effects by causes passes through human consciousness, with the result that men make their own history, although their doing so is neither disinterested nor lacking in motives. In conceding that political will is supported by a factual situation and projects given antagonisms toward their future solution, Thierry Maulnier has for his part granted Marxism all that it asks: since human decision is motivated by the course of events, it will therefore seem—at least in retrospect—to be called forth by these events, so that no rupture or hiatus between effects and causes will ever be discoverable in completed history. In this respect *Violence et conscience* formulates the consequences of a historical method in politics with perfect clarity. "From the moment it has been clearly understood that history is never given to men like an empty space where they may construct what they like but is given to them like a certain state of things produced by anterior causes which they cannot cause not to be and which they must keep in mind, whether they like it or not, in ordering their conduct—from this moment the freedom it leaves them is just the freedom to have a better or worse understanding of the world in which they find themselves and to behave to greater or less advantage in that world. From this point of view, if the fact of consciousness contains an infinite number of possible representations and modes of behavior, there is scarcely more than one possible representation and mode of behavior contained in the highest degree of consciousness. It is in the highest degree of consciousness that man simultaneously perfects and destroys the freedom which history has left him, just because he is conscious."[15]

As a matter of fact, from 1938 on the only thing that set Thierry Maulnier apart from Marxism was his manner of describing the basic situation of our time. As we said before, he saw in it two *equally essential* facts: first, the appearance in modern societies of a class antagonism which destroys national unity, with the proletariat justifiably feeling alien in a country where one is allowed to sell one's labor without retaining possession of the products of this labor; and, second, the resistance of the nation and of the middle classes in particular to this process of decomposition. He viewed as abstract any analysis of the present which omitted either of these two facts or tried to subordinate

---

[14] *Ibid.*, p. 209.
[15] *Violence et conscience*, p. 139.

one to the other. His complaint against Marxism was precisely that it provided only a fleshless schema of history because it reduced history to economic history and deformed even this latter by treating the resistance of the middle classes to proletariatization and their attachment to the values of national civilizations as a surface phenomenon. Thierry Maulnier thought it true that modes of being and thinking depend at every moment on the modes of production, but no less true that the manner of working and producing in a given country at a given moment depends on the mores, the accepted values, and the psychology of the country in question. The class struggle itself takes place only within a national community, on the basis of the cultural acquisitions which comprise the nation's unity even at the moment it is dividing against itself. "We cannot deduce from economic exchanges (except arbitrarily and verbally) the more complex social exchanges; on the contrary, we must consider the existence of a complex social milieu . . . as the vital condition of all economic exchange, even the most primitive. However considerable a role economic exchange may play in social life from the very beginning (and it is as considerable as the vital organic needs and the ways of satisfying them are in the life of an individual human being), it no more constitutes the structure of society than the need to eat, sleep, or clothe oneself constitutes the structure of individual life."[16]

On this point as well, Thierry Maulnier's criticism was less telling against Marxism itself than against the current accounts of it or against certain formulas which are authentically Marxist but which schematize the doctrine. Marxism is often presented as a *reduction* of cultural phenomena to economic phenomena, or as a reduction of history to *conflicts of interest*. Marxists often speak of the bourgeoisie as of an "economic personage" who always acts with a view to his own interests and for whom ideas and beliefs are only means. It is nonetheless true that these interpretations and formulas remain unequal to Marxism and perhaps miss its central intuition. The greatness of Marxism lies not in its having treated economics as the principal or unique cause of history but in its treating cultural history and economic history as two abstract aspects of a single process. Labor, which is the substructure of history in the Hegelian sense, is not the simple production of riches, but, in a more general way, it is the activity by which man projects a human environment around himself and goes

[16] *Au-dela du nationalisme,* p. 64.

beyond the natural data of his life. The Marxist interpretation of history does not reduce it to the conscious play of interests; it simply admits that all ideologies—even, for example, a morality of heroism which prescribes that men should risk their lives—are bound up with certain economic situations through which they come into existence: only when the morality of the masters is embodied in the economic relation of master and slave and in a society based upon slave labor does it cease to be an individual concept and become an institution and receive historical existence. Marxist materialism consists in admitting that the phenomena of civilization and concepts of rights have a *historical anchorage* in economic phenomena, by means of which they escape the transitoriness of interior phenomena and are deposited outside as Objective Spirit. Economic life is not a separate order to which the other orders may be reduced: it is Marxism's way of representing the inertia of human life; it is here that conceptions are registered and achieve stability. More surely than books or teachings, modes of work hand the previous generations' ways of being on to the new generations. It is true that, in a given society at a given moment, the way of working expresses the mental and moral structure just as a living body's slightest reflex expresses the total subject's fundamental way of being in the world. But economic life is at the same time the historical carrier of mental structures, just as our body maintains the basic features of our behavior beneath our varying moods; and this is the reason one will more surely get to know the essence of a society by analyzing interpersonal relations as they have been fixed and general-ized in economic life than through an analysis of the movements of fragile, fleeting ideas—just as one gets a better idea of a man from his conduct than from his thoughts. Thus Thierry Maulnier's criticism of Marxism as abstract materialism was to a large extent unjust. Thierry Maulnier took no more trouble than De Man—whom he names and from whom he perhaps drew his inspiration—to disen-tangle Marxism from the mechanistic and utilitarian ambiguities to which certain of its formulas may lend themselves. Criticizing these formulas leaves Marxism's principal thought—that there is an incarna-tion of ideas and values—intact; it does not authorize us to transcend or "go beyond" economic analysis or to drop the guideline of the class struggle.

In the end this is just what Thierry Maulnier did. On the pretext that, in each single event, the class struggle is never seen except through the medium of the particularities of a country and a time, and that in this sense it is never pure or uniquely responsible, he proceeded as if certain historical realities escaped its influence. He treated the national community, for example, as an equally essential fact. In short, because historical facts entail moral and psychological conditions in addition to their economic conditions, he refused to put things in perspective. But the plurality of conditions does not rule out treating one of them as the principal condition. This is what scientists do every day: even though everything in nature depends to some extent on everything else and there are no strictly isolatable phenomena, we do have laws—i.e., statistically true schemas which approximately apply to the course of nature—for the intervention of the most distant phenomena in what we observe here and now is only negligible, thanks to a kind of damping effect. Likewise, although economic and other conditions are inextricably combined in events taken one by one, we retain the right to give the former a privileged place in our analysis of phenomena, if it has been established that they give a more faithful indication of the course of things when one is considering a sufficiently broad segment of history. It would be impossible in any case to restrict economic analysis to certain sectors of history: it is all-pervasive. The reaction of the middle classes to the threat of proletariatization is not a phenomenon distinct from the class struggle and does not point to any failure of Marxist analysis; it has its place in the class dialectic, being a new phase and a new illustration of it. The nation, which Thierry Maulnier treats as an irreducible fact, is itself charged with the class struggle, whether it is the bourgeoisie invoking the national interest and the external danger to bring strikers back into line or the proletariat assuming responsibility for the national heritage abandoned by the bourgeoisie, as in 1793, 1871, or even in 1944. A strange postulate is involved in Thierry Maulnier's setting the proletarian movement against the demands of national safety, the proletarian fact against the national fact. For it may come about that the proletarian movement is the condition of the nation's safety instead of a threat to it. There are really two nations: the nation as crude reality, with its existing bourgeois framework—this nation undoubtedly threatened by the class struggle; and the nation as a fundamental mode of life and behavior, hard to imagine as having anything to fear from a worldwide proletarian revolution. One cannot cite the national fact as a residue which Marxist analysis is unable to assimilate, since we have seen how this "fact" splits in two precisely under the influence of the historical factors discovered by Marxist analysis. Any politics which claims to be based on the proletarian fact *and* the national fact, as if the first did not encompass the second, is, beneath the flattering guise of a "concrete" politics, really just a "diversionary" effort, as Thierry Maulnier now says fascism was.[17]

Only let us admit that we are better prepared to recognize these truths today than in 1938. Then we were facing fascism on the rise—that is to say, a forest of bayonets but also a "social" and "revolutionary" staging, which intellectuals at least found impressive. We learned what propaganda was after four years of reading articles in *Oeuvre* about "socialist" Europe and the work standard and then confronting them with the reality of Germany at war. Beneath our very eyes fascism *became,* first, an army in combat and, finally, a pile of scrap-iron and ruins where worn-out populations, with no political idea or will, somehow subsisted. It requires effort for us to remember how fascism looked seven years ago, to distinguish it from the war into which it sank, and to restore the prestige it enjoyed as a new society, "beyond Marxism." In another connection, Vichy and the sacrifice of so many French workers made it evident to us that anti-Communism could lead to treason and that the will to revolution could assume responsibility for the nation. Lastly, now that France has clearly ceased to be a power of the first magnitude and national existence seems to depend so strictly upon world imperialisms, our diminished power no longer permits us solemnly to set the drama of worldwide economic organization against the French national fact, as if they were facts of equal weight: our humiliation will perhaps free us of the *provincialism* that was so striking in prewar French politics, and especially in the politics of *Action Française*. These years of looking to the world for our salvation have perhaps taught us to pose problems in worldwide terms, and the knowledge we have gained of infrastructures makes it impossible for us any longer to remain unaware of the matter of history, just as a sick person can no longer remain unaware of his body.

What is certain is that Thierry Maulnier does justice to Marxism in his new book as he has never done before and proposes a view of history which retains all the essential Marxist elements. The idea of historical "mystification" seems to have illuminated the whole Marxist

[17] *Violence et conscience,* p. 93.

conception of history for him. "When capitalistic society has reached a certain stage of decay," he writes, "capitalism can no longer find any safeguard except in a resolutely anti-conservative attitude. The capitalistic caste can no longer find anyone capable of struggling against the proletarian revolt unless it looks outside its own ranks; the economic structure which entails the plundering of labor and the domination of money can no longer count on anything but the myths of disinterestedness and heroism to protract its slow decline. It is no longer a question of a head-on shattering of the anti-capitalistic revolutionary *élan* but is a question of giving that *élan* an oblique orientation which will diminish the force of the shock and preserve part of the existing institutions."[18] Since Thierry Maulnier elsewhere excludes the interpretation of fascism as an "authoritarian disguise for large-scale capitalism," he therefore means that for nearly everyone this holding maneuver is preconscious.[19] He is not sure after all that any member of the bourgeoisie—with the exception of a few "masters"—ever conceived the Fascist diversion as a deliberate project. The mysterious thing about history is precisely that, without any preconceived plan, individuals behave in all particulars as if they had an infinite power of foresight: for example, the "bourgeois" choice of views and values in all domains (politics, morality, religion, the art of war) falls with infallible certainty upon those which will in fact make it possible to maintain capitalism. Plot, premeditation, or coincidence? We asked ourselves this at the Pétain trial. It probably was none of these. But, as if by a sort of reflex, Pétain—formed and defined as he was by fifty years in a military, and ten years in a pre-Fascist, environment— adopted in every circumstance and, for example, when faced with the problem of the armistice, the attitude which ran the least risk of liberating the revolutionary forces. The logic of history does not operate in terms of clear ideas and individual projects; its instruments are the complex politics and anonymous projects which give a group of individuals a certain common style, "fascist," for example, or "proletarian." Insofar as we have not understood that our actions take on a certain statistical and objective meaning (which may be quite different from that which we give them) when they pass from us into things, we are surprised by them, do not recognize them, and are misled by the "mysterious power of autodetermination" with which, as Thierry

18 *Ibid.*, p. 104.
19 *Ibid.*, p. 93.

Maulnier says, history seems endowed.[20] This is what accounts for that look of barely awakened sleepers seen in certain "traitors" when events suddenly show them the unfamiliar configuration of their own lives. It is neither ideas alone nor interests recognized as such which go to make up history, but interests disguised as ideas and ideas which have sunk to the state of worries and vague anxieties in the confused give-and-take of existence. "If the determining factors of the Second World War can in no case be reduced to the play of economic causes, and if the role played by the economic causes of the war cannot easily be disentangled from the confused web in which they operate, there is nonetheless in this historical complex—which includes the routes, angles of attack, and interferences of all the forces governing society —a system of disequilibrium the influence of which seems to guide the ebb and flow of the great struggle, almost in the way that the movements of the ocean are guided by a planetary gravitation. That the war of 1939 was to a considerable degree the war of peoples for possession of the great sources of raw materials and for domination by means of these sources of raw materials is beyond doubt." [21] Here one sees the idea of a sort of global or lateral economic determinism, which allows the other sort of conditions free play in each particular case, content to deflect them in its own direction. The discussion of Marxism has long been conducted as if it were a question of assigning *the cause* of history and as if each event had to have a relationship of linear causality with another event, about which it then had to be determined whether it was "economic" or "ideological," and Marxism was thought vanquished when one pointed to example of "ideological" causality. But it goes without saying that the ideology in turn cannot be separated from its economic context. If a materialistic history is rejected for being abstract, then an idealistic or spiritualistic history should be rejected on the same grounds. One will then conclude that each event entails all orders of determinants, and there are some who still believe that this slant gets them beyond Marxism, since no perspective is absolutely excluded. They do not see that it is precisely this idea, that nothing can be isolated in the total context of history, which lies at the heart of Marxism, with, in addition, the idea that because of their greater generality economic phenomena make a greater contribution to historical discourse—not that they explain everything

[20] *Ibid.*, p. 46.
[21] *Ibid.*, p. 120.

that happens but that no progress can be made in the cultural order, no historical step can be taken unless the economy, which is like its schema and material symbol, is organized in a certain way. "We must be careful . . . ," says Thierry Maulnier, "not to let ourselves be carried too far by this apparent victory over 'materialism.' We have driven the 'production of material conditions' from the 'foundation' where Marx placed it, only to reintroduce it at the 'core' of social reality. It is not a question now of once again ousting productive labor from this core of human social reality where we came upon it, completely immersed in but also completely immersing that reality, associated with all its forms and manifestations by an infinite mutual penetration and full reciprocity. It is not a question of relegating the 'production of material conditions' to the outbuildings of history, the kitchens or waiting rooms of human society, as do the idealistic historians, ashamed and disgusted. Production of the material conditions of life is not the foundation of human history, but neither is it the passive, disgraced servant; it is securely installed in this history, exerting a continual, powerful influence upon it, determining it and determined by it—*on an equal footing,* as it were. We can neither hypostatize it as some kind of transcendent priority nor relegate it to a shameful or contemptible area. The producer of material conditions, the man who wrenches the life of his fellows from the world, this man is not the creator of human society considered in its historical being—for he is himself created by it, along with his work—but neither is he its slave: he is the instrument of the powerful transformations it works upon itself through the medium of nature, which it combats and often controls. History does not spring from him; it does not pass over him; it passes through him. . . . It would be useless to deny the preponderant part which *homo faber's* efforts to assure man's continued survival in nature play in the activities of human society; and it goes without saying that this effort—itself radiating from every part of the social totality of which it is a function—does much to determine the other forms of human activity: the production and transformation of laws, customs, beliefs, styles of civilization, and, in sum, the comportment and content of consciousness. Thus we can conclude that although the superstructures of the social totality are not determined by an economic substratum which could be said to have produced them, one can say that this totality determines itself, mainly through the intermediary of the activities by means of which it assures its survival and transforms surrounding nature."[22] How much Thierry Maulnier has changed can be measured by recalling his summary protests against American and Soviet mechanism in *La Crise est dans l'homme*. If the economy is to the society what the heart is to the organism, the problem is not how to regiment economic progress; we must instead be on the lookout for what Balzac called "the mystery of civilization," of which such progress is perhaps the visible outline.

Thierry Maulnier would seem to have reversed his original positions. In a history in which a strange logic holds everything together, the man with a real political sense will not try to play on human passions in order to reach arbitrarily chosen goals. Thrown with other men into a drama which will not necessarily end well but which at all events is moving toward some end, he understands that conservatism is a utopia, finds nothing insignificant in either men or things, questions and listens to them; for he cannot make them into anything but what they are. The time of juvenile cynicism is long gone: "To govern man by his passions is to augment them dangerously. Flattery and constraint are the two faces of contempt: they do, of course, turn man into a good instrument—but making an instrument of man, that indeed is contempt."[23] Yet one changes philosophies faster than morals and morals faster than politics. If we leave the philosophy of history and turn to practical conclusions, we will find Thierry Maulnier lagging behind his own ideas.

•   •   •

If it is true that the class struggle is an essential fact, that class antagonism shatters the constituted forms of culture, and, lastly, that step by step the economic decay of capitalism corrupts all the ideas, all the values it had sanctioned, then it seems natural to conclude that the only way to return to an "organic" economy and civilization is by expropriating the property-holders and, as Lenin said, "stealing what had been stolen." Thierry Maulnier, on the other hand, imposes such a series of meticulous conditions on this recovery by man of his own life that for all practical purposes they are tantamount to refusing the revolution. Indeed he admits that the problem is to do away with wage-earning and to re-establish the link between the producer and his product. That fraction of labor which serves in the capitalistic system

22 *Ibid.*, pp. 151, 153.
23 *Ibid.*, p. 116.

to multiply capital should be paid for, if not in money and with the right to use that money to buy consumable goods (for the possibility of new investments and a new technical development would then disappear along with the accumulation of wealth), then at least in a "currency of production" which would make the worker co-owner of the enterprises to be created. On this point Thierry Maulnier adds: "As for the owners of the present instruments of production, they may find themselves reasonably satisfied in that case to be left in possession of their property, only without the right to use this property for gratuitous self-appropriation of the surplus value of their employees' labor, so as to assure themselves a monopoly in the creation and ownership of new wealth."[24] And so the very author who described occupation of the State by the bourgeoisie in almost the same terms as the Marxists is expecting the revolution in a State which has not been liberated by the expropriation of the property-holders. How can one help seeing that one of two things will happen: either Thierry Maulnier's "reforms" really will abolish capitalism—in which case it would be naïve to believe that the owners of the instruments of production will be "reasonably satisfied" with the toy one has left them—or else their power will be maintained by some indirect means, in which case they will tolerate the reform but it will no longer be anything but a new mystification. Concretely speaking, *who* will bring about the reform? A parliamentary majority? But, as we shall see, it is not certain that Thierry Maulnier will accept just any form of democracy; and besides, we know full well the means which the powerful have at their disposal—precisely under the aegis of freedom of the press—to stir up currents of opinion and manifestations which paralyze a parliamentary majority. The proletarian problem has been posed, says Thierry Maulnier; there is competition to solve it. "Who the winner of the universal contest will be and whether he holds sword, scepter, or hammer in his right hand does not make much difference to us, but only what his guiding thought will be."[25] And elsewhere: "Let us imagine the political means of a radical transformation of society (i.e., of the political State) in the hands of one man or a group of men endowed with enough boldness, decisiveness, and historical consciousness to abolish the proletariat *qua* class, that is, to impose upon society an

[24] *Ibid.,* p. 173.
[25] *Ibid.,* p. 58.

economic structure which abolishes wage-earning. . . ."[26] So that is
what we end up with: socialism brought about by the decrees of *one
man* or *a group* of enlightened men! Did we think that Thierry Maulnier was won over to the idea—which is perhaps the most incontestable
of Marxist ideas—that an effective politics is not one conceived by a few
individuals gathered around their table but one which carries the
movement of history farther and which is borne by historical forces?
Who will support the decisions of our reformers if not those they are
going to set free, and how are they to support them if not by strikes and
seizing factories? Must one then explain to them that they are not to
take possession of or even direct the factories which they occupy? And
what if they continue to occupy them? Who is going to evacuate the
factories if not the police. and who will benefit from this if not the
present owners? Was it worth the trouble of reflecting about Marxism
and peremptorily rejecting all manner of reformism just to end up with
this new "plan"? If socialism is not an intellectual's notion but, as
Thierry Maulnier said back in 1938, "that which demands to be born,"
the form of social existence which is taking shape in the alienation of
the proletariat and its revolt against this alienation, then a nonprole-
tarian socialism is a square circle.

As *Epoque's* commentator was well aware, Thierry Maulnier could
afford to get rid of his prejudices on the philosophical level, since they
remain effective when one gets down to concrete problems, which,
after all, are the only ones that count in politics. His thought at this
point becomes weak and banal. It is no longer himself speaking. Control of management by labor? "That involves an absurd contamina-
tion of the programs of economic reform by the theoretical principles of
democracy,"—that is, "by methods which have proved their paralyzing
slowness and inefficiency in the political order."[27] That is easy to say.
Is he serious in comparing political democracy, in which everyone is
called upon to give his opinion on abstract problems and, above all,
where a whole series of influences (which Thierry Maulnier himself
has pointed out) come between the voter and legislative decisions, with
the daily management of business by workers? Has he forgotten that
among the workers are a certain number of engineers and directors
who are as "competent" as the owner of the business or the chairman of
the board in general business matters? One only needs to have observed

26 *Ibid.,* p. 165.
27 *Ibid.,* p. 193.

a workshop in operation, a combat section under fire, or a fishing boat at sea to understand that technical authority is never challenged when it is not used to mask inadmissible interests. Men may not be good, but they are not all that stupid; and when one thinks of the great many sacrifices which they have not only endured but finally accepted when it was not at all evident that they had to, one may well wonder whether they would not accept even greater sacrifices to ensure the success of an economy in which they would feel personally involved and which would be *their* affair. The question is not whether the revolution would disrupt production at the start but what solutions there are to the proletarian problem besides this one. A politics "for the people" which is not developed "by the people" in the end is not developed at all: this is the ABC's of a *historical* politics. We are reminded of the results of De Man's experiment in Belgium. The plan, which was adopted by the Belgian Workers Party in particular, had been set forth before "concentrations" of the people which were to be crowned by a giant "concentration" in Brussels, along with the threat of a general strike. There were two possible methods: the reformist or parliamentary method and the revolutionary method. Either workers at all levels would regain possession of the economic apparatus and impose a welfare constitution on the government—which would be going from the revolution to political power; or else the workers would remain at work and the plan would be put into effect by maturely deliberated legislative decisions—which, said De Man, would be going from political power to the revolution. De Man chose the second method, in conformity with the ideology of a planned economy. We all know what happened: the plan was never put into operation. If one's goal is to liberate the proletariat, it is *historically* ridiculous to try to attain that goal by non-proletarian means, and choosing such means clearly indicates that one is renouncing one's pretended goal. End and means can only be distinguished in intellectual conceptions, not on the terrain of history, and any politics which does not admit this principle remains inferior to Marxism on the pretext of "going beyond" it.

Let no attempt be made here to disguise a reactionary politics with the excuse that the revolution must be directed. The problem of directing the revolution exists, but it arises after the economy has been freed of its parasites, not before. A man like Lenin did, of course, run into it along his way. He did not think there was any speculatively perfect solution: a politics cannot be built either on mass opinion alone or solely on the decrees of the party or its leaders. The secret of Leninism was in the communication he managed to establish between the masses and the leaders, between the working class and its "conscience." This presupposes leaders who do not shut themselves up in their offices and who know how to explain to the masses what is being proposed to them; it presupposes a dialogue and an exchange between the masses, which are a constant barometer of the state of the *effective* revolution, and the center, where revolutionary *conceptions* and perspectives are worked out. It no doubt means opening the door to eloquence and introducing a possibility of deceit into the system. But we must admit that if there is any solution, it is this.

One senses a second conservative theme in *Violence et conscience:* the idea that culture is a fragile thing and that a proletarian revolution would destroy it along with its capitalistic props. The proletariat, which "has no homeland" because it is excluded from its nominal homeland, is a result of the decay of capitalism. How is it supposed to have the strength within itself to erect a new culture? "One of the most ingenious, but also one of the most debatable points of the Marxist interpretation of life undoubtedly is this fusion, in a single dialectical movement, of the principles of decline and dissociation with the principles of renewal, of the disintegrating with the constructive forces of life."[28] Marxism is not unaware of the problem. It makes a distinction between a proletariat drained of all cultural substance (and, moreover, of all revolutionary energy)—Marx's *Lumpenproletariat*—and a proletariat which remains capable of historical and cultural creation. Marx's analysis should be extended and renewed on this point: the decay of capitalism, which is much more advanced today than a century ago, and the "rotting" of the revolution, especially in its fascist form, have corrupted, morally ruined, and politically annulled broad social strata which would have been capable of revolutionary action. All one need do to become convinced of this is think of the proletarian elements who were involved in traffic with the Germans during the Occupation or who remain in black market circles as something other than consumers. Such annulment may make it unlikely that a revolutionary consciousness will be formed in the immediate future. However, it must be understood that the restoration of culture is equally compromised, for, according to Thierry Maulnier himself, since economic phenomena are at the heart of a society, economic decomposition will

[28] *Ibid.,* p. 68.

not leave the cultural heritage intact. It is a fact that, in our present situation, there is not one term in the moral vocabulary which has not become ambiguous, not one traditional value which has not been contaminated. If one is to be able to speak favorably of work, family, or country some day, it will be on the condition that these values have first been purified by the revolution of the ambiguities they served to foster. Which means that there can be no question of saving them from proletarian violence, since this violence is the only thing that can make them honorable once more. The only way to preserve what merits being kept of the past is by laying the foundation of a new future. A classless society will reunite the negative conditions of a renewed culture. Thierry Maulnier will ask whether the positive conditions will also be reunited; and it is here that a choice must be made. If one views humanity as Maurras did, i.e., as a completely fortuitous result of a few exceptional men and a few improbable circumstances, then the revolution necessarily seems the greatest possible risk. But Thierry Maulnier has rejected this basically pessimistic view. Against such a view should be set, not the basic optimism of the 18th century, but a methodical optimism, as it were. For, after all, however rare great and beautiful things may be, it is a remarkable fact that they are fairly generally understood and admired. Man might be defined by this ability of his to conceive or in any case to respect what he is not and has not. All several men need do is live together and be associated with the same task for some rudimentary rules and a beginning of law to emerge from their life in common. Looking at things in this way, one gets the feeling that man has immense resources. One need only go back to that very widespread idea that reason is rare, and one could show that in one sense it is everywhere in men, that they are in a way caught up in it, and that this opening to the possible is exactly what makes their instincts much less stable than those of animals, as Pascal— who was no optimist—was well aware. There is something to be said in favor of the "natural light." Men somehow secrete culture without even wanting to. The human world, however different it may be from the natural or animal world, is somehow *natural for man*. One could find many traces of 19th-century evolutionism in Maurras' pessimistic philosophy; if there is a radical difference between human and animal existence, one might doubtless be a little less suspicious of man. The stakes are high, of course, and the risk is great. We should perhaps avoid running it, if we could. But if the alternatives are socialism or chaos, then imprudence is on the side of those who help aggravate the chaos on the pretext that the revolution is risky. Boiled down to its essence, Marxism is not an optimistic philosophy but simply the idea that another history is possible, that there is no such thing as fate, that man's existence is open-ended. It is the resolute try for that future which no one in the world or out of the world can know will come or, if it comes, what it will be.

•   •   •

Has Thierry Maulnier therefore absolutely no grounds for being hesitant about Marxism? On the contrary, we think his hesitation has a profound significance once it has been unburdened of its "reactionary" themes, and it is for the very purpose of extracting what we will call "the Marxist problem" in all its purity that we have formulated the above criticisms.

We know that Marx and Lenin imagined that the State as a coercive power would "wither away" in a late phase of socialist society, because it seemed to them that constraints become superfluous in a society where there is no more oppression or exploitation and where the class struggle has really been abolished. This meant assuming that the contradictions between the individual and society only occur in a capitalistic society and that once this society has been destroyed man will become integrated into all forms of collective existence effortlessly and without any problems. On this point Thierry Maulnier writes: "There is one kind of alienation which can be abolished because it is the result of a certain reformable state of the society. But there is another, irreducible kind: the only way that man could regain complete possession of himself is by ceasing to live in contact with his fellows."[29] The passage would be weak if one took it as an argument against the revolution, for even if there is an alienation of the *for others* to which no revolution will put an end and even if the individual does experience the law as yet another constraint once the revolutionary *élan* has subsided, these are not reasons to turn him aside from the revolutionary act in which, at least for a while, he assumes existence with others and which has a chance of reducing the constraints of co-existence to the inevitable minimum. Although this passage cannot serve to justify a reactionary politics, it does, however, show us what sep-

[29] *Ibid.*, p. 87.

arates Thierry Maulnier from most Marxists: he considers certain contradictions of the human condition definitive; he believes that it is basically irrational. Thierry Maulnier never says this in so many words, but it seems to us that the truth of his book, over and beyond its prejudices, lies in his having clearly perceived in history what J. Hyppolite calls "dialectical facts," without his being able to adhere to the idea of a unique dialectic of history. We are not concerned here with an external criticism of Marxism, which could be curtailed by a more complete examination of the doctrine; our real concern is with an internal difficulty which deserves the attention of the Marxists themselves.

Marxism, as we know, recognizes that nothing in history is absolutely contingent, that historical facts do not arise from a sum of mutually foreign circumstances but form an intelligible system and present a rational development. But the characteristic thing about Marxism—unlike theological philosophies or even Hegelian idealism—is its admission that humanity's return to order, the final synthesis, is not necessitated but depends upon a revolutionary act whose certainty is not guaranteed by any divine decree or by any metaphysical structure of the world. A Marxist believes both that the Russian Revolution of 1917 was not fated—that, for example, it might have failed for want of leaders capable of thinking the situation out and orienting the masses—and that the very presence of a remarkable revolutionary directorate as well as the weakness of the middle-class political personnel in the Russia of 1917 were no chance and were bound up with Russia's total situation at that moment: on the one hand, the radicalism of a newborn proletariat formed by levying a labor force from rural areas and, on the other, the semi-colonial regime in Russia, which foreign capitalism had forced to undergo rapid industrialization. It is therefore characteristic of Marxism to admit that history is both logical and contingent, that nothing is absolutely fortuitous but also that nothing is absolutely necessary—which is what we meant just now when we said that there are dialectical facts. But this completely empirical and experimental character of Marxism immediately poses a problem. If we admit that an event, whatever its probability, can always miscarry at any moment, just as chance may renew its offensive, it may turn out in the end that logic and history go separate ways and that what seems to be the logical consequence of history never materializes in empirical history. Doesn't the revolution cease to be the fundamental dimension of history when it loses the character of a necessary future; and, with regard to effective history—which, after all, is the only thing that matters—isn't the person who judges everything from the angle of the class struggle putting things into an arbitrary perspective? There are two ideas contained in the notion of a "logic of history": first, the idea that events of any order—and economic events in particular—have a human significance, that in all its aspects history is integral and makes up a single drama; and, second, the idea that the phases of this drama do not orderlessly follow one another but move toward a completion and conclusion. The contingency of history means that even if the diverse orders of events form a single intelligible text, they are nonetheless not rigorously bound together, that there is a certain amount of free play in the system. For example, economic development may be ahead of ideological development, ideological maturity may supervene when objective conditions are not yet or are no longer favorable for the revolution; or, on the other hand, the dialectic of history may get bogged down or veer off toward chance ventures without solving the problems which it brought to light. If we resolutely give up the theological idea of a rational basis of the world, the logic of history becomes nothing more than one possibility among others. Even though we are better able to understand a greater number of events through Marxist analysis than through any other analysis, we still do not know whether effective history is going to consist of a series of *diversions*—of which fascism was the first and of which Americanism or the Western bloc could be other examples—for as long as we live and perhaps even for centuries. The Marxist historian will of course always be able to show in retrospect that these systems were just so many forms of "resistance" to the class struggle, but one wonders if the most efficient politics for a given country might not consist in trying to make some sort of place for itself in this world of accidents such as it is, rather than ordering all its behavior in relation to the class struggle, which is a *general* principle of history. It no longer makes any sense to treat the class struggle as an *essential* fact if we are not sure that effective history will remain true to its "essence" and that its texture will not be the product of accidents for a long time or forever. History would then no longer be a coherent discourse whose conclusion we could await with assurance and in which each phrase had its necessary place. Instead, like the words of a drunken man, it would sketch an idea which would soon grow faint—only to keep on reappearing and disappearing without necessarily attaining its full expression. Marxism could then only be stated in terms of negative propositions: the world economy cannot be organized, and its internal contradictions cannot be overcome (barring the continuous sequence of chances upon which man, as a reasonable being, cannot count), as long as socialistic ownership of the instruments of production is not everywhere established. But we know neither that a universal socialist production would achieve equilibrium nor that the course of events, with all the accidents which help to shape it, is heading toward that outcome. Marxism would remain a politics which is as justified as any other. It would even be the only universal and human politics. But it would not be able to take advantage of a pre-established harmony with the course of events: the universal proletariat bearing down on all sides on the capitalistic apparatus and destroying it in order to substitute a socialistic civilization—that would be not a fact but a vow, not an existing force from which we could draw support but a force we would have to create, since the nations' working classes are in fact seduced by the "diversions" of history.

It might be easier to admit this as a problem for Marxism if we put it in terms of everyday politics. The foundations of the proletarian revolution were laid in Russia in 1917 and nowhere else as yet. That is a fact for which hindsight can undoubtedly furnish reasons: it was no accident, one might say, that the most economically backward country in Europe was the first to have its revolution. It was just because Russia, unlike the Western countries, had not effected its own industrialization that it offered a semi-colonial country, as it were, to the capital of "advanced" countries; and the brutal establishment there of modern production methods was bound to provoke a crisis which would lead directly to the proletarian revolution, without passing through a long democratic and bourgeois phase as in the countries of the West. One can even speak of a law of "unequal development," according to which the phases of social and economic evolution may be upset by the interaction of "advanced" and "backward" countries. But this law was only discovered after the event, and since it was likewise only after the event that the Russian phenomenon was reintegrated into the logic of history, other incidences and other after-effects, which cannot be foreseen with the help of given explanatory schemas, cannot be excluded from the future. Not only is this possible, it is inevitable. For even after the unexpected event has been classified under a new law and linked to the Marxist dialectic, its consequences and its interaction with the configuration of the world continue to confuse Marxist schemata. Once the foundations of socialism had been established in Russia, the politics of the new State was profoundly affected by the double necessity of accomplishing an industrialization supposedly given in Marxist schemata of the proletarian revolution and of protecting the new State against a possible coalition of capitalist powers. If the government of the U.S.S.R. brought "bourgeois" motives into its industrial-equipment enterprise, if it established salary differences comparable to or greater than those existing under a capitalist regime, the reason for this is doubtless to be found in the fact that the U.S.S.R. could not apply the socialist ideology in a country which had not yet acquired the infrastructure of socialism and that its problem was precisely the problem of first erecting this infrastructure. On the other hand, it is difficult not to agree that if the Russian Revolution had not looked "well-behaved" to the capitalist powers, if the U.S.S.R. had pursued a policy of supporting proletarian movements outside its borders, then either the coalition against Germany could not have been formed or else the Germans would have succeeded in splitting it apart. Even today, if the U.S.S.R. was not signing an agreement with Chiang Kai-Shek and was openly supporting the Chinese Communists, World War III would be close at hand. But all this comes down to the recognition that the politics of the U.S.S.R. can no longer be a universalist politics, with which Marxists of all countries can immediately concur. For a French Communist, the paths of revolution are at present very different from those foreseen by the doctrine; Marx's nice, simple guideline, "Workers of the world, unite," is no longer available to help him judge everything in politics and know what to do in every case. Whereas for traditional Marxism there could be no contradiction or even any difference between the revolution and everyday politics, between doctrine and tactics, between revolutionary energy and efficacy, between morality and politics, we have returned to the politics of cunning. Because the U.S.S.R. stood alone, we are not even sure that it is the "cunning of reason," and this unforeseeable fact shattered the rationality of history. The result is that if we want to apply Marxist analysis to the events which fill our time, our Marxism loses its way in cross-phenomena and unexpected reactions, runs after events without catching up to them, or in any case without ever getting ahead of them; and a clear-thinking Marxist comes to wonder, as he sees how the schema of the class struggle becomes diversified and takes on different shades of meaning, if the course of history from one diversion to another will really end up as the history of the class struggle or if he is not simply dreaming with his eyes open.

This central difficulty of Marxism is today more obvious than ever.[30] Generally speaking, Marxism is weak when faced with concrete events taken moment by moment. This should not make us forget how strong it appears when applied to a somewhat prolonged sequence of events. We are perhaps misled by the importance we inevitably assign to the present in which we live. If the class struggle should reappear tomorrow—as is possible or even probable after a war—and should show up in all the countries of the world, the broad Marxist lines of history would once again appear. When Lenin, in exile in Switzerland, was reflecting on Marxism, what indication was there that a few months later it would become a reality, even in one part of the world?

The only thing certain is that, having seen history multiply its diversions, we can no longer assert that it will not keep on inventing others until the world sinks into chaos, and consequently we can no longer count on an immanent force in things guiding them toward an equilibrium which is more probable than chaos. We are sure that the world will not become organized, will not stop rending itself, will not extricate itself from precarious compromises or rediscover beliefs and values unless the men who are least involved with the special interests of imperialisms regain possession of the economic apparatus. We know neither whether this necessary condition will be realized nor whether it is a sufficient condition, and consequently we do not know what is the correct value to assign to these pauses, these instants of peace which may be procured through capitalist compromises. It is up to us to observe the world during these years when it begins to breathe again, once the bottom has fallen out of fascism, once consciences have been demobilized. If the class struggle once again becomes the motivating force of history and, definitely, if the alternative of socialism or chaos becomes clearer, it is up to us to choose a proletarian socialism—not as a guaranty of happiness, since we do not know whether man can ever be integrated into co-existence or whether each country's happiness is

---

[30] This is what Lenin had in mind in *La Maladie infantile du communisme* when he sought the criterion of validity for a Marxist compromise with the bourgeoisie. It would be appropriate to extend the practical conclusions which he adopts onto the theoretical plane. A theory of contingency in history could be drawn from his Marxist "perception" of situations.

compossible with that of the others, but as that unknown *other future* which we must reach, or die. Thierry Maulnier would find his *real* conclusion—which he has not written and which he may some day write—in this Marxism without illusions, completely experimental and voluntary, to which he unwittingly committed himself when he recognized both the logic and the contingency of history.

August 1945

I4. THE CRISIS OF
THE UNDERSTANDING

Max Weber's notions of freedom and of truth are both very exacting and very vague.[1] But he was aware that they occur only in certain cultures, by means of certain historical choices which are never completely realized. They do not fully assimilate the confused world out of which they have arisen. They are thus not of divine right and have no other justification than that which they effectively bring to man, no other titles than those which are acquired in a struggle in which they are in principle at a disadvantage, since they cannot subsist without struggle; before they can arise it is equally essential that they legitimatize their adversaries and confront them. Because he remains faithful to the spirit of search and of knowledge, Weber is a liberal. His liberalism is completely new because he admits that truth always leaves a margin of doubt, that it does not exhaust the reality of the past and still less that of the present, and that history is the natural seat of violence. It does not ingenuously consider itself to be the law of things, as did previous liberalisms; it perseveres in becoming such a law through a history in which it is not predestined.

In the first place, Weber believes that he is able to juxtapose the order of truth and that of violence. We know history in the same way that Kant says we know nature; the historian's understanding, like the

Maurice Merleau-Ponty, "The Crisis of the Understanding," *The Primacy of Perception and Other Essays,* Part III, Ch. 6, trans. by Nancy Metzel and John Flodstrom (Evanston, Illinois: Northwestern University Press, 1964), pp. 193–210. Reprinted by permission.

[1] "La crise de l'entendement,"*Les aventures de la dialectique* (Paris, 1955), pp. 15–42.

physicist's, forms an "objective" truth to the degree that it is constructed. The objective element is only one aspect of a coherent representation which can be definitely corrected and made more precise but never merges with the thing in itself. The historian cannot look at the past without finding a meaning, without contrasting the important and the subordinate, the essential and the accidental, plans and accomplishments, preparations and declines. These vectors which are traced through the dense whole of facts have already distorted the original reality in which everything is equally real. We have imposed our own interests upon it. The historian's invasion of history cannot be avoided, but care must be taken to guarantee that the historical understanding, like the Kantian subject, works according to certain rules which assure intersubjective value to its representation of the past. The meanings—or, as Weber calls them, the ideal types—that the historian introduces into the facts must not be taken as keys to history. They are only precise guideposts for appreciating the divergence between what we think and what has been, and for bringing into the open what has been left out of our interpretation. Each perspective is there only in order to prepare for others. It is well founded only if we understand that it is partial and that the real is still beyond it. Knowledge is never categorical; it is always conditional. We can never be the past; it is only a spectacle before us, which is there for us to question. The questions come from us, and thus the responses in principle do not exhaust historical reality, since historical reality does not depend upon them for its existence.

On the contrary, the present is us; it awaits our consent or our refusal. Suspension of judgment, which is obligatory with respect to the past, is here impossible. To wait for things to take shape before deciding is to decide to let them happen in their own manner. The proximity of the present, which is what makes us responsible for it, nevertheless does not give us access to the thing itself. In fact, because of lack of distance we can see only one side of it. Knowledge and practice confront the same infinitely complex historical reality, but they respond to it in two opposed fashions: knowledge by multiplying views through provisional, open, motivated (that is to say, conditional) conclusions; practice through absolute, partial, unjustifiable decisions.

But how can we abide by this dualism of the past and of the present? It is evidently not absolute. I will tomorrow have to construct an image of that which I now see. I cannot pretend not to know it when I see it.

The past which I contemplate has been lived. From the moment when I first desire to study its origins, I cannot deny that it has been a present. Because of the fact that the order of knowledge is not the only order, because it is not enclosed in itself, and because it contains at least the gaping chasm of the present, the whole of history is still action and action already history. History is the same whether we contemplate it as a spectacle or assume it as a responsibility. The condition of the historian is not very different from that of the acting man. He puts himself in the place of those whose actions have been decisive, reconstitutes the horizon of their decision, and redoes what they have done (with this difference: he knows the context better than they, and he is already aware of the consequences). Not that history consists in penetrating the states of mind of great men. Even the search for motives, says Weber, involves ideal types. It is not a question of coinciding with what has been lived but rather of deciphering the total meaning of what has been done. In order to understand an action, its horizon must be restored—not merely the perspective of the actor but also the "objective" context.

History could thus be said to be imaginative action or even the spectacle that one has of an action. Conversely, action consults history, which teaches us, says Weber, not indeed what must be willed but the true meaning of our volitions. Knowledge and action are two poles of a single existence. Our relationship to history is not merely a relation of understanding, that of spectacle and spectator. We would not be spectators if we were not involved in the past. Action would not be serious if it did not bring some sort of finality to the whole enterprise of the past, if it did not give the drama its last act. History is a strange object, an object which is ourselves. Our irreplaceable life, our fierce liberty find themselves already prefigured, already implicated, already played out in other freedoms which today are past. Weber is obliged to go beyond the regime of the double truth, the dualism of the objective understanding and moral feeling, and look beyond the formula of this singular situation.

He has nowhere given this formula. His methodological writings postdate his scientific practice. It is for us to discover in his work as historian how he accommodates himself to this object, which centers around individual subjects, and how he forges a method out of this difficulty. By going beyond the past considered as spectacle, he attempts to comprehend the past itself by making it enter our own lives. We cannot be content with the past as we ourselves have seen it. The very attempt to discover the past as it actually was always implies a spectator, and there is a danger that we will discover the past only as it is for us.

Perhaps it is of the nature of history to be undefined in the present, and to become completely real only when it has once been given as a spectacle to a posterity which passes judgment upon it. Is it perhaps the case that only successive generations (*"generations appelantes,"* as Péguy called them) are in the position to see whether that which has been brought about really deserved to be, to correct the deceptions of recorded history, and to reinstate other possibilities? Is our image of the past preceded only by sequences of events which form neither a system nor even perspectives and whose truth is in abeyance? Is it perhaps the definition of history to exist completely only through that which comes after, to be in this sense suspended into the future? If this is true, the intervention of the historian is not a defect in historical knowledge. That facts interest the historian, that they speak to a man of culture, that they can be recaptured in the intentions of the historical subject threaten historical knowledge with subjectivity. But they also promise it a superior objectivity, if only one can successfully distinguish that which belongs to reason from that which is arbitrary, and determine the close relationships which our "metamorphoses" violate but without which they would be impossible.

Let us now attempt to understand the relationship between Protestantism and the capitalistic spirit. The historian begins by abstracting these two historical types. Weber does not consider speculation, or venture capitalism, which depends upon power politics. He takes as his object an economic system within which one can expect continuous returns from a durable and profitable enterprise—a system which involves a minimum of accountancy and organization, encourages free labor, and tends toward a regular market. In the same way he limits his discussion of the Protestant ethic to the Calvinism of the sixteenth and seventeenth centuries, considered more as it was generally interpreted than as it was originated by Calvin. These facts are chosen as interesting and historically important because they reveal a certain logical structure which is the key to another series of facts. How does the historian know this when he begins? Strictly speaking, he doesn't know. He foresees certain results that are indicated by his analysis. This analysis is justified to the extent that it renders readable those facts which are not contributed by the initial definitions. However, it is not certain that they designate essences. They were not developed by the next genus and specific difference and do not follow, as geometric definitions do, the genesis of an ideal being. They give only, as Weber says, a "provisional illustration" of the point of view chosen, and the historian chooses this point of view in the same way that you remember the word of an author or someone's gesture: when you first approach the work you become aware of a certain style.

It was one of Franklin's works that led Weber to his first view of the relationship between Calvinism and capitalism. Dating from the age of the maturity of Puritanism and preceding the adult age of capitalism, Franklin represented the transition from one to the other. His famous words are striking and illuminating because they express an ethic of labor: It is a duty to augment your capital and to increase it without enjoying that which you have gained. Production and accumulation are in themselves holy. You miss the essential point if you believe that Franklin attempts here to disguise interest as virtue. On the contrary, he goes so far as to say that God uses interest to lead him to the faith. If he writes that time is money, it is because he has learned from the Puritan tradition that spiritually time is precious and that we are in the world to give evidence at each moment of the glory of God. The useful could only become a value after it had been sanctified. What inspired the pioneers of capitalism was not the philosophy of the enlightenment and immanence, the joy of life that will come later. The "righteous, strict, and formalistic" character that brought them success can only be understood in terms of their feeling for the temporal calling and the economic ethic of Puritanism. Many of these elements of capitalism have existed here and there throughout history, but if it is only in Western Europe that you find the rational capitalistic enterprise in the sense that Weber defines it, this is perhaps because no other civilization has a theology which sanctifies temporal labor, demands a disciplined conduct of life, and joins the glory of God to the transformation of nature. Franklin's work presents us with a vital choice in its pure state, a mode of *Lebensführung* which relates Puritanism to the capitalistic spirit, defines Calvinism as disciplined conduct of life and capitalism as rationalization; finally, if the initial intuition is confirmed it discovers an intelligible transition from one to the other. If, in extending the ethic of labor back to its Calvinistic origins and toward its capitalistic consequences, Weber succeeds in understanding the basic structure of the facts, it is because he has discovered an objective meaning in them. It is because he has pierced the appearances in which reason is enclosed and gone beyond provisional and partial perspectives to reestablish the anonymous intention, the dialectic of a whole.

Going back from the disciplined conduct of life to its premises, Weber finds in Calvinism the feeling of an infinite distance between God and his creatures. In themselves they merit only eternal death; they can do nothing and are worth nothing and have no control over their destiny. God decides their election or their dereliction. They do not even know what they truly are. Alone on the other side of things, only God knows if they are to be saved or damned. The Calvinistic consciousness oscillates between culpability and vindication, both of which are equally unmerited, between an anguish without limits and a security without conditions. Both other people and the world have this same relation to God. Because of this infinite distance no third party can intervene in the relationship. The ties which man has with others and with the world are of a different order than those which he has with God. He cannot expect, on the whole, any succor from a church where the sinners are as numerous as the righteous or any aid from sermons and sacraments which will do nothing to alter the *decretum horrible*. The church is not a place where man will find another natural life. It is an institution created by will and attached to predetermined ends. For the Catholic it is as if a running account is open to him, and it is not until the end of his life that the balance is made of what he has and what he owes. The solitude of the Calvinist signifies that he confronts the absolute continually and that he does so futilely because he knows nothing of his destiny. At each moment the whole question of his salvation or damnation is posed and remains unanswered. There is no gain in Christian life; it can never be self-sufficient. "The glory of God and personal salvation remain always above the threshold of consciousness."[2]

Summoned to break the vital alliance that we have with time, with others, and with the world, the Calvinist pushes to its limits a demystification that is also a depoetization or a disenchantment [*Entzauberung*]. The sacraments, the church as the place of salvation, human feelings which always would sanctify creatures are rejected as magic.

[2] Max Weber, *Die Protestantische Ethik und der Geist des Kapitalismus* (Tübingen, 1934), p. 37.

This absolute anguish finds no relaxation in brotherly relations with created things. The created is the material upon which one works. It is to be transformed and organized to manifest the glory of God. The conscious control which is useless for salvation draws man into a temporal enterprise that takes on the value of a duty. Plans, methods, balance sheets are useless from God's point of view, since from that side everything is done and we can know nothing. All that is left to us is to put the world in order, to change the natural aspect and to rationalize life. This is the only means that we have to bring God's reign to earth. Salvation will not result from any of our acts. But the same anguish which we feel before that which we do not control, the same energy that we would expend to implement our salvation, even though we cannot do so, is expended in a temporal enterprise which is under our control. This temporal enterprise becomes even in Puritanism a presumption of salvation. The terror of man in the face of a supernatural destiny over which he has no control weighs heavily upon every one of the Puritan's activities in the world. By an apparent paradox, because he wishes to respect the infinite distance between God and man, he endows the useful and even the comfortable with a dignity and a religious meaning. He discredits leisure and even poverty in order to bring the rigors of asceticism into worldly use. In the Calvinist's estimation the goods of the world are precipitated by, and survive in relationship to, being and the absolute.

Let us now return from the consideration of the Calvinist ethic to the spirit of capitalism. Weber cites one of Wesley's phrases that marks this transition: "Religion necessarily produces the spirit of industry and frugality, and these cannot but produce riches. But as wealth increases so will pride, passion, and the love of worldly things. So although the form of religion remains, the spirit gradually declines." Franklin's generation left to its successors the possibility of becoming rich in good conscience. But they will forget the motive and concentrate on gaining the best of this world and the next. Once crystallized in the world by the Protestant ethic, capitalism will develop according to its own logic. Weber does not believe that it is sustained by the motive that brought it into existence or that it is the truth of Calvinism.

> The capitalistic economy is currently an immense cosmos into which individuals are born. It is for them, in so far as they are individuals, given as an actual, unalterable order within which they have to live. It imposes upon them, in so far as they are involved in market relation-

ships, the norms of their economic behavior. Today's capitalism, newly come to the domination of economic life, trains and produces through economic selection the economic subjects that it needs, whether they be entrepreneurs or laborers. However, it is at this point that we begin to understand the limits of the concept of selection in the explanation of historical facts. In order that the type of behavior [*Lebensführung*] could be chosen with respect to the calling suitable for capitalism, it had not only to exist in several individuals but it must have appeared as a manner of life common to human groups. It is this appearance that needs to be explained.[3]

There are thus a religious efficacy and an economic efficacy. Weber describes them as interwoven, exchanging positions so that first one and then the other plays the role of tutor. The effect turns back on its cause, carrying and transforming it in its turn. Furthermore, Weber does not simply integrate spiritual motives and material causes. He renews the concept of historical matter. An economic system is, as he says, a cosmos, a human choice become a situation. It is because of this that he can examine the disciplined conduct of life in terms of its religious motives and the descent of its capitalistic downfall as they are all connected in a single fabric. History has a meaning, but there is no pure development of the idea. Its meaning comes into contact with contingency at the moment when human initiative founds a system of life in taking up again the various givens. And the historical understanding which reveals an interior to history still leaves us in the presence of empirical history, with its depth and its chances which it does not subordinate to any hidden reason. Such is the philosophy without dogmatism which one observes all through Weber's studies. To go beyond this we must interpret freely. Let us do this without imputing to Weber more than he would have wished to say.

These intelligible nuclei of history are typical ways of treating natural being, of responding to others and to death. They appear at the point where men and the givens of nature or of the past meet, arising as symbolic matrices which have no preexistence and which can, for a longer or shorter time, influence history itself and then disappear, not by external forces but through an internal disintegration or because one of their secondary elements becomes predominant and changes their nature. The "rationalization" by which Weber defines capitalism is a fecund scheme of the kind that can also be used to explain art, science, the organization of the state, mysticism, or Western economy.

[3] *Ibid.*, p. 37.

It emerges here and there in history and, like historical types, is borne out only through the encounter of these givens, when, each confirming the other, they organize themselves into a system. For Weber capitalism presupposes a certain technology of production and therefore presupposes science in the Western sense. But it also presupposes a certain type of law, a government based upon formal rules, without which adventurous and speculative capitalism is possible but not the bourgeois enterprise. To these conditions Weber adds a "rational conduct of life," which has been the historical contribution of Protestantism. Law, science, technology, and Western religion are prime examples of this "rationalizing" tendency. But only after the fact. Each of these elements acquires its historical meaning only through its encounter with the others. History has often produced one of them in isolation (Roman law, the fundamental principles of calculus in India), without its being developed to the degree that it would have to be in capitalism. The encounter of these givens establishes the rationality which each possesses in outline form. To the degree that interactions accumulate, the development of the system in its own sense becomes more and more probable. Capitalistic production pushes more and more in the direction of the development of technology and the applied sciences. At the start it is not an all-powerful idea; it is a sort of historical imagination which sows here and there elements capable of one day being integrated. The meaning of a system in its beginnings is like the pictorial meaning of a painting which directs the painter's movements less than it is a result of them and progresses with them. Or again, it can be compared to the meaning of a spoken language, which is not transmitted in conceptual terms in the minds of those who speak, or in some ideal model of language, but which is, rather, the focal point of a series of verbal operations which converge almost by chance. Historians come to talk of "rationalism" or "capitalism" when the affinity of these products of the historical imagination becomes clear. But history does not work according to a model; it is in fact the very advent of meaning. To say that there has been an affinity between the elements of rationality before they crystallize into a system is only a manner of saying that, taken up and developed by human intentions, they ought to confirm one another and form a whole. Just as before the coming of the bourgeois enterprise, the elements which it joins did not belong to the same world, each must be said to be drawn by the others to develop a meaning which is common to them all, but which no one of them embodies.

The disciplined conduct of life whose principles have been established by Calvinism is finished by capitalism, but finished in both senses of the word. It is realized because it is, even more so than capitalism, activity in the world; it is destroyed as rigorous code because capitalism strives to eliminate its own transcendent motives. There is, Weber says, an elective affinity between the elements of an historical totality:

> Given the prodigious interweaving of the reciprocal influences among the material foundations, the forms of social and political organization, and the spiritual content of the cultural age of the Reformation, we must first of all try to discover whether and to what point certain elective affinities [*Wahlverwandtschaften*] can be recognized between such a form of religious belief and the ethic of a calling. We will also clarify, in so far as this can be done, the modalities and the general direction of the influence which the religious movement, by reason of these elective affinities, exercised upon the material culture. Only when this is sufficiently clarified can we attempt to determine to what extent the contents of modern culture can be imputed, in their historical development, to religious motives and to what extent to others.[4]

This relation is supple and reversible. If Protestant morality and capitalism are two institutional ways of stating the relationship of man to man, there is no reason why Protestant morality should not in such a case support the incipient capitalism. Nor is there anything to prevent capitalism from perpetuating certain typically Protestant modes of behavior in history, or even from displacing it as the driving force of history and substituting itself for it, allowing certain motives to perish and asserting others as its exclusive theme. The ambiguity of historical facts, their *Vielseitigkeit,* the plurality of their aspects, far from condemning historical knowledge to the realm of the provisional (as Weber said at first), is the very thing that agglomerates the dust of facts, which allows us to read in a religious fact the first draft of an economic system, or in an economic system a position taken with regard to the Absolute. Religion, law, and economy make up one single history because any fact in any one of the three orders arises, in a sense, from the two others. This is so because they are all bound up in the unique fiber of human choices.

This is a difficult position to hold and one which is threatened on both sides. Since Weber tries to preserve the individuality of the past while still situating it in a developmental process, perhaps even in

[4] *Ibid.,* p. 83.

a hierarchy, he will be reproached at times for concluding too little and at times for presuming too much. Does he not leave us without the means to criticize the past? Does he not give the same degree of reality and the same value to all civilizations, because the system of real and imaginary means by which man has managed his relations with the world and with other men has always managed to function, somehow or other? If we wish to go so far as to try to understand the past even in its phantasms, are we not inevitably led to justify it and thereby rendered unable to judge it? On the other hand, when Weber presents us with a logic of history, the objection can always be made that, as Malraux has shown, the decision to investigate and understand all civilizations is a deed which belongs to a civilization which is different from them, which transforms them. It transforms the crucifix into a work of art. That which had been a means of capturing the holy becomes an object of knowledge.

One final objection can be made. Historical consciousness is caught in this indefensible paradox: fragments of human life, each of which had been lived as absolute and which are in principle concealed to the disinterested onlooker, are brought together in the imagination in a single act of attention, compared, and considered as moments in a single developmental process. We must choose, then, between a history which judges, situates, and organizes—at the risk of finding in the past only a reflection of the troubles and problems of the present—and an indifferent, agnostic history which strings civilizations together as individuals which cannot be compared.

Weber is not oblivious of these difficulties; indeed it is they which have set his thought in action. The path which he seeks lies between history considered as a succession of unique facts and the arrogance of a philosophy which lays claim to have grasped the past in its categories and reduces it to our thoughts about it. He is opposed to both of them because of our interest in the past; it is ours and we are its. The dramas which have been lived inevitably remind us of our own and of us; we must view them from a single perspective, either because our own acts present us with the same problems in a clearer manner or, on the contrary, because our own difficulties have been more accurately defined in the past. We have just as much right to judge the past as the present. Moreover, it precedes the judgments we pass upon it. It has judged itself; having been lived by men, it has introduced values into history, and we cannot describe it without confirming or weakening their historical status. In most past mystifications those involved were to a certain extent aware of the deception. To be "objective" we are asked only to approach the past with its appropriate criteria. Weber reconciles evaluative history with objective history by calling upon the past to testify concerning itself. It is through Wesley that he can disclose the moment at which religion becomes mystification. An ideology which is a mystification is never completely ignorant of the fact. It requires a great deal of complaisance to justify the capitalistic world by means of Calvinistic principles; if these principles are fully articulated they will expose the ruse of attempting to turn them to one's own purposes. The men of the past could not completely hide the truth of their era from themselves; they did not need us in order to catch a glimpse of it. It is there, ready to appear; we have only to make a sign to reveal it.

Thus the very attempt to understand the past completely presupposes that we have already ordered the facts, placed them in a hierarchy, in a progression or a regression. In so doing we recapture the very movement of the past. It is true that the *Kulturmensch* is a modern type. History appears as a spectacle only to those who have a personal interest in all the various solutions which have been put at their disposal. History thus stands in contrast to both the narrow and the profound passions which it considers. Truth, says Weber, "is that which *seeks* to be recognized by all those who *seek* the truth."[5]

The decision to question each time a fundamental choice that is diffused in his thoughts, his desires, and his actions and of which he has never made an accounting is the result of living in a time that has tasted of the tree of knowledge. Scientific history is in principle opposed to naïve history—which it would, however, like to recapture. It is presupposed in that which it reconstructs. But this is not a vicious circle; it is the postulate of all historical thought. And Weber steps in conscientiously at this point. As Karl Löwith has shown, Weber is aware that scientific history is itself a product of history, a moment of the "rationalization," a moment of the history of capitalism.[6]

This same history turns back upon itself, presuming that clarification is possible. This presumption cannot be demonstrated. It is justified only in so far as it can give us a coherent image of the universal

[5] *Gesammelte Aufsätze zur Wissenschaftslehre* (Tübingen, 1922), p. 184.
[6] "Max Weber und Karl Marx," *Archiv für Sozialwissenschaft und Sozialpolitik,* LVII (1932).

history of culture. Nothing guarantees in advance that the attempt will be successful, but it is sufficient to know that to choose any other hypothesis is to choose chaos and that the truth which is sought is not, in principle, beyond our grasp. Of that we are certain. We discover that we possess the power of a radical choice by which we give meaning to our lives, and through this power we become sensitive to all the uses that humanity has made of it. Through it other cultures are opened up to us and made understandable. What we assume in order to understand history is that freedom understands the uses of freedom. What we contribute ourselves is only the prejudice of not having any prejudices, the fact that we belong to a cultural order where our choices, even those which are opposed to each other, tend to be complementary. "Culture is a closed segment abstracted from the infinity of events which is endowed with meaning and signification only for man. The transcendental condition of all cultural science is not that we find this or that culture valuable but the fact that we are 'cultural men,' endowed with the capacity consciously to take a position with regard to the world and to give meaning to it. Whatever this meaning might be, its consequence is that in living we abstract certain phenomena of human coexistence and in order to judge them we take a position (positive or negative) with regard to their significance."[7]

Historical understanding thus does not introduce a system of categories arbitrarily chosen; it only presupposes the possibility that we have a past which is ours and that we can recapture in our freedom the work of so many other freedoms. It assumes that we can clarify the choices of others through our own and ours through theirs, that we adjust one by the other and finally arrive at the truth.

There is no greater respect, no more profound objectivity than this claim of going to the very source of history. History is not an external god, a hidden reason of which we need only record our conclusions. It is the metaphysical fact that the same life, our own, is played out both within us and outside us, in our present and in our past, and that the world is a system to which we have various accesses or, if you prefer, various likenesses.

Because this type of economy, this type of knowledge, law, and religion depend upon the same fundamental choice and are historical accomplices, we can assume, the circumstances permitting, that the facts will arrange themselves, that the development can interpret the

[7] *Gesammelte Aufsätze zur Wissenschaftslehre,* pp. 180–81.

logic of an initial choice, and that history can become an experience of mankind. Even if the Calvinistic choice has transcendent motives which capitalism ignores, we can still say that in tolerating certain ambiguities it takes responsibility for what follows, and thus we can treat this sequence as a logical development. The Calvinist confronts and juxtaposes the finite and the infinite, carries to the extreme the consciousness that we have of not being the source of our own being, and organizes the obsession with the other world, at the same time closing the routes of access to it. In so doing he paves the way for the fanaticism of the bourgeois enterprise, authorizes the ethic of labor, and eliminates the consideration of the transcendent. Thus the course of history clarifies the errors and the contradictions of the fundamental choice, and the historical failure proves counter to Calvinism. In the factual sciences there is no proof by absurdity or crucial experiment. We know that certain solutions are impossible. We do not gain an enveloping understanding from the working operations of history which would reveal a true situation. At best we rectify errors which occur along the way, but the new aim is not immune to errors which will have to be rectified anew. History eliminates the irrational; but the rational continues to be imagined and to be created, and it has not the power of replacing the false with the true.

One historical solution of the human problem, one end of history could be conceived only if humanity were a thing to be known—if in it knowledge were able to exhaust being and could come to a state that really contained all that it had been and all that it could ever be. Whereas, on the contrary, in the depth of social reality each decision brings unexpected consequences, and man responds to these surprises be inventions which transform the problem. There is no situation without hope, but there is no choice which terminates the deviations or which can extenuate its inventive power and exhaust its history. There are only advances. The capitalistic rationalization is one of them, since it is the resolution of taking our given condition in hand through knowledge and action. It can be demonstrated that the appropriation of the world by man, that demystification, is better because it faces difficulties that other historical regimes have avoided. But this progress is bought by regressions, and there is no guarantee that the progressive elements of history will be disengaged from experience and be added up later. Demystification is also de-poetization and disenchantment. We must keep the capitalistic refusal of the sacred as external but renew in it the demands of the absolute that it has abolished. We have no grounds for affirming that this recovery will be made.

Capitalism is a shell that the religious animal has secreted for his domicile, and it survives him. "No one knows yet who will inhabit this shell in the future: whether at the end of its prodigious development there will be new prophets or a vigorous renaissance of all thoughts and ideals or whether finally, if none of this occurs, mechanism will produce only petrification [*Versteinerung*] hidden under a kind of anxious importance. According to this hypothesis, the prediction will become a reality for the last men of this particular development of culture. Specialists without spirit, libertines without heart, this nothingness imagines itself to be elevated to a level of humanity never before attained."[8] If the system comes to life again, it will be through the intervention of new prophets or by a resurrection of past culture, by an invention or reinvention which does not come from anything in that system. Perhaps history will eliminate, together with false solutions to the human problem, certain valid acquisitions as well. It will not locate its errors precisely in a total system. It does not accumulate truths; it works on a question that is confusedly posed and is not sheltered from regressions and setbacks. Projects change so much in the course of things that the generations of men who make the accounting are not those who have had the experience. What the facts have taught them has not been passed on.

Weber's phenomenology is thus not systematic like Hegel's. It does not lead to an absolute knowledge. Man's freedom and the contingency of history exclude definitively "the idea that the end of the cultural sciences, even though remote, is to construct a closed system of concepts in which reality will be confined according to a definitive order and from which it can be deduced. The course of unforeseeable events is transformed endlessly, stretching to eternity. The problems that move men are constantly posed anew and from other aspects. That which becomes meaningful and significant in the infinite flow of the individual constantly changes the field and it becomes a historical concept, just as the relations of thought are variable under which it is considered and posited as an object of science. The principles of the cultural sciences will keep changing in a future without limits as long as a sclerosis of life and of spirit does not disaccustom humanity, as in China, to posing new questions to an inexhaustible life.

[8] *Ibid.*, p. 204.

A system of the cultural sciences, even if confined to an area which is systematic and objectively valid for questions and for the domains which these questions are called upon to treat, will be nonsense in itself. An attempt of this type could only reassemble pell-mell the multiple, specific, heterogeneous, disparate points of view under which reality is presented to us each time as 'culture,' i.e., each time it is made significant in its specificity."[9]

The intelligible wholes of history never cease to confront contingency, and the movement by which history turns back on itself to attempt to grasp itself, to dominate itself, to justify itself, is also without guarantee. History admits of dialectical facts of adumbrative significations. It is not a coherent system. Like a distracted interlocutor it allows the debate to become sidetracked; it forgets the data of the problem along the way. Historical epochs become ordered around a question of human possibilities rather than around an immanent solution of which history will be the result.

Because its aim is to recover the fundamental choices of the past, science is, for Weber, a methodical extension of the experience of the present. But have this experience and its practical options benefited from historical understanding? For only if they have would Weber have reconciled theory and practice.

Weber is not a revolutionary. It is true that he writes that Marxism is "the most important instance of the construction of ideal types" and that all those who have employed its concepts know how fruitful they are—on the condition that they take as *meanings* what Marx describes as *forces*. But for him this transposition is incompatible with both Marxist theory and practice. As historical materialism, Marxism is a causal explanation through economics; and in its revolutionary practices Weber never sees the fundamental choice of the proletariat appear. It thus happens that, as has been said, this great mind judges the revolutionary movements which he witnessed in Germany after 1918 as if he were a provincial, bourgeois German. The Munich riot had placed at the head of the revolutionary government the most moralistic of its students. ("God, in his wrath, has made him a politician," Weber will say while defending him before the tribunal at the time of the repression.)[10] Weber confines himself to these minor facts and does not see a new historical significance in the revolutions after 1917. He is

[9] *Ibid.*, p. 185.
[10] Marianne Weber, *Max Weber, ein Lebensbild* (Tübingen, 1926).

against the revolution because he does not consider it to be a revolution—that is to say, the creation of a historical whole. He describes it as essentially a military dictatorship and for the rest, a carnival of intellectuals dressed up as politicians.

Weber is a liberal. But as we said at the beginning, his is a different kind of liberalism from those which preceded him. Raymond Aron writes that his politics is, like that of Alain, a "politics of the understanding." Only, from Alain to Weber the understanding has learned to doubt itself. Alain recommends a policy which is not quite adequate: do each day that which is just and don't worry about the consequences. However, this maxim is inoperative every time we approach a critical situation, and understanding is then against his principles, sometimes revolutionary, sometimes submissive. Weber himself well knows that it functions easily only within certain critical limits, and he consciously gives himself the task of keeping history within the region where it is free from antinomies. He does not make an isolated instance of it. Since we cannot even be sure that the history within which we find ourselves is in the end rational, those who choose truth and freedom cannot find those who make other choices guilty of absurdity, nor can they even flatter themselves of having "gone beyond" them. "It is the destiny of a cultural epoch which has tasted of the tree of knowledge to know that we cannot decipher the meaning of world events, regardless of how completely we might study them. We ought, rather, to be in the condition to create it ourselves and to know that world-views can never be the product of factual knowledge. Thus the highest ideals, those which move us most powerfully, can only become valid by being opposed to the ideals of other men, which are as sacred to them as ours are to us."[11]

Weber's liberalism does not demand a political utopia. It does not consider the formal universe of democracy to be an absolute. He admits that all politics is violence—even, in its own fashion, democratic politics. His liberalism is militant, suffering, heroic. He recognizes the rights of his adversaries, refuses to hate them, does not try to avoid confronting them, and in order to refute them relies only upon their own contradictions and upon the discussions which expose them. Though he rejects nationalism, Communism, and pacifism, he does not want to outlaw them; he does not cease trying to understand them. He who under the Empire decided against submarine warfare and in favor

[11] *Gesammelte Aufsätze zur Wissenschaftslehre,* p. 154.

of a white peace declared himself jointly responsible with the patriot who would kill the first Pole who entered Danzig. He opposed the pacifist left, which made Germany alone responsible for the war and exonerated in advance the foreign occupation, because he thought that these abuses of self-accusation paved the way for a violent nationalism in the future. Still, he testified in favor of the students who were involved in pacifist propaganda. Though he did not believe in the revolution, he made public his esteem for Liebknecht and Rosa Luxemburg.

Weber is against political discrimination within the university. Perhaps, he says, anarchist opinions might allow a scholar to see an aspect of history of which he would not have become aware had it not been for them. Though he scrupulously left out of his teaching anything which might have favored some cause or have exhibited his personal beliefs, he is in favor of professors who become engaged in politics. However, they should do this outside the classroom—in essays which are open to discussion and in public gatherings where the adversary can respond. The academic soliloquy should not be fraudulently used for the purposes of propaganda. . . . Thus he holds both ends of the chain. He thereby makes truth work together with decision, knowledge with struggle. In this way he makes sure that freedom should never be made the point of honor of a repression.[12]

Is this better than a compromise? Has he succeeded in uniting, except in his own person, the meanings of force and of freedom? When he wished to found a political party upon these bases, Weber was so easily eliminated and he returned so quickly to his studies that it was thought he did not adhere to it too strongly. It was thought that he felt there was an insurmountable obstacle in it and that a party which did not play according to the rules of the game would be a utopia. Nevertheless this failure is perhaps only Weber's. Perhaps it leaves intact the political wisdom which he sketched out at least once, even if he did not know how to put it into practice. For he does not content himself with setting values and efficacity, feeling and responsibility in opposition to one another. He makes an attempt to show what must be done to get beyond these alternatives. The taste for violence, he says, is a hidden weakness; the ostentation of virtuous feelings is a secret violence. These are two sorts of histrionics or neurosis, and there is a *force,* that of true politics, which is beyond these.

His secret is to not try to form an image of himself and of his life.

[12] On all these points see Marianne Weber, *op. cit.*

Because he has set himself and success at a distance, he does not become complacent in his intentions; he does not accept the judgment of others without recourse. Because his action is a "work," a devotedness to a "thing" [*Sache*] which grows outside him, it has a rallying power of the sort which is always lacking in undertakings which are done out of vanity. "Lack of distance" from oneself, from things, and from others is the professional disease of academic and intellectual circles. For them action is only a flight from oneself, a decadent mode of self-love. On the contrary, having once and for all decided to "bear the irrationality of the world," the politician is patient or intractable when he must be—that is to say, when he has compromised as much as he will allow himself and when the very sense of what he is doing is involved. Precisely because he is not a man of the ethics of the heart, when he says no to others and to things, even this is an action, and it is this which shows the inadequacy of the sterile promises of the politics of the heart. "When today, in the agitation of a time which we believe to be productive although agitation is not always a true passion, suddenly we see politics of the heart appearing everywhere, its advocates proclaiming, 'It is the world that is stupid and common, not I; I refuse the responsibility for the consequences'—then I often point out that there must be a degree of interior equilibrium that lies behind this ethics of the heart. I have the impression that in nine cases out of ten they are braggarts who do not really feel the seriousness of their action and who are intoxicated by romantic sentiments. This does not particularly arouse my humane interest or disturb me at all; on the contrary, what is disturbing is that a mature man, regardless of whether he is young or old, who feels actually responsible with his whole soul for consequences and who practices the ethics of responsibility, can come to the point of saying: *here I stand; I cannot do otherwise.* There is something here which is humanely pure and which grips you. But each one of us who is not internally dead ought to find ourselves in that situation. The ethics of heart and the ethics of responsibility are not absolutely opposed but complementary, and only the man in whom they are joined has the political calling."[13]

It will be said that this talisman is a small thing, that it is only a question of ethics, that a major political viewpoint extends the history of a time, and that it gives it its formula. But this objection ignores the most certain conclusion Weber establishes. If history does not have a

13 *Politik als Beruf,* p. 66.

direction like a river but only a meaning, not a truth but only errors to be avoided, if practice is not deduced from a dogmatic philosophy of history, it is not superficial to base a politics on the analysis of the political man. After all, once a politics is separated from the official legends, what makes it important is not the philosophy of history which inspires it and which in other hands would only produce upheavals. It is the human quality that causes the leaders truly to love the political apparatus, and their most personal acts are the most important thing. It is this rare quality that elevates Lenin and Trotsky above the other authors of the 1917 revolution. The course of things is only meaningful to those who know how to read it, and the principles of a philosophy of history are dead letters as long as you cannot recreate them in contact with the present. But in order to succeed we must possess the capacity of living history of which Weber speaks. The truth of politics is only this art of inventing what will later appear to have been required by the times. Certainly Weber's politics will have to be elaborated. It is not by chance that the art of politics is found in some places and not in others. We can think of it more as a symptom of the "intentions" of history than as a cause. We can try to read the present more attentively than Weber did, to perceive "elective affinities" that escaped him. But that which he has shown definitively is that a philosophy of history which is not a historical novel does not break the circle of knowledge and reality and that it is more a meditation upon that circle.

We began this study with Weber because at a time when the Marxist dialectic was becoming an actuality he showed under what conditions a historical dialectic is possible. There had been Marxists who understood this, and they were the best. There had been a rigorous and consequential Marxism which also was a theory of the historical understanding of the *Vielseitigkeit* of the creative choice, and a philosophy which questioned history. It is only after Weber and this Weberian Marxism that the adventures of the dialectic of the past thirty-five years can be understood.

On the Problem of
God and Religion

While Merleau-Ponty never developed in any complete way a philosophy of God or religion, the problem of God and religion does appear more than sporadically in his writings. Nevertheless, the selections in Part Seven are not of the same centrality to his thought as those in other sections. The first selection deals with the questions of proving God's existence, the second with the historical relationship between Christianity and philosophy, and the third with the relationship between Christianity and human society and history.

I5. GOD
AND
PHILOSOPHY

It is striking to find that today one no longer proves the existence of
God, as Saint Thomas, Saint Anselm, and Descartes did. The proofs
are ordinarily presupposed, and one limits one's self to refuting the negation of God either by seeking to find some gap in the new philosophies through which the constantly presupposed notion of the necessary
being may be made to reappear or, if these philosophies place this
notion decidedly in question, by abruptly disqualifying them as *atheism*. Even such relatively serene reflections as those of Father de Lubac
on atheistic humanism, and those of M. Maritain on the meaning of
contemporary atheism are carried on as if philosophy, when it is not
theological, is reduced to the negation of God. Father de Lubac takes
as the object of his study an atheism which truly wishes, he says, "to
replace what it destroys," which, therefore, begins by destroying what
it wishes to replace, and which is rather, like that of Nietzsche, a sort
of deicide. Maritain examines what he rather curiously calls positive
atheism, and which soon comes to appear to him as an "active combat
against everything that suggests God," an "antitheism," an "act of
inverted faith," a "refusal of God," a "defiance against God." This
antitheism certainly exists, but since it is an inverted theology, it is
not a philosophy, and by focusing the whole discussion on it, one shows
perhaps that it holds locked up within itself the very theology it is
attacking. But at the same time one reduces everything to a controversy

Maurice Merleau-Ponty, *In Praise of Philosophy,* trans. by John Wild and James
M. Edie (Evanston, Illinois: Northwestern University Press, 1963), pp. 42–47.
Reprinted by permission.

between theism and anthropotheism as they re-echo the troubles of religious alienation, and forgets to ask whether the philosopher really has to choose either the theology and the apocalypse of Wonderland or the "mystique of the superman," and whether any philosopher has ever endowed man with the metaphysical functions of omnipotence.

Philosophy works itself out in another order, and it is for the same reasons that it eludes both Promethean humanism and the rival affirmations of theology. The philosopher does not say that a final transcendence of human contradictions may be possible, and that the complete man awaits us in the future. Like everyone else, he knows nothing of this. He says—and this is something altogether different—that the world is going on, that we do not have to judge its future by what has happened in the past, that the idea of a destiny in things is not an idea but a dizziness, that our relations with nature are not fixed once and for all, that no one can know what freedom may be able to do, nor imagine what our customs and human relations would be in a civilization no longer haunted by competition and necessity. He does not place his hope in any destiny, even a favorable one, but in something belonging to us which is precisely not a destiny—in the contingency of our history. The denial of this is a fixed (non-philosophical) position.

Must we then say that the philosopher is a humanist? No, if one understands by "man" an explanatory principle which ought to be substituted for the others. One explains nothing by man, since he is not a force but a weakness at the heart of being, a cosmological factor, but also the place where all cosmological factors, by a mutation which is never finished, change in sense and become history. Man is as effective in the contemplation of an inhuman nature as in the love of himself. His existence extends to too many things, in fact to all, for him to become the object of his own delight, or for the authorization of what we can now reasonably call a "human chauvinism." This same wide-ranging flexibility, which eludes every religion of humanity, also takes the wind from the sails of theology. For theology recognizes the contingency of human existence only to derive it from a necessary being, that is, to remove it. Theology makes use of philosophical wonder only for the purpose of motivating an affirmation which ends it. Philosophy, on the other hand, arouses us to what is problematic in our own existence and in that of the world, to such a point that we shall never be cured of searching for a solution, as Bergson says, "in the notebooks of the master."

Father de Lubac discusses an atheism which means to suppress this searching, he says, "even including the problem as to what is responsible for the birth of God in human consciousness." This problem is so little ignored by the philosopher that, on the contrary, he radicalizes it, and places it above the "solutions" which stifle it. The idea of necessary being, as well as that of "eternal matter" and "total man," appear prosaic to him in comparison with this constant manifesting of religious phenomena through all the stages of world history, and this continual rebirth of the divine which he is trying to describe. In this situation, he is well able to understand religion as one of the expressions of the central phenomenon of consciousness. But the example of Socrates reminds us that it is not the same thing, but almost the opposite, to understand religion and to accept it. Lichtenberg, of whom Kant said that each of his phrases hid a profound thought, held something of the following kind: one should neither affirm the existence of God nor deny it. As he explained: "it is not necessary that doubt should be anything more than vigilance; otherwise, it can become a source of danger." It is not that he wished merely to leave certain perspectives open, nor to please everyone. It is rather that he was identifying himself, for his part, with a consciousness of self, of the world, and of others that was "strange" (the word is his) in a sense which is equally well destroyed by the rival explanations.

This decisive moment when certain particles of matter, words, and events allow themselves to be animated by a meaning, the nearest contours of which they suggest without containing, is above all the fundamental keynote of the world which is already given with the least of our perceptions. Both consciousness and history echo this. It is the same thing to establish them against any naturalistic explanation as it is to release them from any sovereign necessity. Hence one bypasses philosophy when one *defines* it as atheism. This is philosophy as it is seen by the theologian. Its negation is only the beginning of an attention, a seriousness, an experience on the basis of which it must be judged. Furthermore, if one remembers the history of the word *atheism,* and how it has been applied even to Spinoza, the most positive of philosophers, we must admit that all thinking which displaces, or otherwise defines, the sacred has been called atheistic, and that philosophy which does not place it here or there, like a thing, but at the joining of things and words, will always be exposed to this reproach without ever being touched by it.

A sensitive and open thought should not fail to guess that there is an affirmative meaning and even a presence of the spirit in this philosophical negativity. Indeed Maritain finally comes to justify the continuous criticism of idols as essential to Christianity. The saint, he says, is a "complete atheist" with respect to a God who would be only the guarantor of the natural order, who would consecrate not only all the world's goodness but all the world's evil as well, who would justify slavery, injustice, the tears of children, the agony of the innocent by sacred necessities, who would finally sacrifice man to the cosmos as "the absurd Emperor of the world." The Christian God who redeems the world and is accessible to prayer, according to Maritain, is the active negation of all this. Here, indeed, we are close to the essence of Christianity. The philosopher will only ask himself if the natural and rational concept of God as necessary being is not inevitably that of the Emperor of the world, if without this concept, the Christian God would not cease to be the author of the world, and if the criticism we are now suggesting is not the philosophy which presses to the limit that criticism of false gods which Christianity has introduced into our history? Yes, *where* will one stop the criticism of idols, and *where* will one ever be able to say the true God actually resides if, as Maritain writes, we pay tribute to false gods "every time we bow before the world"?

16. CHRISTIANITY AND PHILOSOPHY

One of the tests in which philosophy best reveals its essence is its confrontation with Christianity. Not that there is Christianity unanimous on one side and philosophy unanimous on the other. On the contrary, what was striking in the famous discussion of this subject which took place 'twenty-five years ago[1] was that behind disagreement about the idea of Christian philosophy or about the existence of Christian philosophies, one detected a more profound debate concerning the nature of philosophy, and that on this point neither Christians nor non-Christians were agreed.

Gilson and Maritain said that philosophy is not Christian in its *essence* but only according to its status, only through the intermingling of religious thought and life in the same age and ultimately in the same man. And in this sense they were not so far from Bréhier, who distinguished philosophy as a rigorous system of ideas from Christianity as the revelation of a supernatural history of man, and concluded, for his part, that no philosophy as philosophy can be Christian. When on the other hand Brunschvicg,[2] thinking of Pascal and Malebranche, reserved the possibility of a philosophy which confirms the discordancy between existence and idea (and thus its own insufficiency), and

Maurice Merleau-Ponty, "Everywhere and Nowhere," *Signs,* Part II, Ch. 5, trans. by Richard C. McCleary (Evanston, Illinois: Northwestern University Press, 1964), pp. 140–46. Reprinted by permission.

[1] "La notion de philosophie chrétienne," *Bulletin de la Société française de Philosophie,* Séance du 21 mars, 1931.

[2] Léon Brunschvicg, twentieth-century French philosopher and professor who influenced the young Merleau-Ponty.—Trans.

thereby serves as an introduction to Christianity as an interpretation of existing man and the world, he was not so far from Blondel, for whom philosophy *was* thought realizing that it cannot "close the gap," locating and palpating inside and outside of us a reality whose source is not philosophical awareness. Once a certain point of maturity, experience, or criticism has been passed, what separates men or brings them together is not so much the final letter or formulation of their convictions but rather the way in which, Christians or not, they deal with their own duality and organize within themselves relationships between idea and reality.

The real question underlying debate about Christian philosophy is that of the relation between essence and existence. Shall we assume that there is an essence of philosophy or a purely philosophical knowledge which is jeopardized in human life (in this case, religious life) but nevertheless remains what it is, strictly and directly communicable, the eternal word which illuminates every man who comes into this world? Or shall we say on the contrary that philosophy is radical precisely because it digs down beneath what seems to be immediately communicable, beneath available thoughts and conceptual knowledge, and reveals a tie between men, as it does between men and the world, which precedes and founds ideality?

To prove that this alternative governs the question of Christian philosophy, we need only follow the twists and turns of the discussion which took place in 1931. Some of the discussants, having granted that in the order of principles, ideas, and possibilities, philosophy and religion are both autonomous, admit when they turn toward facts or history that religion has made a contribution to philosophy, whether it be the idea of creation, of infinite subjectivity, or of development and history. Thus in spite of essences there is an exchange between religion and reason which entirely recasts the question. For if matters of faith can in fact provide food for thought (unless faith is only the opportunity for an awareness which is equally possible without faith), we must admit that faith reveals certain aspects of being, that thought (which ignores them) does not "tie it all up," and that faith's "things not seen" and reason's evidence cannot be set apart as two *domains*. If on the contrary we follow Bréhier in going straight to history in order to show that there has been no philosophy which was Christian, we succeed only by rejecting as alien to philosophy the ideas of Christian origin which block our efforts, or by seeking their antecedents outside

Christianity at no matter what cost—which proves clearly enough that we are referring to a history which has been prepared and doctored in accordance with the idea of philosophical immanence. Thus two alternatives were presented in the discussion. We may ask a factual question; but since Christian philosophy can be neither affirmed or denied on the level of "pure" history except in a wholly nominal way, the supposed factual judgment will be categorical only if it includes a conception of philosophy. Or we may openly ask the question in terms of essences, and then everything has to be begun again as soon as we pass to the order of mixtures and existing philosophies. In both cases, we miss the problem, which exists only for an historico-systematic thought capable of digging beneath essences, accomplishing the movement back and forth between them and facts, challenging essences with facts and "facts" with essences, and in particular putting its own immanence in question.

For this "open" thinking the question is in a sense settled as soon as it is asked. Since it does not take its "essences" as such for the measure of all things, since it does not believe so much in essences as in knots of significations which will be unraveled and tied up again in a different way in a new network of knowledge and experience, and which will only continue to exist as its past, we cannot see in the name of what this projecting thought would refuse the title of philosophy to indirect or imaginative modes of expression and reserve it for doctrines of the intemporal and immanent Word which are themselves placed above all history. Thus there is certainly a Christian philosophy, as there is a Romantic or a French philosophy, and a Christian philosophy which is incomparably more extensive, since in addition to the two philosophies we have mentioned it contains all that has been thought in the West for twenty centuries. How can we take ideas like those of history, subjectivity, incarnation, and positive finitude away from Christianity in order to attribute them to a "universal" reason with no birthplace?

What is not thereby settled—and what constitutes the real problem of Christian philosophy—is the relationship between this instituted Christianity, a mental horizon or matrix of culture, and the Christianity effectively lived and practiced in a positive faith. To find a meaning and an enormous historical value in Christianity and to assume it personally are two different things. To say yes to Christianity as a fact of culture or civilization is to say yes to St. Thomas, but also to St. Augustine and Occam and Nicholas of Cusa and Pascal and Malebranche, and this assent does not cost us an ounce of the pains each one of them had to take in order to be himself without default. Historical and philosophical consciousness transmutes the struggles they sustained, at times in solitude and to the death, into the benevolent universe of culture. But the philosopher or historian, precisely because he understands them all, is not one of them. Furthermore, the historian pays the same attention and infinite respect to a bit of broken pottery, formless reveries, and absurd rituals. He is only concerned with knowing what the world is made of and what man is capable of, not with getting himself burned at the stake for this proposition or having his throat cut for that truth. For the philosopher, the Christianity which fills our philosophy is the most striking sign of self-transcendence. For the Christian, Christianity is not a symbol; it is the truth. In a sense, the tension between the philosopher who understands everything as human questioning and the narrow, profound practice of the very religion he "understands" is greater than it was between a rationalism which claimed to explain the world and a faith which was only nonsense to it—because the distance between the two is shorter.

So once again philosophy and Christianity are in conflict, but the conflict is one we meet within the Christian world and within each Christian in the form of the conflict between Christianity "understood" and Christianity lived, between universality and choice. Within philosophy too, when it collides with the Manichaeism of *engagement.* The complex relationship between philosophy and Christianity would be disclosed only if a Christianity and a philosophy worked upon internally by the same contradiction were compared to one another.

The "Thomist peace" and the "Cartesian peace," the innocent coexistence of philosophy and Christianity taken as two positive orders or two truths, still conceal from us the hidden conflict of each with itself and with the other, as well as the tormented relationships which result from it.

If philosophy is a self-sufficing activity which begins and ends with conceptual understanding, and faith is assent to things not seen which are given for belief through revealed texts, the difference between them is too great even for there to be conflict. There will be conflict when rational adequation claims to be exhaustive. But if only philosophy recognizes, beyond the possibilities it is judge of, an actual world order whose detail arises from experience, and if the revealed given is taken as a supernatural experience, there is no rivalry between faith and reason. The secret of their agreement lies in infinite thought, whether it is conceiving of possibilities or creating the actual world. We do not have access to all it thinks, and its decrees are known to us only by their effects. We are thus in no position to understand the unity of reason and faith. What is certain is that it is brought about in God.

Reason and faith are thus in a state of equilibrium of indifference. Some have been astonished to see that Descartes, after having defined natural light so carefully, accepts a *different light* without difficulty, as if as soon as there are two, at least one must become relatively obscure. But the difficulty is no greater—and no differently met—than that of admitting the distinction which the understanding makes between soul and body, and, in another context, their substantial unity. There is the understanding and its sovereign distinctions, and there is the existing man (the understanding aided by imagination and joined to a body) whom we know through the practice of life because we are that man; and the two orders are a single one because the same God is both the sustainer of essences and the foundation of our existence. Our duality is reflected and surmounted in Him as the duality of his understanding and his will. We are not required to understand how. God's absolute transparency assures us of the fact, and for our part we can and must respect the difference between the two orders and live in peace on both levels.

Yet this is an unstable concordat. If man is really grafted onto the two orders, their connection is also made in him, and he should know something about it. His philosophical and his religious relationships to God should be of the same type. Philosophy and religion must symbolize. In our view, this is the significance of Malebranche's philosophy. Man cannot be part "spiritual automaton," part religious subject who receives the supernatural light. The structures and discontinuities of religious life are met with again in his understanding. In the natural order understanding is a sort of contemplation; it is vision in God. Even in the order of knowledge, we are neither our own light to ourselves nor the source of our ideas. We are our soul, but we do not have the idea of it; we only have feeling's obscure contact with it. All there can be in us of light and of intentional being comes from our participation in God. We do not have the power to conceive; our whole initiative in understanding is to address—this is what is called "attention"—a "natural prayer" to the Word which has only obligated itself to grant it always. What is ours is this invocation and the passive experience of the knowledge-events which result from it—in Malebranche's terms, "perception" and "feeling." What is also ours is this present, livelier pressure of intelligible extension on our soul, which makes us believe we see the world. In fact we do not see the world in itself. This appearance *is* our ignorance of ourselves, of our souls, and of the genesis of its modalities; and all there is of truth in our experience of the world is the fundamental certainty of an actual world existing beyond what we see and depending on which God makes us see what we do see. The slightest sense perception is thus a "natural revelation." Natural knowledge is divided between idea and perception, as religious life is divided between the light of mystical life and the chiaroscuro of revealed texts. The only thing that allows us to say that it is natural is that it obeys laws, and that God, in other words, intervenes in it only through general acts of will.

And even so the criterion is not an absolute one. If natural knowledge is woven out of religious relationships, the supernatural in return imitates nature. It is possible to sketch out a sort of dynamics of grace and glimpse laws and an order according to which the incarnate Word usually exercises its mediation. For the longitudinal cleavage between philosophy (the realm of pure understanding) and the created and existing world (the realm of natural or supernatural experience), Malbranche substitutes a transversal cleavage, and distributes the same typical structures of light and feeling, of ideal and real, between reason and religion. Natural philosophy's concepts invade theology; religious concepts invade natural knowledge. We no longer limit ourselves to evoking the infinite, which is for us incomprehensible, and in which orders that are for us distinct are believed to be unified. The articulations of nature hold only through God's action; almost all the interventions of grace are subjected to rules. God as cause is required by each idea we think of, and God as light is manifest in almost all His acts of will. No one has ever been closer to the Augustinian program: "True religion is true philosophy; and true philosophy, in turn, is true religion."

Thus Malebranche tries to think about the relationship between religion and philosophy instead of accepting it as a fact about which there is nothing to say. But can this relationship be formulated in terms of identity? Taken as contradictory, reason and faith coexist without difficulty. Similarly, and inversely, as soon as they are made identical they become rivals. The community of categories underlines the discordancy between natural revelation and natural prayer, which are open to all, and supernatural revelation and supernatural prayer, which were taught at first only to some; between the eternal and the incarnate Word; between the God we see as soon as we open our eyes and the God of the Sacraments and the Church, who must be gained and merited through supernatural life; and between the Architect divined in His works and the God of love who is reached only in the blindness of sacrifice. It is this very discordancy that one would have to take as one's theme if one wanted to construct a Christian philosophy; it is in it that one would have to look for the articulation of faith and reason. In so doing one would draw away from Malebranche, but one would also be inspired by him. For although he communicates something of reason's light to religion (and at the limit makes them identical in a single universe of thought), and although he extends the positivity of understanding to religion, he also foreshadows the invasion of our rational being by religious reversals, introducing into it the paradoxical thought of a madness which is wisdom, a scandal which is peace, a gift which is gain.

What would the relationship between philosophy and religion be in this case? Maurice Blondel[3] wrote: "Within and before itself philosophy hollows out a void which is prepared not only for the discoveries which it subsequently makes on its own grounds but also for the illuminations and contributions which it does not itself and never can really originate." Philosophy reveals a lack, a being out of focus, the expectation of forward movement. Without necessitating or presupposing positive options, it paves the way for them. It is the negative of a certain positive; not just any sort of void but precisely the lack of what faith will bring; and not hidden faith but the universally confirmable premise of a faith which remains free. We do not go from one to the other either by prolongation or simply by adjunction, but by a reversal which philosophy motivates without accomplishing.

Is the problem solved? Or does it not arise again at the suture of negative philosophy and positive faith? If, as Blondel would have it, philosophy is universal and autonomous, how could it leave responsibility for its conclusions to an absolute decision? What it roughs out with the broken lines of conceptual terms in the peace of the universal receives its full meaning only in the irreparable partiality of a life. But

---

[3] Maurice Blondel, twentieth-century French philosopher. For further judgments of his thought by Merleau-Ponty, see *In Praise of Philosophy.*—Trans.

how could it help wanting to be a witness to this very passage from universal to particular? How could it possibly dwell in the negative and abandon the positive to a "wholly other" solicitation? It must itself recognize in a certain fullness what it sketched out beforehand in the void, and in practice at least something of what it has seen in theory. Philosophy's relationship to Christianity cannot be simply the relationship of the negative to the positive, of questioning to affirmation. Philosophical questioning involves its own vital options, and in a sense it maintains itself within a religious affirmation. The negative has its positive side, the positive its negative, and it is precisely because each has its contrary within itself that they are capable of passing into one another, and perpetually play the role of warring brothers in history.

Will this always be the case? Will there ever be a real exchange between philosopher and Christian (whether it is a matter of two men or of those two men each Christian senses within himself)? In our view this would be possible only if the Christian (with the exception of the ultimate sources of his inspiration, which he alone can judge) were to accept without qualification the task of mediation which philosophy cannot abandon without eliminating itself. It goes without saying that these lines commit their signer alone, and not the Christian collaborators who have so kindly agreed to give him their assistance. It would be a poor recognition of their aid to create the slightest ambiguity between their feelings and his. Nor does he give these lines as an introduction to their thought. They are more in the nature of reflections and questions he is writing in the margin of their texts in order to submit them to them.

These texts themselves (and on this point we are no doubt in unanimous agreement) give us a lively sense of the diversity of Christian inquiries. They remind us that Christianity has nourished more than one philosophy, no matter what privilege one of them may have been granted, that as a matter of principle it involves no single and exhaustive philosophical expression, and that in this sense—no matter what its acquisitions may be—Christian philosophy is never *something settled*.

17. FAITH AND GOOD FAITH

Pierre Hervé was right in his recent reply to Father Daniélou.[1] To give Catholicism its due, it is easy to cite Christian and pontifical texts or individual acts which promote freedom and oppose the interests of established regimes. But it is even easier to find texts in the Catholic tradition which are hostile to freedom. Above all, historical Catholicism is not merely a certain number of texts nor a sum of individuals; it is a machine, an institution or a movement with an over-all logic, which is unquestionably operating in a reactionary direction despite certain texts and individual sentiments, or even with the help of the ambiguity which these create. There was once a young Catholic who was led "to the Left" by the demands of his faith. This was the time when Dollfuss inaugurated Europe's first Christian Socialist government by shelling the working-class sections of Vienna. A magazine inspired by Christians protested to President Miklas, and the protest was said to be supported by the most progressive of our great religious orders. The young man was welcomed at the table of some monks belonging to this order. In the middle of lunch he was astonished to hear that, after all, the Dollfuss government was the established power, that it had the right to a police force since it was the proper government, and that the Catholics, as Catholics, had nothing against it, although as citizens

Maurice Merleau-Ponty, "Faith and Good Faith," *Sense and Non-Sense,* Part III, Ch. 12, trans. by Hubert L. Dreyfus and Patricia Allen Dreyfus (Evanston, Illinois: Northwestern University Press, 1964), pp. 172–81. Reprinted by permission.
[1] *Action,* Dec. 14, 1945.

they were free to censure it. In later life the young man never forgot this moment. He turned to the Father (a bold and generous man, as was seen later) who had first voiced these opinions and told him simply that this justified the workers' opinion of the Catholics: in social questions they can never fully be counted on.

Hervé's criticism is, however, incomplete. It puts the sentiments of the Catholics back into the context of institutional Catholicism and pontifical diplomacy. It shifts the discussion from the plane of ideas to that of facts. But this is the very reason it will never convince Father Daniélou. One can imagine him reading Hervé's conclusive text but remaining unconvinced. How could he separate Catholicism from what he himself thinks and wants? In his own eyes the Catholic is progressive, although for others the Catholic is reactionary. Reverend Father Daniélou feels that he is free, just, and bold in his political thinking, and as a matter of fact he is. But we see him only through the social body which he inhabits, just as we see an alien consciousness only through that unchanging physical body, that frozen past, which carries so little weight for the consciousness itself. Father Daniélou will agree that the past gives him the lie—but he will add that the problem is constantly to recall Christianity to itself, to reawaken its hunger and thirst for justice. He will plead guilty for the past and innocent for the future. He will appeal from the outside to the inside, from historical Catholicism to its conscience, from a history which today's Catholics never made to the one they want to create from now on. He will always have the right to think that bad luck was behind any reactionary manifestations of the Catholic religion and that the institution and the luck may change.

The question could be settled only by illuminating the relationship of the religion itself to the conservative spirit and the revolutionary spirit. We must understand why organized Christianity has assumed a certain guise throughout history, why the Christian is not the same for others as for himself. In the last analysis, our bodies bear witness to what we are; body and spirit express each other and cannot be separated. The Catholic's social conduct cannot be criticized without touching on his inner life. We cannot rest content with blaming the political and social infrastructure of Catholicism; along with the critique of the underlying structure there must go a critique which would grasp Catholicism in its totality and define it globally as a certain stand about the world and men which yields both generous sentiments and conservative conduct. There must be an ambiguity in Catholicism as a spiritual way of life to correspond to its ambiguity as a social phenomenon.

•   •   •

Catholicism posits a belief in both an interior and an exterior God. This is the religious formulation of its contradictions.

"Turn inward," said St. Augustine. "Truth dwells within the inner man." One finds God by turning away from things. Whether God is the model according to which my spirit was created or whether I experience and, so to speak, touch God when I become conscious of myself as spirit, God is in any case on the side of the subject rather than on the side of the world. He is "within me more myself that I," *intimior intimo meo,* to quote St. Augustine once again. He is fully that clarity, that light which I am at my best moments. What is evident for me cannot be less so for Him, since it is precisely upon my inner experience of the truth that I base my affirmation of an absolute Truth and of an absolute Spirit which thinks it. Since God is truth, I always serve Him in saying what I think, on the sole condition that I have done my utmost to clarify my ideas. To be faithful is to be sincere. Faith is good faith.

Obedience to God does not, therefore, consist in yielding to an alien and obscure will but consists in doing what we really want, since God is more ourselves than we. To confess God in words is nothing: "The letter kills, but the spirit quickens." All that is valuable is the evidence which the spirit within us gives to itself. It exists in men who do not call God by name but who recognize Him in spirit and truth. As for the others, force is powerless to save them. Force may impose gestures but not an inner conviction. Canon Law states: "No one can be constrained by force to embrace the Catholic faith." Religion can be neither attacked nor defended by arms. "Who lives by the sword shall die by the sword." Here religion is placed in a dimension of eternity where it is invulnerable. God, unlike things, does not need time and space in order to exist: He is everywhere, and nowhere in particular. He is not diminished when men turn away from Him. In this sense, sin is unreal. If my actions go against my conscience, I cease to be spirit, I cease to be myself, I do nothing positive; and evil is only the absence of good. The expression "to *do* good" loses its sense because good resides only in the spirit and finally in God, who is eternal. There is always an element of Stoicism in the idea of God: if God exists, then perfection has already been achieved outside this world; since perfection cannot be increased, there is, strictly speaking, nothing to do. "My kingdom is not of this world." Good works are the by-products of religion. They do not add to the total Good, just as infinity is not increased by the addition of another unit. Our fate here matters little in the other world because God is worthy of our adoration no matter what. Let us find our rest in Him. Quietism. Our fate here below is unimportant in any case; we have only to take it as it comes, for better or for worse. After all, we do not have any claim on life. "Thy will be done." Man renounces his claim on his life. He lives in the will of God as children live in the will of their parents. As Hegel said, it is the reign of the Father.

The Incarnation changes everything. Since the Incarnation, God has been externalized. He was seen at a certain moment and in a certain place, and He left behind Him words and memories which were then passed on. Henceforth man's road toward God was no longer contemplation but the commentary and interpretation of that ambiguous message whose energy is never exhausted. In this sense Christianity is diametrically opposed to "spiritualism." It reopens the question of the distinction between body and spirit, between interior and exterior. Catholicism does not like reflexive proofs of God and only grudgingly does it make room for them. One can prove the existence of God with the human spirit as a starting point, but only by taking it as one part of Creation with the same standing as the heavens and the earth which "declare the glory of God." The human soul can signal God's place at the origin of the world, but it can neither see nor understand Him and cannot therefore be centered in Him. The world ceases to be like a flaw in the great eternal diamond. It is no longer a matter of rediscovering the transparence of God outside the world but a matter of entering body and soul into an enigmatic life, the obscurities of which cannot be dissipated but can only be concentrated in a few mysteries where man contemplates the enlarged image of his own condition. Pascal said, and Jacques Rivière says now, that the dogmas of the Incarnation and Original Sin are not clear but are valuable because they reflect man's contradictions of body and soul, nobility and wretchedness. The parables of the Gospel are not a way of presenting pure ideas in images; they are the only language capable of conveying the relations of religious life, as paradoxical as those of the world of sensation. Sacramental words and gestures are not simply the embodiment of some thought. Like tangible things, they are themselves the carriers of their meaning, which is inseparable from its material form. They do not evoke the idea of God: they are the vehicle of His presence and action. In the last analysis the soul is so little to be separated from the body that it will carry a radiant double of its temporal body into eternity.

Hegel said that the Incarnation is "the hinge of universal history" and that all history thereafter has only developed its consequences. And the God-Man and the Death of God do, in effect, transform spirit and religion. As if the infinite God were no longer sufficient, as if something moved in Him, as if the world and man became the necessary moments of a greater perfection instead of being a useless decline from the originating perfection. God can no longer be fully God, and Creation cannot be completed unless man freely recognizes God and returns Creation to Him through Faith. Something is happening; the world is not futile; there is something to be done. Man could not return to God unless he had been separated from Him. "Fortunate the fault which merited such a Redeemer." One should not regret paradise lost: in it man lived like an animal under the natural law of God. It is through sin that he acquired the knowledge of good and evil, that he became consciousness and became man. *Omnia cooperantur in bonum, etiam peccata.* Sin is real. It serves the glory of God. It is no longer a question of man's withdrawing from the world like the Stoics or regaining purity and sincerity in the Socratic manner, by the exercise of his understanding. His relation to God is ambiguous because it does not exist without separation. Kierkegaard thought it impossible to say "I am a Christian" in the way one says "I am tall" or "I am short," because being a Christian means living the contradiction of good and evil, and so it also means not being a Christian. Never absolutely good or absolutely bad, man cannot be sincere, for sincerity supposes a definite nature which one can assess without ambiguity. It is a matter not of contemplating oneself but of constructing and going beyond oneself. "Faith is in things unseen." It is an adherence that goes beyond the guarantees which one is given and therefore excludes an ever-present sincerity. The Christian should not "deny in darkness what he has seen in light." He will not challenge his God and his Church even if he does not at first understand their decrees; he will not doubt the sacraments even though they afford him no happiness.

The paradox of Christianity and Catholicism is that they are never satisfied with either an interior or an exterior God but are always *between* one and the other. We must go beyond ourselves; we must "lose our life," but in its loss is its salvation. Faith is reliance, but the Christian knows whom he is relying on: *scio cui credidi*. Catholicism does not want to give everything over to Christian faith. The Syllabus states that no one is a Catholic who doubts reason's ability to prove the existence of God, and modernists have been censured for wanting to *replace* the God of philosophers and scholars with the God perceived by the heart. Catholicism finds distasteful a philosophy which is merely a transcription of Christian experience, doubtless because such a philosophy, when carried to its logical extreme, would be a philosophy of man instead of a theology. *Tu es vere Deus absconditus.* There is nothing one can say about this hidden God inaccessible to speculation, whose affirmation lies in the shadowy regions of faith, and in the end He would appear to be a postulate of human life rather than the most certain of beings. One does not of course challenge Christian experience and Pascal's description of it: one just maintains it on the indistinct plane of existence, the essences of which are still judged by speculative philosophy and Thomism.

The Incarnation is not followed out in all its consequences. The first Christians felt abandoned after the death of Christ and looked everywhere for a trace of Him. Centuries later the Crusaders plunged into the search for an empty tomb. And this was because they worshiped the Son in the spirit of the religion of the Father. They had not yet understood that God was with them now and forever. The meaning of the Pentecost is that the religion of both the Father and the Son are to be fulfilled in the religion of the Spirit, that God is no longer in Heaven but in human society and communication, wherever men come together in His name. Christ's stay on earth was only the beginning of his presence, which is continued by the Church. Christians should not remain polarized by an historical episode, no matter how decisive it might have been, but should live out the marriage of the Spirit and human history which began with the Incarnation. Catholicism arrests and freezes this development of religion: the Trinity is not a dialectical movement; the Three Persons are co-eternal. The Father is not surpassed by the Spirit; the religion of the Father lives on in the religion of the Spirit, for Love does not eliminate the Law or the fear of God. God is not completely with us. Behind the incarnate Spirit there remains that infinite gaze which strips us of all secrets, but also of our liberty, our desire, and our future, reducing us to *visible objects*. Likewise, the Church is not rooted in human society but is crystallized on the margin of the State. The Spirit is everywhere, but its privileged dwelling place is the Church. For a second time men are alienated by this second gaze which weighs upon them and which has more than once found a *secular arm* to serve it. What is surprising about this? Not only is it tempting, it is urgent to hold men in check when one *knows* that they are wasting their time in an idle search while on the reverse side of things an infinite Knowledge has already settled everything. And so love changes to cruelty, the reconciliation of men with each other and with the world will come to naught, the Incarnation turns into suffering because it is incomplete, and Christianity becomes a new form of guilty conscience.

The ambiguity of Christianity on the political plane is perfectly comprehensible: when it remains true to the Incarnation, it can be revolutionary, but the religion of the Father is conservative. Hindsight may reveal that sin helps create the general good and that man's trespass had fortunate results. But one cannot say this at the moment of decision, for at that moment sin is still forbidden. Adam would therefore have done better to avoid sin. Perfection is behind rather than before us. The Christian always has the right to accept existing evil but may never purchase progress with a crime. He can rally to a revolution that is already over, he can absolve it of its crimes, but he cannot start it. Even if a revolution makes just use of power, it remains seditious as long as it is unsuccessful. The Catholic as Catholic has no sense of the future: he must wait for that future to become part of the past before he can cast his lot with it. Fortunately, the will of God is not always clear, and the only way to know it, as Coûfontaine says in *l'Otage,* is to try to oppose it.[2] And, fortunately again, the Catholic as citizen is always free to join a revolution—but he will keep the best part of himself separate from it, and as a Catholic he will be indifferent to it. Claudel and Jacques Rivière were right in saying that the Christian is a nuisance to the Establishment because he is always somewhere else

[2] English translation of Claudel's play by P. Chavannes, *The Hostage* (New Haven, 1917).—Trans.

and one can never be sure of him. But the Christian makes revolutionaries uneasy for the very same reason: they feel he is never completely
with them. He is a poor conservative and an unsafe bet as a revolutionary. There is just one case where the Church itself calls for insurrection: when a legal power violates divine law. But one has never
in fact seen the Church take a stand against a legal government for the
simple reason that it was unjust or back a revolution simply because it
was just. On the contrary, it has been seen to favor rebels because they
protected its tabernacles, its ministers, and its property. God will not
fully have come to the earth until the Church feels the same obligation
toward other men as it does toward its own ministers, toward the
houses of Guernica as toward its own temples. There is such a thing as
A Christian revolt, but it is very localized, appearing only when the
Church is threatened. The Church is conservative insofar as it demands the boldness and heroism of the faithful for itself alone and
makes them live on two different levels. This, in short, is what the
Hegelian and Marxist theories of alienation say; and this is what
Christianity itself says with complete awareness: "No man can serve
two masters." No one loves well what he does not love best of all. But
since Christians also believe in the Incarnation, since it is supposed to
animate their lives, they can come as close to the revolutionaries as
they wish—at least for a while—as shown by the example of Bergamin
and several others. There is no doubt that they then have that second-
class sincerity which consists of saying what one thinks. One does not
see how they could have that sincerity of the first order which consists
of purging oneself of the equivocal.

•   •   •

Are we therefore to take up Gide's phrase, "Simple faith exempts
one from good faith," once again? Gide himself made all the comment
necessary: "It is not freedom which brings man happiness but rather
the acceptance of a duty."[3] If sincerity is one's highest value, one will
never become fully committed to anything, not to a Church or to a
party, not to a love or a friendship, not even to a particular task; for
commitment always assumes that one's affirmation surpasses one's
knowledge, that one believes by hearsay, that one gives up the rule of

[3] Preface to *Vol de nuit*. [English translation by Stuart Gilbert, *Night Flight*
(New York and London, 1932).]

sincerity for that of responsibility. The intellectual who refuses his commitments on the pretext that his function is to see all sides is in fact contriving to live a pleasant life under the guise of obeying a vocation. He resolves to avoid all resolutions and to supply strong reasons to those weak in conviction. He who is not with me is against me. Not being a Communist is being anti-Communist. Sincerity itself is deceitful and turns into propaganda. From the moment we do something, we turn toward the world, stop self-questioning, and go beyond ourselves in our action. Faith—in the sense of an unreserved commitment which is never completely justified—enters the picture as soon as we leave the realm of pure geometrical ideas and have to deal with the existing world. Each of our perceptions is an act of faith in that it affirms more than we strictly know, since objects are inexhaustible and our information limited. Descartes even said that believing two and two makes four demands an act of will. How can the Catholic be blamed for living equivocally if everybody dwells in the same state and if bad faith is the very essence of consciousness?

In reality there is no such dilemma as faith versus good faith. There can be no question of *sacrificing* good faith to faith, and only a dead or sectarian faith demands such a sacrifice. Completely devoid of sincerity, faith becomes sheer obedience or madness. "The party is no place for robots! Let no lips be sealed!" exclaimed Thorez one day.[4] Today's overly docile neophyte is the turncoat of tomorrow. Sincerity is not enough in a creature such as man, who is at every instant thrown beyond himself by knowledge as well as action and therefore is unable to give an exact account of his motives at every instant. "When a man is sincere, he doesn't think about it or put it on display. The very act of calling oneself sincere implies a double point of view, a reflection which corrupts one's vaunted sincerity and reduces it to an attitude. . . . Making a value of sincerity is precisely characteristic of an insincere society, which turns inward upon itself instead of acting upon the world."[5] Sincerity is not a goal, but, for exactly the same reasons, insincerity must never be a system, a rule, or a habit. If commitment goes beyond reasons, it should never run contrary to reason itself. Man's value does not consist in either an explosive, maniac sincerity or an unquestioned faith. Instead, it consists of a higher awareness which enables him to determine the moment when it is reasonable to

---

[4] Louis Aragon, "Maurice Thorez et la France," *Labyrinthe* (Dec. 15, 1945).
[5] P. Hervé, *La libération trahie,* p. 96.

take things on trust and the moment when questioning is in order, to combine faith and good faith within himself, and to accept his party or his group with open eyes, seeing them for what they are.

Lenin intimated something of this sort in his formula "democratic centralism." The party must welcome discussion but must also maintain discipline. The decisions must express the will of the active members, and at the same time the members must consider themselves committed to party decisions even if these run contrary to their personal views. The revolution is *both* a reality which the spontaneous course of events is preparing and an idea being worked out in the minds of those individuals who are most aware of what is happening. If the Communist attracts no followers after defending his view of the truth before the party, it means that his proposed solutions are premature or historically false, since they do not reflect the wishes of the party and the masses, who are the revolution in action. This has nothing to do with asceticism or fideism or an anti-individualist point of view. Rather, it is the idea that political action is more than an intellectual exercise and presupposes an effective contact with history as it takes shape; the idea that one's commitment to the party does not depend solely on an intellectual consent but also upon involvement in effective history, which counterbalances and regulates theory. Lenin was fully aware of the tension which sometimes exists between the individual and the party, between judgment and loyalty. Although it is impossible and would be unhealthy to ignore this conflict, he thinks it is transcended by the individual's life in the party which is *his* party. If the individual goes along with the party and against his own private opinion, it is because the party has proven its worth, because it has a mission in history, and because it represents the proletariat. There is no such thing as unmotivated commitment. What makes the Marxist notion of the party different from all others, what makes it a new cultural phenomenon and explains its place in modern literature and thought, is precisely this conception of an exchange, a vital communication between individual judgment and historical reality through the intermediary of the party.

"In any political structure the directors are necessarily granted a certain measure of trust, indeed, of orthodoxy, even if one doesn't like to admit it. This orthodoxy is undoubtedly relative, based on reason and constantly re-examined, but it is nevertheless beyond the competence of any citizen to analyze, unravel, and judge everything by himself in the complexity of world politics. Where one places one's trust is determined by a direct personal examination of those facts one is in a position to judge and, for the rest, by just plunging in, which in no way means blindly swearing allegiance, nor does it exclude the effort to understand. Let us frankly admit that a certain bias is involved, but a bias which is much closer to the spirit of free questioning and honest objectivity than the false objectivity of the intellectuals detached from ordinary custom. . . ."[6] I repeat that it involves an exchange between private judgment and party decisions, a give-and-take, living actively *with* the party, not just passively obeying it. In speaking of a bias which can be carefully scrutinized, an objective subjectivity, a vigilant trust, faith which is good faith and freedom which is commitment, Hervé is describing that communication between opposites which a frivolous author recently attributed to "reactionary philosophy." One can well believe that it is difficult to maintain an equilibrium between these opposites, since Communist criticisms of existentialism—of which there have recently been many—certainly give off more heat than light and reveal more faith than good faith.

[6] *Ibid.*, pp. 32–35.

PART EIGHT

Epilogue

This last selection was prepared by Merleau-Ponty in connection with his candidacy for election to the Collège de France. It represents a very valuable statement for the student of his thought, for in it he summarizes his philosophical work to date and projects it into the future. Since no major original work was completely finished between the time this statement was written and his untimely death, this selection gives the reader an important clue as to the direction Merleau-Ponty's work would have taken if he had lived.

18. AN UNPUBLISHED TEXT BY MAURICE MERLEAU-PONTY: A PROSPECTUS OF HIS WORK

We never cease living in the world of perception, but we bypass it in critical thought—almost to the point of forgetting the contribution of perception to our idea of truth.[1] For critical thought encounters only *bare propositions* which it discusses, accepts or rejects. Critical thought has broken with the naive evidence of *things,* and when it affirms, it is because it no longer finds any means of denial. However necessary this activity of verification may be, specifying criteria and demanding from our experience its credentials of validity, it is not aware of our contact with the perceived world which is simply there before us, beneath the level of the verified true and the false. Nor does critical thought even define the positive steps of thinking or its most valid accomplishments.

My first two works sought to restore the world of perception. My

Maurice Merleau-Ponty, "An Unpublished Text by Maurice Merleau-Ponty: A Prospectus of His Work," *The Primacy of Perception and Other Essays,* Part I, Ch. 1, ed. by James M. Edie, trans. by Arleen B. Dallery (Evanston, Illinois: Northwestern University Press, 1964), pp. 3–11. Reprinted by permission.

[1] "Un inédit de Maurice Merleau-Ponty," *Revue de métaphysique et de morale,* no. 4 (1962), 401–409. This text was preceded by the following "Introductory Note" signed by Martial Gueroult: "The text given below was sent to me by Merleau-Ponty at the time of his candidacy to the Collège de France, when I was putting together a report of his qualifications for presentation to the assembly of professors. In this report Merleau-Ponty traces his past and future as a philosopher in a continuous line, and outlines the perspectives of his future studies from *L'Origine de la vérité* to *L'Homme transcendental.* In reading these unpublished and highly interesting pages, one keenly regrets the death which brutally interrupted the élan of a profound thought in full possession of itself and about to fulfill itself in a series of original works which would have been landmarks in contemporary French philosophy."

works in preparation aim to show how communication with others, and thought, take up and go beyond the realm of perception which initiated us to the truth.

The perceiving mind is an incarnated mind. I have tried, first of all, to re-establish the roots of the mind in its body and in its world, going against doctrines which treat perception as a simple result of the action of external things on our body as well as against those which insist on the autonomy of consciousness. These philosophies commonly forget— in favor of a pure exteriority or of a pure interiority—the insertion of the mind in corporeality, the ambiguous relation which we entertain with our body and, correlatively, with perceived things. When one attempts, as I have in *The Structure of Behavior,* to trace out, on the basis of modern psychology and physiology, the relationships which obtain between the perceiving organism and its milieu one clearly finds that they are not those of an automatic machine which needs an outside agent to set off its pre-established mechanisms. And it is equally clear that one does not account for the facts by superimposing a pure, contemplative consciousness on a thing like body. In the conditions of life—if not in the laboratory—the organism is less sensitive to certain isolated physical and chemical agents than to the constellation which they form and to the whole situation which they define. Behaviors reveal a sort of prospective activity in the organism, as if it were oriented toward the meaning of certain elementary situations, as if it entertained familiar relations with them, as if there were an *"a priori* of the organism,"* privileged conducts and laws of internal equilibrium which predisposed the organism to certain relations with its milieu. At this level there is no question yet of a real self-awareness or of intentional activity. Moreover, the organism's prospective capability is exercised only within defined limits and depends on precise, local conditions.

The functioning of the central nervous system presents us with similar paradoxes. In its modern forms, the theory of cerebral localizations has profoundly changed the relation of function to substrate. It no longer assigns, for instance, a pre-established mechanism to each perceptual behavior. "Coordinating centers" are no longer considered as storehouses of "cerebral traces," and their functioning is qualitatively different from one case to another, depending on the chromatic nuance to be evoked and the perceptual structure to be realized. Finally, this functioning reflects all the subtlety and all the variety of perceptual relationships.

The perceiving organism seems to show us a Cartesian mixture of the soul with the body. Higher-order behaviors give a new meaning to the life of the organism, but the mind here disposes of only a limited freedom; it needs simpler activities in order to stabilize itself in durable institutions and to realize itself truly as mind. Perceptual behavior emerges from these relations to a situation and to an environment which are not the workings of a pure, knowing subject.

In my work on the *Phenomenology of Perception* we are no longer present at the emergence of perceptual behaviors; rather we install ourselves in them in order to pursue the analysis of this exceptional relation between the subject and its body and its world. For contemporary psychology and psychopathology the body is no longer merely *an object in the world,* under the purview of a separated spirit. It is on the side of the subject; it is our *point of view on the world,* the place where the spirit takes on a certain physical and historical situation. As Descartes once said profoundly, the soul is not merely in the body like a pilot in his ship; it is wholly intermingled with the body. The body, in turn, is wholly animated, and all its functions contribute to the perception of objects—an activity long considered by philosophy to be pure knowledge.

We grasp external space through our bodily situation. A "corporeal or postural schema" gives us at every moment a global, practical, and implicit notion of the relation between our body and things, of our hold on them. A system of possible movements, or "motor projects," radiates from us to our environment. Our body is not in space like things; it inhabits or haunts space. It applies itself to space like a hand to an instrument, and when we wish to move about we do not move the body as we move an object. We transport it without instruments as if by magic, since it is ours and because through it we have direct access to space. For us the body is much more than an instrument or a means; it is our expression in the world, the visible form of our intentions. Even our most secret affective movements, those most deeply tied to the humoral infrastructure, help to shape our perception of things.

Now if perception is thus the common act of all our motor and affective functions, no less than the sensory, we must rediscover the structure of the perceived world through a process similar to that of an archaeologist. For the structure of the perceived world is buried under the sedimentations of later knowledge. Digging down to the perceived world, we see that sensory qualities are not opaque, indivisible "givens," which are simply exhibited to a remote consciousness—a favorite idea of classical philosophy. We see too that colors (each surrounded by an affective atmosphere which psychologists have been able to study and define) are themselves different modalities of our co-existence with the world. We also find that spatial forms or distances are not so much relations between different points in objective space as they are relations between these points and a central perspective—our body. In short, these relations are different ways for external stimuli to test, to solicit, and to vary our grasp on the world, our horizontal and vertical anchorage in a place and in a here-and-now. We find that perceived things, unlike geometrical objects, are not bounded entities whose laws of construction we possess *a priori,* but that they are open, inexhaustible systems which we recognize through a certain style of development, although we are never able, in principle, to explore them entirely, and even though they never give us more than profiles and perspectival views of themselves. Finally, we find that the perceived world, in its turn, is not a pure object of thought without fissures or lacunae; it is, rather, like a universal style shared in by all perceptual beings. While the world no doubt co-ordinates these perceptual beings, we can never presume that its work is finished. Our world, as Malebranche said, is an "unfinished task."

If we now wish to characterize a subject capable of this perceptual experience, it obviously will not be a self-transparent thought, absolutely present to itself without the interference of its body and its history. The perceiving subject is not this absolute thinker; rather, it functions according to a natal pact between our body and the world, between ourselves and our body. Given a perpetually new natural and historical situation to control, the perceiving subject undergoes a continued birth; at each instant it is something new. Every incarnate subject is like an open notebook in which we do not yet know what will be written. Or it is like a new language; we do not know what works it will accomplish but only that, once it has appeared, it cannot fail to say little or much, to have a history and a meaning. The very productivity or freedom of human life, far from denying our situation, utilizes it and turns it into a means of expression.

This remark brings us to a series of further studies which I have undertaken since 1945 and which will definitively fix the philosophical significance of my earlier works while they, in turn, determine the route and the method of these later studies.

I found in the experience of the perceived world a new type of relation between the mind and truth. The evidence of the perceived thing lies in its concrete aspect, in the very texture of its qualities, and in the equivalence among all its sensible properties—which caused Cézanne to say that one should be able to paint even odors. Before our undivided existence the world is true; it exists. The unity, the articulations of both are intermingled. We experience in it a truth which shows through and envelops us rather than being held and circumscribed by our mind.

Now if we consider, above the perceived world, the field of knowledge properly so called—i.e., the field in which the mind seeks to possess the truth, to define its objects itself, and thus to attain to a universal wisdom, not tied to the particularities of our situation—we must ask: Does not the realm of the perceived world take on the form of a simple appearance? Is not pure understanding a new source of knowledge, in comparison with which our perceptual familiarity with the world is only a rough, unformed sketch? We are obliged to answer these questions first with a theory of truth and then with a theory of intersubjectivity, both of which I have already touched upon in essays such as "Le doute de Cézanne," "Le Roman et la métaphysique,"[2] and, on the philosophy of history, in *Humanisme et terreur* [1947]. But the philosophical foundations of these essays are still to be rigorously elaborated. I am now working on two books dealing with a theory of truth.

It seems to me that knowledge and the communication with others which it presupposes not only are original formations with respect to the perceptual life but also they preserve and continue our perceptual life even while transforming it. Knowledge and communication sublimate rather than suppress our incarnation, and the characteristic operation of the mind is in the movement by which we recapture our corporeal existence and use it to symbolize instead of merely to co-exist. This metamorphosis lies in the double function of our body. Through its "sensory fields" and its whole organization the body is, so to speak, predestined to model itself on the natural aspects of the world. But as an active body capable of gestures, of expression, and finally of language, it turns back on the world to signify it. As the observation of

[2] These are the first two essays in *Sens et non-sens* (Paris, 1948).—*Trans.*

apraxics shows, there is in man, superimposed upon actual space with its self-identical points, a "virtual space" in which the spatial values that a point *would receive* (for any other position of our corporal co-ordinates) are also recognized. A system of correspondence is established between our spatial situation and that of others, and each one comes to symbolize all the others. This insertion of our factual situation as a particular case within the system of other possible situations begins as soon as we *designate* a point in space with our finger. For this pointing gesture, which animals do not understand, supposes that we are already installed in virtual space—at the end of the line prolonging our finger in a centrifugal and cultural space. This mimic usage of our body is not yet a conception, since it does not cut us off from our corporeal situation; on the contrary, it assumes all its meaning. It leads us to a concrete theory of the mind which will show the mind in a relationship of reciprocal exchange with the instruments which it uses, but uses only while rendering to them what it has received from them, and more.

In a general way expressive gestures (in which the science of physiognomy sought in vain for the sufficient signs of emotional states) have a univocal meaning only with respect to the situation which they underline and punctuate. But like phonemes, which have no meaning by themselves, expressive gestures have a diacritical value: they announce the constitution of a symbolical system capable of redesigning an infinite number of situations. They are a first language. And reciprocally language can be treated as a gesticulation so varied, so precise, so systematic, and capable of so many convergent expressions [*recoupements*] that the internal structure of an utterance can ultimately agree only with the mental situation to which it responds and of which it becomes an unequivocal sign. The meaning of language, like that of gestures, thus does not lie in the elements composing it. The meaning is their common intention, and the spoken phrase is understood only if the hearer, following the "verbal chain," goes beyond each of its links in the direction that they all designate together.

It follows that even solitary thought does not cease using the language which supports it, rescues it from the transitory, and throws it back again. Cassirer said that thought was the "shuttlecock" of language. It also follows that perhaps, taken piece by piece, language does not yet contain its meaning, that all communication supposes in the listener a creative re-enactment of what is heard. Language leads us to a thought which is no longer ours alone, to a thought which is presumptively universal, though this is never the universality of a pure concept which would be identical for every mind. It is rather the call which a situated thought addresses to other thoughts, equally situated, and each one responds to the call with its own resources. An examination of the domain of algorithm would show there too, I believe, the same strange function which is at work in the so-called inexact forms of language. Especially when it is a question of conquering a new domain for exact thought, the most formal thought is always referred to some qualitatively defined mental situation from which it extracts a meaning only by applying itself to the configuration of the problem. The transformation is never a simple analysis, and thought is never more than relatively formal.

Since I intend to treat this problem more fully in my work *L'Origine de la vérité,* I have approached it less directly in a partially written book dealing with literary language. In this area it is easier to show that language is never the mere clothing of a thought which otherwise possesses itself in full clarity. The meaning of a book is given, in the first instance, not so much by its ideas as by a systematic and unexpected variation of the modes of language, of narrative, or of existing literary forms. This accent, this particular modulation of speech—if the expression is successful—is assimilated little by little by the reader, and it gives him access to a thought to which he was until then indifferent or even opposed. Communication in literature is not the simple appeal on the part of the writer to meanings which would be part of an *a priori* of the mind; rather, communication arouses these meanings in the mind through enticement and a kind of oblique action. The writer's thought does not control his language from without; the writer is himself a kind of new idiom, constructing itself, inventing ways of expression, and diversifying itself according to its own meaning. Perhaps poetry is only that part of literature where this autonomy is ostentatiously displayed. All great prose is also a re-creation of the signifying instrument, henceforth manipulated according to a new syntax. Prosaic writing, on the other hand, limits itself to using, through accepted signs, the meanings already accepted in a given culture. Great prose is the art of capturing a meaning which until then had never been objectified and of rendering it accessible to everyone who speaks the same language. When a writer is no longer capable of thus founding a new universality and of taking the risk of communicating, he has outlived his time. It seems to me that we can also say of other institutions that they have ceased to live when they show themselves incapable of carrying on a poetry of human relations—that is, the call of each individual freedom to all the others.

Hegel said that the Roman state was the prose of the world. I shall entitle my book *Introduction à la prose du monde*.[3] In this work I shall elaborate the category of prose beyond the confines of literature to give it a sociological meaning.

For these studies on expression and truth approach, from the epistemological side, the general problem of human interrelations—which will be the major topic of my later studies. The linguistic relations among men should help us understand the more general order of symbolic relations and of institutions, which assure the exchange not only of thoughts but of all types of values, the co-existence of men within a culture and, beyond it, within a single history. Interpreted in terms of symbolism, the concept of history seems to escape the disputes always directed to it because one ordinarily means by this word— whether to accept it or to reject it—an external Power in the name of which men would be dispossessed of consciousness. History is no more external to us than language. There *is* a history of thought: the succession of the works of the spirit (no matter how many detours we see in it) is really a single experience which develops of itself and in whose development, so to speak, truth capitalizes itself.[4] In an analogous sense we can say that there is a history of humanity or, more simply, *a* humanity. In other words, granting all the periods of stagnation and retreat, human relations are able to grow, to change their avatars into lessons, to pick out the truth of their past in the present, to eliminate certain mysteries which render them opaque and thereby make themselves more translucent.

The idea of a single history or of a logic of history is, in a sense, implied in the least human exchange, in the least social perception. For example, anthropology supposes that civilizations very different from ours are comprehensible to us, that they can be situated in relation to ours and vice-versa, that all civilzations belong to the same universe of thought, since the least use of language implies an idea of truth. Also we can never pretend to dismiss the adventures of history as something

---

[3] This work was never published as such, though some of the studies it occasioned are the basis of the early chapters of *Signes* (Paris, 1960).—*Trans.*

[4] That is, truth becomes Truth by "building up its capital."—*Trans.*

foreign to our present action, since even the most independent search for the most abstract truth has been and is a factor of history (the only one, perhaps, that we are sure is not disappointing). All human acts and all human creations constitute a single drama, and in this sense we are all saved or lost together. Our life is essentially universal.

But this methodological rationalism is not to be confused with a dogmatic rationalism which eliminates historical contingency in advance by supposing a "World Spirit" (Hegel) behind the course of events. If it is necessary to say that there is a total history, a single tissue tying together all the enterprises of simultaneous and successive civilizations, all the results of thought and all the facts of economics, it must not be in the guise of a historical idealism or materialism—one handing over the government of history to thought; the other, to matter. Because cultures are just so many coherent systems of symbols and because in each culture the modes of work, of human relations, of language and thought, even if not parallel at every moment, do not long remain separated, cultures can be compared and placed under a common denominator. What makes this connection of meaning between each aspect of a culture and all the rest, as between all the episodes of history, is the permanent, harmonious thought of this plurality of beings who recognize one another as *"semblances,"* even when some seek to enslave others, and who are so commonly situated that adversaries are often in a kind of complicity.

Our inquiries should lead us finally to a reflection on this *transcendental man,* or this "natural light" common to all, which appears through the movement of history—to a reflection on this Logos which gives us the task of vocalizing a hitherto mute world. Finally, they should lead us to a study of the Logos of the perceived world which we encountered in our earliest studies in the evidence of things. Here we rejoin the classical questions of metaphysics, but by following a route which removes from them their character as *problems*—that is to say, as difficulties which could be solved cheaply through the use of a few metaphysical entities constructed for this purpose. The notions of Nature and Reason, for instance, far from explaining the metamorphoses which we have observed from perception up to the more complex modes of human exchange, make them incomprehensible. For by relating them to separated principles, these notions mask a constantly experienced moment, the moment when an existence becomes aware of itself, grasps itself, and expresses its own meaning.

The study of perception could only teach us a "bad ambiguity," a mixture of finitude and universality, of interiority and exteriority. But there is a "good ambiguity" in the phenomenon of expression, a spontaneity which accomplishes what appeared to be impossible when we observed only the separate elements, a spontaneity which gathers together the plurality of monads, the past and the present, nature and culture into a single whole. To establish this wonder would be metaphysics itself and would at the same time give us the principle of an ethics.

BIBLIOGRAPHY

Primary Sources

IN FRENCH

[NOTE: Articles marked (SNS) are included in the collection *Sens et non-sens* (1948); those marked (S) are collected in *Signes* (1960).]

1942

La structure du comportement. Paris: Presses Universitaires de France, 1942; 4th ed., 1960.

1945

La phénoménologie de la perception. Paris: Nouvelle Revue Française, Gallimard, 1945; 4th ed., 1962.

"Roman et métaphysique." *Cahiers du Sud,* No. 270 (March, 1945), pp. 194–207. (SNS)

"Le cinéma et la nouvelle psychologie." *Les Temps modernes,* No. 2 (November, 1945), pp. 930–43. (SNS)

"La guerre a eu lieu." *Les Temps modernes,* No. 1 (October, 1945), pp. 48–66. (SNS)

"La querelle de l'existentialisme." *Les Temps modernes,* No. 2 (November, 1945), pp. 344–56. (SNS)

"Le doute de Cézanne." *Fontaine,* No. 47 (December, 1945), pp. 80–100. (SNS)

1946

"Pour la vérité." *Les Temps modernes,* No. 4 (January, 1946), pp. 577–600. (SNS)

"Foi et bonne foi." *Les Temps modernes,* No. 5 (February, 1946), pp. 769–82. (SNS)

"Autour du Marxisme." *Fontaine,* Nos. 48–49 (February, 1946), pp. 309–31. (SNS)

"L'existentialisme chez Hegel." *Les Temps modernes,* No. 7 (April, 1946), pp. 1311–19. (SNS)

"Marxisme et philosophie." *Revue internationale,* Vol. I, No. 6 (June–July, 1946), pp. 518–26. (SNS)

"Le Yogi et le Prolétaire." *Les Temps modernes,* No. 13 (October, 1946), pp. 1–29; No. 14 (November, 1946), pp. 253–87; No. 16 (January, 1947), pp. 676–711. [Later collected in *Humanisme et terreur* (1947).]

1947

"La primat de la perception et ses conséquences philosophiques." *Bullosophie,* No. 4 (October, 1947), pp. *letin de la Société française de phi-* 119–53.

"Indochine S.O.S." *Les Temps modernes,* No. 18 (March, 1947), pp. 1039–52. [Printed anonymously; reprinted (S) under the title "Sur l'Indochine."]

"Apprendre à lire." *Les Temps modernes,* No. 22 (July, 1947), pp. 1–27. (Reprinted as Preface to *Humanisme et terreur.*)

"La métaphysique dans l'homme." *Revue de métaphysique et de morale,* Nos. 3–4 (July, 1947), pp. 290–307. (SNS)

"En un combat douteux." *Les Temps modernes,* No. 27 (December, 1947), pp. 961–64.

"Lecture de Montaigne." *Les Temps modernes,* No. 27 (December, 1947), pp. 1044–60. (S)

"Jean-Paul Sartre, un auteur scandaleux." *Figaro littéraire,* December 6, 1947. (SNS)

Humanisme et Terreur. Paris, Gallimard (Nouvelle Revue Française), 1947. (A collection of articles and the preface indicated above, with corrections and additions.)

1948

"Complicité objective." *Les Temps modernes,* No. 34 (July, 1948), pp. 1–11.

"Communisme et anti-communisme." *Les Temps modernes,* No. 34 (July, 1948), pp. 175–88. [(S) under the title "La politique paranoïaque."]

Sens et non-sens. Paris: Nagel, 1948.

1949

"Note sur Machiavel." *Les Temps modernes,* No. 48 (October, 1949), pp. 577–93. (S)

"Marxisme et superstition." *Les Temps modernes,* No. 50 (December, 1949), pp. 1119–21. (S)

1950

"Les jours de notre vie." *Les Temps modernes,* No. 51 (January, 1950), pp. 1153–68. [In collaboration with J.-P. Sartre; (S) under the title "L'U.R.S.S."]

"L'adversaire est complice." *Les Temps modernes,* No. 57 (July, 1950), pp. 1–11.

1951

"Le philosophe et la sociologie." *Cahiers internationaux de sociologie,* X (July, 1951), pp. 50–69. (S)

"L'homme et l'adversité." Paper given at the *Rencontres internationales de Genève,* September 10, 1951. (S)

"Sur la phénoménologie du langage." In *Problèmes actuels de la phéno-*

ménologie. Ed. by H. L. Van Breda, O. F. M. Brussels: Desclée de Brouwer, 1952, pp. 89–109. (S)

1952

"Le langage indirect et les voix du silence." *Les Temps modernes,* No. 80 (June, 1952), pp. 2113–44; No. 81 (July, 1952), pp. 70–94. (S)
"Un inédit de Merleau-Ponty." Paper given for his candidacy to the Collège de France in 1952. [Later published in *Revue de Métaphysique et de Morale,* No. 4 (October, 1962), pp. 401–09.]

1953

Éloge de la philosophie. Paris: Nouvelle Revue Française, Gallimard, 1953.
"Le monde sensible et le monde de l'expression: Recherches sur l'usage littéraire du langage." *Annuaire du Collège de France,* 1953, pp. 145–55.

1954

"Où sont le nouveaux-maîtres?" *L'Express,* No. 71 (October 2, 1954).
"La philosophe est-il un fonctionnaire?", *L'Express,* No. 72 (October 9, 1954).
"Le libertin est-il un philosophe?", *L'Express,* No. 73 (October 16, 1954). [(S) under the title "Sur l'érotisme."]
"La France va-t-elle se renouveler?" *L'Express,* No. 74 (October 23, 1954).
"Les femmes sont-elles des hommes?"

L'Express, No. 76 (November 6, 1954).
"Les peuples se fâchent-ils?" *L'Express,* No. 80 (December 4, 1954).
"Le goût pour les faits divers est-il malsan?" *L'Express,* No. 82 (December 18, 1954). [(S) under the title "Sur les faits divers."]
"Le problème de la parole: Matériaux pour une théorie de l'histoire." *Annuaire du Collège de France,* 1954, pp. 175–87.

1955

"D'abord comprendre les communistes." *L'Express,* No. 85 (January 8, 1955).
"A quoi sert l'objectivité?" *L'Express,* No. 88 (January 29, 1955).
"Comment répondre à Oppenheimer?" *L'Express,* No. 91 (February 19, 1955).
"Claudel était-il un génie?" *L'Express,* No. 93 (March 5, 1955). [(S) under the title "Sur Claudel."]
"M. Poujade a-t-il une petite cervelle?" *L'Express,* No. 95 (March 19, 1955).
"Le marxisme est-il mort à Yalta?" *L'Express,* No. 98 (April 9, 1955), [(S) under the title "Les papiers de Yalta."]
"Einstein et la crise de la raison." *L'Express,* No. 103 (May 14, 1955). (S)
"Où va l'anti-communisme?" *L'Express,* No. 108 (June 25, 1955).
"L'avenir de la révolution." *L'Express,* No. 118 (August 27, 1955). (S)
Les Aventures de la dialectique. Paris: Nouvelle Revue Française, Gallimard, 1955.

"L'institution dans l'histoire personelle et publique: Le problème de la passivité, le sommeil, l'inconscient, la mémoire." *Annuaire du Collège de France,* 1955, pp. 157–64.

1956

"Premier dialogue Est-Ouest à Venise." *L'Express,* No. 278 (October 19, 1956).

"Réforme ou maladie sénile du communisme." *L'Express,* No. 283 (November 23, 1956), pp. 13–17. [(S) under the title "Sur la déstalinisation."]

"Partout et nulle part." Preface to *Les philosophes célèbres.* Ed. by M. Merleau-Ponty. Paris: Mazenod, 1956. (S)

"La philosophie dialectique: Textes sur la dialectique." *Annuaire du Collège de France,* 1956, pp. 175–80.

1957

"La démocratie peut-elle renaître en France?" *L'Express,* No. 368 (July 3, 1957).

"Le concept de nature." *Annuaire du Collège de France,* 1957, pp. 201–17.

1958

"Sur Madagascar, à la suite d'un séjour effectué en oct.–nov. 1957." *L'Express* (August 21, 1958). (S)

"Du moindre mal à l'union sacrée." *Le Monde* (June 5, 1958). [(S) under the title "Sur le 13 mai 1958."]

"La France en Afrique." *L'Express,* No. 375 (August 21, 1958).

"R. Martin du Gard." *L'Express,* No. 376 (August 21, 1958).

"Le concept de nature (suite): L'Animalité, le corps humain, passage à la culture." *Annuaire du Collège de France,* 1958, pp. 213–19.

1959

"Le philosophe et son ombre." In "E. Husserl (1859–1959)." *Phenomenologica,* No. 4 (1959). (S)

"De Mauss à Lévi-Strauss." *La Nouvelle Revue française,* No. 82 (October, 1959), pp. 615–31. (S)

"Bergson se faisant." *Bulletin de la Société française de Philosophie,* No. 1 (January, 1960), pp. 35–45. (S)

1960

Preface to A. Hesnard, *L'oeuvre de Freud et son importance dans le monde moderne.* Paris: Payot, 1960, pp. 5–10.

Signes. Paris: Nouvelle Revue Française, Gallimard, 1960. (Preface dated February and September, 1960.)

1961

"L'oeil et l'esprit." *Art de France,* No. 1, pp. 187–208. (Reprinted in *Les Temps modernes,* special issue No. 184–185, pp. 193–227.)

"L'ontologie cartésienne et l'ontologie d'aujourd'hui: Philosophe et non-philosophe d'après Hegel." *Annuaire du Collège de France,* 1961, p. 163.

1962

"Un inédit de Merleau-Ponty." *See above,* 1952.

1964

Le visible et l'invisible. Paris: Nouvelle Revue Française, Gallimard, 1964. (Portions of a book on which Merleau-Ponty was working at the time of his death.)

In English

In Praise of Philosophy. Tr. by John Wild and James M. Edie. Evanston, Ill.: Northwestern University Press, 1963.

Phenomenology of Perception. Tr. by Colin Smith. New York: Humanities Press, 1962.

The Primacy of Perception and Other Essays. Ed. by James M. Edie. Evanston, Ill.: Northwestern University Press, 1964.

Sense and Non-Sense. Tr. by Herbert L. Dreyfus and Patricia Allen Dreyfus. Evanston, Ill.: Northwestern University Press, 1964.

Signs. Tr. by Richard C. McCleary. Evanston, Ill.: Northwestern University Press, 1964.

The Structure of Behavior. Tr. by Alden L. Fisher. Boston: Beacon Press, 1963.

Secondary Sources in English

BALLARD, EDWARD G. "The Philosophy of Merleau-Ponty." *Tulane Studies in Philosophy,* Vol. 9 (1960).

BANNAN, JOHN F. "Philosophical Reflection and the Phenomenology of Merleau-Ponty." *Review of Metaphysics,* Vol. 8 (1955), pp. 418–42.

—— *The Philosophy of Merleau-Ponty.* New York: Harcourt, Brace and World, 1967.

BAYER, RAYMOND. *Merleau-Ponty's Existentialism.* Buffalo, N.Y.: University of Buffalo Studies, 1951.

CARR, DAVID. "Maurice Merleau-Ponty: Incarnate Consciousness." In George A. Schrader, ed., *Existential Philosophers: Kirkegaard to Merleau-Ponty.* New York: McGraw-Hill, 1967, pp. 396–429.

KAELIN, EUGENE F. *An Existentialist Aesthetic: The Theories of Sartre and Merleau-Ponty.* Madison: University of Wisconsin Press, 1962.

KWANT, REMY C. *The Phenomenological Philosophy of Merleau-Ponty.* Pittsburg: Duquesne University Press, 1963.

LANGAN, THOMAS D. *Merleau-Ponty's Critique of Reason.* New Haven: Yale University Press, 1966.

LAUER, QUENTIN. "Four Phenomenologists." *Thought,* Vol. 33 (Summer, 1958), pp. 183–204.

SCHARFSTEIN, BEN-AMI. "Bergson and Merleau-Ponty: A Preliminary Comparison." *Journal of Philosophy,* Vol. 52 (1955), pp. 380–86.

SPIEGELBERG, HERBERT. "The Phenomenological Philosophy of Maurice Merleau-Ponty." In *A History of the Phenomenological Movement.* The Hague: Nijhoff, 1960, Vol. II, pp. 516–62.